The Executive Effect:
Concepts and Methods for Studying Top Managers

STRATEGIC MANAGEMENT POLICY AND PLANNING:
A Multivolume Treatise, VOLUME 2

General Editors: *Howard Thomas,* Department of Business Administration, University of Illinois, Urbana-Champaign and *Dan E. Schendel,* Krannert Graduate School of Management, Purdue University

Strategic Management Policy and Planning
A Multivolume Treatise

General Editors:

Howard Thomas
Department of Business Administration
University of Illinois at Urbana-Champaign

and

Dan E. Schendel
Krannert Graduate School of Management
Purdue University

FORTHCOMING
(Additional volumes and volume numbers will be assigned at a future date)

Planning and Control Systems
Edited by **John H. Grant,** *Graduate School of Business, University of Pittsburgh*

Strategic Issues in State-Owned Organizations
Edited by **Taleb Hafel,** *Ecole des Hautes Etudes Commerciales, Universite de Montreal*

Industry and Competative Analysis
Edited by **John McGee,** *Templeton College, Oxford University*

Strategy Models
Edited by **Aneel Karani,** *School of Business Administration, University of Michigan*

Research Methodology and Strategic Management
Edited by **N. Venkatraman,** *Sloan School of Management, Massachusetts Institute of Technology,* **D. Sudharshan** and **Howard Thomas,** *Department of Business Administration, University of Illinois*

Strategy Valuation
Edited by **Carolyn Woo,** *Krannert Graduate School of Management, Purdue University*

The Executive Effect:
Concepts and Methods for Studying Top Managers

edited by: **DONALD C. HAMBRICK**
Graduate School of Business
Columbia University

 **JAI PRESS INC.**

Greenwich, Connecticut   *London, England*

LIBRARY OF CONGRESS
Library of Congress Cataloging-in-Publication Data

The Executive effect : concepts and methods for studying top managers
/ edited by Donald C. Hambrick.
        p.   cm.—(Strategic management policy and planning ; v. 2)
    Includes bibliographies.
    ISBN 0-89232-804-5
    1. Executives.   2. Chief executive officers.   I. Hambrick, Donald
C.   II. Series.
HD38.2.E93 1988
568.4—dc19   88-21833
                                                                    CIP

Copyright © 1988 JAI PRESS INC.
55 Old Post Road, No. 2
Greenwich, Connecticut 06830

JAI PRESS LTD.
3 Henrietta Street
London WC2E 8LU
England

Library of Congress Catalog Number: 88-21833

ISBN: 0-89232-804-5

Manufactured in the United States of America

CONTENTS

PART III.   EXECUTIVE TRANSITIONS

LIST OF CONTRIBUTORS

Gerard L. Brandon	Landy, Jacobs and Associates
Robert B. Duncan	School of Business Northwestern University
John J. Gabarro	Harvard Business School Harvard University
Anil Gupta	College of Business Administration University of Maryland
Donald C. Hambrick	Graduate School of Business Columbia University
Ellen F. Jackofsky	Cox School of Business Southern Methodist University
John R. Kimberly	Kellogg School of Management Northwestern University
Frances J. Milliken	Graduate School of Business New York University
Shelley R. Robbins	School of Business University of Wisconsin Milwaukee
Elaine Romanelli	Fuqua School of Business Duke University
John J. Slocum, Jr.	Cox School of Business Southern Methodist University

Jeffrey A. Sonnenfeld   Harvard Business School
                                        Harvard University

William H. Starbuck   Graduate School of Business
                                        New York University

Richard M. Steers   College of Business Administration
                                        University of Oregon

Michael L. Tushman   School of Business
                                        Columbia University

Gerardo R. Ungson   College of Business Administration
                                        University of Oregon

Edward J. Zajac   Kellogg School of Management
                                        Northwestern University

PREFACE

This is a book about top managers and the effects they have on their organizations. After focusing for twenty years on environments, processes, structures, portfolios, and competitive dynamics, strategic management researchers have shown a recent interest in returning to the study of the individuals who are formally charged with directing organizations. These theorists are drawing upon a variety of theoretical foundations and rationales in their inquiries into executive leadership. However, a significant and gratifying number have attempted particularly to test, extend, and refine the "upper echelons" perspective proposed by Phyllis Mason and me a few years ago (Hambrick and Mason, 1984). According to the upper echelons view, the organization is a reflection of its top managers; if we want to improve our explanations for why organizations behave and perform as they do, we must look to the top managers—their experiences, values, cognitive styles, and aptitudes—as an important source of variation.

The logic of the upper echelons view relies on early work by theorists of the Carnegie School who argued that complex decisions are largely the result of behavioral factors rather than techno-economic optimization (Cyert and March, 1963; March and Simon, 1958). In their view, bounded rationality, multiple and conflicting goals, ill-defined options, and varying aspiration levels—and hence actions or inaction—all are derived from idiosyncratic beliefs, knowledge, assumptions and values that each decision maker brings to the administrative setting.

In psychologists' parlance, the upper echelons view argues that responses are more a function of the subject and his or her personalized interpretation of stimuli, than of the stimuli themselves. Prevailing psychological theory supports such a view when the stimuli are many and ambiguous; conversely, such theory supports the predominant role of stimuli in determining actions, when the stimuli are few and unambiguous. As an example of the latter, flames leaping from a corner of a room tend to drive everyone to an exit on the opposite side of the room, regardless of the individuals' upbringing, values, education, and so on.

The validity of the upper echelons views depends, then, upon how multitudinous and ambiguous the stimuli are which confront senior executives. There is no way reliably or universally to gauge these magnitudes, and intuitive guesses would probably be misleading. However, a variation of an illustration used by cybertneticians to demonstrate complexity of systems may help frame things.

Assume we have a square grid of 100 electric switches, 10 switches wide and 10 switches high. Each switch has two possible states, on or off. The variety of this grid is 2^{100}. If we wanted to search all possible states of this system, and could do so at the supercomputer speed of one billion patterns per second, it would take 32 trillion years to complete the full search.

Yet, compared to well documented portrayals of general management work (Mintzberg, 1973; Kotter, 1983), the 10x10 switch grid is utterly trivial. A senior manager deals not with 10 variables but possibly 10s or even 100s, each having not just two possible states but many. Clearly, the manager cannot search the whole "grid," either in everyday actions or even in rare, momentous decisions. Instead, he or she falls back on experience, gravitates to what is personally most interesting or desirable, takes mental shortcuts, attends to the personally interpretable, and listens to familiar and pleasing voices. In short, the senior manager injects a great deal of him or herself into actions and outcomes.

Granted, managers may not always matter to the same degree. An articulate camp has argued that organizations are largely inertial, hemmed in by external forces and their own inability to change; under such a view, managers are incidental (e.g., Lieberson and O'Connor 1970; Hannan and Freeman, 1977).

This extreme view may apply to a small subset of organizations whose managers have little discretion (Hambrick and Finkelstein, 1987). However, the top managers of most firms have some (and sometimes substantial) leeway for altering their organizations. Take the cases of these four healthy firms: Greyhound, Primerica, National Intergroup and Trinova. Within the last five years these very large, old companies have completely ceased all operations in their original lines of business. Their founders would not recognize them. Not even their CEOs in 1960 (or possibly even in 1970) would recognize them today. They are fundamentally different because of choices made by top managers. And those managers made choices on the basis of their highly individualized aspiration levels, assumptions, knowledge of alternatives, and propensities.

If we can observe such wholesale changes in these large mature enterprises, then to observe a lack of change in other organizations is not to confirm a nonrole for leaders; rather, it is simply an illustration of the effects of lethargic, unimaginative, or homogenized leaders. Namely, to observe widespread organizational inertia is to document widespread leadership inertia. The managers do matter.

Researchers who recognize the central role of executive leadership in organizational functioning and performance have embarked on a new wave of investigations. So many projects are underway at so many institutions that it is safe to say that executive leadership will be the central thrust of the field of strategic management in the 1990s, as competitive strategy was in the 1980s. However, with some important exceptions, the realm of executive leadership is uncharted territory. We lack a coherent platform from which to proceed.

This book is an attempt to provide such a platform. While it does not propose a single, overarching framework for viewing executives, it does pull together ten new, original papers by some of today's most active thinkers on the topic. The authors were carefully selected both for their known thoughtfulness and insights as well as for their diversity of views and methods. After all, such diversity is what is needed at this early point in this research stream. We must doggedly avoid premature closure on paradigms, vantages, and techniques for studying top managers. Rival approaches need full airings.

In fact, at this point, even speculative approaches are needed. I have encouraged the authors to go beyond the known, the tested, the palatable, even at times beyond the plausible. The result is a rich mixture of established and vanguard ideas.

The first part of the book deals with the factors that underlie executive behavior. Included are papers on executive values, executive perceptions, cultural determinants of executive action, and executive rewards.

The second part of the book focuses on executive behavior in context. These four papers address executive roles over the evolution of the organization; the associations (descriptive and prescriptive) among environment, strategy, and executive characteristics; relations between the chief executive and the board of directors; and the role of top management in instilling a strategic vision in the organization.

The final section focuses on the important issue of executive transitions, particularly the challenges of assuming a new general management position, and, at the other end, the immense difficulty and trauma encountered by CEOs—who often come to think of themselves as heroes—in leaving office. In short, the book addresses a cross-section of some of the most important and timely topics in the sphere of executive leadership.

My indebtedness for help on the book extends in many directions. Foremost, thanks go to the authors who signed on for this venture and then responded so admirably to my constant cajoling. Deep appreciation goes to my colleagues and students at Columbia and at Penn State (where the project was launched while on sabbatical), who stimulated and steered the project in ways they may not have known. Margaret Hambrick was of immense help in managing the editorial process. And, our support staff at Columbia—Debbie Washington, Maxine Braiterman, and Colette Neven—deserve cheers for their help in preparing the manuscript.

REFERENCES

Cyert, R.M., and March, J.G. *A Behavioral Theory of the Firm*. Englewood Cliffs, NJ: Prentice-Hall, 1963.

Hambrick, D.C., and Finkelstein, S. "Managerial Discretion: A Bridge Between Polar Views of Organizational Outcomes." In *Research in Organizational Behavior*, pp. 369-406. Edited by L.L. Cummings and B.M. Staw. Greenwich, CT: JAI Press, 1987.

Hambrick, D.C., and Mason, P.A. "Upper Echelons: The Organization as a Reflection of Its Top Managers." *Academy of Management Review* 9 (1984): 193-206.

Hannan, M.T., and Freeman, J.H. "The Population Ecology of Organizations." *American Journal of Sociology* 82 (1977): 929-964.

Kotter, J.P. *The General Managers*. New York: Free Press, 1982.

Lieberson, S., and O'Connor, J.F. "Leadership and Organizational Performance: A Study of Large Corporations." *American Sociological Review* 37 (1972): 117-130.

March, J.G., and Simon, H.A. *Organizations. New York: Wiley, 1958.*

Mintzberg, H. *The Nature of Managerial Work*. New York: Harper & Row, 1973.

PART I

BASES FOR EXECUTIVE BEHAVIOR

EXECUTIVE VALUES

Donald C. Hambrick and Gerard L. Brandon

The possible role of executive values in strategic decision making both intrigues and perplexes students of organizations. For example, observers have pointed to the late J.W. Marriott's values as a devout Mormon as an explanation for why his firm did not join the other large hospitality chains in the casino business in the late 1970s ("The Marriott Man," 1979). Then one is left wondering why Marriott allowed liquor to be served in his establishments. Or, one could consider John Teets, the current chairman of Greyhound Corporation. In explaining why Teets has been extremely aggressive with Greyhound's unions, observers claim that as a boy Teets was indelibly impressed by difficulties his father, a small contractor, had with unions and their enforcers. At the same time, Teets takes a dim view of employees at any level working extra hours. "Your family is more important than your job," he says to his staff ("A Body Builder...," 1985: 130).

Unfortunately, our understanding of managerial values is too incomplete to be able to neatly reconcile paradoxical observations such as these. Although some research has attempted to measure and typify managers' values, relatively little work has been done on the links between their values and actions.

The idea that organizational outcomes are based in part on managerial values is a central tenet of the "upper-echelons" theory proposed by

Hambrick and Mason (1984). In their view, the organization is a reflection of its top managers—their values, cognitive bases, cognitive styles, and various aptitudes. In the face of the ambiguity and ill-defined options that typify strategic decisions, no two managers or management teams will necessarily opt for—or even identify—the same solutions. To understand why managers differ in their choices, Hambrick and Mason argued that we need to understand the managers themselves.

The logic of the upper echelons perspective rests on early work by Carnegie theorists who argued that complex decisions are largely the result of behavioral factors rather than techno-economic optimizing attempts (Cyert and March, 1963; March and Simon, 1958). In their view, bounded rationality, multiple and conflicting goals, ill-defined options, and varying aspiration levels all derive from "givens" that each decision maker brings to the administrative situation. These "givens" are of two types: (1) beliefs—knowledge or assumptions about future events, alternatives, and consequences attached to alternatives; and (2) values—principles for ordering consequences or alternatives according to preferences.

The purpose of this chapter is to review, integrate, and extend the literature on managerial values, in an attempt to provide a cohesive platform from which research on this important topic might continue. Following this introductory section will be a brief discussion of values as a concept in behavioral and social theory. Then will be a review and critique of the major approaches to measuring values, their relevance to managerial settings, and distillation down to a limited set of the most potent value dimensions for understanding executive action. The next major section will address the origins of executive values. Namely, where do executives get their values? How persistent are they? Can organizations shape values? To what extent do managers feign certain values for symbolic purposes? The chapter will then turn to the link between executive values and action, attempting to model how and where values manifest themselves in organizational outcomes. The last major section will deal with the normative implications of executive values, and particularly whether either strength or homogeneity of values within a management team affects organizational performance. We will conclude with discussion of needed research and a summary.

VALUES AS A CONCEPT

Investigating the literature on personal values is onerous and frustrating. It is a massive body, since theorists in the fields of psychology, sociology, anthropology, economics, political science, philosophy, and theology all have rightfully claimed the importance of values to what they study. They have all set forth definitions, methods, and models in abundance. More often than not, each offering ignores the others, resulting in a vast theoretical underbrush.

Although there is not complete agreement on a definition of values, prominent theorists actually are not at serious odds about how they define the term. For instance, Rokeach (1973: 159-60) states:

> to say that a person 'has a value' is to say that he has an enduring belief that a specific mode of conduct or end-state of existence is personally and socially preferable to alternative modes of conduct or end-states of existence.

Hofstede's (1980) definition is very similar: "a broad tendency to prefer certain states of affairs over others" (p. 19). Our definition is a minor modification of those of Rokeach and Hofstede. We define a value as *a broad and relatively enduring preference for some state of affairs.*

As we proceed to elaborate on our definition, it seems prudent to start with a discussion of the only substantive difference between our definition and those of Hofstede and Rokeach. Namely, we drop the requirement that a value can only be conceived in relative terms. In support of his view, Hofstede (1980: 24) says:

> A rating of one value is as meaningful as the sound of one hand clapping. Most of us will value both "freedom" and "equality," but the difference between people will only appear when we look at the relative value attached to freedom over quality, or vice versa, in case of conflict.

In our view, the absolute importance of a value to an individual is as important as, and conceptually distinct from, the relative difference between two values. For instance, assume there is a reliable way to gauge a person's values on a 10-point scale. Executive A scores 4 on "power" and 6 on "family security," while Executive B scores 7 and 9, respectively. Both executives place the same relative 2-point premium on family security, but Executive B is far more intense about both values. While other theorists emphasize the prediction that both executives will tend to resolve conflicts in favor of family security, we wish to retain both that prediction as well as others that might be allowed by knowing about the absolute intensity of the person's values—possibly predictions about his or her search behavior, dissonance in the face of value conflict, and so on.[1]

Beyond this important difference, our conception of values is in line with most prominent theorists. Since some common threads have emerged in the definition of values, it is useful to elaborate on them.

First, most theorists allow for both personal and social values. Personal values are conceptions of what the person desires (e.g., prestige, family security, wealth, or wisdom). Social values have to do with what the person finds desirable in others or in the broader social system (e.g., rationality, honesty, courage, world at peace). Obviously, there is not a clear demarcation between the two sets. In fact, it could be said that all social values can be applied at the personal level. To the extent they do not agree— say that I value honesty in others but not so much in myself—we have the origins of hypocrisy and double standards. Similarly, to the extent personal values have higher intensity than social values, we have the origins of selfishness and isolation. Interestingly, we know of no recent theories or research which have studied the interplay between personal and social values.

Values can also be either instrumental or terminal, that is, dealing either with means or ends. For example, courage and honesty are primarily modes of conduct, whereas salvation and self-respect are end-states that a person may value to some degree. Here, again, there is no clear-cut demarcation. And, here too, little research has been done on the relationships between the two types. An interesting issue is the degree of clustering or concordance between certain terminal and instrumental values. For instance, given that a person considers equality a very important terminal value, what tend to be his or her dominant instrumental values?

Such a question takes us to consideration of the concept of a value system, a widely used term among theorists to refer to the complete network and associated valences of values held by an individual. As noted earlier, values cannot meaningfully be examined in isolation. As each value is learned or modified, it becomes integrated into an overall system of values in which each value has its own amount of priority. For instance, managers typically are confronted by situations in which they cannot satisfy all their values. They may have to choose between behaving compassionately or behaving competently; they may have to choose between pleasure and accomplishment. A hierarchy, or value system, thus exists for each person.

However, the concept of a value hierarchy presumes nothing about gradations between levels. For example, we suspect that the vast majority of possible values are jumbled together in the person's inner being with relatively little salience and little opportunity for exercise. At the top of each person's system are a small handful of dominant values of paramount importance.[2]

A final definitional feature of values is that they are relatively enduring, thus, standing in contrast to ephemeral attitudes or emotions. However, values are not entirely fixed over a person's adult life. Rokeach (1973: 11) commented on a theoretical conception that allows for both stability and change in a person's value system:

> It is stable enough to reflect the fact of sameness and continuity of a unique personality socialized within a given culture and society, yet unstable enough to permit

rearrangements of value priorities as a result of changes in culture, society, and personal experience.

Having summarized the major characteristics of values, it is useful to distinguish them from closely-related attributes—especially attitudes and beliefs. An attitude represents a feeling for a specific object or situation— say, towards promote-from-within policies, severance pay, or decentralization. A value, on the other hand, is a broader preference. Values shape attitudes, not the other way around (Becker and Connor, 1986). As Rokeach noted (1973: 160): "a value, unlike an attitude, is a standard or yardstick to guide actions, comparisons, evaluations, and justifications of self and others."

Values also stand in contrast to beliefs. A value has to do with what is desired or desirable, whereas a belief has to do with what is thought to exist (now or in the future) (Jacob, Flink, and Shuchman, 1962). As noted earlier, then, beliefs include knowledge or assumptions about future events, alternatives, or consequences attached to alternatives. For example, a manager might have a belief that incentive compensation does not bring about extra effort from employees. The manager might also highly value equality. One deals with what is, the other with what should be. As one could expect, and as we shall see below, values and beliefs influence and reinforce each other, but they are conceptually distinct (Kluckhohn, 1951).

REVIEW AND DISTILLATION OF FOUR MAJOR VALUE SCHEMES

One goal of this chapter is to review and integrate the approaches taken by researchers in the study of values. Such an analysis cannot possibly be exhaustive, since hundreds of different value measures and conceptualizations have been set forth (Bales and Couch, 1969). However, four schemes have achieved substantial recognition and have spawned major programs of research. Two of these—the Allport-Vernon-Lindzey instrument and Rokeach's Value Survey—were originated for the study of individuals in general. The other two—England's Personal Values Questionnaire and Hofstede's Work-Related Values instrument—were designed primarily for the study of managers and other organizational members. We will briefly review these four approaches, concentrating on their underlying assumptions and measures.

Allport-Vernon-Lindzey

The Allport-Vernon-Lindzey (A-V-L) "Study of Values" (1970) was developed out of the theoretical perspective of the philosopher Eduard

Spranger. In his book, *Types of Men* (1928), Spranger argued that the personalities of individuals are best known through examination of their values. He identified six major values which he believed to be held by individuals in varying degrees. These formed the basis for the six dimensions of the A-V-L instrument, listed and briefly defined as follows (1970, pp. 4-5):

Theoretical: "The dominant interest of the theoretical man is the discovery of *truth*.

Economic: The economic man is characteristically interested in what is *useful*.

Aesthetic: The aesthetic man sees his highest value in *form and harmony*.

Social: The highest value for this type is *love of people*.

Political: The political man is interested primarily in *power*.

Religious: The highest value of the religious man may be called *unity*.

Allport et al., measured the relative strength of these six values by a series of forced-choice questions, such as the following: "Which of the following branches of study do you expect ultimately will prove more important for mankind? (a) mathematics; (b) theology." In this instance, a person's response would be recorded as contributing to his theoretical or religious scores. A fixed total of 240 points are thus divided across the six categories.

Substantial reliability tests (test-retest and split-half) have been conducted with satisfactory results. Validity tests have also been conducted with supportive results. For instance, Mawardi (1952) found that the A-V-L test, when given in college, was highly predictive of occupational careers followed by students 5 to 15 years later.

Guth and Taguiri (1965) used the A-V-L scheme for their well-known study of values held by business executives. In a sample of participants in a senior executive education program, Guth and Taguiri found, not surprisingly, that economic values were rated the highest. Social values were rated the lowest. For comparison, groups of scientists and research managers were also studied, with both groups scoring highest on theoretical and lowest on social values.

Badr, Gray, and Kedia (1982) examined the differences in values of American and Egyptian business students, using the A-V-L system. They found that the two groups differed significantly, with the American students rating economic and political values most highly, and the Egyptian students rating theoretical and religious values most highly. In addition, the authors found that the students' values were strongly related to decision alternatives they picked in 14 written business situations. Whether the values would predict actual business decisions is, however, an open and unexplored question.

Beyond the obvious question of whether the A-V-L instrument can actually be used to predict managerial behaviors, two other limitations can be raised as well. First, the typology deals solely with the lofty side of human nature. Allport et al. (1970: 3) agree, as they describe Spranger's original scheme: "The neglect of sheerly sensuous values is a special weakness in his typology. His attempt to reduce hedonistic choices partly to economic and partly to aesthetic values seems unconvincing."

A second limitation is in the "fixed-pie," or ipsative, scoring system. Each respondent gets a total of 240 points, regardless of his or her actual value intensity across the six dimensions. Here again, Allport et al. note the flaw in Spranger's conception (1970: 3): "He does not allow for formless or valueless personalities, nor for those who follow an expedient or hedonistic philosophy of life." As noted above, the fixed-sum measurement approach is probably as much a result of attempts to avoid socially desirable responses (high scores on all values) as much as from a conceptual mandate.

Rokeach

A prominent figure in the study of values, Rokeach (1973) was explicit about the assumptions that guided his research: (1) There are a small number of values which all people hold to varying degrees; (2) values are an important and integral part of the individual's belief system; (3) values are a function of the culture, the society, and the personality of the individual; (4) finally, the consequences of values are manifested in nearly any phenomenon of interest to social scientists.

In developing his measurement system, Rokeach distinguished between two types of values—terminal and instrumental. As noted earlier, terminal values are preferences for certain end-states, and instrumental values deal with modes of conduct. Thus, Rokeach developed two separate inventories of 18 items each and asked respondents to rank them "in order of importance to you, as guiding principles in your life" (1973: 27). The 18 terminal values included items such as "a sense of accomplishment" and "true friendship." The instrumental values included items such as "ambitious" and "logical." The items were distilled from literature reviews, open-ended interviews, and exhaustive lists of personality-trait words. Test-retest reliabilities have been consistently satisfactory,and values profiles tend to correspond meaningfully with occupational categories, race, political party, and attitudes on major social issues (summarized in Rokeach, 1973).

However, application to managerial groups has been relatively limited. Sikula (1973), in a study of government executives, generally replicated Rokeach's profile of business executives—finding an emphasis on "competency" values (such as wise, logical, intellectual) and "initiative" values (such as imagination and courage). Munson and Posner (1980) found that the Rokeach instrument could be used to discriminate managers from nonmanagers in two large computer companies.

In an attempt to bring some parsimony to the total of 36 items in the Rokeach instrument, Howard, Shudo, and Umeshima (1983) conducted a factor analysis of responses from Japanese and American executives. They found six factors that closely resembled the factor structure observed by Rokeach (1973) in a study of a general population. For example, the factor "Competence vs. Morality" consisted of items such as forgiving and helpful (both loading positively); and intellectual, logical, and capable (loading negatively). The six-factor structure only accounted for 34 percent of variance but still greatly aids parsimony. For example, as a result of their factor analysis, Howard et al., were able to observe broad-based, robust differences between American and Japanese managers. In line with popular conceptions, the authors found that the American managers valued individuality, while the Japanese managers valued socially-oriented qualities.

England

England and his colleagues primarily have been interested in the study of values of managers in different cultures (e.g., England, 1967; England and Lee, 1974; England, Negandhi, and Wilpert, 1979; Whitely and England, 1980). As such, England is the only major theorist we are examining here who has been explicitly interested in managers. Thus, his explicit assumptions are of great pertinence to us:

1. Personal value systems influence a manager's perception of situations and problems he faces.

2. Personal value systems influence a manager's decisions and solutions to problems.

3. Personal value systems influence the way in which a manager looks at other individuals and groups of individuals; thus they influence interpersonal relationships.

4. Personal value systems influence the perception of individual and organizational success as well as their achievement.

5. Personal value systems set the limits for the determination of what is and what is not ethical behavior by a manager.

6. Personal value systems influence the extent to which a manager will accept or will resist organizational pressures and goals.

England's measurement scheme is by far the most complex of those we examine here. His Personal Values Questionnaire (PVQ) consists of 66 items in five categories: goals of business organizations, personal goals of individuals, groups of people, ideas associated with people, and ideas about general topics. Managers are asked to rate each of the 66 as either of high, average, or low importance. In addition, respondents are asked to indicate why the item has the indicated importance—because it is "right," "successful," or "pleasant." Then, by examining the items marked as high in importance, England quantitatively assesses whether the respondent's values were driven by pragmatism (values held because they are "successful"), moral ("right"), or feeling ("pleasant").

Through his various studies, England observed several strong patterns. For instance, he found that American managers are particularly pragmatic (England, 1967). That is, they rate values as highly important primarily because they consider those values to be associated with success. Pragmatism was found later to be the dominant orientation of both male and female American managers (Watson and Ryan, 1979). While a variety of intercultural differences have been observed, results indicate that, regardless of culture, managers who hold dynamic, pragmatic, and achievement-oriented values are more successful professionally (at least in the narrow terms of age-adjusted salary) than managers who value social welfare, obedience, and security (England and Lee, 1974).

Addressing the complexity of the 66-item instrument, Whitely and England (1980) conducted a factor analysis of responses from over 2,000 managers in the United States, Australia, India, Korea, and Japan. They found that 12 factors could be extracted, accounting for 48 percent of total variance. Examples of the factors are "Entrepreneurialism" (consisting of change, risk, and competition) and "Extrinsic Rewards" (consisting of money and property). The factor reduction achieves some parsimony, but the scheme remains very cumbersome.

The PVQ has the advantage of not assuming a fixed-pie of values. Namely, respondents can conceivably rate all items as unimportant or highly important. While appealing conceptually, it is not clear what such approach yields in the way of reliability. In fact, data on reliability and validity of the PVQ are somewhat limited.

Hofstede

Like England, Hofstede was primarily interested in cross-cultural comparisons of values (Hofstede, 1980, 1983). He administered 32 value questions to matched samples of employees of a large multinational corporation in 50 countries. Respondents used Likert-type scales to indicate their degree of agreement with such statements as: "How important is it to you to have an opportunity for advancement to higher level jobs?" and "How satisfied are you with the freedom you have to adopt your own approach to the job?" Hofstede developed his list of items by having a prior conception of some major value dimensions he thought to be relevant. Compared to the other approaches we have reviewed, Hofstede asked about relatively specific likes and dislikes—preferences which approximate attitudes as we have defined them.

Interestingly, Hofstede's primary emphasis was on using individual responses within a country to characterize the values and culture of the overall country. By factor analyzing results from 40 countries, he found that four dimensions emerged, accounting for 50 percent of variance. The four dimensions, and brief interpretations, are as follows (Hofstede, 1984: 390):

Power distance:	defines the extent to which inequality in power is seen as normal.
Individualism:	assumption that individuals look primarily after their own interest and those of their immediate family (as opposed to collectivism).
Masculinity:	an assumption of very different social roles for men and women— that men be assertive, competitive, and striving for material success; that women serve and care for the nonmaterial quality of life.
Uncertainty Avoidance:	the extent to which people are made nervous by situations they consider to be unstructured, unclear, or unpredictable.

Hofstede not only found that nationality accounted for major differences in these values, but also that occupational category, age, and sex accounted for differences as well. No predictive associations with other tangible behaviors have been established; however, Jackofsky and Slocum, in this volume, present anecdotal evidence of how executive behavior is a function of the values proposed by Hofstede.

Toward a Core Set of Executives Values

Theorists obviously have set forth many value dimensions—far too many for the researcher to fully reconcile or employ. Adding to the frustration is that none of the major theorists have pointedly addressed how or why their own value typologies differ from the others. The result, as noted by Becker and Connor (1986) in a review of the values literature, is severe disjointedness.

In order for theory-building and research on executive values to advance, a distillation of a core set of values pertaining to executives must be accomplished. Fortunately, close inspection of the extant value schemes reveals striking overlaps in support of such an aim. We will now present our own such attempt.

Our intent is not to develop an exhaustive scheme. Rather, we wish to identify a limited set of value dimensions which, (a) have support or precedent in two or more of the major frameworks we have reviewed; and

Table 1. A Distilled Set of Six Significant Executive Value Dimensions

Executive Value Dimension	Allport, Vernon Lindzey (1960)	Analogues in Other Value Schemes		
		Rokeach (1973)[1]	England (1967)[2]	Hofstede (1980)
Collectivism	Social	Personal vs. Social World at Peace National Security Equality	Social Equality Social Welfare Liberalism Equality Compassion Employee Welfare	Individualism (−)
Duty		Inner vs. Other-Directed Obedient Polite Helpful Clean	Personal Loyalty Loyalty Trust Obedience Honor Dignity	
Rationality	Theoretical	Competence vs. Morality Intellectual Logical Capable	Irrational Behavior (−) Conflict Emotions Prejudice	Masculinity
Novelty			Entrepreneurialism Change Risk Competition	Uncertainty Avoidance (−)
Materialism	Economic	Delayed vs. Immediate Gratification Pleasure A Comfortable Life An Exciting Life	Extrinsic Rewards Money Property	
Power	Political		Personal Influence Prestige Power Influence	Power Distance

[1]Listed are factor names and component elements from a factor analysis of Rokeach's items conducted by Howard et al. (1983), on samples of American and Japanese executives.

[2]Listed are factor names and component elements from a factor analysis of England's items conducted by Whitely and England (1980) on a sample of executives from several countries.

(b) are expected to have a significant effect on a broad array of organizational actions and attributes. Thus, we exclude dimensions such as aesthetic and religious factors, which, even though of general importance, probably do not play major roles in a broad array of organizational circumstances.[3] We also exclude dimensions which we expect would yield little variance among senior executives—for example, achievement.

Based on those criteria, we believe the following six value dimensions represent a parsimonious set of central importance to observers of executive behavior:

Collectivism:	to value the wholeness of humankind and of social systems; regard and respect for all people.
Duty:	to value the integrity of reciprocal relationships; obligation and loyalty.
Rationality:	to value fact-based, emotion-free decisions and actions.
Novelty:	to value change, the new, the different.
Materialism:	to value wealth and pleasing possessions.
Power:	to value control of situations and people.

Table 1 portrays how these six dimensions align with the values proposed by the theorists discussed above. Coalescing prior research, our framework greatly reduces the disjointedness of the earlier schemes. In fact, striking commonalities exist among these previously disparate approaches. We will draw upon our typology later in the chapter, particularly in hypothesizing how the six value dimensions might be associated with specific organizational actions and attributes.

ORIGINS OF EXECUTIVE VALUES

Values only exist in a social, or relational, context. While one can speak of "needs" in infants, one can speak of "values" only in maturing or mature individuals who have been regularly exposed to models, rules, and sanctions of a social system. The social system exists in several layers, including national culture, regional society, family, and employing organizations.

As indicated above, the influence of national culture in shaping values of executives has been heavily examined. Studies by Bendix (1956), Sutton, Harris, Kaysen, and Tobin (1956), and Chatov (1973) all concluded that the values which American business executives bring to their tasks are predominantly due to a national system of beliefs. England (1975), in statistical research comparing managers from the United States, Japan, Australia, Korea, and India, found that countries accounted for 30 to 45 percent of the variations in values. Hofstede (1980) similarly documented the strong role of national culture in accounting for values. His results were particularly persuasive since his subsamples consisted of employees of a single multinational firm which itself had a strong unifying culture; moreover the sub-samples were matched according to education and occupational category.

While national culture accounts for a substantial portion of value development, other layers of the social system operate as well. Cohort history, and particularly the occurrence of wars, depressions, disasters, or major social movements, can sharply affect the values of a body of individuals in a society (e.g., Kluckhohn, 1951; Jacob, Flink, and Schuchman, 1962; Schmidt and Posner, 1983). For example, the actions and outlooks of two U.S. cohorts are routinely attributed in part to the indelible impressions of the Great Depression of the 1930s and the antiestablishment movement of the 1960s.

Family influences are also a critical determinant of values. For example, Rokeach found that family characteristics such as class, race, and religious upbringing were all strongly associated with value variations within a culture (Rokeach, 1969a, 1969b; Rokeach and Parker, 1970). Thus, by early adulthood an individual's value system tends to have a relatively distinct form.

Then, professional selection and socialization processes—originating at both the occupational and organizational levels—serve to reinforce and modify values. We can expect that the values of executives, even more so than those of other members, are greatly shaped by employing organizations, since executives typically have lengthy cumulative exposure to their organizations' norms; and since, almost by definition, they have achieved success by adherence to those norms.

At the occupational level, a self-selection process occurs, such that individuals entering a certain line of work tend to have values that differ from the population as a whole. For example, Allport et al. (1970) reported that the values of students majoring in business administration were significantly different from students in other fields—notably emphasizing economic and political values and deemphasizing social and religious values. Rawls and Nelson (1975) similarly found that there was a significant correspondence between MBA students' values (measured by the A.V.L. instrument) and their intentions to enter certain types of industries.

Selection processes continue to operate after entry to an occupation, and socialization processes also occur. To the extent the occupation has a codified body of standards and norms which are repeatedly reinforced, members can be expected to strengthen their values (e.g., Blau and McKinley, 1979; Cafferata, 1979). Moreover, if the person is highly successful within his or her occupation, the initial values which formed the basis for selection are reinforced (Mortimer and Lorence, 1979).

In this vein, the recent proliferation of management publications, executive education programs and visible executive "heroes" (e.g., Iacocca, Welch, and Perot), almost certainly have led to a vastly more pronounced "executive culture" than existed earlier in the United States. That is, executives today may have more extreme and homogeneous values than their predecessors.

The employing organization also exerts its own pressure on values. This too occurs both through selection and socialization. Organizations convey something of themselves in attracting employment candidates and, in turn, seek to hire individuals whose values "fit" the setting. After the entry screen, socialization occurs (Feldman, 1981). Organizations use a combination of such methods as training, mentoring, ceremonies, rewards, legends, and myths to shape the values of members (Louis, Posner, and Powell, 1983; Pfeffer, 1981). The longer a member stays in the organization, the more his or her values can be expected to resemble those preferred by the organization (Wiener, 1982). Members who achieve extraordinary success by abiding by and transmitting organizational values—members such as executives—can be particularly thought to embrace those values.

In sum, senior executives can be expected to have relatively entrenched value sets. Their extended exposure to value-shaping stimuli, their self-selection into settings compatible with their values, and the reinforcement they have received through their successes, all give rise to a well-defined value profile. This is not to say that executives' values are particularly noble or of a higher order than other individuals', but rather that their values are relatively deeply held and fixed.

LINK BETWEEN EXECUTIVE VALUES AND ACTION

Despite the abundant literature on values, very little theory or research has been set forth on how values are converted into action. With limited exceptions (e.g., England, 1967), the few investigators who have explored the association between managerial values and actions have been primarily interested in cross-sectionally documenting that such a link might exist, rather than the operative process by which it occurs (e.g., Guth and Taguiri, 1965; Farris, 1973; England, 1973; Lee, 1975). Similarly, the broader literature on executive action and complex decision making usually implies a role for values; however, that role and its mechanisms for occurrence are not specified (e.g., Cyert and March, 1963; Bower, 1970; Allison, 1970; MacCrimmon and Taylor, 1976).

Accordingly, any attempt to model the link between executive values and action must be taken as preliminary and incomplete. Our purpose in this section is to propose such a model. We will start with a general model, including several propositions; we will then propose a variation which accounts for constraints on executive discretion.

A General Model

Our general model, portrayed in Figure 1, indicates that values influence action in two ways. First, there is a direct influence which occurs when the executive selects a course of action strictly because of his or her preferences. Facts may be well or poorly grasped, but they are immaterial (Simon, 1957). The person's values dictate a behavior. For example, an executive who has strong egalitarian values might hold managerial perquisites to a minimum, regardless of available data—even data he or she fully comprehends—on positive motivational consequences of such perquisites. In this case, values alone guide the behavior. We will use England's (1967) term "behavior channeling" to refer to this direct influence of values on action.

Far more common, however, is an indirect effect in which values influence the manager's perceptions of stimuli; those perceptions, in turn, shape action. In this mode, the manager "sees what he wants to see," "hears what she wants to hear" (Weick, 1979). This well known process of "perceptual screening" (England, 1967) has been documented by numerous psychologists but primarily derives from early work by Postman, Bruner, and McGinnies (1948). To return to the above instance of the executive with strong egalitarian values, it is likely that he or she would seek and embrace any data unsupportive of executive perquisities and would discount any supportive data. A decision not to have such perquisites can again be expected.

In order to posit ideas about the relative roles and impacts of these two pathways—behavior channeling and perceptual screening—one must make some assumptions about the awareness of executives toward their values and their decision styles. First, it is logical, and not at all circular, to expect that executives have values about the roles of their values in decision making. For example, as we shall note below, one's values toward duty and rationality might greatly affect the degree to which other values are manifested through behavior channeling versus perceptual screening. Second, executives (as do all individuals) have the capacity to juggle their own values, to sense which of their values are most overdue for fulfillment, or, conversely, which values are currently relatively sated. Consciously or unconsciously, the executive will take turns honoring her various values. Third, the executive has some capacity for considering how others perceive her values and her exercise of them. This means she may try to feign certain values or to hide others. She may realize that she can only fulfill important values if she appears to operate without regard for them. Since, in most cultures, executives are not supposed to cater to their own values, such masking may be common, even a preoccupation.

Figure 1.   General Model of the Link Between
Executive Values and Actions

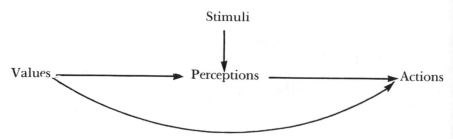

In general, then, executives have some tendency to "step outside" their values—to consider their existence, their fulfillment and how they are perceived. Executives differ in the degree of this tendency, but few are devoid of it. Therefore, the typical view that executives unwittingly allow their values to creep continually into their actions may be a serious over-simplification.

We now turn to several propositions dealing with the modes by which values are manifested in executive behavior.

P1.   Dominant values (those that are very strongly held) operate more through behavior channeling than do weak values.

If the value is strong, it is a guiding force that can surmount and supercede data. In fact, data are not even needed. Action can be taken on the basis of the preference alone. Conversely, if the value is weaker, the executive will be less likely to decide strictly on the basis of preference. He or she will have greater need to bolster the decision with supportive data, applying reality tests, so to speak. Moreover, the executive is less willing to appear ideological in pursuit of a weak value, and, therefore, is less inclined to take an action, or appear to take an action, simply because of personal preference. Instead, data will be sought and screened; the eventual decision will seem less value-laden.

P2.   The more complex and ambiguous the stimuli, the greater the role for perceptual screening than for behavioral channeling.

Ambiguity evokes equivocality. The executive will be less inclined to directly favor a value if available stimuli are abundant and vague. Moreover, such stimuli heighten the possibility that the executive can locate plausible data supportive of his or her view and thus avoid the appearance of a strictly ideological stance.

The next three propositions return to our view that one's values affect the role of values in decision making.

P3. The more the executive values rationality, the more his or her values will operate through perceptual screening than through behavior channeling.

The believer in rationality strives to gather and evaluate facts, no matter how subjective, and is not inclined to act strictly on the basis of preference. This is not to say that such a person achieves an objective, undistorted interpretation of available stimuli. In fact, we would expect value-based distortions to play their usual major role.

P4. The more the executive values duty, the more he or she will submerge his other values when making major decisions; however, his or her other values may be strongly reflected in minor decisions.

P5. The more the executive values power, the more he or she will exercise values in large decisions; however, his or her values may be submerged in minor decisions.

Here, we are arguing that certain values can be pivotal in affecting the role of other values in decisions. The duty-bound executive is expected to try to hold his other preferences aside in making decisions for the organization. Behavioral channeling particularly will be limited. It may be in small, minor decisions that the executive allows himself any value favors. Conversely, the power-seeking executive will inject his values into major choices as he attempts fundamentally to mold the organization to terms that suit him. However, he may waive his values in small actions to allow placative side-payments to various constituencies.

This concludes discussion of our general model. We have argued that values are transmitted to executive action in two ways: (1) directly through behavioral channeling, and (2) indirectly through perceptual screening. We have also suggested that the executive's values will affect the relative predominance of the two modes, as well as the general degree to which the executive's values will be manifested in organizational outcomes.

A Moderated Model

We now turn to a more subtle view, in which we examine the moderating influences of context on the link between values and action. Specifically, we will argue that any such link depends on how much discretion the executive possesses. Schematically, this model is portrayed as Figure 2.

Figure 2.   Discretion as a Moderator of the Value-Action Link

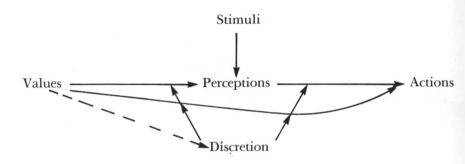

It is well known that executives do not always have complete latitude of action (Lieberson and O'Connor, 1972; Hannan and Freeman, 1977). It is only to the extent they have discretion that their values will appear in organizational outcomes. Hambrick and Finkelstein (1987) argue that discretion is determined by three sets of forces: (1) the degree to which the *environment* allows variety and change; (2) the degree to which the *organization* itself is amenable to an array of possible actions and empowers the executive to formulate and execute those actions; and, (3) the degree to which the *executive* personally is able to envision or create multiple courses of action.

The role of discretion in moderating the effects of executives on their organizations has been documented directly or indirectly from a variety of vantages. Lieberson and O'Connor (1972) found that more variance in profitability could be attributed to CEO's in industries with high advertising intensity and high growth rates—both of which signal discretion (Hambrick and Finkelstein,1987)—than in more commodity-like or low-growth industries. Carroll (1984) found that newspapers had a disproportionately high death rate following the departure of a founder who served both as publisher and editor, and who thus possessed substantial discretion. Reinganum (1985) found that the stock market responds to the departure of a CEO only if the firm is small, the predecessor departs the scene, and the successor comes from the outside—all attributes conferring discretion. Miller and Toulouse (1986) found that CEO personality was more strongly related to strategy and structure in small firms in dynamic environments than in larger firms in stable environments. As a final example—and perhaps the most pointed of those noted—Hage and Dewar (1973) found that the values of the entire elites of health and welfare organizations were better predictors of subsequent innovations than were the values of the executive directors alone. As professional and typically pluralistic organizations, one could expect that the executive directors in these agencies had limited discretion.

Examples of executives with limited discretion include the CEO who heads a regulated utility in a mature market; who heads a firm which has a dominating stockholder or former chairman still on the board; or who himself is without energy or capacity for search. We would expect to find that these executives' values would not greatly manifest themselves in organizational outcomes. Major actions are relatively few, and any such actions emanate from forces other than the executive.

Conversely, we would expect a far stronger link between an executive's values and organizational outcomes in situations of high discretion: firms in high-growth, differentiable-product industries; firms that are relatively young and not very capital intensive; and situations where the executive is a dominant shareholder and has breadth of perspective so as to be aware of multiple options on various fronts.

Since discretion is in part determined by the executive's own attributes, we can expect that values help to shape discretion (the dotted line in Figure 2). For example, an executive who values rationality may be relatively inclined to conduct exhaustive searches for alternatives and, in doing so, will improve the chances of locating options that suit his or her other values (e.g., novelty or collectivism) as well. Similarly, an executive who values novelty will be relatively inclined to generate radical, innovative options. There is a greater chance that the options identified will bear closer relationships to the executive's other values than would occur if the executive were more content with the status quo.

Clearly, any attempts to study the transmission of executive values into organizational outcomes must be sensitive to the amount of discretion the executive possesses. We anticipate that executives often have limited discretion, and, hence, organizational outcomes may bear no correspondence to managerial values. However, the absence of any such links is not in itself evidence about the executive's values or lack thereof.

Alternatively, it may be that executive selection processes favor candidates whose values—both areas and intensities of values—match the amount of discretion the executive will be afforded. Executives with strong values in low-discretion situations could be extremely frustrated or frustrating to the system. Over time, an executive who is restrained from exercising his or her values in major organizational choices has five major options:

- They inject their values into relatively minor organization choices (e.g., parking lot policy, memo format policy, office decor).

- They inject their values into affairs outside the organization (civic, church, family, clubs).
- They modify (neutralize) their values to suit the lack of discretion.
- They experience disillusionment and frustration over lack of value fulfillment.
- They depart in search of a setting where values can be better exercised.

We cannot surmise the relative frequency with which these various responses to values blockages occur, nor the sequence in which they tend to occur for a given executive. Scholarly pursuit of such issues could help shed light on major dilemmas in organizational and executive behavior. At this point it might simply be said that mismatches between executive values and discretion are of potentially major significance.

Some Expected Associations

Having discussed the mechanisms by which values are transmitted into action, as well as the possibility that limited discretion may dampen any such relationships, we can now specify some general associations that can be expected to exist between executives' values and the attributes of their organizations. We rely on the scheme laid out by Galbraith and Nathanson (1978) for categorizing various managerial levers: strategy, structure, information/decision processes, rewards and people. We use the distilled list of values set forth earlier in the chapter (Table 1). These two schemes allow the matrix presented as Table 2.

Our aim is only to portray some illustrative possibilities. Thus, even though several hypothesized entries could probably be developed for every cell, we restrict ourselves to some of the more interesting associations that might be expected between executive values and organizational attributes. For example, we expect that executives who highly value rationality will develop relatively comprehensive, analytic decision processes (Fredrickson, 1984). Executives who value novelty will tend to undertake "prospecting" strategies of on-going product/market initiatives (Hage and Dewar, 1973; Miles and Snow, 1978); and so on.

Although the occurrence of these associations depends on the executive's degree of discretion, it still is clear from Table 2 that the potential impact of top executive values on the organization is farreaching. Values of top managers may affect the organization's competitive actions, the way in which it makes decisions, and, perhaps most importantly, the types of people who are selected and retained. It is through the latter mechanism—selecting and retaining certain types of people—that values can create an ever-tightening spiral resulting in extremely homogeneous outlooks. We now turn to the implications that this condition, and others stemming from executive values, may have for organizational performance.

Table 2. Some Hypothesized Links between Executive Values and Actions

| | | | Organizational Actions and Attributes | | |
| | | | | | |
Executive Value	Strategy	Structure	Information/ Decision Processes	Rewards	People
Collectivism	Significant corporate philanthropy; Related diversification with many inter-unit flows	Flat structure; many committees	Participative decision processes	Rewards heavily tied to overall firm performance	Promote-from-within policies; lifetime employment
Duty	Long-term vertical relationships (suppliers and customers); little contract litigation against firm		Open, two-way communication channels; Well-developed audit and control systems	Executive perquisites/ bonuses tightly tied to market norms	Long tenures; few layoffs
Rationality	Incremental strategies based primarily on "calculable" factors (e.g., prices, costs, capacities)	Highly formalized structure	Comprehensive/ analytic processes	Highly formalized pay systems (e.g., Hay); emphasis on quantitative performance measures)	Routinized personnel policies (e.g., selection, evaluation, advancement); large personnel staffs
Novelty	Prospecting (many product-market initiatives)	Frequent reorganizations; structural ambiguity (matrix, etc.)	Spontaneity; decision-making outside formal channels and processes	Frequent changes in reward system; Large incentives for innovation	Heterogeneous management cadre; limited pressure for conformity
Materialism	Portfolio churning (frequent acquisitions and divestitures)	Small staffs; Low administrative intensity		Extraordinary executive pay and perks	Opportunistic hiring and firing of key executives
Power		Highly Centralized	Tight control of information and resources at top of organization; Top-down decision-making	Subjective criteria for awarding (large) incentives	Pliant, supplicant subordinates

EXECUTIVE VALUES AND
ORGANIZATIONAL ACCOMPLISHMENT

If values affect choices, then they also must affect organizational achievements. Viewed positively, values may be thought of as providing a central focus for action, a superordinate vision, or as the glue for binding the organization's members together. Viewed negatively, values can be thought of as the reason organizational resources are sometimes diverted to the selfish aims of individuals or cliques; as rationales for exclusion; or as the cause of insular homogeneity in some organizations.

Very little concrete evidence exists as to the normative implications of executive values. Over a decade ago, Connor and Becker (1975: 557) wrote: "there are few data which allow anything except speculation about the relationship between values and organizational effectiveness." Regrettably, the situation today remains essentially the same. Almost no systematic research has been done on the links between executive values and performance. With limited exception (to be discussed below), the closest thing has been a stream of research that has examined the associations between executives' values and their own "success" in their organizations (e.g., England and Lee, 1974; Munson and Posner, 1980; Ryan, Watson, and Williams, 1981; Jaskolka, Beyer, and Trice, 1985). Accordingly, our own thoughts on the issue of values and organizational achievement are preliminary.

Values and Organizational Performance

We turn first to the conventional conception of organizational performance and will try to assess whether and how executive values might affect the attainment of stakeholder purpose. Our discussion will focus on two major issues: Are stakeholders disserved by executives who inject their own values into decision making? Is organizational performance helped or hurt by homogeneous values within a management team?

Should Values Be Reined In?   Of central concern is whether the organization will perform better or worse if executives attempt to set their values aside in making decisions. One line of reasoning is that executives are stewards of the organization's resources and, as such, should try to submerge their own preferences in favor of the interests of the broader coalition. However, this is an unrealistic and probably harmful view.

As discussed earlier, values operate largely at the unconscious level in shaping the executive's perceptions of situations. Admittedly, we argued earlier that executives have some capacity for comprehending their own values. However, we doubt that this is a well-honed aptitude, and particularly doubt that it extends to an ability to understand the processual implications of one's values. Values enter early in the decision process to affect information acquisition, screening, and distortion (Cyert and March, 1963; Mintzberg et al., 1976). Executives thus make—or at least think they make—decisions on the basis of "factual" support. What they do not always recognize—and can probably never fully reconstruct—is how their values have shaped their interpretation of facts. In short, setting executive values aside in decision making is not possible.

As importantly, it may not be desirable. Andrews (1971: 108) spoke of managerial values impinging on choices: "We must accept not only the inevitability but the desirability of this intervention." In his view, executive commitment and energy can only be expected when the executive has a preference for what he or she is doing. Pursuing a strategy that runs counter to one's values is to elicit half-heartedness or, worse, even the inward hope that the offending initiative will fail.

Barnard (1938) addressed the positive role of executive values somewhat differently, arguing that values are the mechanisms that keep executives from "overloading." In Barnard's view, a "moral code" is the basis for sorting the bewildering load of information and options that confront the executive. In its absence, the executive bogs down. An attempt to neutralize the executive's value system would presumably bring the same result.

If controlling forces—boards of directors or trustees—are concerned about executive values, the place to address it is in executive selection. As argued by agency theorists (e.g., Jensen and Meckling, 1976; Fama, 1980), the board may have additional opportunity to moderate or bend executive values through a system of rewards and controls. But, for the most part, the values of individuals chosen to run the firm will run their course.

Homogeneity of Team Values. An important issue is whether homogeneity or heterogeneity of managerial values leads to higher organizational performance. Barnard (1938) framed the two sides very well. On the one hand, he argued that "compatibility" of executives is an important factor in organizational success, and that such compatibility derives from similarity of values. On the other hand, he noted that "excessive compatibility or harmony is deleterious, resulting in 'single track minds' and excessively crystallized attitudes" (p. 225).

Unfortunately, the limited literature on group values does not resolve the question. There is some evidence that extreme homogeneity of values (such as portrayed in Figure 3-1) helps organizational performance by creating a unity of vision and smoothing communication, (e.g., Jacob, Flink, and Schuchman, 1962; Reddy and Sheets, 1979; Beyer and Trice, 1978). However, evidence also exists that homogeneity hurts performance by severely restricting information processing capabilities (Janis, 1972; DeWoot,

Heyvaert, and Martou, 1977), and, by extension, that diversity of values (Figure 3-2) is desirable.

A variation suggested by some theorists is that the top management team should have similar values but dissimilar cognitive experiences and expertise (Janis, 1972; Shaw, 1976). The ideal team would be tightly clustered on key value dimensions (such as in Figure 3-1) but broadly dispersed on experience dimensions. To achieve sufficient dissimilarity of cognitions would require a mix of individuals with different tenures in the organization, different types of education, different functional and business backgrounds, and different outside affiliations. Such diversity could help ensure that a wide range of information is accessible to and considered by the team in its deliberations. However, the chief problem with such an approach is that the team's homogeneous values still may serve as severe filters and distorters of incoming information, thus quite possibly overriding the supposed diversity the members are expected to contribute.

Another compromise solution would be to have a homogeneous set of dominant values among the majority of the team but strive to include a limited number of members who have different values. In the extreme (Figure 3-3), the team would then include token deviants whose values differ sharply from the rest of the team. However, these "voices in the wilderness" can be expected to encounter sharp discounting of their ideas, isolation, and short tenures (Wagner, Pfeffer, and O'Reilly, 1984).

A perhaps more promising approach would be to have a nucleus of individuals who hold the core values and a limited number of people who differ from the mode in varying degrees (Figure 3-4). This approach would allow for mediators or interpreters who could span between the views of extreme members and those comprising the values-nucleus.[4]

We do not envision a universal answer to the question of the desirability of values homogeneity. However, extending some ideas of Hambrick and Mason (1984), our thoughts so far lead to these conclusions:

1. As long as the organization's strategy is stable and generally suits conditions in the environment (a period of what Tushman and Romanelli [1985] would call "convergence"), homogeneity of values will yield effective decisions and a very efficient process for arriving at those decisions. An efficient decision process is fast and consumes relatively few organizational resources.
2. When the environment is disruptive and discontinuous, heterogeneity of values will yield the most effective decisions. The team will not be particularly efficient; for example, dissensus and "political loops" will abound (Mintzberg, Raisinghani, and Theoret, 1976). However, eventual decision quality will surpass what could be achieved by a homogeneous team.
3. Since environmental disruptions can occur at any time and without warning (Kaufman, 1985), an organization maximizes its chances of long-term survival by having at least some diversity of values within its top management team.

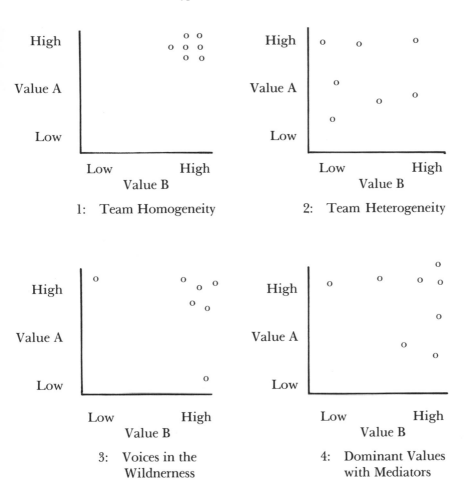

Figure 3. Alternative Team Profiles on
Two Hypothetial Value-Dimensions

1: Team Homogeneity

2: Team Heterogeneity

3: Voices in the
Wildnerness

4: Dominant Values
with Mediators

Values and Instructive Extremism—A New View

So far, in discussing how executive values affect organizational achievement, we have drawn on the customary way of evaluating organizations: according to their effectiveness in meeting immediate stakeholders' goals (profits, stability, employee welfare, and so on). However, individual organizations fulfill another important need. They serve as experiments, examples, and object lessons for other organizations and society at large. Organizations provide demonstration of what is possible, what works, what does not work. What might be called "accomplishment" of an organization thus amounts to the sum total of what the organization yields to the larger social system, both through substantive performance as well as useful instruction and insight.

Under this definition, all other things equal, bland, unimaginative organizations that strictly imitate other organizations do not contribute as much as radical, innovative organizations. Regardless of whether they succeed or fail, bold organizations accomplish something. They are the way in which limits are tested and re-defined—limits of product design, process technology, organizational and employment practices. Thus, Freddie Laker, the British pioneer of cut-rate no-frills air travel, accomplished an immense amount, regardless of his firm's failure. Donald Burr, the founder of People Express Airlines, exploited the Laker legacy and then contributed his own— a visible experiment with employee stock ownership, job rotation, and flat organizational structure. Burr's experiment worked for awhile, then it collapsed. However, at this writing, other airlines are experimenting with modified approaches to Burr's formula. Thus, Burr literally created knowledge, insight, and options for others. His organization thus accomplished a great deal even though it failed.

Our central premise is that organizations provide extraordinary instruction only when they are headed by executives with very strongly held values. For the most part, only firms led by executives who strongly value novelty will yield major innovations. Only firms led by executives who strongly value collectivism (as apparently Burr did) will undertake major social experiments. None of this is to say that strong executive values will always be fulfilled, but rather that non-extreme values lead to non-extreme organizations.

Gray, unintense executive value systems tend to yield gray, neutral organizational behavior. The gray organization's "performance," in the conventional sense, may be satisfactory. (As an imitator, even that probably will not be exceptionally high or sustainable.) However, the organization's accomplishment in the larger social system will be moderate at best.

SUMMARY AND NEEDED RESEARCH

This chapter has attempted to review and integrate major portions of the literature on executive values. Following an initial discussion of values as a concept, we examined the major value typologies and measurement approaches that have been used in prior research. We distilled the following six value dimensions as a preliminary core set for studying executives: collectivism, duty, rationality, novelty, materialism, and power. Next, we considered the origins of executive values—national culture, family, cohort, and profession, particularly emphasizing the selection and socialization processes that occur both at the occupational and the organizational levels.

We then examined the processes by which executive values may become reflected in actions. Following England (1967), we argued that values may directly affect choices or may indirectly affect them by shaping perceptions. We hypothesized a relatively complete set of organizational attributes that could be expected to follow from each of the six types of executive values noted above. Finally, the paper examined the prescriptive implications of executive values. We argued that long-run and short-run performance may be balanced by having a top team whose majority embraces a core set of values, but with some members who deviate from the core in varying degrees. As a closing observation, we suggested that extreme executive values provide the basis for experimentation and re-defining organizational capabilities.

Although this chapter follows a vast literature and itself addresses numerous issues, an understanding of executive values—their forms, origins, and effects—still lies ahead of us. Future research should build on the foundation set by prior theorists, but new directions and emphases are needed as well.

Methods and instruments need to be given renewed attention. Existing questionnaires have certain strengths and weaknesses which need to be carefully assessed, perhaps as part of an attempt to develop a new, brief, synthesized instrument. In addition, projective techniques, interviews, and simple experiments should be part of the overall effort to gauge executive values. Unfortunately, overt behaviors cannot be used as direct indices of values, since they are the hypothesized outcomes of the values (Kluckhohn, 1951).

Projects need to be conducted on a variety of important issues. Turning first to the origins of values, we need research on values of executives with different regional and family upbringings, educational and career experiences. Especially needed are longitudinal studies of how values change or become strengthened over one's career. The researcher would want to be alert to possible life-stage effects, socialization effects, and—particularly pertinent for successful executives—reinforcement effects. It is expected that values do not remain constant in their intensity over one's career, but the process and triggers for change are not well understood.

Research on the effects of executive values is needed, as well. The process by which values affect perceptions in complex decision-making warrants inquiry. The straightforward association between executive values and actions has so far gone largely untested, and is thus an area of great need and opportunity. Guth and Taguiri (1967) posited that values would be reflected in organizational outcomes; and in this paper we hypothesized numerous specific relationships (Table 2). However, empirical evidence is needed. If the relationship between values and outcomes is found to be weak, research must be undertaken to explain the observed poor correspondence, possibly including moderators such as discretion (Hambrick and Finkelstein, 1987), power (Pfeffer, 1981; Mintzberg, 1983), or inertia (Hannan and Freeman, 1977). In turn, a research question arises: What are the effects on organizations and on the executives themselves when they are somehow disallowed from exercising their values?

Research needs to extend beyond the single person at the top. Studies of values within top management teams could yield important information on processes of selection, cohesion, and communication. In addition, we need to know the circumstances under which homogeneous team values help and hurt organizational performance.

Finally, at the simply descriptive level, more research is needed to document the value tendencies of executives and the degree to which they differ from other groups within societies. As the stewards of much of our human and material resources, there are major implications if executives possess, or are tending toward, extreme or aberrant values.

Admittedly, to study executive values is to delve into the murkiest of organizational phenomena. Yet, the role of values in influencing organizational processes, memberships, and outcomes is enormous. We encourage researchers to explore this topic of great organizational and social importance.

ACKNOWLEDGMENTS

This paper is based on research sponsored by Columbia University's Strategy Research Center. Jim Fredrickson, Steve Grover, Jim Kuhn, Carol Marais, Lance Sandelands, and John Slocum made helpful comments on earlier drafts.

NOTES

1. Interestingly, the definitional emphasis other theorists place on the relative weighting of values may have been forced upon them by their measurement methods. As we shall see below, the prominent attempts to measure values tend to rely on "zero-sum" approaches— rank ordering or dividing up a "value-pie." These approaches were thought necessary because of the threat of socially desirable responses to open-sum gauges. Thus, methodological considerations may have greatly restricted both theoretical and empirical insights.

2. One thoughtful colleague has commented to us that the hierarchical metaphor is misleading, a distinctly male-oriented view which imposes too much order, sense of win versus lose, and sense of top versus bottom on values phenomena. Such a concern is probably legitimate, yet our own attempt to identify a clear, concise alternative portrayal has not yielded much. The idea of a person's "values hierarchy" must be taken as a crude contrivance.

3. Our exclusion of religious values warrants more explanation, particularly in light of the opening Marriott anecdote. On the one hand, we expect religious values to be of great importance in some organization contexts. On the other hand, and contrary to Spranger (1928),

we do not believe that "religious" can meaningfully be considered a scalar dimension. Followers of different religions hold often widely differing values, many of which are captured, we believe, by the six dimensions we propose. Obviously, treatment of religious values poses a challenge for theorists. Our own approach stems from practical grounds.

4. See Brunson (1985) for an illustration of a clustering procedure for studying top management team values.

REFERENCES

Allison, G.T. *Essence of Decision*. Boston, MA: Little, Brown, 1971.

Allport, G.W., Vernon, P.E., and Lindzey, G. *Study of Values*. New York: Houghton Mifflin, 1970.

Andrews, K.R. *The Concept of Corporate Strategy*. Homewood, IL: Dow Jones-Irwin, 1971.

Badr, H.A., Gray E.R., and Kedia, B.L. "Personal Values and Managerial Decision Making: Evidence From Two Cultures." *Management International Review* 12 (1982): 65-73.

Bales, R.F., and Couch, A.S. "The Value Profile: A Factor Analytic Study of Value Statements." *Sociological Inquiry* 39 (1969): 3-18.

Barnard, C.I. *Functions of the Executive*. Cambridge, MA: Harvard Univers-ity Press, 1938.

Becker, B.W., and Connor, P.E. "On the Status and Promise of Values Research." *Management Bibliographies and Reviews* 12 (1986): 3-17.

Bendix, R. *Work and Authority in Industry*. New York: Wiley, 1956.

Beyer, J.M., and Trice, H.M. *Implementing Change*. New York: Free Press, 1978.

Blau, J.R., and McKinley, W. "Ideas, Complexity, and Innovation." *Administrative Science Quarterly* 24 (1979): 200-219.

"A Body Builder Lifts Greyhound." *Fortune* 25 October 1985, pp. 124-134.

Bower, J.L. *Managing the Resource Allocation Process*. Boston, MA: Division of Research, Harvard Business School, 1970.

Brunson, R.W. "A Top Management Personal Values Typology: Inverted Factor Analysis to a Conglomerate." *Group and Organization Studies* 10 (1985): 118-134.

Cafferata, G.L. "An Attribution Theory of Professional Ideology." Working paper, University of Rochester, NY, 1979.

Carroll, G.R. "Dynamics of Publisher Succession in Newspaper Organizations." *Administrative Science Quarterly* 29 (1984): 93-108.

Chatov, R. "The Role of Ideology in the American Corporation." In *The Corporate Dilemma*, pp. 50-75. Edited by D. Votaw and S.P. Sethi. Englewood Cliffs, NJ: Prentice-Hall, 1973.

Connor, P.E., and Becker, B.W. "Values and the Organization: Suggestions for Research." *Academy of Management Journal* 18 (1975): 550-561.

Cyert, R.M., and March J.G. *A Behavioral Theory of the Firm*. Englewood Cliffs, NJ: Prentice-Hall, 1963.

Dewoot, P., Heyvaert, H., and Martou, F. "Strategic Management: An Empirical Study of 168 Belgian Firms." *International Studies of Management and Organization* 7 (1977-78): 60-75.

England, G.W. "Personal Value Systems of American Managers." *Academy of Management Journal* 10 (1967): 53-68.

England, G.W. "Personal Value Systems and Expected Behavior of Managers —A Comparative Study in Japan, Korea, and the United States." In *Management Research: A Cross-Cultural Perspective*, pp. 270-292. Edited by D. Graves. San Francisco, CA: Jossey-Bass, 1973.

England, G.W. *The Manager and His Values*. Cambridge, MA: Ballinger, 1975.

England, G.W., and Lee, R. "Organizational Goals and Expected Behavior Among American, Japanese and Korean Managers—A Comparative Study." *Academy of Management Journal* 14 (1971): 425-438.

England, G.W., and Lee, R. "The Relationship Between Managerial Values and Managerial Success in the United States, Japan, India, and Australia." *Journal of Applied Psychology* 59 (1974): 411-419.

England, G.W., Negandhi, A., and Wilpert, G. *Organizational Functioning in a Cross-Cultural Perspective.* Kent: Comparative Administration Research Institute, 1979.

Fama, E. "Agency Problems and the Theory of the Firm." *Journal of Political Economy* 88 (1980): 288-306.

Farris, M.T. "Purchasing Reciprocity and Antitrust." *Journal of Purchasing* 27 (February 1973): 15-27.

Feldman, D.C. "The Multiple Socialization of Organization Members." *Academy of Management Review* 6 (1981): 309-318.

Fredrickson, J.W. "The Comprehensiveness of Strategic Decision Processes: Extensions, Observations, Future Directions." *Academy of Management Journal* 27 (1984): 445-466.

Galbraith, J.R., and Nathanson, D.A. *Strategy Implementation: The Role of Structure and Process.* St. Paul, MN: West, 1978.

Guth, W.D., and Tagiuri, R. "Personal Values and Corporate Strategy." *Harvard Business Review* 43(5) (1965): 123-132.

Hage, J., and Dewar, R. "Elite Values Versus Organizational Structure in Predicting Innovations." *Administrative Science Quarterly* 18 (1973): 279-290.

Hambrick, D.C., and Finkelstein, S. "Managerial Discretion: A Bridge Between Polar Views of Organizational Outcomes." In *Research in Organizational Behavior,* pp. 369-406. Edited by L.L. Cummings, and B.M. Staw. Greenwich, CT: JAI Press, 1987.

Hambrick, D.C., and Mason, P.A. "Upper Echelons: The Organization as a Reflection of Its Top Managers." *Academy of Management Review* 9 (1984): 193-206.

Hannan, M.T., and Freeeman, J.H. "The Population Ecology of Organizations." *American Journal of Sociology* 82 (1977): 929-964.

Hofstede, G. *Culture's Consequences: International Differences in Work-Related Values.* Beverly Hills, CA and London: Sage, 1980.

Hofstede, G. "Dimensions of National Cultures in Fifty Countries and Three Regions." In *Expiscations in Cross-Cultural Psychology,* pp. 335-355. Edited by J.B. Deregowski, S. Dziurawiec, and R.C. Annis. Netherlands: Swets and Zeitlinger, 1983.

Hofstede, G. "The Cultural Relativity of the Quality of Life Concept." *Academy of Management Review* 9 (1984): 389-398.

Howard, A., Shudo, K., and Umeshima, M. "Motivation and Values Among Japanese and American Managers." *Personnel Psychology* 36 (1983): 883-898.

Jacob, P.E., Flink, J.J., and Shuchman, H.L. "Values and Their Function in Decision-Making." *American Behavioral Scientist* 5 (Supplement 9 1962): 6-38.

Janis, I.L. *Victims of Groupthink.* Boston, MA: Houghton Mifflin, 1972.

Jaskolka, G., Beyer, J.M., and Trice, H.M. "Measuring and Predicting Managerial Success." *Journal of Vocational Behavior* 26 (1985): 189-205.

Jensen, M.C., and Meckling, W.H. "Theory of the Firm: Managerial Behavior, Agency Costs and Ownership Structure." *Journal of Financial Economics* 3 (1976): 305-360.

Kaufman, H. *Time, Chance, and Organizations.* Chatham, NJ: Chatham House, 1985.

Kluckhohn, C., et al. "Values and Value-Orientations in Theory of Action: An Exploration of Definition and Classification." In *Toward a General Theory of Action,* pp. 388-433. Edited by T. Parsons and E.A. Shils. Cambridge, MA: Harvard University Press, 1951.

Lee, R. "The Relationship Between Managerial Values and Managerial Behavior: A Cross-Cultural, Cross-Validation Study." Ph.D. dissertation, University of Minnesota, 1975.

Lieberson, S., and O'Connor, J.F. "Leadership and Organizational Performance: A Study of Large Corporations." *American Sociological Review* 37 (1972): 117-130.

Louis, M.R., Posner, B.Z., and Powell, G.N. "The Availability and Helpfulness of Socialization Practices." *Personnel Psychology* 36 (1983): 857-866.

MacCrimmon, K.R., and Taylor, R.N. "Decision Making and Problem Solving." In *Handbook of Industrial and Organizational Psychology,* pp. 1397-1453. Edited by M.D. Dunnette. Chicago, IL: Rand McNally, 1976.

March, J.G., and Simon, H.A. *Organizations.* New York: Wiley, 1958.

"The Marriott Man." *Nation's Business* 37 (October 1978): 51-53.

Mawardi, B.H. "The Allport-Vernon Study of Values as a Tool in Vocational Guidance with Liberal Arts College Women." Master's thesis, Wellesley College, 1952.

Miles, R.E., and Snow, C.C. *Organizational Strategy, Structure, and Process.* New York: McGraw-Hill, 1978.

Miller, D., and Toulouse, J.M. "Chief Executive Personality and Corporate Strategy in Small Firms." *Management Science* 32 (1986): 1389-1409.

Mintzberg, H. *Power In and Around Organizations.* Englewood Cliffs, NJ: Prentice-Hall, 1983.

Mintzberg, H., Raisinghani, D., and Théorêt, A. "The Structure of 'Unstructured' Decision Processes." *Administrative Science Quarterly* 21 (1976): 246-275.

Mortimer, J.T., and Lorence, J. "Work Longitudinal Study." *American Journal of Sociology* 84 (1979): 1361-1385.

Munson, J.M., and Posner, B.Z. "Concurrent Validation of Two Value Inventories in Predicting Job Classification and Success for Organizational Personnel." *Journal of Applied Psychology* 65 (1979): 536-542.

Pfeffer, J. *Power in Organizations.* Marshfield, MA: Pitman, 1981.

Pfeffer, J. "Management as Symbolic Action: The Creation and Maintenance of Organizational Paradigms." In *Research in Organizational Behavior,* Vol. 3, pp. 1-52. Edited by L.L. Cummings, and B.M. Staw. Greenwich, CT: JAI Press, 1981b.

Postman, J., Bruner, J.S., and McGinnies, E. "Personal Values as Selective Factors in Perception." *Journal of Abnormal and Social Psychology* 43.2 (1948): 142-154.

Rawls, J.R., and Nelson, O.T., Jr. "Characteristics Associated With Preferences for Certain Managerial Positions." *Psychology Reports* 36 (1975): 911-918.

Reddy, A.B., and Sheets, R.G. "Projects, Ideologies, and Interorganizational Change." Working paper, Sangamon State University, MI, 1979.

Reinganum, M.R. "The Effect of Executive Succession on Stockholder Wealth." *Administrative Science Quarterly* 30 (1985): 46-61.

Rokeach, M. *Beliefs, Attitudes, and Values.* San Francisco, CA: Jossey-Bass, 1968.

Rokeach, M. "Value Systems in Religion." *Review of Religious Research* 11 (1969a): 3-23.

Rokeach, M. "Religious Values and Social Compassion." *Review of Religious Research* 11 (1969b): 24-38.

Rokeach, M. *The Nature of Human Values.* New York: The Free Press, 1973.

Rokeach, M., and Parker, S. "Values as Social Indicators of Poverty and Race Relations in America. *The Annals of the American Academy of Political and Social Science* 388 (1970): 97-111.

Ryan, E.J., Jr., Watson, J.G., and Williams, J. "The Relationship Between Managerial Values and Managerial Success of Female and Male Managers." *Journal of Psychology* 108 (1981): 67-72.

Schmidt, W.H., and Posner, B.Z. *Managerial Values in Perspective.* New York: American Management Associations, 1983.

Shaw, M. *Group Dynamics: The Psychology of Small Group Behavior.* New York: McGraw-Hill, 1976.

Sikula, A.F. "The Values and Value Systems of Governmental Executives." *Public Personnel Management* 25 (January/February 1973): 16-22.

Simon, H.A. *Administrative Behavior*. 2nd ed. New York: MacMillan, 1957.

Spranger, E. *Types of Men*. Translated by P.J.W. Pigors. Halle: Max Niemeyr Verlag, 1966.

Sutton, F.X., Harris, S.E., Kaysen, C., and Toblin, J. "Value Orientations and the Relationship of Managers and Scientists." *Administrative Science Quarterly* 10 (1956a): 39-51.

Sutton, F.X., Harris, S.E., Kaysen, C., and Toblin, J. *The American Business Creed*. Cambridge, MA: Harvard University Press, 1956b.

Tushman, M.L., and Romanelli, E. "Organizational Evolution: A Metamorphosis Model of Convergence and Reorientation." *Research in Organizational Behavior*, pp. 171-222. Edited by L.L. Cummings, and B. M. Staw. Greenwich, CT: JAI Press, 1985.

Wagner, W.G., Pfeffer, J., and O'Reilly, C.A., III. "Organizational Demography and Turnover in Top-Management Groups." *Administrative Science Quarterly* 29 (1984): 74-89.

Watson, J.G., and Ryan, E.J., Jr. "A Comparative Study of the Personal Values of Female and Male Managers." *Journal of Psychology* 102 (1979): 302-316.

Weick, K.E. "Cognitive Processes in Organizations." In *Research in Organizational Behavior*, pp. 41-74. Edited by B.M. Staw. Greenwich, CT: JAI Press, 1979.

Wiener, Y. "Commitment in Organizations: A Normative View." *Academy of Management Review* 7 (1982): 418-425.

Whitley, W., and England, G.W. "Variability in Common Dimensions of Managerial Values Due to Value Orientation and Country Differences." *Personal Psychology* 33 (1980): 77-89.

EXECUTIVES' PERCEPTUAL FILTERS:

WHAT THEY NOTICE AND

HOW THEY MAKE SENSE

William H. Starbuck and Frances J. Milliken

Management magazines, academic journals, and textbooks almost always presume that analyses of past events reveal how those events actually unfolded. Such writings also frequently portray strategy formulation and implementation as a causal sequence, in which executives perceive some reality, analyze the options offered by this reality, decide to pursue one or more of these options, and obtain results when their organizations' environments react. Thus, according to this causal sequence, organizations' environments act as impartial evaluators of executives' perceptions, analyses, and actions. When the results are good, executives receive credit for accurately perceiving opportunities or threats, for analyzing these correctly, and for taking appropriate actions. When the results are bad, executives get blamed for perceiving erroneously, for making analytic mistakes, or for taking inappropriate actions.

35

This chapter argues that, prevalent though they are, retrospective explanations of past events encourage academics to overstate the contributions of executives and the benefits of accurate perceptions or careful analyses. Because retrospective analyses oversimplify the connections between behaviors and outcomes, prescriptions derived from retrospective understanding may not help executives who are living amid current events. As Fischhoff (1980: 335) observed, "while the past entertains, ennobles, and expands quite readily, it enlightens only with delicate coaxing."

The chapter describes some of the influences on the perceptual filtering processes that executives use as they observe and try to understand their environments. It has four major sections. The first of these explains how retrospection distorts people's understanding of their worlds by emphasizing one or the other of two logical sequences. The ensuing section characterizes perceptual filtering, and argues that filtering can provide a nonjudgmental framework for looking at past, present, and future events. The next-to-last and longest section reviews evidence about how filtering processes vary with executives' characteristics—such as their habits, beliefs, experiences, and work settings. This review divides perception into noticing and sensemaking. The chapter ends by considering how a focus on perceptual filtering changes one's understanding of the noticing and sensemaking tasks of executives. Noticing may be at least as important to effective problem solving as sensemaking. Sensemaking focuses on subtleties and interdependencies, whereas noticing picks up major events and gross trends.

RETROSPECTION

"The French people are incapable of regicide."—Louis XVI, King of France, 1789

"The Army is the Indian's best friend."—General George Armstrong Custer, 1870

"I don't need bodyguards."—Jimmy Hoffa, June 1975

"Nobody can overthrow me. I have the support of 700,000 troops, all the workers, and most of the people. I have the power."—Mohammed Reza Pahlevi, Shah of Iran, March 6, 1978

Observers of the past can discern executives:

who drew erroneous inferences from their observations,
who sensibly diversified and spread their risks, or
who saw meaningful connections where everyone else saw unrelated events.

By contrast, observers of the present and future have less confidence that they can identify executives:

who are failing to anticipate important trends,
who are not implementing effectively strategies that might work, or
who are putting all of their eggs into the right baskets.

People seem to see past events as much more rationally ordered than current or future events, because retrospective sensemaking erases many of the causal sequences that complicate and obscure the present and future (Fischhoff, 1975; Fischhoff and Beyth, 1975; Greenwald, 1980; Hawkins and Hastie, 1986). The past seems to contain fewer of the sequences in which

the goodness or badness of results remains unclear, or
incorrect actions by executives yield good results, or
correct actions by executives yield bad results, or
executives' actions have no significant effects on results, or
bad analyses by executives lead to correct actions, or
good analyses by executives lead to incorrect actions, or
analyses by executives do not significantly affect their actions, or
inaccurate perceptions by executives undermine good analyses, or
accurate perceptions by executives get lost in bad analyses, or
executives' own perceptions exert no significant effects on their analyses.

For instance, in a study of a large government project, Ross and Staw (1986) noted that public declarations of commitment to the project became occasions for erasing information that had cast doubt upon it. Such erasing may occur quite involuntarily as people's memories automatically take account of subsequent events (Fischhoff, 1975; Loftus, 1979; Snyder and Uranowitz, 1978; Wohlwill and Kohn, 1976). As Fischhoff (1980: 341) put it, people "not only tend to view what has happened as having been inevitable but also to view it as having appeared 'relatively inevitable' before it happened."

Observers who know the results of actions tend to see two kinds of analytic sequences:

Good results → Correct actions → Flawless analyses → Accurate perceptions
Bad results → Incorrect actions → Flawed analyses → Inaccurate perceptions

Knowing, for example, that bad results occurred, observers search for the incorrect actions that produced these bad results; the actual results guide the observers toward relevant actions and help them to see what was wrong with these actions (Neisser, 1981). Knowing that actions were incorrect, observers seek flawed analyses; the incorrect actions point to specific analyses, and the actions' incorrectness guarantees the presence of flaws in these analyses. Knowing which analyses contained flaws, observers look for inaccurate perceptions; observers inspect the perceptions that fed into the flawed analyses, feeling sure that some of these perceptions must have contained errors.

Thus, after the space shuttle exploded and destroyed the Challenger spacecraft, a Presidential Commission searched for the human errors that caused this disaster. Physical evidence from the sea bottom, laboratory tests, and television tapes ruled out several initial hypotheses and focused attention on design flaws in the wall of the solid-rocket booster. Confident that mistakes had occurred when NASA decided to continue using this booster, the Presidential Commission could then review these processes and identify the mistakes. The Commission did spot some data that should have been taken more seriously, some rules that should have been enforced more stringently, some opinions that should have been given more credence, some communication channels that should have been used, and some specific people who had played central roles in the faulty decision processes. Many of these same actions had occurred before previous flights—the same rules had been bent, the same kinds of discussions had taken place, and the same communication channels had been ignored. But, after previous flights, no participant said these actions had been mistakes; and when inspectors noted defects in the solid-rocket boosters, NASA personnel concluded that these defects were not serious.

Retrospective perceivers are much more likely to see bad results, and hence mistaken actions and analyses, if they did not themselves play central roles in the events; and perceivers are much more likely to see good results if they did play central roles (Nisbett and Ross, 1980). Festinger, Riecken, and Schachter (1956) observed a religious cult that waited expectantly for a flying saucer to arrive and carry them off so that they would be safe when the world came to an end at midnight. At dawn, facing the fact that the expected events had not transpired, the cult members retreated in confusion and disappointment to their meeting house. But they soon emerged with revitalized faith, for they had realized that it was their unquestioning faith the night before that had convinced God to postpone Armageddon.

The two dominant analytic sequences not only simplify observers' perceptions, they put executives' perceptions at the beginnings of causal sequences and imply that executives' perceptual accuracy strongly influences their organizations' results. For example, nearly all explanations of crisis, disaster, or organizational decline focus on how executives failed to spot major environmental threats or opportunities, failed to heed well-founded warnings, assessed risks improperly, or adhered to outdated goals and beliefs (Dunbar and Goldberg, 1978; Mitroff and Kilmann, 1984;

Starbuck, Greve and Hedberg, 1978). On the other hand, explanations of organizational success generally cite executives' accurate visions, willingness to take wise risks or refusals to take foolish risks, commitments to well-conceived goals, or insightful persistence in the face of adversity (Bennis, 1983; Peters and Waterman, 1982). In foresight, however, one is hard pressed to distinguish accurate perceivers from inaccurate ones. Examples abound, of course. In 1979, Harding Lawrence, Chairman of the Board of Braniff Airlines, was hailed for "his aggressive response to deregulation. . .another brilliant, strategic move that should put Braniff in splendid shape for the 80s" (*Business Week,* March 19, 1979); a few years later, industry experts were blaming Braniff's bankruptcy on Lawrence's overly aggressive response to deregulation. In 1972, James Galton, publisher of the Popular Library, told Macmillan that Richard Bach's best-selling novel, "*Jonathan Livingston Seagull* will never make it as a paperback"; Avon Books bought the rights and sold seven million copies in ten years. Immediately after World War II, IBM offered computers for sale, but looked upon this offer as merely a way to publicize the company's participation in an avant-garde wartime project; at that time, Chairman of the Board Thomas J. Watson speculated, "I think there is a world market for about five computers."

The two dominant kinds of analytic sequences also conform to norms about what ought to happen in a rational world:

> Accurate perceptions ought to go with flawless analyses, and flawless analyses ought to lead to correct actions, and correct actions ought to yield good results.

This rationalization helps observers to understand their environments and it gives observers the comfort of knowing that their worlds are working as they should work. Unfortunately, such understanding can only exist after results have occurred and the results' goodness or badness clarifies, because good and bad results may arise from very similar processes. For example, executives who insightfully persisted in the face of adversity may also have failed to heed well-founded warnings that nearly came true. Their research led Starbuck, Greve, and Hedberg (1978:114) to conclude that "the processes which produce crises are substantially identical to the processes which produce successes."

Of course, even hindsight usually leaves the past complex and ambiguous. Some results manifest themselves much later than others, and results have numerous dimensions that elicit different evaluations from observers who hold divergent values, so observers disagree about results' goodness and see multiple and inconsistent interpretations of their causes. Retrospection only makes the past clearer than the present or future; it cannot make the past transparent. But the past's clarity is usually artificial enough to mislead people who are living in the present and looking toward the future. In particular, retrospection wrongly implies that errors should have been anticipated and that good perceptions, good analyses, and good decisions will yield good results.

The present is itself substantially indeterminate because people can only apprehend the present by placing it in the context of the past and the future, and vice versa. Imagine, for instance, that this is Thursday, October 24, 1929: Stock prices plummeted today. Is this an exceptional opportunity to buy underpriced stocks that will rebound tomorrow, or does today's drop portend further declines tomorrow? To understand today's prices, one needs a forecast of tomorrow's, and this forecast derives from one's past experiences. But the past has already been reconstructed to fit the present; and as future events unfold, the past will be reconstructed again and again. Not only is the future unclear, it is fundamentally unpredictable. Indeed, a prediction that is "correct" in the sense that some highly probable events could bring the predicted situation into being may actually invalidate itself by triggering reactions that make the projected events highly improbable. For example, the Club of Rome sponsored a computer-simulation study of the future, titled *The Limits to Growth* (Meadows, Meadows, Randers, and Behrens, 1972). This study predicted that if current trends continue, then before the year 2100 major ecological catastrophes will bring an end to civilization as we know it, because resources are being consumed so rapidly, populations are expanding so rapidly, and ecological problems are escalating. This forecast evoked furor; it alerted people by dramatizing the ecological trends; and it stimulated some immediate, superficial, short-run efforts toward conservation. But the forecast may not have triggered enough fundamental and long-run changes in human behavior to render itself incorrect.

PERCEPTUAL FILTERING

One thing an intelligent executive does not need is totally accurate perception. Such perception would have no distortion whatever. Someone who perceived without any distortion would hear background noise as loudly as a voice or music, and so would be unable to use an outdoor telephone booth beside a noisy street, and would be driven crazy by the coughs and chair squeaks at symphony concerts. A completely accurate perceiver might find it so difficult to follow a baseball's path that batting or catching would be out of the question. The processes that amplify some stimuli and attenuate others, thus distorting the raw data and focusing attention, are perceptual filters.

Effective perceptual filtering amplifies relevant information and attenuates irrelevant information, so that the relevant information comes into the perceptual foreground and the irrelevant information recedes into the background. The filtered information is less accurate but, if the filtering is effective, more understandable. People filter information quite instinctively: for example, a basketball player can shoot a foul shot against a turbulent backdrop of shouting people and waving hands, and a telephone user can hear and understand a quiet voice despite interference from street noise that is many times louder.

In complex environments, effective perceptual filtering requires detailed knowledge of the task environment. Systems engineers sometimes try to design filters that minimize the errors in perceived information—errors might include extraneous information, biases, noise, static, or interference between simultaneous messages (Sage, 1981). To design an error-minimizing filter for some task, an engineer would make assumptions about the possible sources of stimuli, and would distinguish relevant from irrelevant sources. An error-minimizing filter makes predictions about where errors are going to occur in perception and then either removes these errors or prevents them from occurring. In a task environment as complex as most real-life environments, an error-minimizing filter would incorporate numerous complex assumptions (Ashby, 1960), and for the filter actually to minimize perceptual error, these assumptions must be correct.

In real life, people do not know all of the sources of stimuli, nor do they necessarily know how to distinguish relevant from irrelevant information. They must discover the characteristics of sources and tasks experimentally. Some combinations of tasks and task environments occur often enough and with enough consistency that people learn to make useful discriminations. For example, batters can practice tracking baseballs until they develop good models of baseball trajectories and learn to distinguish baseballs from other stimuli. Even though batters may move around from one ballpark to another, they encounter enough consistency that their learning transfers. Batters also see immediate consequences of their actions, so they get prompt feedback concerning the effectiveness of their perceptions.

Executives, by contrast, find it difficult to practice strategizing: Long lags may intervene between executives' actions and the visible outcomes of those actions, and these outcomes have multiple causes; so executives lack clear feedback about the effectiveness of their perceptions and the relevance of information. Constant changes in their environments mean that executives' knowledge rapidly grows obsolete and that they gain few benefits from practice. Executives' experience may even be deceptive. Some research indicates that industries and strategic groups change bimodally: long periods of gradual incremental development get interrupted by occasional bursts of radical change (Astley, 1985; Astley and Fombrun, 1987; Fombrun and

Starbuck, 1987; Tushman and Anderson, 1986). Therefore, executives' learning mainly occurs during the periods of relative stability, but their strategic skills are mainly tested during the bursts of change. It is during the bursts of change that executives most need to act creatively rather than on the basis of experience and that perceptual errors may cause the greatest damage.

The theories about effective perceptual filtering assume that it occurs within perceivers, not their environments, and that the unfiltered stimuli are facts. However, perceivers are inseparable from their environments because each depends on the other, and perceptions can either validate or invalidate themselves when people act on their environments (Ittelson, Franck, and O'Hanlon, 1976). For example, people in hierarchies pay more attention to messages from their superiors than to ones from their subordinates, so they actually receive more information from their superiors even though more messages originate from their subordinates (Porter and Roberts, 1976). Another example was suggested by Hayek (1974), who argued that an emphasis on quantitative measures and mathematical models caused economists to develop mistaken beliefs about macroeconomic systems, and that these erroneous beliefs led them to formulate policies that produced unexpected consequences and actually made the macroeconomic systems less manageable and less self-correcting. In particular, at one time, economists generally taught that inflation and unemployment worked against each other: an economic policy could achieve full employment only if it suffered some inflation, or it could suppress inflation by maintaining a high level of unemployment. In the 1960s, economists moved into governmental policy-making positions and began creating institutions that were designed to control inflation while minimizing unemployment. One result, said Hayek, was an economy in which unemployment rises whenever inflation stops accelerating.

Perceivers who act on their environments need perceptual filters that take account of the malleability of task environments. Perceptual errors have smaller consequences in environments that resist change, and larger consequences in more malleable environments. But errors may yield benefits as well as costs—as when faulty perceptions lead people to pursue energetically goals that would look much less attainable if assessed in utter objectivity, but the pursuers' enthusiasm, effort, and self-confidence bring success. Brunsson pointed out that actions are more likely to succeed if they are supported by strong commitments, firm expectations, and high motivation. He said:

> organizations have two problems: to choose the right thing to do, and to get it done. There are two kinds of rationality corresponding to the two problems: decision rationality and action rationality. Neither is superior to the other, but they serve different purposes and are based

Table 1. *Types of Perceptual Filtering*

Distortions in noticing (where to look and what to see)
> Paying too much or too little attention to stimuli with certain properties
>> stimuli in certain environmental domains
>> changes or regularities
>> familiar or unusual stimuli
>> expected or unexpected stimuli
>> desirable or undesirable stimuli
>> dramatic or undramatic stimuli
> Letting some stimuli draw too much attention to themselves, and other stimuli evade attention

Distortions in sensemaking (what it means)
> Distortions in framing
>> Perceiving or classifying events in the wrong frameworks (schemata)
>> Applying existing frameworks in radically novel situations
>> Perceiving illusory stimuli that fit evoked frameworks, or ignoring stimuli that violate evoked frameworks
>> Assigning high credibility to stimuli that fit evoked frameworks, and discounting stimuli that violate evoked frameworks
>> Assigning importance to covariations that fit evoked frameworks, and discounting covariations that violate evoked frameworks

> Distortions in predicting
>> Forming expectations by applying the wrong frameworks (schemata)
>> Amplifying good events and attenuating bad events
>>> Underestimating or not seeing serious, imminent threats
>>> Overestimating insignificant, remote, or doubtful opportunities
>> Amplifying bad events and attentuating good events
>>> Underestimating or not seeing significant, immediate opportunities
>>> Overestimating minor, very distant, or improbable threats
>> Underestimating or overestimating
>>> the effects of environmental changes
>>> the ranges of environmental events likely to occur
>>> the ranges of probable outcomes from proposed actions, policies, or strategies
>>> risks associated with proposed actions, policies, or strategies

> Distortions in causal attributions
>> Making attributions by applying the wrong frameworks (schemata)
>> Attributing outcomes produced by many causes to only a few causes, or vice versa
>> Amplifying or attenuating the influence of
>>> environmental causes
>>> an organization's actions
>>> executives' actions
>> Failing to notice or allow for
>>> contingency variables
>>> feedback loops
>> Perceiving uncontrollable events as controllable, or vice versa

on different norms. The two kinds of rationality are difficult to pursue simultaneously, because rational decision-making procedures are irrational in an action perspective. They should be avoided if action is to be more easily achieved. (1985: 27)

It is generally impossible to decide, at the time of perception, whether perceptions will prove accurate or inaccurate, correct or incorrect, because perceptions are partly predictions that may change reality, because different perceptions may lead to similar actions, and because similar perceptions may lead to different actions. Many perceptual errors, perhaps the great majority, become erroneous only in retrospect. Even disagreement among people who are supposedly looking at a shared situation does not indicate that any of these divergent perceptions must be wrong. People may operate very effectively even though they characterize a shared situation quite differently, and people's unique backgrounds may reveal to them distinct, but nevertheless accurate and valid, aspects of a complex reality.

Trying to learn from past errors oversimplifies the complexity and ambiguity of the task environments that people once faced, and it assumes that the future will closely resemble the past. Furthermore, although in the present, people can distinguish their perceptions from the alternative actions they are considering, people looking at the past find such distinctions very difficult because they revise their perceptions to fit the actions that actually occurred (Loftus, 1979; Neisser, 1981). Therefore, it makes sense to deemphasize errors and to analyze perception in a nonjudgmental, nonaccusatory framework. One way to do this is to emphasize filtering processes.

Table 1 identifies some filtering processes that may be important in understanding environmental scanning and strategy formulation (McArthur, 1981; Taylor and Crocker, 1981). All of these filtering processes distort the raw data that executives could perceive. In some situations, these distortions enable executives to operate more effectively in their environments by focusing attention on important, relevant stimuli; whereas in other situations, these same distortions make executives operate less effectively by focusing attention on unimportant, irrelevant stimuli. Further, these types of filtering may persist over time and so characterize organizations or individual executives.

INFLUENCES UPON FILTERING PROCESSES

Executives who work in the same organization frequently disagree about the characteristics of that organization, and executives whose firms compete in the same industry may disagree strongly about the characteristics of that industry (Downey, Hellriegel, and Slocum, 1977; Duncan, 1972; Payne and Pugh, 1976; Starbuck, 1976). The stimuli that one executive receives may be precisely the same stimuli that another executive filters out. Furthermore, executives who notice the same stimuli may use different frameworks to interpret these stimuli and therefore disagree about meanings or causes or effects. Understanding how organizational and individual characteristics influence executives' filtering processes may both help executives themselves to behave more effectively and help researchers to predict the types of filtering processes that executives use (Jervis, 1976).

The analyses to follow divide perception into noticing and sensemaking. This is admittedly a difficult distinction in practice because people notice stimuli and make sense of them at the same time, and each of these activities depends upon the other. For instance, what people notice becomes input to their sensemaking, and in turn, the sense that people have made appears to influence what the people notice (Goleman, 1985). Noticing involves a rudimentary form of sensemaking in that noticing requires distinguishing signal from noise, making crude separations of relevant from irrelevant. Similarly, sensemaking involves a form of noticing when a perceiver reclassifies remembered signal as noise, or remembered noise as signal, in order to fit a new interpretive framework.

Nevertheless, like others (Daft and Weick, 1984; Kiesler and Sproull, 1982), we believe a distinction between noticing and sensemaking sometimes exists and has theoretical value. For example, Daft and Weick (1984) distinguished scanning, a process that collects data, from interpretation, a process that gives meaning to data. Thus, Daft and Weick's scanning corresponds to noticing, and their interpretation corresponds to sensemaking. We prefer the term noticing to scanning on the ground that scanning seems to imply formal and voluntary actions, whereas noticing may be quite informal and involuntary; and we prefer the term sensemaking to interpretation because sensemaking seems more self-explanatory.

Noticing: Where to Look and What to See

> The range of what we think and do
> is limited by what we fail to notice.
> And because we fail to notice
> *that* we fail to notice
> there is little we can do
> to change
> until we notice
> how failing to notice
> shapes our thoughts and deeds.
> R. D. Laing (Goleman, 1985:24)

Noticing is an act of classifying stimuli as signals or noise. Noticing results from interactions of the characteristics of stimuli with the characteristics of perceivers. In particular, some stimuli are more available or more likely to attract attention than others (McArthur, 1981; Taylor and Crocker, 1981; Tversky and Kahneman, 1974). However, the characteristics of perceivers, including their current activities, strongly affect both the availabilities of stimuli and the abilities of stimuli to attract attention (Wohlwill and Kohn, 1976); even colorful or loud stimuli may be overlooked if people are used to them or are concentrating on critical tasks, and novel events or sudden changes may remain unseen if people are looking elsewhere. Furthermore, executives tend to have more control over their own behaviors than over the stimuli that interest them most. Therefore, we emphasize the characteristics of perceivers, either as individuals or as members of organizations, more than the characteristics of stimuli. Noticing is influenced by perceivers' habits, their beliefs about what is, and their beliefs about what ought to be.

People classify stimuli by comparing them either to other immediately available stimuli or to standards arising from their experiences and expectations. Psychologists call the smallest differences that people can detect reliably "just-noticeable differences," and they have devoted extensive research to ascertaining just-noticeable differences in laboratory settings.

In the 1830s, E. H. Weber studied people's abilities to identify the heavier of two weights, and posited that just-noticeable differences are approximately constant percentages of the absolute magnitudes of stimuli. By this hypothesis, a just-noticeable difference in wealth, for example, would be some percentage of a person's wealth, so a rich person would be much less likely to notice a $1 difference in wealth than a poor person. Studies indicate that Weber's hypothesis seems to describe hearing and vision accurately over a wide range of stimuli, but it describes touch, smell, and taste less accurately (Luce and Galanter, 1963). It does, nonetheless, suggest some ideas about executives' perceptions. For instance, an executive in a volatile industry might be less likely to notice absolutely small changes in prices or sales volumes than an executive in a stable industry. Similarly, an executive in a small firm might tend to be more sensitive to the needs of an individual employee than an executive in a large firm.

Psychologists' studies of just-noticeable differences measure what people can perceive under controlled conditions, and these studies emphasize comparisons between simultaneous or nearly simultaneous stimuli. In real life, people not only compare stimuli to standards arising from nearly simultaneous stimuli, they also compare stimuli to standards evolved over long periods, and to models and enduring expectations about their environments. Furthermore, a yes-no characterization of noticing seems to misrepresent its subtlety and continuity. If need be, people can often recall stimuli that they had been unaware that they had noticed or that they had classified as background noise; this recall suggests that people perceive unconsciously or subliminally as well as consciously. You may, for instance, have had the experience of hearing a question but not quite hearing it, so you ask the questioner to repeat her question, but before she does so, you suddenly realize that you know the question and you answer it.

Bargh (1982) pointed out that people seem to have two modes of noticing, one of them controlled and volitional, and one automatic and involuntary. Although the two modes interact on occasion, they operate independently of each other most of the time. Bargh observed that people who are fully absorbed in performing tasks nevertheless notice it when someone speaks their names. Nielsen and Sarason (1981) found that someone can virtually always capture another person's attention by speaking sexually explicit words.

The standards that determine what people notice in real life seem to be of several not-entirely-distinct types: People notice familiar and unfamiliar stimuli, as well as what they believe to be relevant, important, significant, desirable, or evil.

Looking for the Familiar or Overlooking the Familiar. Helson (1964) observed that perceptual thresholds reflect experience, but that adaptation both sensitizes and desensitizes. On the one hand, people grow less sensitive to stimuli as these stimuli become more familiar. For example, an executive who moves into a new industry would initially notice numerous phenomena, but many of these would fade into the background as the industry becomes more familiar. On the other hand, some sensory functions improve with practice (Gibson, 1953), and as people become more familiar with a domain of activity, they grow more sensitive to subtle changes within that domain (Schroder, Driver, and Streufert, 1967). Thus, an executive who moves into a new industry would initially overlook some phenomena that seem unimportant, but would gradually learn to notice those phenomena as experience clarifies their significance. Although these two processes produce opposite effects that may, in fact, counteract each other, they generally interact as complements: decreasing sensitivity pushes some stimuli into the background, while increasing sensitivity brings other stimuli to the foreground.

Helson studied the relative effects of foreground and background events on what it is that people do not notice. He (1964) argued that experience produces standards for distinguishing or evaluating stimuli, and he called these standards "adaptation levels." People do not notice the stimuli that resemble adaptation levels, or they act as if they are indifferent to such stimuli. In studies of vision and weight-sensing, Helson found that the adaptation level associated with a sequence of alternating stimuli resembles an average in which the foreground stimuli receive around three times the weight of the interspersed background stimuli, implying that foreground events actually exert much more influence on not-noticing than background events do. Nonsimultaneity evidently helps perceivers to concentrate on foreground events and to deemphasize background events in cognition. On the other hand, Helson's experiments showed that the adaptation level associated with a combination of simultaneous stimuli resembles an average in which the background stimuli have around three times the weight of foreground stimuli, implying that simultaneous background events actually exert much more influence on not-noticing than foreground events do. Simultaneous background events impede perceivers' abilities to concentrate on foreground events, and so the background events gain influence in cognition; where background events greatly outnumber foreground events, as in an ordinary photograph, the background events dominate the adaptations that determine not-noticing. An extrapolation might be that general, societal events (occurring simultaneously with events in executives' task environments) affect the executives' expectations about what is normal and unremarkable more strongly than do the specific, immediate events in their task environments.

Because simultaneous background stimuli strongly influence what people do not notice, people tend not to notice them. In particular, people tend to notice subtle changes in foreground stimuli while overlooking substantial changes in background stimuli, and so background stimuli may have to change dramatically to attract notice (McArthur, 1981; Normann, 1971). One reason is that familiarity enables people to develop programs and habits for noticing foreground stimuli, whereas they attend less systematically and consistently to background stimuli. Like experience, moreover, programs and habits may have complementary effects, in that they may also deaden sensitivity and convert foreground events into background events (Tuchman, 1973). Programs and habits make noticing less reflective, and by routinizing it, inject extraneous detail.

Lyles and Mitroff (1980:116) found that "managers become aware of significant problems through informal sensing techniques"; they surmised that either "the formal reporting systems do not identify the relevant indicators or, more possibly, . . .managers tend to ignore the indicators when they are *formally* reported." Formalized information systems often try to make up for inflexibility by providing extensive detail, so they bog down in detail and operate slowly: irrelevant detail becomes noise, and slow processing makes the data outdated. For instance, in the late 1950s, executives in the Tar Products Division of the Koppers Company decided that computers could provide inputs to operating decisions, so they purchased a computer-based system that produced weekly and monthly reports of the plants' daily inventories and outputs. The collected data were voluminous but riddled with large errors, both unintentional data-entry errors and intentional misrepresentations of the plants' situations. But personnel at divisional headquarters remained quite unaware of these errors because they paid almost no attention to the computer-generated reports. The headquarters personnel in production scheduling could not wait for the computer-generated data, so they maintained daily contact with the plants by telephone; the headquarters personnel in purchasing and sales looked mainly at annual totals because they bought and sold through annual or longer contracts.

Successful experience may tend to make foregrounds smaller and backgrounds larger. For instance, IBM, which dominated the mainframe computer business, virtually ignored the initial developments of minicomputers, microcomputers, and supercomputers; these developments were obviously foreground events for Digital Equipment, Apple, and Cray. Success gives individual people and organizations the confidence to build upon their experience by creating buffers, which insulate them from environmental variations, and programs, which automate and standardize their responses to environmental events. The buffers and programs identify certain stimuli as foreground events and they exclude other stimuli from consideration. Starbuck (1976: 1081) observed:

> organizations tend to crystallize and preserve their existing states of knowledge whenever they set up systems to routinely collect, aggregate, and analyze information, whenever they identify and allocate areas of responsibility, whenever they hire people who possess particular skills and experiences, and whenever they plan long-range strategies and invest in capital goods.

Thus, organizational scanning systems formalize their members' beliefs and expectations as procedures and structures that may be difficult to change.

However, like sexually explicit words, social and technological changes may make themselves difficult to ignore: IBM did eventually enter the minicomputer and microcomputer businesses.

Looking for What Matters.   People also define foregrounds and backgrounds on the basis of their definitions of what phenomena are relevant, important, insignificant, desirable, or evil (Goleman, 1985). For instance, in recent years, two amateur astronomers, one Australian and one Japanese, who specialized in this activity, have spotted a great majority of the known comets; presumably professional astronomers assign lower value to comet spotting in comparison to alternative uses of their time. Rosenhan (1978) remarked that the staff members in psychiatric hospitals tend not to notice that patients are in fact behaving normally; possibly these staff members would notice the normal behaviors if they saw them outside of the hospital context.

Weick (1979) pointed out that people "enact" their environments; by this, he meant that people's beliefs and expectations define what they regard as relevant, and so beliefs and expectations define what parts of task environments draw people's notice. Deciding that certain markets and prices are worth scanning, executives may assign subordinates to monitor these markets and prices, thereby making them part of their organization's foreground. But no organization can afford to monitor everything, so by not assigning subordinates to monitor other markets and prices, the executives are implicitly defining a background (Normann, 1971). For example, Mitroff and Kilmann (1984) argued that business firms overlook saboteurs, terrorists, and other "bizarre characters" in their environments because managers find it "unthinkable" that anyone might commit sabotage or terrorism against their firms. Another example occurred at the Facit company, a manufacturer of mechanical calculators: When Facit's top managers wanted to assess the threat posed by electronic calculators, they instructed their salesmen to interview Facit's customers about their attitudes toward this new technology. The salesmen continued to report that Facit's customers almost unanimously preferred mechanical to electronic calculators. . .even while the number of customers was plummeting.

Executives' values about how their businesses should be run also influence their definitions of foregrounds and backgrounds. Donaldson and Lorsch (1983), for instance, commented that executives' values about organizational self-sufficiency seem to influence their organizations' actions; in particular, CEOs who believe that long-term debt indicates inadequate self-sufficiency tend to avoid strategies that require borrowing. One reason executives' values have such effects on actions is that they influence what the executives and their organizations notice. Thus, executives who believe in the no-debt principle are likely to relegate potential lenders and financial markets to the background, and so remain uninformed about available loan terms or changes in interest rates.

The influence of executives' definitions of what matters may gain strength through the uncoupling of executives' decisions about what to observe from their subordinates' acts of perception. This uncoupling and the asymmetry of hierarchical communications impair feedback, and so executives' perceptions adapt sluggishly to the actual observations made by their subordinates. Organizations encourage the creation of formalized scanning programs, they assign specialists to monitor foreground events, and they discourage subordinates from reporting observations that fall outside their assigned responsibilities. Even when subordinates do notice events that have been formally classified as background, they tend not to report these upward, and superiors tend to ignore their subordinates' messages (Dunbar and

Goldberg, 1978; O'Reilly, 1983; Porter and Roberts, 1976). For instance, on the morning of the Challenger disaster, a crew was dispatched to inspect ice formation on the shuttle and launch pad. The crew noticed very low temperatures on the solid rocket boosters, but this observation was not relevant to their assignment, so they did not report it (Presidential Commission, 1986).

Sensemaking: What It Means

On the day following the 1956 election in which a *Republican* President and *Democratic* Congress were elected, two colleagues remarked to me that the voters were becoming more discriminating in splitting their ballots. But the two individuals did not mean the same thing by the remark, for one was a staunch Republican and the other a strong Democrat. The first referred with satisfaction to the election of a Republican President; and the second approved the election of a Democratic Congress.—Harry Helson, 1964: 36.

Daft and Weick (1984: 286) remarked: "Managers. . .must wade into the ocean of events that surround the organization and actively try to make sense of them." Sensemaking has many distinct aspects—comprehending, understanding, explaining, attributing, extrapolating, and predicting, at least. For example, understanding seems to precede explaining and to require less input; predicting may occur without either understanding or explaining; attributing is a form of explanation that assigns causes. Yet, concrete examples seem to illustrate the commonalities and interdependencies among these processes more than their differences.

What is common to these processes is that they involve placing stimuli into frameworks (or schemata) that make sense of the stimuli (Goleman, 1985). Some sensemaking frameworks seem to be simple and others complex; some appear to describe static states of affairs and others sequential procedures; some seem to delineate the boundaries between categories and others to describe central tendencies within categories; some seem more general and others more specific; some appear more abstract and others more concrete (Dutton and Jackson, 1987; Hastie, 1981). These sensemaking frameworks, like the frameworks for noticing, reflect habits, beliefs about what is, and beliefs about what ought to be.

Perceptual frameworks categorize data, assign likelihoods to data, hide data, and fill in missing data (Taylor and Crocker, 1981). At least frameworks often imply that certain data ought to exist or ought not to exist. Sherlock Holmes was, of course, remarkable for his ability to draw elaborate inferences from a few, seemingly trivial and incongruous clues. Nonfictional people, however, should contemplate the probabilities that the filled-in data may actually exist but not be seen until sought, or they may be seen in fantasy but not actually exist, or they may not actually exist until sought. Errors seen in retrospect often exemplify the latter. For instance, the faults in the space shuttle's solid-rocket booster were only a few of multitude design characteristics. Before January 28, 1986, NASA had classified some of these design characteristics as not dangerous and others as dangerous; dangerous characteristics were not errors, however. The investigation of the disaster categorized a few of these design characteristics as errors, but doing so involved making some tests and ruling out some alternatives.

Similarly, nonfictional people should allow for the probabilities that existing data may not be taken into account because they violate perceptual frameworks or may be distorted badly to make them fit perceptual frameworks. In March 1961, shortly before the U.S. Central Intelligence Agency launched an invasion of the Bay of Pigs, the CIA's private internal reports stated: "Many people in Camaguey believe that the Castro regime is tottering and that the situation can at any moment degenerate into bloody anarchy" (Report CS-3/467: 630). "It is generally believed that the Cuban Army has been successfully penetrated by opposition groups and that it will not fight in the event of a showdown" (Report CS-3/470: 587).

In spite of their propensities for seeing what ought to exist, people do sometimes strive to see beyond their blind spots. They get opportunities to discover their blind spots when they observe incongruous events that do not make sense within their perceptual frameworks (McCall, 1977). Management by exception is an action strategy that depends on spotting situations in which current events are diverging from familiar patterns. Such observations may be either very disorienting or very revealing, or both. Incongruous events are disorienting as long as they make no sense, and they become revealing when they induce perceivers to adopt new frameworks that render them explicable. For instance, Starbuck (in press) and his colleagues set out to discover the abnormalities that cause a few organizations to run into serious, existence-threatening crises. But the researchers were inundated with examples, and so it gradually dawned on them that they were seeing normality because crises are common. Facing this incongruity brought the researchers to see that the causes of crises are essentially the same as the causes of success.

Watzlawick, Weakland, and Fisch (1974) said that all perceptual frameworks have blind spots that prevent people from solving problems and that link behaviors into self-reinforcing cycles (Goleman, 1985; Masuch, 1985). To solve problems that blind spots have made unsolvable, people need new perceptual frameworks that portray the problematic situations differently. Watzlawick, Weakland, and Fisch proposed four basic strategies for reframing such problematic situations: (1) redefine undesirable elements to make them appear desirable, or vice versa; (2) re-label elements so that they acquire new meanings; (3) ignore elements that you cannot change; and (4) try overtly to achieve the opposite of what you want. For example, a man with a bad stammer had to work as a salesman, but this role heightened his worries about his speech defect and so made it worse. His psychotherapists advised him that potential customers generally distrust salesmen precisely because of their slick and clever spiels that go on insistently, whereas people listen carefully and patiently to someone with a speech handicap. Had he considered what an incredible advantage he actually had over other salesmen? Perhaps, they suggested, he should try to maintain a high level of stammering even after experience made him feel more at ease and his propensity to stammer abated.

Framing Within the Familiar.   Normann (1971) pointed out that people in organizations can understand and readily respond to events in the domains with which they interact frequently, but that they are likely to misapprehend events in unfamiliar domains, or to have difficulty generating responses to them. Different parts of organizations are familiar with different domains, and these domains both shape and get shaped by organizations' political systems and task divisions: Hierarchical, functional, geographic, and product differentiations affect the ways people interpret events, and these differentials foster political struggles that interact with strategic choices and designs for organizational perception systems (Dearborn and Simon, 1958).

For instance, people with expertise in newer tasks tend to appear at the bottoms of hierarchies and to interpret events in terms of these newer tasks, and they welcome changes that will offer them promotion opportunities and bring their expertise in the fore. Conversely, people at the tops of organizational hierarchies tend to have expertise related to older and more stable tasks, they are prone to interpret events in terms of these tasks, and they favor strategies and personnel assignments that will keep these tasks central (Starbuck, 1983). Some research also suggests that people at the tops of organizational hierarchies tend to have simpler perceptual frameworks than their subordinates. One reason is that top executives have to span several domains of expertise, each of which looks complex to specialists (Schroder, Driver, and Streufert, 1967). Another reason is that top executives receive so much information from so many sources that they experience overloads (Ackoff, 1967; Hedberg, 1981). A third reason is that top executives receive much of their information through intermediaries, who filter it (Starbuck, 1985). Still another reason is that their spokesperson roles force top executives to put ideas and relationships into simply expressed terms (Axelrod, 1976; Hart, 1976, 1977).

Repeated successes or failures lead people to discount accidents as explanations, to look for explicit causes, and eventually to expect the successes or failures to continue. Repeated failures may lead people to view themselves as having weak influence over events and to blame the failures on external causes such as bosses, enemies, strangers, foreign competition, economic cycles, or technological trends (Langer and Roth, 1975). By contrast, repeated successes may cause people to see themselves or their close associates as having strong influence on events. NASA, for instance, experienced many years of successes in meeting technological challenges. It would appear that this made people at NASA grow confident that they could routinely overcome nearly insurmountable technological hurdles. They became used to the technologies with which they were working, and they gradually grew more complacent about technological problems as more flights worked out well. Thus, the NASA personnel came to see the space shuttle as an "operational" technology, meaning that it was safe enough to carry ordinary citizens such as Senators and schoolteachers.

Framing Within the Expected.   Expectations may come from extrapolating past events into the future. In a world that changes slowly and in which everyone else is deriving their expectations incrementally and so behaving incrementally, most of the time it is useful to formulate expectations incrementally oneself. It also appears that simple extrapolations generally work better than complex ones. Makridakis and Hibon (1979) tested 22 mechanistic forecasting techniques on 111 economic and business time series. They found that simple rules do surprisingly well in comparison to complex rules, and in particular, that the no-change rule

$$\text{next period} = \text{this period}$$

provides excellent forecasts. Another effective forecasting rule is a weighted average in which more recent events receive more weight. Simple rules extrapolate well because they 'hedge' forecasts towards recent experience and therefore they make fewer large errors. Complex forecasting rules amplify short-term fluctuations when they project and thus make large errors more often.

Because extrapolations normally deviate no more than incrementally from experience, they set up past-oriented perceptual frameworks that do not encourage innovation. Expectations, however, may also come from models and general orientations that are transmitted through socialization, communication, or education; and the expectations that come from transmitted models may differ radically from experience. For example, members of the religious cult observed by Festinger, Riecken, and Schachter (1956) obviously had no experience indicating that they would be carried off in a spaceship before the world came to an end at midnight. Thus, transmitted models have the capacity to generate expectations that correspond to other people's experiences, that encourage innovation, that enable people to see problems from new perspectives, or that interrupt cycles of self-reinforcing behaviors. Unfortunately, transmitted models may be difficult to disconfirm. During World War II, the Germans developed a secret code that they believed to be unbreakable (Winterbotham, 1975); but the Allies broke the code early in the war, with the result that the Allied commanders often knew of the Germans' plans even before the German field commanders heard them. The Germans never did discover that their code had been broken, partly because the Germans believed so strongly in their cryptographers, and partly because the Allies were careful to provide false explanations for their successes.

Stereotypes are categorical expectations, or central-tendency schemata. People transmit stereotypes to one another, and labels enable people to evoke stereotypes for one another; so to facilitate communication, organizations tend to foster labeling and to make labels more definitive. A stereotype may embody useful information that helps a person decide how to behave in new situations or with new people; an effective stereotype enables a person to act more appropriately than if the person had no information. On the other hand, a stereotype may caricature situations or people and become a self-fulfilling prophecy (Danet, 1981). At best, a stereotype describes the central tendency of a group of situations or a group of people, and specific instances deviate from this central tendency.

Fredrickson (1985) investigated the degrees to which the labels 'problem' or 'opportunity' may represent shared schemata. In strategic-management courses, he presented two strategy cases to MBA students and to upper-middle-level executives; the cases sometimes labeled the described situations as problems and other times as opportunities. He found that the labels correlated with differences in the problem-solving processes recommended by MBA students, but not by the executives. Fredrickson traced these differences to the MBA students' extensive experience with teaching cases, as compared to the executives' relative inexperience with them. It might appear that the strategic-management courses had taught the MBA students that these two labels denote stereotypes, but that executives at large had not been influenced strongly by the courses, do not hold these stereotypes, and do not assign these labels shared meanings. However, Jackson and Dutton (1987) found evidence that the labels 'threats' and 'opportunities' do evoke shared schemata among executives. Jackson and Dutton asked participants in an executive-development program to think of experiences that they would classify as opportunities or as threats, and then to characterize these experiences in terms of 56 attributes. The participants tended to agree that opportunities and threats differ in at least three attributes: opportunities are positive and controllable, and they offer possible gains; whereas threats are negative and uncontrollable, and they portend possible losses. The participants also perceived opportunities and threats to have seven attributes in common, including pressure to act, urgency, difficulty, and importance. Thus, problems, threats, and opportunities may possess more shared attributes than distinct attributes. Jackson and Dutton (1987: 34) observed: "These simple labels do not have simple meanings."

Fredrickson's study suggests that labeling a situation as a problem or threat might have no discernible effects on the way an executive perceives it; but Jackson and Dutton's study suggests that labeling a situation as an opportunity might lead an executive to perceive it as more controllable and to notice its positive aspects, whereas labeling the situation as a threat might cause the executive to see its negative and uncontrollable elements. However, both Fredrickson and Jackson and Dutton imposed labels on the participants in their studies; the participants did not choose or generate these labels themselves, so these studies say nothing about how often executives use various labels spontaneously. Kepner and Tregoe (1965) observed managers who participated in training programs to improve group problem-solving skills. They noted that managers use the label "problem" to denote: (1) evidence that events differ from what is desired, (2) events that cause discomfort or require effort, (3) conjectures about why events differ from what is desired, (4) possible sources of events that cause discomfort, and (5) actions that ought to be taken. Managers also use this label interchangeably with other labels such as "issue," "question," "trouble," and "situation." Kepner and Tregoe concluded that the differing labels and the differing meanings of these labels engender a lot of confusion, misdirected disagreement, and wasted talk (Maier, 1963; Starbuck, 1983). One implication might be that, expecting labels to be used inconsistently, executives treat them as ambiguous; another implication might be that by developing shared stereotypes, organizations would improve group problem solving.

Rotter related controllability itself to noticing and sensemaking. After reviewing various studies, he (1966: 25) concluded that:

> the individual who has a strong belief that he can control his own destiny is likely to. . .be more alert to those aspects of his environment which provide useful information for his behavior;. . .[and to] place greater value on skill or achievement reinforcements and [to] be generally more concerned with his ability, particularly his failures.

Rotter defined locus of control as "a generalized expectancy" about who or what controls rewards and punishments; supposedly, a person with an internal locus of control sees herself as exerting strong influence over outcomes, whereas one with an external locus believes she has weak influence. As one driver reported to an insurance company, "The telephone pole was approaching. I was attempting to swerve out of its way when it struck my front end." However, research indicates that the behavioral consistencies associated with generalized personal characteristics, such as locus of control or dogmatism or cognitive complexity, are much smaller than the behavioral variations associated with different situations (Barker, 1968; Goldstein and Blackman, 1978; Mischel, 1968).

Framing Within What Matters. ". . .a nuclear war could alleviate some of the factors leading to today's ecological disturbances that are due to current high-population concentrations and heavy industrial production" Official of the U.S. Office of Civil Defense (Schell, 1982: 7).

Beliefs about "what matters" not only define what phenomena are relevant, important, insignificant, desirable, or evil, they also influence sensemaking by determining the frames of reference that give meaning to phenomena (Jervis, 1976). These beliefs include both generalized images of how the world should be and more specific ideas about what should be organizations' missions, structures, and strategies. For example, CEOs who believe that long-term debt indicates inadequate self-sufficiency may also tend to see borrowing as risky and burdensome, debt as constraining, and lenders as controlling (Donaldson and Lorsch, 1983). Similarly, in 1962, Joseph F. Cullman III, the President of Philip Morris, advised his company's stockholders that "There is growing evidence that smoking has pharmacological. . .effects that are of real value to smokers."

Because values and norms differ considerably from one arena to another, perceivers may discover that the beliefs that guided them well in one arena take them astray in another. In 1985, for instance, the U.S. Department of Justice indicted General Dynamics Corporation and several of its current and former top executives. The prosecutors charged that one of General Dynamics' defense contracts required it to absorb costs above a \$39 million ceiling, but the company had fraudulently charged \$3 million of the work on that project to two other contracts, one for general research and development and one for the preparation of bids and proposals. Eighteen months later, the Department of Justice withdrew these charges and explained that the contract in question was far more flexible than the prosecutors had originally surmised; in particular, the contract did allow General Dynamics to charge additional costs to other defense contracts. Evidently, the actual words of the contract were not at issue. Rather, the prosecutors had originally assumed that the contract provisions meant what they would mean outside the context of defense contracting, but the prosecutors later discovered that the language of defense contracts often appears to say something other than what it actually says. Thus, even though this contract appeared to set a ceiling on costs, both General

Dynamics and the U.S. Department of Defense understood that costs above this ceiling would be paid through other channels.

Jönsson and Lundin (1977) found that organizational sensemaking frameworks evolve cyclically. They observed that Swedish industrial-development companies went through waves of enthusiasm that were punctuated by intermittent crises. Each wave was associated with a shared myth, or key idea, that appeared as the solution to a preceding crisis. A new myth would attract adherents, filter perceptions, guide expectations, provide rationalizations, and engender enthusiasm and wishful thinking; vigorous action would occur. But eventually, new problems would be seen arising, enthusiasm for the prevailing myth would wane, and alternative "ghost" myths would appear as explanations for what was wrong. As alternative perceptual frameworks, these ghost myths would highlight anomalies connected with the prevailing myth, cast doubt upon its relevance, and so accelerate unlearning of it. When enough anomalies accumulated, organization members would discard the prevailing myth and espouse one of the ghost myths.

LIVING WITH COMPLEXITY

A focus on filtering processes makes it clear that the past, present, and future intertwine inseparably. Familiar events, expectations, and beliefs about what matters form overlapping categories than cannot be cleanly distinguished from one another. Expectations about the future, for instance, grow out of past experience and simultaneously express models that verge very close to wishful thinking; these expectations also lead people to edit their past experience and to espouse goals that look feasible. Such complexity matches the worlds in which people live.

Simon (1957: 20) pointed out that "principles of administration. . ., [are] like proverbs, they occur in pairs. For almost every principle one can find an equally plausible and contradictory principle." For instance, the injunction to minimize spans of control runs up against the injunction to minimize the number of hierarchical levels. Simon pointed out that if one tries to render one of these injunctions more valid by narrowing its scope, the injunction no longer solves so many problems. Hewitt and Hall (1973) remarked that societies offer numerous "quasi-theories," which are widely accepted recipes that can explain observed events and that apply to very diverse situations. For example, the quasi-theory of time claims that events can be expected to occur at certain times, and so an occurrence can be explained by saying that its time has come, or a nonoccurrence can be explained by saying that its time has not yet come. Edelman (1977: 5) argued that:

In every culture people learn to explain chronic problems through alternative sets of assumptions that are inconsistent with one another; yet the contradictory formulas persist, rationalizing inconsistent public policies and inconsistent individual beliefs about the threats that are widely feared in everyday life.

He illustrated this point by asserting that everyone, whether poor or affluent, learns two contrasting characterizations of the poor, one as victims of exploitative institutions and one as independent actors responsible for their own plight and in need of control to compensate for their inadequacies. Westerlund and Sjöstrand (1979) identified numerous myths that organizations sometimes bring forth to frame problem analyses. Most of these myths occur in mutually contradictory pairs. For example, the myth of organizational limitations states that an organization has boundaries that circumscribe its abilities; but this myth contradicts the one of the unlimited environment, which claims that the organization's environment offers innumerable opportunities. Similarly, the fairy tale of optimization convinces organization members of their competence by asserting that the organization is acting optimally; but it contradicts the fairy tale of satisfaction, which says that satisfactory performances are good enough.

Fombrun and Starbuck (1987) explained that such contradictions are so prevalent because processes affecting social systems inevitably call forth antithetical processes having opposing effects. For instance, laws forbidding certain businesses make it highly profitable to engage in these businesses illegally, so law enforcement unintentionally fosters criminality. One ubiquitous antithetical effect is that the handicaps of individuals motivate the creation of compensating social supports, and another prevalent antithetical effect is that organizations' strategic choices create opportunities for their competitors. Antithetical processes mean that social systems tend to remain stable, complex, and ambiguous. A process that tends to displace a social system from its current state gets offset by processes that tend to restore that current state; a process that tends to eliminate some characteristics gets offset by processes that tend to preserve the existing characteristics or to add new ones; and so the social system remains a complex mixture.

Facing such a world, realistic people have to have numerous sensemaking frameworks that contradict each other. These numerous frameworks create plentiful interpretive opportunities—if an initial framework fails, one can try its equally plausible converse, or try a framework that emphasizes different elements. Thus, meanings are generally cheap and easily found, except when people confront major tragedies such as divorces or the deaths of loved ones . . .and even these often become "growth experiences." People have confidence that they can eventually make sense of almost any situation because they can.

Of course, some sensemaking frameworks lead to more effective behaviors than others do, but the criteria of effectiveness are many and inconsistent, and perceivers usually can appraise effectiveness only in retrospect. The most accurate perceivers may be either ones who change their minds readily or ones who believe strongly enough to enact their beliefs, and the happiest perceivers may be the least accurate ones. The ambiguity and complexity of their worlds imply that perceivers may benefit by using multiple sensemaking frameworks to appraise events; but perceivers are more likely to act forcefully and effectively if they see things simply, and multiple frameworks may undermine organizations' political structures (Brunsson, 1985; Wildavsky, 1972). Malleable worlds imply that perceivers may benefit by using frameworks that disclose opportunities to exert influence, but people who try to change their worlds often produce unintended results, even the opposite of what they intended. Perceivers who understand themselves and their environments should appreciate sensemaking frameworks that recognize the inevitability of distortions and that foster beneficial distortions, but such wise people should also doubt that they actually know what is good for themselves, and they should recognize that the most beneficial errors are often the most surprising ones. Fortunately, people seem to have a good deal of latitude for discretion. People investigate hypotheses from the viewpoint that they are correct, and as long as results can be interpreted within current frameworks, the frameworks need not change, or even be evaluated (Snyder, 1981). Further, sensemaking may or may not determine whether people respond appropriately to environmental events: sometimes people act first and then later make sense of the outcomes (Starbuck, 1983; Weick, 1983).

Because sensemaking is so elusive, noticing may be at least as important as sensemaking. Perhaps sensemaking and noticing interact as complements in effective problem solving: sensemaking focuses on subtleties and interdependencies, whereas noticing picks up major events and gross trends. Noticing determines whether people even consider responding to environmental events. If events are noticed, people make sense of them; and if events are not noticed, they are not available for sensemaking. Thus, it makes a great difference how foregrounds, backgrounds, and adaptation levels adjust to current stimuli and experience. Insofar as people can control these adjustments voluntarily, they can design noticing systems that respond to changes or ignore them, that emphasize some constituencies and deemphasize others, or that integrate many stimuli simultaneously or concentrate on a few stimuli at a time.

In the late 1950s, residents of Seattle noticed small pits scarring their automobile windshields. As time passed, more and more auto owners reported finding these pits, and public concern escalated. One widespread hypothesis held that recent Soviet atomic-bomb tests had hurled radioactive salts into the atmosphere; and upon being captured by Seattle's moist atmosphere, these salts were creating a glass-etching dew on windshields, where their damage was highly visible. Another popular hypothesis was that rain and macadam from extensive new highway construction were creating acid salts, with the result that autos were throwing droplets of acid onto each other. As the reports of pitting multiplied, the officials of Seattle finally appealed to Governor Rosollini for help; the Governor in turn appealed to President Eisenhower; and the President dispatched a team of investigators from the National Bureau of Standards. The Federal investigators spent no time pursuing either of the prevalent hypotheses: instead they measured the frequency of windshield pits and discovered that they were no more common than ever. Seattle had not experienced a plague of windshield pitting, but an epidemic of windshield noticing.

ACKNOWLEDGMENTS

We thank Janice Beyer, Janet Dukerich, Jane Dutton, and Donald Hambrick for contributing helpful comments and suggestions.

REFERENCES

Ackoff, R.L. "Management Misinformation Systems." *Management Science* 14 (1967): B147-B156.

Ashby, W.R. *Design for a Brain.* 2nd ed. New York: Wiley, 1960.

Astley, W.G. "The Two Ecologies: Microevolutionary and Macroevolutionary Perspectives on Organizational Change." *Administrative Science Quarterly* 30 (1985): 224-241.

Astley, W.G., and Fombrun, C.J. "Organizational Communities. An Ecological Perspective." In *Research in the Sociology of Organizations,* Vol. 5. Edited by S. Bacharach and N. Di Tomaso. Greenwich, CT: JAI Press, 1987.

Axelrod, R.M., ed. "Results." *Structure of Decision: The Cognitive Maps of Political Elites,* pp. 221-248. Princeton, NJ: Princeton University Press, 1976.

Bargh, J.A. "Attention and Automaticity in the Processing of Self-Relevant Information." *Journal of Personality and Social Psychology* 43 (1982): 425-436.

Barker, R.G. *Ecological Psychology.* Stanford, CA: Stanford University Press, 1968.

Bennis, W.G. "The Artform of Leadership." In *The Executive Mind: New Insights on Managerial Thought and Action,* pp. 15-24. Authored by S. Srivastva and Associates. San Francisco, CA: Jossey-Bass, 1983.

Brunsson, N. *The Irrational Organization: Irrationality as a Basis for Organizational Action and Change.* Chichester: Wiley, 1985.

Central Intelligence Agency. Report CS-3/467: 630.

Central Intelligence Agency. Report CS-3/470: 587.

Daft, R.L., and Weick, K.E. "Toward a Model of Organizations as Interpretation Systems." *Academy of Management Review* 9 (1984): 284-295.

Danet, B. "Client-Organization Relationships." In *Handbook of Organizational Design,* Vol. 2, pp. 382-428. Edited by P.C. Nystrom and W.H. Starbuck. New York: Oxford University Press, 1981.

Dearborn, D.C., and Simon, H.A. "Selective Perception: A Note on the Departmental Identifications of Executives." *Sociometry* 21 (1958): 140-144.

Donaldson, G., and Lorsch, J.W. *Decision Making at the Top: The Shaping of Strategic Direction.* New York: Basic Books, 1983.

Downey, H.K., Hellriegel, D., and Slocum, J.W., Jr. "Individual Characteristics as Sources of Perceived Uncertainty." *Human Relations* 30 (1977): 161-174.

Dunbar, R.L.M., and Goldberg, W.H. "Crisis Development and Strategic Response in European Corporations." *Journal of Business Administration* 9(2) (1978): 139-149.

Duncan, R.B. "Characteristics of Organizational Environments and Perceived Environmental Uncertainty." *Administrative Science Quarterly* 17 (1972): 313-327.

Dutton, J.E., and Jackson, S.E. "Categorizing Strategic Issues: Links to Organizational Action." *Academy of Management Review* 12 (1987): 76-90.

Edelman, M. *Political Language: Words That Succeed and Policies That Fail.* New York: Academic Press, 1977.

Festinger, L., Riecken, H.W., and Schachter, S. *When Prophecy Fails.* Minneapolis, MN: University of Minnesota Press, 1956.

Fischhoff, B. "Hindsight or Foresight: The Effect of Outcome Knowledge on Judgment Under Uncertainty." *Journal of Experimental Psychology: Human Perception and Performance* 1 (1975): 288-299.

Fischhoff, B. "For Those Condemned to Study the Past: Reflections on Historical Judgment." In *New Directions for Methodology of Behavioral Science*, pp. 79-93. Edited by R.A. Shweder and D.W. Fiste. San Francisco, CA: Jossey-Bass, 1980.

Fischoff, B., and Beyth, R. "I Knew It Would Happen: Remembered Probabilities of Once-Future Things." *Organizational Behavior and Human Performance* 13 (1975): 1-16.

Fombrun, C.J., and Starbuck, W.H. "Variations in the Evolution of Organizational Ecology." Working paper, New York University, 1987.

Fredrickson, J.W. "Effects of Decision Motive and Organizational Performance Level on Strategic Decision Processes." *Academy of Management Journal* 28 (1985): 821-843.

Gibson, E. "Improvement in Perceptual Judgments as a Function of Controlled Practice or Training." *Psychological Bulletin* 50 (1953): 401-431.

Goldstein, K.M., and Blackman, S. *Cognitive Style: Five Approaches and Relevant Research.* New York: Wiley, 1978.

Goleman, D. *Vital Lies, Simple Truths: The Psychology of Self-Deception.* New York: Simon and Schuster, 1985.

Greenwald, A.G. "The Totalitarian Ego: Fabrication and Revision of Personal History." *American Psychologist* 35 (1980): 603-618.

Hart, J.A. "Comparative Cognition: Politics of International Control of the Oceans." In *Structure of Decision: The Cognitive Maps of Political Elites*, pp. 180-217. Edited by R.M. Axelrod. Princeton, NJ: Princeton University Press, 1976.

Hart, J.A. "Cognitive Maps of Three Latin American Policy Makers." *World Politics* 30 (1977): 115-140.

Hastie, R. "Schematic Principles in Human Memory." In *Social Cognition, The Ontario Symposium*, Vol. 1, pp. 39-88. Edited by E.T. Higgins, C.P. Herman, and M.P. Zanna. Hillsdale, NJ: Erlbaum, 1981.

Hawkins, H.A., and Hastie, R. "Hindsight: Biased Processing of Past Events in Response to Outcome Information." Working paper, Carnegie-Mellon University and Northwestern University, 1986.

Hayek, F.A. von. *The Pretence of Knowledge.* Stockholm: The Nobel Foundation, 1974.

Hedberg, B.L.T. "How Organizations Learn and Unlearn." In *Handbook of Organizational Design*, Vol. 1, pp. 3-27. Edited by P.C. Nystrom and W.H. Starbuck. New York: Oxford University Press, 1981.

Helson, H. *Adaptation-Level Theory.* New York: Harper & Row, 1964.

Hewitt, J.P., and Hall, P.M. "Social Problems, Problematic Situations, and Quasi-Theories." *American Sociological Review* 38 (1973): 367-374.

Ittelson, W.H., Franck, K.A., and O'Hanlon, T.J. "The Nature of Environmental Experience." In *Experiencing the Environment,* pp. 187-206. Edited by S. Wapner, S. Cohen, B. Kaplan. New York: Plenum, 1976.

Jackson, S.E., and Dutton, J.E. "What Do 'Threat' and 'Opportunity' Mean? A Complex Answer to a Simple Question." Working paper, New York University, 1987.

Jervis, R. *Perception and Misperception in International Politics.* Princeton, NJ: Princeton University Press, 1976.

Jönsson, S.A., and Lundin, R.A. "Myths and Wishful Thinking as Management Tools." In *Prescriptive Models of Organizations,* pp. 157-170. Edited by P.C. Nystrom and W.H. Starbuck. Amsterdam: North-Holland, 1977.

Kepner, C.H., and Tregoe, B.B. *The Rational Manager.* New York: McGraw-Hill, 1965.

Kiesler, C.A., and Sproull, L.S. "Managerial Responses to Changing Environments: Perspectives on Problem Sensing from Social Cognition." *Administrative Science Quarterly* 27 (1982): 548-570.

Langer, E.J., and Roth, J. "Heads I Win, Tails It's Chance: The Illusion of Control as a Function of the Sequence Outcomes in a Purely Chance Task." *Journal of Personality and Social Psychology* 32 (1975): 951-955.

Loftus, E.F. "The Malleability of Human Memory." *American Scientist* 67 (1979): 312-320.

Luce, R.D., and Galanter, E. "Discrimination." In *Handbook of Mathematical Psychology,* Vol. 1, pp. 191-243. Edited by R.D. Luce, R.R. Bush, and E. Galanter. New York: Wiley, 1963.

Lyles, M.A., and Mitroff, I.I. "Organizational Problem Formulation: An Empirical Study." *Administrative Science Quarterly* 25 (1980): 102-119.

McArthur, L.Z. "What Grabs You? The Role of Attention in Impression Formation and Causal Attribution." In *Social Cognition, The Ontario Symposium,* Vol. 1, pp. 201-246. Edited by E.T. Higgins, C.P. Herman, and M.P. Zanna. Hillsdale, NJ: Erlbaum, 1981.

McCall, M.W., Jr. "Making Sense With Nonsense: Helping Frames of Reference Clash." In *Prescriptive Models of Organizations,* pp. 111-123. Edited by by P.C. Nystrom and W.H. Starbuck, 1977.

Maier, N.R.F. *Problem-Solving Discussions and Conferences: Leadership Methods and Skills.* New York: McGraw-Hill, 1963.

Makridakis, S., and Hibon, M. "Accuracy of Forecasting: An Empirical Investigation." *Journal of the Royal Statistical Society,* Series A 142 (1979): 97-145.

Masuch, M. "Vicious Circles in Organizations." *Administrative Science Quaterly* 30 (1985): 14-33.

Meadows, D.H., Meadows, R.L, Randers, J., and Behrens, W.W., III. *The Limits to Growth.* New York: Universe Books, 1972.

Mischel, W. *Personality and Assessment.* New York: Wiley, 1968.

Mitroff, I.I., and Kilmann, R.H. *Corporate Tragedies: Product Tampering, Sabotage, and Other Catastrophes.* New York: Praeger, 1984.

Neisser, U. "John Dean's Memory: A Case Study." *Cognition* 9 (1981): 1-22.

Neilsen, S.L., and Sarason, I.G., "Emotion, Personality, and Selective Attention." *Journal of Personality and Social Psychology* 41 (1981): 945-960.

Nisbett, R.E., and Ross, L. *Human Inference: Strategies and Shortcomings of Social Judgment.* Englewood Cliffs, NJ: Prentice-Hall, 1980.

Normann, R. "Organizational Innovativeness: Product Variation and Reorientation." *Administrative Science Quarterly* 16 (1971): 203-215.

O'Reilly, C.A., III. "The Use of Information in Organizational Decision Making: A Model and Some Propositions." In *Research in Organizational Behavior*, Vol. 5, pp. 103-139. Edited by L.L. Cummings and B.M. Staw. Greenwich, CT: JAI Press, 1983.

Payne, R.L., and Pugh, D.S. "Organizational Structure and Climate." In *Handbook of Industrial and Organizational Psychology*, pp. 1125-1173. Edited by M.D. Dunnette. Chicago, IL: Rand McNally, 1976.

Peters, T.J., and Waterman, R.H., Jr. In *Search of Excellence*. New York: Harper & Row, 1982.

Porter, L.W., and Roberts, K.H. "Communication in Organizations." In *Handbook of Industrial and Organizational Psychology*, pp. 1553-1589. Edited by M.D. Dunnette. Chicago, IL: Rand McNally, 1976.

Presidential Commission on the Space Shuttle Challenger Accident *Report to the President*. Washington: U.S. Government Printing Office, 1986.

Rosenhan, D.L. "On Being Sane in Insane Places." In *Contemporary Readings in Psychopathology*, pp. 29-41. Edited by J.M. Neale, G.C. Davison, and K.P. Price. New York: Wiley, 1978.

Ross, J., and Staw, B.M. "Expo 86: An Escalation Prototype." *Administrative Science Quarterly* 31 (1986): 274-297.

Rotter, J.B. "Generalized Expectancies for Internal Versus External Control of Reinforcement." *Psychological Monographs* 80(1) (1966): 1-28.

Sage, A.P. "Designs for Optimal Information Filters." In *Handbook of Organizational Design*, Vol. 1, pp. 105-121. Edited by P.C. Nystrom and W.H. Starbuck. New York: Oxford University Press, 1981.

Schell, J. *The Fate of the Earth*. New York: Knopf, 1982.

Schroder, H.M., Driver, M.J., and Streufert, S. *Human Information Processing*. New York: Holt, Rinehart and Winston, 1967.

Simon, H.A. *Administrative Behavior*. 2nd ed. New York: Macmillan, 1957.

Snyder, M. "Seek, and Ye Shall Find: Testing Hypotheses About Other People." In *Social Cognition, The Ontario Symposium*, Vol. 1, pp. 277-303. Edited by E.T. Higgins, C.P. Herman and M.P. Zanna. Hillsdale, NJ: Erlbaum, 1981.

Snyder, M., and Uranowitz, S.W. "Reconstructing the Past: Some Cognitive Consequences of Person Perception." *Journal of Personality and Social Psychology* 36 (1978): 941-950.

Starbuck, W.H. "Organizations and Their Environments." In *Handbook of Industrial and Organizational Psychology*, pp. 1069-1123. Edited by M.D. Dunnette. Chicago, IL: Rand McNally, 1976.

Starbuck, W.H. "Organizations as Action Generators." *American Sociological Review* 48 (1983): 91-102.

Starbuck, W.H. "Acting First and Thinking Later: Theory Versus Reality in Strategic Change." In *Organizational Strategy and Change*, pp. 336-372. Edited by J.M. Pennings and Assoc. San Francisco, CA: Jossey-Bass, 1985.

Starbuck, W.H. "Why Organizations Run into Crises. . .and Sometimes Survive Them." In *Information Technology and Management Strategy*. Edited by K. Laudon and J. Turner. Englewood Cliffs, NJ: Prentice-Hall, in press.

Starbuck, W.H., Greve, A., and Hedberg, B.L.T. "Responding to Crises." *Journal of Business Administration* 9(2) (1978): 111-137.

Taylor, S.E., and Crocker, J. "Schematic Bases of Social Information Processing." In *Social Cognition, The Ontario Symposium*, Vol. 1, pp. 89-134. Edited by E.T. Higgins, C.P. Herman and M.P. Zanna. Hillsdale, NJ: Erlbaum, 1981.

Tuchman, G. "Making News by Doing Work: Routinizing the Unexpected." *American Journal of Sociology* 79 (1973): 110-131.

Tushman, M.L., and Anderson, P. "Technological Discontinuities and Organizational Environments." *Administrative Science Quarterly* 31 (1986): 439-465.

Tversky, A., and Kahneman, D. "Judgement Under Uncertainty: Heuristics and Biases." *Science* 185 (1974): 1124-1131.

Watzlawick, P., Weakland, J.H., and Fisch, R. *Change: Principles of Problem Formation and Problem Resolution.* New York: Norton, 1974.

Weick, K.E. *The Social Psychology of Organizing.* 2nd ed. Reading, MA: Addison-Wesley, 1979.

Weick, K.E. "Managerial Thought in the Context of Action." In *The Executive Mind: New Insights on Managerial Thought and Action,* pp. 221-242. Authored by S. Srivastva and Associates. San Francisco, CA: Jossey-Bass, 1983.

Westerlund, G., and Sjöstrand, S. *Organizational Myths.* London: Harper & Row, 1979.

Wildavsky, A.B. "The Self-Evaluating Organization." *Public Administration Review* 32 (1972): 509-520.

Winterbotham, F.W. *The Ultra Secret.* New York: Dell, 1975.

Wohlwill, J.F., and Kohn, I. "Dimensionalizing the Environmental Manifold." In *Experiencing the Environment,* pp. 19-54. Edited by S. Wapner, S. Cohen, and B. Kaplan. New York: Plenum, 1976.

CEO ROLES ACROSS CULTURES

Ellen F. Jackofsky and John W. Slocum, Jr.

Despite the importance of the CEO to the firm, there is a dearth of knowledge about CEOs (Worrell, Davidson, Chandy and Garrison, 1986). What has been written focuses either on executive succession (Dalton and Kesner, 1985) or on demographic statistics (Norburn, 1986). This paper explores the possibility that societal value systems are reflected in the processes by which the CEO enacts his/her role(s). Mintzberg (1973), Harris and Moran (1986), Jauch and Kraft (1986), among others, have stated that the effect of societal values on various aspects of strategic management have too often been neglected. We clearly recognize and will briefly discuss other variables, such as environmental characteristics, business strategy, and so on, that affect the process by which the CEO enacts his/her role. We contend that relationships between these variables reflect, at least in part, culturally specific values. To explore this major premise, we first review salient literature on comparative management research, and then propose a paradigm that coalesces research from divergent literatures to investigate how cultural values impact upon CEO role behaviors. Anecdotal evidence from popular business presses will be used to illustrate our paradigm.

PROBLEMS IN CROSS-CULTURAL RESEARCH

While it is well recognized that innumerable factors influence organizations (March and Simon, 1958), the question of cross-cultural effects are still debated (Lammers and Hickson, 1979; Lincoln, Hanada and McBride, 1986; Terpstra and David, 1985; Tosi and Slocum, 1984). There are researchers who contend that theories of organizations are dependent on the society in which a particular organization is located (Crozier, 1964; Glasier, 1971). Other researchers posit that theories of organizations only become such when one discovers relationships between organizational attributes that apply across cultural settings (Heydebrand, 1973). The former approach is known as the "culture-specific argument" and the latter as the "culture-free or contingency argument."

The "culture-specific concept" is based on the thesis that different societies reflect distinct and relatively stable cultures (Child and Kieser, 1979). Cultural frameworks are persistent because they are shared among individuals in a society within a particular time frame and then transmitted between generations. Organizations in different cultures may develop, for example, similar structures in response to environmental exigencies:

> Hence, a comparison of the systemic relationships between social structures and organizations and of the processes by which they are manifested in each national situation alone can enable one to develop a theory of organizations. . . . (Maurice, 1979: 47).

Contrary to this culture-specific approach, the culture-free argument is based on the premise that scientific reasoning is not possible without the potential for external validity across cultures (Negandhi, 1975). Research should focus on developing universal theories of organizations that extend beyond national boundaries and/or cultural specifics. This suggests that industrialization has a greater impact on the way that an organization forms and is sustained over time than culture (Kerr, Dunlop, Harbison and Myers, 1960). A similar argument has been advanced by Galbraith (1967) who suggested that the form of a particular institution is more dependent on economic factors than cultural ones. The "culture-free" advocates point out that it is not the absolute differences between levels of variables (e.g., size, strategy, technology, and structure) across cultures that are of concern, but the stability of relationships between these variables across cultures that affect theories of organizations (Hickson, McMillan, Azumi and Horvath, 1979). In a review of studies that examined formalization, structural specialization, and centralization across several countries, Hickson et al. (1979) found partial support for the stability of relationships between contextual variables across cultures.

These two lines of reasoning concerning the effects of culture on organizational functioning have been brought together by Child and Kieser (1979). They suggest that cultural influences are likely to affect the links in a model that bridges organizational context and structure, individual roles and individual behaviors. However:

> the cultural factor has most bearing upon modes of individual conduct and inter-personal relationships, and it is precisely at this level that one would expect the products of socialization to be manifested most strongly (Child and Kieser, 1979: 268).

In addition to the Child and Kieser work, Hofstede (1980a) has found that researchers have a tendency to design cross-cultural research so that similarities or differences will be found. If the researcher looks for similarities, research that is more general in nature versus specific will be designed. Differences are usually found between cultures when individual or group level outcomes have been examined (Bhagat and McQuaid, 1982), but not as frequently when structural, strategic, and technological variables have been researched. This bias in design may be related to another problem: the ecological fallacy (Adler, 1984; Hofstede, 1980a). An ecological fallacy occurs when the researcher does not stipulate whether the level of analysis of variables is individual, group, or organizational. In this case, similarities and/or differences in cultures are posited by employing theories based on individual processes (cognitions, attributions, personalities) to conceptualize national/cultural effects.

The level of the analysis problem underscores the importance of clearly defining the concept of culture in any particular research effort (Drenth and Groenendijk, 1984). It is unclear in cross-cultural research whether differences and/or similarities are the result of the "designated variables or the meaning of the concepts used" (Drenth and Groenendijk, 1984: 120). Hofstede (1980a) points out that the referent group makes a difference in individuals' reactions to leadership behavior. The individual from a society where social class differences are emphasized is more likely to refer to a leader from his/her own group, as opposed to someone from a society where class differences are less demarcated. In this latter situation, reference to a leader would not necessarily be based on group membership.

By not clearly defining culture, it is less likely that researchers can classify differences found between organizations as cultural (Drenth and Groenendijk, 1984). To be consistent in classification, Ajiferuke and Boddewijn (1970) suggested that culture be defined either on the societal or individual level. The definition of culture must be congruent with the level of theory being investigated. If the research is designed to address individual behavior, the effects of cultural values on personal orientations to work behavior should be utilized. On the other hand, if the research is based on macro issues (e.g., industrialization), then culture must be operationalized on a global level.

In summarizing research reports that address the potential for cultural differences between organizations, Lammers and Hickson (1979) found that culture is a determinant of behavior in organizations. Cultural patterns affect organizational forms and processes in three fundamental ways. First, dominant values of a particular culture are reflected in the standards imposed on organizations by its environment (e.g., government, customers, suppliers). Second, the founders of an organization have learned certain values from their culture and these are imprinted on the organization from its beginning. Even when organizations are reconstructed, they are affected by the cultural values of "dominant elites" (Hambrick and Mason, 1984). Third, organizational members (i.e., those other than the "dominant elites") behave in a manner that is reinforced by cultural values.

This chapter examines the effect that cultural values have on the dominant elites' orientations toward management in their respective organizations. By designating "dominant elites" as chief executive officers (i.e., those located at the head of their organizations), we are able to identify similarities and/or differences in configurations of roles utilized by CEOs in carrying out their functions. The specific orientations that we will focus on are more fully explained in the next section of the paper.

FORCES INFLUENCING CEO ROLE BEHAVIORS

A chief executive's role behavior is not random. These behaviors are orientations affected by a set of five forces (see Figure 1). Four of these forces—task environment, strategy, organization structure and managerial characteristics—have been examined by others (Hambrick and Finkelstein, 1987; Kets de Vries and Miller, 1986; Huff, 1982). Various linkages between these four forces have been proposed and tested. According to this literature, the chief executive's decision-making domain is a function of (1) the degree to which the task environment permits variety and change (Hrebiniak and Joyce, 1985); (2) the degree to which the structure of the organization itself (and its culture) is amenable to change and reinforces the CEOs' behaviors (Mintzberg, 1984); (3) the strategy pursued by the firm (Porter, 1980); and (4) particular managerial characteristics (e.g., personality traits, educational backgrounds, interpersonal skills) of the CEO (Miller, Kets de Vries and Toulouse, 1982; Channon, 1979; Kofodimos, Kaplan and Drath, 1986).

The fifth force, culture, has been neglected by most previous researchers. According to Mintzberg (1973: 197), researchers "know almost nothing about work variations by cultures. . . .The influence of cultural factors on the manager's job. . .certainly requires investigation." Our model indicates

Figure 1. Factors Affecting CEO Role Behaviors

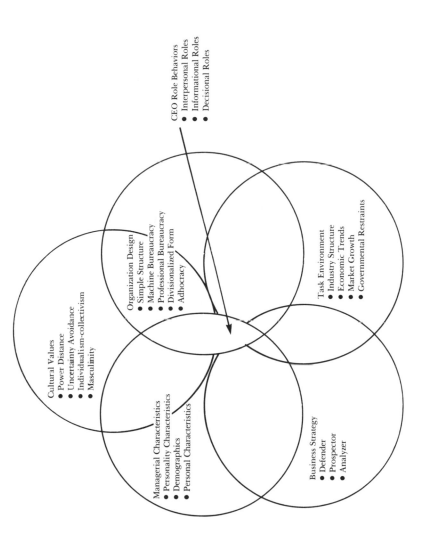

that a society's culture will impact both the CEO's managerial characteristics and the design of the organization's hierarchy. Evidence to support our model is based on the work of Lincoln et al. (1986), Meyer and Rowan (1977), Child and Kieser (1979), and Kofodimos et al. (1986), among others. Lincoln et al. (1986), for example, compared U.S. and Japanese manufacturing firms on a number of structural and technological dimensions. Not only did these researchers find structural differences between these firms, they also found that the processes by which decisions were implemented varied by culture. In Japan, closer supervisor-subordinate interaction facilitated work-group dynamics (a characteristic of the nenko system) and encouraged decision making at lower levels than in U.S. companies. These researchers conclude that "it is the processes whereby task contingencies" affect design decisions that reflect cultural differences. We have found no evidence to suggest that a corporation's task environment and its enacted business strategy are directly related to a society's values.

Cultural Values

One of the major problems in studying cultural values is the vagueness of both terms. According to Kluckhohn (1951: 395), "a value is a conception, explicit or implicit, distinctive of an individual or a group, of the desirable which influences the selection from available modes, means and ends of actions." Therefore, values are ends and not means. As such, values have both intensity and direction. Individual values are mutually related to form value systems. However, these value systems need not be in a state of congruence, as, for example, freedom and equality.

The values people hold about what is desirable and undesirable are embedded in the culture. According to Hofstede, culture is defined as the "collective mental programming of the people in an environment" (1980a: 25). Culture is not a characteristic of individuals, but of a collection of individuals who share common values. Just as culture determines the identity of a group of people, personality determines the identity of an individual. In studying values, the focus is on the individual. In studying cultures, the focus is on societies. Therefore, in studying how cultures affect chief executive roles, we are primarily interested in how CEO roles reflect the cultural values of a society. Mintzberg (1973), for example, empirically determined the basic characteristics of managerial work. Mintzberg found that meetings, either scheduled or unscheduled, consume 70 percent of a manager's 8-hour day. Doktor, Lie, and Redding (1986) found that Korean and Japanese managers held meetings of longer duration than managers in the United States. The reason for longer meetings was that Asian managers need time to build consensus, foster team building, and pay dutiful attention to certain rites and rituals. In both these societies, group consensus is highly valued, whereas in the United States, individualism is highly valued. Therefore, while values may not directly affect whether the chief executive enacts a role, they impact the processes by which the CEO implements the role behavior(s).

Hofstede (1980a, 1980b, 1983, 1984) has proposed a paradigm to study the impact of culture on individuals. To develop this paradigm, he originally studied the values and beliefs of over 116,000 employees from a large U.S.-based multinational corporation (IBM) that had operations in 40 countries around the world. His classification system has been supported by Adler (1984, 1986), Bhagat and McQuaid (1982), Ronen and Shenkar (1985), Dorfman, Howell, and Bautista (1986) among others, as an indicator of cultural mores and beliefs. Goodstein (1981) and Hunt (1981) have criticized his methodology and managerial implications, but both agree that cultural values affect managerial behaviors. To counter these criticisms, Hofstede clearly indicates that not every person in a culture shares all the characteristics ascribed to that culture.

In the current work, we used Hofstede's typology because it permitted us to relate four common cultural elements to CEO role behaviors. These elements are: power distance, uncertainty avoidance, individualism-collectivism, and masculinity. We shall briefly describe each of these dimensions and present a table that (1) highlights the salient characteristics of that dimension and (2) lists several countries that Hofstede (1980a) noted as examples of cultures which are high and low on each dimension. For extensive development of these concepts, see Hofstede (1980a).

Power Distance. This refers to the extent to which a culture accepts the inequality of the distribution of power between people (see Table 1). Inequality can occur in a variety of areas, for example, social status, prestige, wealth, and the laws and rules of society. In low power distance societies, such as the United States, Sweden, and Austria, new members can rise more easily into the elite class than in high power distance, or elitist societies, such as the Philippines, Mexico, and India, because belonging to the middle class groups in low power distance societies is a stepping stone into the elitist category.

An unequal distribution of power between managers and subordinates is the essence of organization. However, the processes by which these differences are manifested differ widely. In societies with small power distances, such as Sweden, Israel, and Austria, subordinates and managers are highly interdependent in the completion of tasks, and status differences between them are downplayed. Under these conditions, subordinates prefer a consultative decision style that minimizes the power differences between superior and subordinate. In cultures where there are large power differences, such as the Philippines, Mexico, Venezuela, and India, a more

Table 1.   POWER DISTANCE (PDI)—Degree of Inequality
in Power between Persons*

LOW (Countries—Austria, Israel, Denmark, Sweden, Norway)	HIGH (Countries—Philippines, Mexico, Venzuela, Brazil)
• Managers make decisions after consulting with subordinates.	• Managers employ an autoractic style of management.
• Close supervision is negatively evaluated by subordinates.	• Managers use coercion and legitimate bases of power to get work done.
• Hierarchy is for decision-making convenience.	• Hierarchy means inequality.
• Control systems based on trust in subordinate's ability to complete job.	• Centralization of authority is common.
• All employees have equal rights.	• Powerholders are "entitled" to privileges.

* Adapted from G. Hofstede, *Culture's Consequences* (Beverly Hills, CA: Sage Publications 1980), pp. 92-152.

autocratic management style is not only more common, but also more expected by subordinates (Williams, Whyte and Green, 1966).

Uncertainty Avoidance.   The second dimension, uncertainty avoidance, is the extent to which people in a culture feel threatened by uncertain and ambiguous situations and try to avoid them (Table 2). The concept of uncertainty has been an important one in theories of organizations (see Cyert and March, 1963; Lawrence and Lorsch, 1967; March and Simon, 1958). Hofstede contends that cultures use the same techniques to cope with uncertainty as organizations do (e.g., rules and rituals). High uncertainty avoidance countries, such as Greece, Japan, France, and Peru, have sustained higher economic growth after World War II, generated stronger nationalism, and are less tolerant of citizen protest than low uncertainty avoidance countries, such as Denmark, Sweden, and Ireland. In Crozier's (1964) study of French companies, the reliance on rules and regulations to control the behavior of employees enabled managers to successfully use the bureaucratic approach to manage their firms. In primitive cultures, rites and rituals were prescribed by priests to ensure winning wars or bountiful crops. These rites and rituals permitted tribal members to continue their lives in the face of high degrees of uncertainty. In U.S. corporations, rites and rituals perform similar functions.

According to Hofstede, the consequences for companies operating in either high or low uncertainty avoidances societies are quite pronounced.

Table 2. UNCERTAINTY AVOIDANCE (UAI)—Degree to which People Feel Threatened by Ambiguous and Risky Situations*

LOW (Countries—Denmark, Sweden, Great Britain, U.S.A., India)	HIGH (Countries—Greece, Portugal, Japan, Peru, France)
• Few rules, rituals, and standards.	• Reliance on experts.
• Managers focus on long-range decisions that emphasize strategic planning.	• High formalization, specialization and standardization.
• Deviant behavior tolerated.	• Impersonal control and planning systems based on rules and regulations
• Conflict and competition can be used constructively.	• Managers influence subordinates through the uses of their legitimate power.
• More willing to take risks.	• Concern with security and fewer risks.

* Adapted from G. Hofstede, *Culture's Consequences* (Beverly Hills, CA: Sage Publications 1980), pp. 153-212.

For example, employees whose companies are indigenous to a low (as compared to a high) avoidance uncertainty society may have fewer written rules and procedures to follow, are rewarded to become generalists more than specialists, have fewer rituals, encounter less structuring of their activities, and have managers who are more willing to take risks.

Individualism-collectivism. As shown in Table 3, the third dimension is individualism and its opposite, collectivism. Individualism implies a loosely knit social structure in which people are supposed to take care of themselves and of their immediate families (analogous to tigers in the wild). Collectivism implies a tightly knit social structure in which people differentiate between in-groups and out-groups. People expect that in-groups (such as clans and organizations) will protect their members, and feel that they should be extremely loyal to their in-group. Riesman, Glazer, and Denney, in their book, *The Lonely Crowd* (1953), characterize the American culture as strongly individualistic, whereas the Chinese (as well as other Asian societies) were characterized as highly collective. In Whyte's book, *The Organization Man* (1956), the theme was that large corporations are destroying individualism and exhorting collectivism. Whyte concluded that the strong feelings of individualism in the United States make it unrealistic to think that organizations, as opposed to individuals, will solve the major problems facing society.

The level of individualism-collectivism in a culture will affect an organization's members in a variety of ways. Managers operating in cultures

Table 3. INDIVIDUALISM (IDV)—Extent to which
Society Expects to Take Care of Individuals versus the
Degree to which the Person Should Take Care of Him/Herself*

LOW (*Countries—Venezuela, Columbia, Taiwan, Mexico, Greece*)	*HIGH* (*Countries—United States, Australia, Great Britain, Canada, Netherlands*)
• Managers value traditions & have a high emotional dependence on groups.	• Individual initiative is socially valued.
• Long tenure is valued.	• Short tenure is valued.
• Corporations should assume responsibility for employees (e.g., training, physical welfare).	• Corporation is not responsible for employees.
• Security in position is valued along with orderliness and conformity to group goals.	• Individual decision making and autonomy are high.
• Promotion is from the inside and based on seniority.	• Managers develop policies and practices that reflect individual initiative.

* Adapted from G. Hofstede, *Culture's Consequences* (Beverly Hills, CA: Sage Publications 1980), pp. 213-260.

that place a high value on individualism frequently move from company to company, believe that the corporation is not responsible for the welfare of its employees, engage in networking activities between companies, and generally believe that higher quality decisions are made by individuals than by groups. In cultures that value collectivism, employers are attracted to larger rather than smaller companies, attach more importance to structure than freedom on their jobs, and are more emotionally and morally involved with their companies than those from cultures high on individualism.

Masculinity. The fourth dimension is masculinity, and its opposite, femininity (Table 4). Masculinity refers to the extent to which dominant values in a culture are "masculine" in terms of assertiveness, and acquisition of tangible things. In masculine societies, such as Japan, Austria, and Italy, people believe that a job should provide its incumbent with opportunities for growth, challenge, recognition, and advancement. Douglas McGregor wrote about the successful United States manager as:

a masculine person. The good manager is aggressive, competitive, firm, just. He is not feminine; he is not soft or yielding or dependent or intuitive in a womanly sense (1967: 23).

Table 4.   MASCULINITY (MAS)—Extent to which Assertiveness
and Acquisition of Things are More Important
Than Caring for the "Quality of Life"

LOW *(Countries—Sweden, Denmark,* *Thailand, Finland, Yugoslavia)*	HIGH *(Countries—Japan, Austria,* *Venezuela, Italy, Mexico)*
• Soft, yielding inituitve skills are valued.	• Aggression, competition, and justice are valued managerial skills.
• Work is not central life interest for most people.	• Earnings, individual recognition, advancement, and challenge are important symbols of success.
• Theory Y is practiced.	• Work is central life interest for most people.
• Social rewards are valued.	• Company's interference into private lives accepted.
• Intuition and belief in group decision making is important.	

* Adapted from G. Hofstede, *Culture's Consequences* (Beverly Hills, CA: Sage Publications
1980), pp. 261-311.

In more feminine cultures, such as Sweden, Norway, Thailand, and
Portugal, people place more emphasis on cooperation, working conditions,
and employment security. Feminine cultures stress openness and expression
of emotions that would represent a counter-cultural movement in masculine
societies.

The consequences for organizations have been highlighted by Hofstede.
In masculine societies, there are fewer jobs for women, more industrial
conflict, greater emphasis on individual as opposed to team achievement,
work occupies more of a central life interest, and an organization's
interference in private lives of its employees is more readily accepted than
in more feminine cultures.

Country Clusters.   Because of the difficulties in representing these four
value dimensions in a single diagram, in his original work Hofstede
constructed cultural maps (via cluster analysis) of his 40 countries. The data
in Table 5 summarize these maps. We will utilize these data when discussing
how societal values affect the processes by which CEO roles are manifest.

Table 5 indicates that the United States ranks below average on power
distance and uncertainty avoidance, well above average on masculinity, and
high on individualism (the most individualistic in Hofstede's study). Some
of today's management heroes, such as Lee Iacocca (Chrysler), Ross Perot

Table 5.   Country Clusters and Their Value Systems

Cluster #1	*Cluster #2*
High power distance	High power distance
High uncertainty advoidance	High uncertainty avoidance
Medium to high individualism	Low individualism
Medium masculinity	Low or high masculinity
Belgium	Columbia
*France	Mexico High Masculinity
Argentina	Venezuela
Brazil	
Spain	Chile
	Peru Low Masculinity
	Portugal
Cluster #3	*Cluster #4*
Medium power distance	High power distance
High uncertainty	Low to medium uncertainty avoidance
Medium individualism	Low individualism
High masculinity	Medium masculinity
*Japan	Pakistan
	*Taiwan
	Thailand
	Hong Kong
	India
	Philippines
	Singapore
Cluster #5	*Cluster #6*
High power distance	Low power distance
High uncertainty avoidance	Medium to high uncertainty avoidance
Low individualilsm	Medium individualism
Medium masculinity	Medium to high masculinity
Greece	Austria
Turkey	Israel
Iran	*Germany (F.R.)
	Switzerland
Cluster #7	*Cluster #8*
Low to medium power distance	Low power distance
Low to medium uncertainty avoidance	Low to medium uncertainty avoidance
High individualism	Medium to high individualism
High masculinity	Low masculinity
Australia	Denmark
Canada	*Sweden
United States	Finland
New Zealand	Norway
Ireland	Netherlands
Great Britain	

* Countries examined in current effort.

Source: G. Hofstede, *Culture's consequences* (Beverly Hills, CA: Sage Publications 1980), p. 336.

(EDS and GM), Sam Walton (Wal-Mart Stores), John Opel (IBM), and John Byrne (GEICO Corporation) reflect these values in the designs of their organizations and orientations toward their jobs.

We are cognizant that CEO options are not only constrained by the values of society, but by other forces, as shown in Figure 1. These other forces will be only briefly discussed because other researchers have elaborated on them in previous writings.

Managerial Characteristics

Managerial characteristics are the second set of factors that affect CEO role behaviors (Figure 1). These factors comprise a class of characteristics that the CEO brings to the job. Channon (1979) found in a study of 82 chief executive officers in Great Britain that their socio-demographic profiles strongly suggest that they have similar values. These values are reinforced by attending prestigious schools, serving in particular branches of the military service, and belonging to the elite social structure of London clubs. The cultural values of Great Britain support these behaviors. By attending the proper schools, joining the "elite" clubs, etc., the value of individualism is sustained and transmitted.

Furthermore, the CEO's personality characteristics can influence the strategy and even the structure of a firm. Miller and Friesen (1984) found that characteristics of "stagnant bureaucracies" resemble those of a depressive personality. These organizations were without clearly defined and measurable goals, lacked initiative, reacted slowly to external changes in the task environment, and were generally characterized by high degrees of apathy and frustration.

There have been a myriad of studies that examined the effect of CEOs' personal attributes on decision making (Kofodimos et al., 1986, Norburn, 1986). Some of the more common attributes that have been examined are tolerance for ambiguity, locus of control, cognitive complexity, tolerance for stress, and tenure, among others. In Norburn's study of 354 CEOs in Great Britain, he suggested that intelligence was most closely related to economic performance for companies in growth industries (with creativity a close second), while for companies operating in declining industries, personal integrity was most important. Similarly, in growth industries, CEOs were more likely to have longer tenure, report less stress, and develop a greater variety of outside interests than CEOs operating in more highly turbulent industries. The research by Miller, Kets de Vries, and Toulouse concerning locus of control found "the more internal the executive, the more innovative the firm" (1982: 244).

Similar results have found when other demographic variables have been reported (Norburn, 1986). Variables such as socio-economic status of parents and siblings, types of educational experience (private or public), and early childhood experiences have all been examined, but the results remain inconclusive.

Of course, all of these managerial characteristics—personality, personal attributes and demographics—must be considered when explaining the behavior of CEOs. To simplify our presentation, we have employed a ceterus paribus assumption. We also recognize that no one factor operates independently of others (Hambrick and Mason, 1984).

Organization Design

The third array of factors that impinge on CEO role orientations are those that are internal to the organization. Much has been written about how the structural design of an organization affects CEO decision making (Mintzberg, 1979). The stage of the organization's life cycle (Kimberly and Miles, 1980), its size (Aldrich, 1979), technology (Fry and Slocum, 1984), corporate culture (Schein, 1985), performance-reward systems (Kerr and Slocum, 1987), and capital intensity (Hannan and Freeman, 1977) are among the contingency factors that differentially affect the structuring of an organization, and the roles enacted by the CEO. For example, the liaison, spokesman, and negotiator roles have been found by Mintzberg (1973) and Stewart (1967) to be of greater importance in large publicly held companies than in small, privately held ones.

Our purpose is not to examine the interrelationships among these contingency factors, but to study configurations or clusters of design parameters that reflect the underlying cultural values of CEOs. Mintzberg's framework (1979) was selected as it reflects the authors' views that effective organizations achieve internal consistency among their design parameters. The choice of structural designs reflects values that the CEO has toward work (Mintzberg and Waters, 1982). Mintzberg proposed five structural configurations (see Figure 1). In each configuration, there are different coordination mechanisms, a different part of the organization plays the dominant role, and a different type of decentralization is used. We urge the reader to consult Mintzberg (1979: 299-467) for more information on these types.

Task Environment

The fourth factor that affects the CEO's role is the set of characteristics of the industry in which the CEO's corporation is competing (Porter, 1980). Fluctuations in the economy, which are beyond the control of any company, affect a corporation's performance and impose constraints on the CEO. In addition to major business cycles are changes in interest and unemployment rates, as well as other environmental factors, all of which serve to constrain possible actions of CEOs.

In a seminal work, Lieberson and O'Connor (1972), found that industry and the organization accounted for more of the variance in some dimensions of a firm's financial performance than the leadership behaviors of the company's CEO. Variations in sales, earnings and profit margins were explained more fully by the competitiveness of the industry and other characteristics than by leadership. In Figure 1, we have listed some characteristics of the task environment that prior researchers have found to constrain CEO discretion (Hambrick and Finkelstein, 1987).

Business Strategy

The final factor impinging on CEO roles is business strategy (Huff, 1982; Miles, Snow, Meyer and Coleman, 1978). Miles and his associates have identified three recurring viable strategies that are predicated on the rate at which an organization changes its products or markets. Defenders are organizations that engage in little or no new product development. Often they operate in secure market niches within an industry and compete on the basis of price, service, delivery, and/or quality. Firms pursuing a defender strategy attempt to organize the production and delivery of goods and services as efficiently as possible, tend to have few integrative mechanisms, are not highly differentiated and have information systems that provide the CEO with the needed data to reach a decision. Prospectors attempt to pioneer in new products. They tend to change product lines frequently and try not to get locked into a single technology. They tend to have complex and costly integrative mechanisms (such as matrix structures), develop management philosophies that foster the delegation of decisions down the hierarchy, and rely on participative management techniques. Analyzers are an intermediate type. They tend to make slower product changes than do prospectors, but are less committed to stability and efficiency than are defenders. The internal structure combines aspects of both defenders and prospectors. This typology has received support from various researchers (e.g., Hambrick, 1983; Slocum, Cron, Hansen and Rawlings, 1985).

CEO ROLES

We propose that as a result of the joint effects of managerial characteristics, organizational design, business strategy, task environment, and cultural values (as shown in Figure 1), the chief executive officer of an organization develops and employs (more or less) a pattern of roles that characterizes his/her job.

Mintzberg (1973) proposed that managerial roles can be divided into three major groupings: interpersonal, informational, and decisional. The interpersonal role arises directly from a manager's formal authority and encompasses three behaviors: (1) figurehead, representing the organization in formal ceremonies; (2) liaison, interacting with others outside the organization that can affect the organization's success; and (3) leadership, directing and coordinating the activities of subordinates in order to accomplish organizational goals. The basic function of the interpersonal role is to place the manager in a formal position to receive information and to serve as a focal person for the organization's activities. Through these interpersonal roles, a manager builds a network of contacts which provide the foundation for the next role—informational.

The informational roles involve three additional managerial behaviors: (1) monitor, scanning the environment for information that may affect the organization; (2) disseminator, sharing and distributing information to subordinates; and (3) spokesperson, transmitting information to others in an official capacity. This unique ability to gather and transmit information provides the manager with the resources needed to make strategic decisions, the third role.

In the decisional role, the manager commits the organization to action. There are four different decision roles that the manager can play: (1) entrepreneurial, initiating new projects to change the organization; (2) disturbance handler, responding to threats and conflicts that are usually beyond the manager's immediate control; (3) resource allocator, deciding who will get which resources and how much they will get; and (4) negotiator, dealing with others to obtain competitive advantages for the company.

It is important to note that Mintzberg's intention was to present these roles as one way to classify the activities of managers in a useful manner. Mintzberg used the term "role" to serve as a way of representing behaviors that are organized so that they can be identified with one another. He stated that:

> individual personality may affect how a role is performed, but not that it is performed. Thus, actors, managers, and others play roles that are predetermined, although individuals may interpret them in different ways (1973: 54).

We suggest that CEOs, by virtue of their formal position, have the opportunity to display certain role behaviors. The manner in which the behaviors are differentially displayed by individual CEOs is determined by the way each CEO interprets the roles. The enactment process is strongly affected by the five forces illustrated in Figure 1.

CONSEQUENCES OF CULTURAL VALUES ON CEO ROLES

In the previous sections of this paper, we outlined the various factors that influence a CEO's role. The purpose of this section is to provide illustrations of the potential relationships between cultural values and CEO roles. Instances of CEO behavior that reflect the specific values hypothesized by Hofstede (1980a) will be highlighted. While evidence pertaining to these relationships is elusive, we attempted to piece together the relevant information through specific examples.

Methodology

To provide evidence of these relationships, two computerized searches were undertaken. First, we scanned articles, printed in English, from 1977-1987 that contained the words "CEO, Director, or President" in their titles. This search process generated a list of more than 150 articles, many of which were too brief (e.g., news items in the *Wall Street Journal*) to provide rich enough data for the investigation. *Ward's Business Directory* was then consulted to determine those companies in selected countries (see Table 5) that had the highest sales in 1985. A search was again performed on these top companies and their CEOs. It was our assumption that published data would be available about the CEO in the largest companies, but that for smaller companies, data would be difficult to acquire through secondary sources. We admit that our list is skewed in favor of large corporations and that these CEOs may not adequately reflect all the societal values uncovered by Hofstede.

We are also cognizant that the ecological unit of analysis problem severely restricts our ability to study each individual CEO role (a micro level unit of analysis) using data that were aggregated to provide a national level of analysis. Dorfman et al. (1986) warn researchers of the limitations of this practice. However, we believe that since CEOs' behaviors are critical to the performance of the firm and since we are *not* examining specific individual differences but a set of managerial roles, Hofstede's work is applicable for our purposes. These roles not only reflect the underlying values of a society, they also reflect the various constraints (business strategy, organizational design, managerial characteristics and task environment) that affect the ability of a CEO to display them.

We were not able to gather data from all countries within each cluster (see Table 5). Thus, we chose one country within each cluster whose value system(s) deviated from the 40 country norms by more than two standard deviations (Hofstede, 1980a: 315). We then focused on evidence from countries that were ranked within the top or lower ten countries on each of the four value systems. If values were to be reflected in CEO roles, we would expect these to be pronounced and explicit. For example, Hofstede's data indicate that Japan ranks as the highest society in masculinity and fourth highest in uncertainty avoidance. Therefore, we chose to study CEOs in Japan and to focus on how those particular value systems were manifested through various roles. We eliminated from our investigation those countries that Hofstede indicated have value systems that are in a state of transition (e.g., Finland, Iran, Italy, South Africa). The final criterion was that secondary data, in English, must be available from at least two different sources for the purpose of establishing validity. We recognize that this criterion highlights one of the problems in cross-cultural research—that of the researcher's cultural bias (Adler, 1984, 1986). Our list of CEOs was severely constrained by this criterion.

Ultimately, an examination of cultural values and CEO roles was carried out in five countries, each representing a different cluster (see Table 5). Examples of countries from both Cluster #2 and Cluster #5 were not possible given the limitations discussed above. We also do not present an analysis of a country within Cluster #7. We have instead utilized examples from the United States (a country in Cluster #7) throughout our chapter. Finally, we recognize that all the characteristics of countries in a cluster may not have been represented in the country we selected, thus, posing a problem of external validity (Whiting, 1968). We have used Hofstede's set of abbreviations for the value systems (PDI for power distance; IDV for individualism; UAI for uncertainty avoidance; and MAS for masculinity) when referring to how these impact CEO roles.

Cluster #1

France is an example of a country classified by Hofstede (1980a) as high in PDI, high in UAI, medium to high in IDV, and medium in MAS. The literature search of CEOs operating in France uncovered information about Bernard Hanon of Renault and Jean-Paul Parayre of Peugeot SA. Both men served as CEO of their respective companies and were ultimately forced out of their positions.

Hanon, who was CEO of Renault from 1981 until 1985, had assumed his position with the company at a time when Renault (along with the entire French auto industry) was faltering ("A Change. . .," 1985). Four years later as conditions at Renault worsened, Hanon, while in New York, was awakened by an aide calling from Paris to inform him of a French newspaper's announcement that he was soon to be replaced as chairman of Renault ("Revolving Door. . .," 1985).

Hanon's strategy of directing the state-owned company was termed "tough-minded" ("The Roadblocks. . .," 1984: 60). Even though he may have been autocratic in expressing his own management orientation (high PDI), he was also known for his conservative decisions (high UAI). For example, with the introduction of the R-5, Renault's small car, Hanon supported the design of the new product along the lines of "their old basic model." The changes in the car were all "under the hood where the buyer could not see what had been done" ("The Roadblocks. . .," 1984: 60). The successor to the R-5, the Supercinq, was then introduced into the market. Its launch (and car launches are crucial in France) was unsuccessful because it was not different in image or styling from the R-5. This lack of change in the appearance of the automobile illustrates the cultural value of uncertainty avoidance. To make matters worse, Renault clung to tradition without any really new and different products (high UAI). This mistake was quite costly for Hanon and Renault ("The French. . .," 1985). In another move, Hanon supported a series of job cuts to increase productivity. However, along with this move to reduce the work force, Hanon offered "a series of social emoluments, such as early retirement."

When Hanon was forced to resign as CEO of Renault, his supporters "argued that he was made the scapegoat for factors that were largely beyond his control" ("Revolving Door. . .," 1985: 45). In a time of economic unrest in France, Hanon was regarded as an effective CEO and made sure that Renault operated in a socially acceptable manner. Interestingly, Hanon's downfall was at least partially attributed to the power of France's labor unions in opposing his attempt to unilaterally reduce the number of jobs by 9,000. To reverse the economic downfall, Hanon pushed for a round of deep job cuts for laborers in an effort to increase productivity. The power of labor unions in France is a fact of life. Their existence and strong influence on all facets of an employee's job are expected in a society with a cultural value of high power distance.

While Hanon's administration was high in power distance and, in a way, high in uncertainty avoidance, Parayre thrived on risk and uncertainty. As expressed by one Peugeot executive, "Parayre is very bold and a bit of a gambler" ("Sudden Growth. . .," 1978: 14). When Parayre took over as CEO of Peugeot in 1977, he was the first "outsider" to hold that post. Previously the leadership of the company had been by family members or by men who had spent their working lives at Peugeot (high UAI). Prior to joining Peugeot, Parayre had been a respected civil servant noted for his astute management abilities. It was felt that Parayre was "the model of a French technocrat, a perfect representative of that urbane, self-assured meritocracy" (high PDI) ("A Young. . .," 1978: 120). His demise as CEO was, like Hanon's, partially due to a power struggle with French labor unions (high PDI). This power struggle resulted when two of Peugeot's acquisitions made under the influence of Parayre (Citroën and Chrysler's European operations) suffered large financial setbacks. In fact, when Peugeot took over Citroën, Parayre boasted that "we set up a decentralized management structure. . . ." (low PDI) ("A Young...," 1978: 121). This cultural incongruity may have been one of the problems experienced in the acquisition.

Throughout Parayre's career prior to joining Peugeot, there were strong indications of his penchant for power (high PDI). For example, in his first job as a highway engineer, his management acumen caught the attention of a politician who later became France's Prime Minister. He was then chosen to be a member of the Ministry for Industrial and Scientific Development where he headed a key department to "watch over" the automotive sector of the economy. Impressed with his performance, the Peugeots asked him to leave government service and join them. "It was extraordinary for a man so young to move so quickly to the top of such an important and tradition-minded company" ("A Young. . .," 1978).

In summary, cultural values of France were apparent, to some extent, in the accounts of Hanon's and Parayre's administrations. There was clear evidence of large societal power distances demonstrated by the active involvement of labor unions in the demise of both CEOs. It was also apparent that both men confirmed this high power distance value with their own tough-minded and autocratic styles with which they enacted their roles. Both men developed practices that reflected their own initiative particularly in introducing and acquiring new product lines. However, while Hanon's policies were very much in line with cultural mores of the French, Parayre took risks uncommon to the French value of high uncertainty avoidance. From accounts of his boldness and risky nature, Parayre's behavior was probably more directly influenced by personality characteristics than cultural values.

Cluster #3

According to Hofstede (1980a: 335), Japan represents a cultural area by itself. Japanese values include a medium PDI, high UAI, medium IDV, and high MAS (the highest among the 40 countries surveyed). Much has been written about Japan's workers and managers (e.g., Abegglen, 1958; Cole, 1979; Lincoln et al. 1986; Ouchi, 1981; and Pascale and Athos, 1981). Nonaka and Okumura (1984) compared 229 American and 291 Japanese CEOs on a variety of managerial issues, including the management of their environment, production technology, management strategy, organization structure, and organizational processes. Smith (1985) interviewed seven CEOs, including Ichiro Isoda of Sumintomo Bank, Isao Kakauchi of Daiei and Kazuo Inamori of Kyocera Corporation; and Dun's Review ("Patience, Restraint. . .," 1979) interviewed six others, including Takashi Ishihara of Nissan, Yoshizo Ikeda of Mitsui & Co., and Yoshihiro Inayama of Nippon Steel. Instead of highlighting several CEOs, we have chosen to summarize their role orientations and relate MAS and UAI value systems to these behaviors.

Japanese CEOs practice patience and spend resources on strategic, as opposed to tactical, planning. Making a mistake is very costly; it is better to take no action than to take a serious risk (high UAI). One reason for this patience is that Japanese CEOs believe that the more important objective is to increase market share than to emphasize short-term profits. For example, Ishihara states that it was the accumulation of resources over the long term that enabled Nissan to become a major competitor in the automobile industry. Japanese CEOs are more willing to have more "Dogs" and "Question Marks" in their business portfolio than CEOs from other countries because they reward perseverance in a product market (high UAI). Many of the aforementioned CEOs think in terms of a 12 to 20-year program in a product's life cycle. Market share, new product ratio, and ability to adapt to changes in the environment are important. Because of these emphases, they place high importance on collecting a large amount of diffuse information. This information collection process includes sharing information through group-oriented decision making. Since information is typically widely dispersed in large companies, a high frequency of communication between managers (informally as well as in formal meetings) is necessary for group decision making to be of superior quality. In some ways, this management practice has hindered Japanese CEOs who are operating in unstable task environments, such as international investment in security markets. While decision making by consensus and promotion by seniority permit CEOs to know their business intimately, it can also lead to inflexibility and a lack of imagination.

Most CEOs have had long tenure with one company (for example, Ishihara has been with Nissan for 50 years; Isoda with Sumitomo bank for 35 years, and Inayama with Nippon Steel for almost 50 years) and are dependent on their companies not only for their working lives, but how they spend their leisure time (high MAS). For Inayama, work is his central life interest and his work is an end in itself. Since tenure is rewarded, most CEOs have worked in a variety of capacities for their company. These practices serve to reinforce organizational goals, values and their ability to think multidimensionally.

"In the beginning, there was a strategy" might be a saying attributed to American CEOs, while in Japan, the statement might read, "In the beginning there was the organization." In Japan human resources are developed to fit the structure, while in the U.S. human resources are developed for the purpose of conforming to the strategy (Jackson and Schuler, 1987). A good example of these sayings may be found by analyzing the role behaviors of Ichiro Isoda of Sumitomo Bank (Oka, 1982). Isoda's managerial philosophy is to be decisive and reward generously but punish lightly and delegate authority. When he assumed the top role in 1974, the bank was in serious financial condition. One of its major customers, Ataka (a large trading company) was on the brink of bankruptcy. Because many of Japan's enterprises are under-capitalized, they rely heavily on banks for money. A bank frequently will "nurse" a company until its financial condition improves. Isoda went to another large trading company and helped arrange a friendly merger, but his bank had to absorb a $1 billion loss. Similarly, when Toyo Kogyo (manufacturer of the Mazda) experienced a major sales slump in the 1970s, he sent in senior managers from his bank to occupy key managerial positions until a technical tie-up with Ford Motor Company could be reached. Isoda's decisions in these two instances were aided by members of his executive council. Members of the executive council made presentations and Isoda demanded that presenters from the company know as much about the bank as bank officials knew about the company. Recently, the bank has implemented a total reorganization of the company in which three groups were established, each with its own managing director. The reason for this reorganization was so that the bank could aggressively pursue new customers and managers could be held accountable for their decisions. According to Isoda, the job of the CEO is to make decisions; but to make correct decisions, he must know his work thoroughly (high UAI).

In summary, Japanese CEO behaviors reflect both high masculinity and high uncertainty avoidance. Masculinity was manifested in terms of work as the central life interest, the need to excel, the establishment of clear lines of authority and responsibility, decisions supported by facts, and the company's accepted intrusion into the private lives of workers. The use of groups to make strategic decisions, rites and rituals, impersonal control systems, and discouragement of conflict and competition between members of the same organization are representative of high uncertainty avoidance.

Cluster #4

Taiwan was chosen from the cluster representing, in general, the less developed Asian countries. The cultural values of this cluster were: high PDI, low to medium UAI, low IDV, and medium MAS. While Taiwan generally fell within this cluster, the only cultural value where Taiwan was extreme was low IDV, and we have attempted to focus on that value system. Narratives, while limited, were found for Y. C. Wang, Taiwan's leading industrialist, one of the world's wealthiest men who made the largest proportion of his fortune building and expanding a business based on polyvinyl chloride, a plastic material ("A Plastics. . .," 1983; Tanzer, 1985).

In line with the Buddhist culture, Wang and his family are close, and represent a collective unit. This family closeness extends from social gatherings to business dealings. His family and its foundations own between 26 percent and 60 percent of Wang's three largest companies (about $550 million of holdings) with a high value placed on traditionalism (low IDV). Wang is proud of his heritage and tells stories about his meager beginnings. Pointing to a dish of sweet potatoes at the dinner table, Wang immodestly explained that the potatoes were all he had to eat as a child. This value on tradition is emphasized by the very way that Wang became so wealthy— by producing a "relatively ancient material, polyvinyl chloride, a plastic used in making a myriad of products" (Tanzer, 1985).

Wang is orderly and conforms to his culture's tradition of hard work. He gives "unrelenting attention to details and spends work weeks that would have put most chief executives underground long ago" (Tanzer, 1985). He expects his production workers and executives to follow his example of hard work and long hours. All employees, including himself, must be well trained and use their learned skills on the job. Wang is described as "no armchair capitalist, thriving on the same trench air that his troops breathe." Wang boasts that he doesn't "think the organization is getting out of hand because he is aware of every detail of the operation." In these comments are embedded the very essence of low individualism. There is a high dependence of the CEO on his organization and the organization on him.

The populace of Taiwan operates on the "jen" philosophy—meaningful existence includes the person plus intimate societal and cultural influences. This philosophy is of utmost importance to Wang. In fact, in a 1983 speech at the Wharton School, he expressed his concern over the moral decadence of the West. He said, "It is most alarming that one tends to relax his determination and hardworking habit after one has reached a certain degree of comfort in life" (Tanzer, 1985).

Wang's strategy for his organization is one of vertical integration. The Wang-related companies are expanding in a methodical fashion, acquiring businesses that extend from those that already exist. For example, the initial chemical produced, polyvinyl chloride, is used to produce PVC pipe. Wang's group is now the world's biggest producer and processor of PVC.

In summary, Taiwan's culture is one characterized by collective identity (low IDV) where individual views are influenced by the environment. Wang's emphasis on tradition, family, company, and the collective whole of his organizations is in line with this "jen" philosophy.

Cluster #6

The country selected to represent this cluster was the Federal Republic of Germany. Germany has a value system of low PDI, medium to high UAI, medium IDV and high MAS. The three CEOs studied were Carl H. Hahn of Volkswagen, Karlheinz Kaske of Siemans, and Heinz Nixdorf of Nixdorf Computers, A.G.

According to VW's strong-willed boss, Carl Hahn, VW's competitive edge is its strong German engineering tradition (Richman, 1986; Brady, 1985a; Bail, 1983). Under his leadership, VW plans to stick to its tradition of making styling changes only when needed (high UAI). He believes that VW should maintain its history of quality, road handling ease, and longevity. In 1983 when VW reported a $144 million loss in the U.S., Hahn attributed it to poor quality in the Beetle, while others in the company attributed the loss to Hahn's "screwing around with the Mona Lisa." (This is a good example of how CEO behavior that contradicted the German cultural value of high uncertainty avoidance was seen as inappropriate.) To ensure its competitive edge, VW has invested more than $194 million in Wolfsburg to build one of the world's most highly automated final assembly plants. The plant was designed according to tight engineering specifications and has few wage differentials between hierarchical levels (low PDI). To grow as an international company, Hahn plans to divisionalize VW so that it is not overly dependent on any one car and should be able to withstand sudden currency changes. When VW decided to manufacture its "Golf" car in the U.S., it purchased a Chrysler plant in Westmoreland, PA, and refurbished it. VW adopted this strategy because it was fearful of currency devaluations and possible U.S. protectionist policies. While the plant is losing money, Hahn announced that the company would phase out production at parts plants in other locations, and centralize all U.S. operations in the Westmoreland plant. Hahn's decision to build cars in Spain hinged on whether or not the Spanish-built cars could be manufactured to the rigorous German quality standards (high MAS and high UAI).

At VW, managers have well defined jobs and are given detailed instructions on how to perform their jobs (high UAI). Their motivation to perform is predicated on Hahn's belief that managers have a strong ambition to succeed and a high need for job security (high MAS and high UAI). His basic philosophy is for the manager to do first whatever is necessary for the company to succeed, and then tell people back at headquarters what was done. Performance against well-defined standards is what counts. Managers who succeed are rewarded with money, independence, and job challenge (high MAS).

Siemens, A.G. is West Germany's second largest company and its president is Karlheinz Kaske. It is run with typical German engineering thoroughness and a pedantic approach to management (Brady, 1985b). Kaske has developed a highly centralized organization (high PDI), even though it is differentiated into six relatively autonomous product groups. According to outsiders, the major problem with the company is its stubborn conservatism coupled with a reluctance to take risks (high UAI) and a managerial workforce that isn't strong enough to make decisions or question Kaske's decisions. Kaske, a physicist, tenaciously clings to old managerial practices. The inability to translate technology into saleable products reflects the company's penchant for perfection and product overdesign (high UAI). For example, in the computer-aided tomography market, Siemens took so long to get the prototype to production, that it missed the introductory phase of the product's life cycle that is now dominated by GE. Siemens was also a pioneer in the ultrasonic imaging market, but lost its edge when it tried to engineer the product to meet every possible exigency.

According to Heinz Nixdorf, founder of Nixdorf Computer, "I like profit because it's the best measurement that you are on the right track with a customer" (Brady, 1985c). Nixdorf has stated that one of the best things about German industry is that they train their employees well to do their jobs (high UAI). Through this emphasis on training, Nixdorf's employees have made its office furniture, built the company's new building, made most of the company's own components, trained its own delivery drivers, and provided a day-care center for its employees (low PDI). Since Germany is a high UAI and low PDI country, time is a considerable source of stress, and therefore a company that allows people relief from strict time rules enables them to be a success. Most of Nixdorf's employees work a 38.5-hour work week and get paid to spend 2 of those hours in the company sports center. Only 9 percent of the company's more than 20,000 employees are unionized. Nixdorf believes that if all employees are treated equally (no status distinctions between managers and workers), they bring much needed stability to the company and that, in turn, makes for good relationships with customers (low PDI).

Nixdorf's strategy is to provide tailor-made problem-solving packages for clients in the high-tech market with state-of-the-art telecommunications equipment and point-of-sale terminals. According to him, "I know we did find the way, not only our way, but *the* (italics in the original) way" ("The Ambitious. . .," 1984). In the next four years, he predicts the company will double its sales and eventually become Europe's leader in computers, employing over 70,000 people. To achieve these goals, he will have to sell some equity, but has little intention of "relinquishing any control of the company" (high UAI). Investors will be able to buy only nonvoting shares. Although his net worth is over $1 billion, Nixdorf has little interest in retiring. According to him, "I will not be an artist. I will not be a politician. I think perhaps I will be dead when I retire" (Brady, 1985c: 55).

Several commonalities in these three CEOs' role behaviors are noteworthy because they reflect Germany's values. First, each of these individuals has an unambiguous style in resolving problems. Extensive rules and regulations have been developed to cope with exigencies that might happen (high UAI). Second, the managers who report to these individuals have well defined job responsibilities and are held accountable for financial results. Success is defined by career advancement, challenging jobs, and opportunities for recognition as being a leader in the field (high MAS). Third, the German value of decision making based on fact and truth is manifested in their reliance on engineering principles and their search for the "one best way." Fourth, each person discussed how his values of stable employment, educational training, and the firm's performance directly affected German society. The only apparent anomaly was Kaske's value of high PDI that's not entirely consistent with Hofstede's paradigm.

Cluster #8

Sweden was the country studied as representative of Hofstede's eighth cluster. The nation scores at the extremes of each of the four value dimensions: low PDI, low UAI, high IDV, and low MAS (the lowest among the 40 countries surveyed). Pehr Gyllenhammar of Volvo and Percy Barnevik of ASEA (manufacturer of electrical equipment) were studied.

To describe Pehr Gyllenhammar, one must begin with his individualistic manner. A London broker was quoted as saying, "Pehr Gyllenhammar is a law unto himself" ("Volvo's 'Emperor'. . .," 1986: 45). Gyllenhammar's response to a 1983 board rejection of his proposal to sell Volvo stock in the U.S. was a direct demonstration of his independent ways. He replaced three outside directors with Volvo executives. Another example of his outward aggressive independence was his emphatic "no" when asked whether he was discouraged after his company suffered large losses because of the oil market decline (Berss, 1984).

This individualistic, determined demeanor has been well received in Sweden, a country that exemplifies low uncertainty avoidance. Gyllenhammar has led Volvo through a steady period of growth as an automobile company and, at the same time, directed the company into diverse markets. His latest efforts have been in the biotechnology industry. It is in biotechnology that Gyllenhammar has suffered one of his greatest setbacks. A month after he negotiated a $528 million joint venture with Fermenta, a Swedish biotech and chemical company, the CEO of the company resigned, and Volvo cancelled its plans with the company. Meanwhile Volvo was obligated to pay $35 million of personal debt to Fermenta's resigned CEO.

Despite Gyllenhammar's forceful manner, he maintains a people-oriented style in his management practices (low MAS). "Gyllenhammar's reputation stems more from initiating generous labor settlements than from working wonders with Volvo profits" (Sturm, 1979). Reporters have suggested that as he continues to boost his public image, he is gathering support to run for political office. Gyllenhammar enjoys being a celebrity as demonstrated by his regular appearances on Swedish television, but his greatest popularity is derived from his experiments designed to take "the boredom out of assembly-line work" (Sturm, 1979: 37).

Gyllenhammar's individualism, risk-taking, and concern for others are congruent with Swedish cultural values, although some recent literature points to possible peculiarities of Gyllenhammar that are not in line with the Swedish value of low PDI. Dubbed an "emperor" ("Volvo's 'Emperor' . . .," 1986), Gyllenhammar spearheaded a movement to sell 40 percent of Volvo to the Norwegian government. Management of the largest stockholder (Sweden's Fourth Pension Fund) recommended a negative vote against the sale, but its vote was over-ruled by a group of union and political appointees (high PDI) (Sturm, 1979). His "autocratic" behavior represents an interesting paradox. Gyllenhammar is known best worldwide for his leadership in job enrichment at Volvo's Kalmar plant in the early 1970s. Job enrichment allows employees, in addition to management, the discretion to make decisions (low PDI), which results in the flattening of the organization's hierarchy and the reduction of status differences between levels of employees. Other consequences of job enrichment are high job satisfaction, high quality production, low turnover, and low absenteeism.

The other Swedish CEO we studied was Percy Barnevik of ASEA. ASEA has recently received international attention for its leadership in developing and producing robotics. In 1982, when the company inaugurated its new plant in Belgium, the ribbon-cutting ceremony was performed by a one-armed robot. When the robot reached for flowers to present to the official, it knocked over the vase. Barnevik boasts that such an incident will never happen again as now his robots can "see" by laser!

Prior to the high-tech era in ASEA's history, the company was a conservative manufacturer of electrical equipment. With Barnevik as CEO, a new strategy has emerged that emphasizes change (low UAI) and aggressiveness (high IDV). As Barnevik claims, "The core of the game is to exploit our technology on a worldwide basis" ("Sweden's ASEA. . .," 1984: 104). Barnevik has been ruthless in streamlining Swedish holdings, getting rid of several unprofitable businesses while making the others autonomous profit centers. Barnevik has decentralized responsibility for accounting and profits (low PDI). Within six weeks of becoming CEO, he changed the structure of the company, reorganizing it "from a directionless, top-heavy conglomerate into 40 separate profit centers" ("Sweden's ASEA. . .," 1984: 104).

Barnevik made another integrative and progressive move for ASEA into the high-tech specialty area of long-distance power transmission of high voltage direct current (HVDC). Through ASEA's innovativeness in this area, it has acquired 53 percent of the world's market for HVDC technology. Industry specialists predict rapid growth for HVDC, now comprising only two percent of power line sales worldwide, because of its use with long distance cables ("Sweden's ASEA. . .," 1984).

In summary, available evidence concerning CEOs and their roles in Sweden are in line with Hofstede's (1980a, 1980b) findings along the dimensions of individualism and uncertainty avoidance. Both Gyllenhammar of Volvo and Barnevik of ASEA base their strategic orientations on high risk (low UAI) and individual initiative (high IDV). It is clear from the articles we analyzed that Gyllenhammar manages with a "people-oriented" philosophy (low MAS), but there was no evidence for either low or high masculinity in Barnevik's case. There was strong evidence, however, that Barnevik utilized decentralization as a strategic orientation (low PDI). For Gyllenhammar, this cultural dimension was most confusing. Although he built a reputation through his efforts in job enrichment, a program characterized by low power distances, most recent evidence indicates that he currently maintains a strong hierarchical position (high PDI).

CONCLUSIONS AND DIRECTIONS FOR FUTURE RESEARCH

The purpose of this chapter was to explore the relationships between cultural values and selected CEO roles. While there is a paucity of data on CEOs, our evidence supports the thesis advanced by Child and Kieser (1979) that each culture embodies distinctive attributes and these are manifested by managers in how they enact their roles. We found little evidence to support the "culture free" argument, but additional comparative research must be undertaken before this argument can be dismissed. We also agree with Child and Kieser that the individual should be the unit of analysis, and not the firm. Unfortunately, it was difficult to entirely separate the behavior of the CEO from the behavior(s) of the firm.

The dearth of literature on CEOs was surprising. While Mintzberg's seminal work has generated a vast number of replication studies (Kurke and Aldrich, 1983), with the notable exceptions of Bruce (1986), Kaplan (1986) and Kofodimos et al. (1986) researchers have not extended and/or developed a new paradigm to study CEO behaviors. Those researchers who do focus on CEOs are attempting to coalesce divergent literatures and develop a parsimonious set of variables to explain CEO behaviors. The extant literature on CEOs does not focus on process variables, such as networking, agenda setting and leadership, but instead on outcomes of the enactment process (e.g., ROI, ROE, market share). If future researchers want to study how a culture's values affect CEO behaviors, then attention to the processes by which CEOs make decisions warrants closer scrutiny. The various constraints proposed in our paper were offered as a start. Unfortunately, we were not able to postulate relationships between these variables (managerial characteristics, task environment, organization design, business strategy, cultural values) and our role orientations with the present research status of the field. To do so with any precision would be premature.

These theoretical problems are accompanied by a host of methodological queries when attempting to conduct cross-cultural research. Many researchers who have studied CEOs have focused on their personal attributes and have drawn on macro sociological data to support the inclusion and/ or exclusion of variables. Unfortunately, these researchers have left unspecified the unit of analysis. A clear specification of the unit of analysis is needed in future research. Another problem is language equivalence. To generalize cross-culturally, a research team should be composed of individuals from (or very familiar with) the cultures studied. For example, there are words in the English language that have no counterpart in other languages. Potential confusion could be alleviated if researchers had the ability to think, read, and speak fluently in the language of the countries studied.

We believe that if new paradigms are to be developed, qualitative research strategies are most likely to generate sufficiently rich data to support these theory building efforts. For example, Kofodimos et al.'s (1986) use of the idiographic research method enabled them to intensively study the behavior of a senior executive. From this approach, they were able to conclude that general patterns of character were reflected in managerial actions and these actions were based on cultural values.

Further empirical work needs to be conducted to validate Hofstede's findings as a cross-cultural paradigm. While Hofstede (1980a: 325-339) provides evidence of the validity of his work, critics point out that since he studied one multinational corporation, it is impossible to separate company and cultural effects. Additional studies are needed using multiple companies that are both multinational as well as indigenous to a country. Perhaps if such studies were undertaken, the value systems identified by Hofstede could be more clearly established. It was difficult to discern, for example, in Germany, if that culture's penchant for low PDI was characteristic of IBM or of the German culture. We found conflicting evidence with Hofstede's classification system on that value when studying indigenous German companies.

Despite these theoretical and methodological problems, there are exciting challenges open to those interested in studying the impact of culture on CEO orientations. Since paradigms and methodologies are not yet sufficiently well developed, researchers should focus on good theory building instead of empirically testing hypotheses. A requirement for theory building is for the researcher(s) to develop well crafted parsimonious arguments and clearly define terms. We hope that this article is the first step in this process.

ACKNOWLEDGMENTS

Support for this project was granted from the Bureau of Business Research, Cox School of Business, Southern Methodist University, Dallas, TX. The authors would like to acknowledge the constructive comments offered by Nancy Adler, Don Hambrick, Mike Harvey, Don Hellriegel, Geert Hofstede, Sally McQuaid, and Michael Wooton on earlier drafts of this paper. Portions of this chapter were presented at the Pan Pacific Conference, Taipei, Taiwan, May 17-20, 1987. An abridged version of this chapter appears in *The Academy of Management Executive* 2 (1988): pp. 39-55.

REFERENCES

Abegglen, J. *The Japanese Factory: Aspects of Its Social Organization.* Glencoe, IL: The Free Press, 1958.

Adler, N. "Understanding the Ways of Understanding: Cross-Cultural Management Methodology Reviewed." In *Advances in International Comparative Management,* pp. 31-67. Edited by R. Farmer. Greenwich, CT: JAI Press, Inc, 1984.

Adler, N. *International Dimensions of Organizational Behavior.* Boston, MA: Kent Publishing Company, 1986.

Ajiferuke, M., and Boddewijn, J. "Socio-Economic Indicators in Comparative Management." *Administrative Science Quarterly* 15 (1970): 453-458.

Aldrich, H. *Organizations and Environments.* Englewood Cliffs, NJ: Prentice-Hall, 1979.

"The Ambitious Plan to Hoist Nixdorf to New Heights." *Business Week* 12 March 1984, pp. 40-41.

Bail, R. "Volkswagen's Struggle to Restore Its Name." *Fortune* 27 June 1983, pp. 100-104.

Berss, M. "The Master Builder." *Forbes* 19, November 1984, pp. 242-243.

Bhagat, R., and McQuaid, S. "Role of Subjective Culture in Organizations: A Review and Directions for Future Research." *Journal of Applied Psychology* 67 (1982): 653-685.

Brady, R. "You Will See More to Come." *Forbes* 28 January 1985a, pp. 36-37.

Brady, R. "The Lecture Series." *Forbes* 17 June 1985b, p. 132.

Brady, R. "Nixdorf's Way." *Forbes* 6 May 1985c, pp. 54-55.

Bruce, J. *The Intuitive Pragmatists: Conversations with Chief Executive Officers.* Greensboro, NC: Center for Creative Leadership, 1986.

"A Change of Drivers at Renault." *Fortune* 18 February 1985, p. 11.

Channon, D. "Leadership and Corporate Performance in the Service Industries." *Journal of Management Studies* 12 (1979): 185-201.

Child, J., and Kieser, A. "Organization and Managerial Roles in British and West German Companies: An Examination of the Culture-Free Thesis." In *Organizations Alike and Unlike,* pp. 251-271. Edited by C. Lammers, and D. Hickson. London: Routledge & Kegan Paul, Ltd, 1979.

Cole, R. *Work, Mobility and Participation: A Comparative Study of American and Japanese Industry.* Berkeley, CA: University of California Press, 1979.

Crozier, M. *The Bureaucratic Phenomenon.* Chicago, IL: University of Chicago Press, 1964.

Cyert, R.E., and March, J.G. *A Behavioral Theory of the Firm.* Englewood Cliffs, NJ: Prentice-Hall, 1963.

Dalton, D. and Kesner, I. "Organizational Performance as an Antecedent of Inside/Outside Chief Executive Succession: An Empirical Assessment." *Academy of Management Journal* 28 (1985): 749-762.

Doktor, R., Lie, H., and Redding, S. "A Day in the Life of a CEO—in Japan, South Korea, Hong Kong and United States." In *Organizational Behavior*, 4th ed, p. 13. Edited by D. Hellriegel, J.W. Slocum, Jr., and R. Woodman. St. Paul, MN: West Publishing Company, 1986.

Dorfman, P., Howell, J., and Bautista, J. "Dimensions of National Culture and Work-Related Values: Hofstede Revisited." Paper presented at Academy of Management Meetings, Chicago, 1986.

Drenth, P., and Groenendijk, B. "Work and Organizational Psychology in Cross-Cultural Perspective." In *Handbook of Work and Organizational Psychology*, pp. 1197-1229. Edited by P. Drenth, H. Thierry, P. Willems, and C. deWolf. New York: John Wiley & Sons, 1984.

"The French Car Pile-Up." *Management Today*, September 1985, pp. 58-61.

Fry, L., and Slocum, J.W., Jr. "Structure, Technology and Workgroup Effectiveness: A Test of a Contingency Model." *Academy of Management Journal* 27, (1984): 221-246.

Galbraith, J.K. *The New Industrial State*. London: Hamish Hamilton, 1967.

Glasier, W. "Cross-National Comparisons of the Factory." *Journal of Comparative Administration* (May 1971): 83-117.

Goodstein, C. "Commentary: Do American Theories Apply Abroad?" *Organizational Dynamics* (Summer 1981): 49-54.

Hambrick, D.C. "Some Tests of the Effectiveness and Functional Attributes of Miles & Snow's Strategic Types." *Academy of Management Journal* 26 (1983): 5-26.

Hambrick, D.C., and Finkelstein, S. "Managerial Discretion: A Bridge Between Polar Views of Organizational Outcomes." In *Research in Organizational Behavior*, pp. 369-406. Edited by L.L. Cummings and B.M. Staw. Greenwich, Ct: JAI Press, 1987.

Hambrick, D.C., and Mason, P.A. "Upper Echelons: The Organization as a Reflection of Its Top Managers." *Academy of Management Review* 9 (1984): 193-206.

Hannan, M.T., and Freeman, J.H. "The Population Ecology of Organizations." *American Journal of Sociology* 82 (1977): 929-964.

Harris, P.R., and Moran, R.T. *Managing Cultural Differences*. Houston, TX: Gulf Publishing Company, 1986.

Heydebrand, W. *Comparative Organization: The Results of Empirical Research*. Englewood Cliffs, NJ: Prentice-Hall, 1973.

Hickson, D., McMillan, C., Azumi, K., and Horvath, D. "Grounds for Comparative Organization Theory: Quicksands or Hard Core?" In *Organizations Alike and Unlike*, pp. 25-41. Edited by C. Lammers and D. Hickson. London: Routledge & Kegan Paul, 1979.

Hofstede, G. *Culture's Consequences: International Differences in Work-Related Values*. Beverly Hills, CA: Sage, 1980a.

Hofstede, G. "Motivation, Leadership, and Organization: Do American Theories Apply Abroad?" *Organizational Dynamics* 8 (Summer 1980b): 42-63.

Hofstede, G. "Dimensions of National Cultures in Fifty Countries and Three Regions." In *Explications in Cross-Cultural Psychology*, pp. 335-355. Edited by J. Deregowski, D. Dzivrawiec, and R. Anuis. Liste, Netherlands: Suets & Zeitlinger, 1983.

Hofstede, G. "The Cultural Relativity of the Quality of Life Concept." *Academy of Management Review* 9 (1984): 389-398.

Hrebiniak, L.G., and Joyce, W.F. "Organizational Adaptation: Strategic Choice and Environmental Determinism." *Administrative Science Quarterly* 30 (1985): 336-349.

Huff, A. "Industry Influences on Strategy Reformulation." *Strategic Management Journal* 3 (1982): 119-131.

Hunt, J. "Applying American Behavioral Science: Some Cross-Cultural Problems." *Organizational Dynamics* (Summer 1981): 55-62.

Jackson, S.E., and Schuler, R.S. "Competitive Strategies, Human Resource Management Practices and Industrial Relations Implications." Working paper, Graduate School of Business, University of Michigan, 1987.

Jauch, L., and Kraft, K. "Strategic Management of Uncertainty." *Academy of Management Review* 11 (1986): 777-790.

Kaplan, R. *The Warp and Woof of the General Manager's Job.* Greensboro, NC: Center for Creative Leadership, Technical Report #27, 1986.

Kerr, C., Dunlop, J., Harbison, F., and Myers, C. "Industrialism and World Society." *Harvard Business Review* 38(1) (1960): 113-126.

Kerr, J., and Slocum, J.W., Jr. "Managing Corporate Cultures Through Reward Systems." *Academy of Management Executive* 1 (1987): 99-108.

Kets de Vries, M., and Miller, D. "Personality, Culture and Organization." *Academy of Management Review* 11 (1986): 266-279.

Kimberly, J.R., and Miles, R.H. *The Organizational Life Cycle.* San Francisco, CA: Jossey-Bass Publishers, 1980.

Kluckhohn, C. "Values and Value-Orientations in the Theory of Action: An Exploration in Definition and Classification." In *Toward a General Theory of Action*, p. 395. Edited by T. Parsons and E. Shils. Cambridge, MA: Harvard University Press, 1951.

Kofodimos, J., Kaplan, R., and Drath, W. *Anatomy of an Executive: A Close Look at One Executive's Managerial Character and Development.* Greensboro, NC: Center for Creative Leadership, Technical Report #29, 1986.

Kurke, L., and Aldrich, H. "Mintzberg Was Right!: A Replication and Extension of the Nature of Managerial Work." *Management Science* 29 (1983): 975-984.

Lammers, C., and Hickson, D. *Organizations Alike and Unlike: International and Inter-Institutional Studies in the Sociology of Organizations.* London: Routledge & Kegan Paul, 1979.

Lawrence, P.R., and Lorsch, J.W. *Organization and Environment: Managing Differentiation and Integration.* Homewood, IL: Richard D. Irwin, 1967.

Lieberson, S., and O'Connor, J.F. "Leadership and Organizational Performance: A Study of Large Corporations." *American Sociological Review* 37 (1972): 117-130.

Lincoln, J., Hanada, M., and McBride, K. "Organizational Structures in Japanese and U.S. Manufacturing." *Administrative Science Quarterly* 31 (1986): 338-364.

March, J.G., and Simon, H.A. *Organizations.* New York: John Wiley & Sons, 1958.

Maurice, M. "For a Study of 'the Societal Effect': Universality and Specificity in Organization Research." In *Organizations Alike and Unlike*, pp. 42-60. Edited by C. Lammers, and J.D. Hickson. London: Routledge & Kegan Paul, 1979.

McGregor, D. *The Professional Manager.* New York: McGraw-Hill, 1967.

Meyer, J., and Rowan, B. "Institutional Organizations: Formal Structure as Myth and Ceremony." *American Sociological Review* 83 (1977): 340-363.

Miles, R.E., Snow, C.C., Meyer, A., and Coleman, H. "Organizational Strategy, Structure, and Processes." *Academy of Management Review* 3 (1978): 546-562.

Miller, D., and Friesen, P.H. *Organizations: A Quantum View.* Englewood Cliffs, NJ: Prentice-Hall, 1984.

Miller, D., Kets de Vries, M.F., and Toulouse, J.M. "Top Executive Locus of Control and Its Relationship to Strategy-Making, Structure, and Environment." *Academy of Management Journal* 25 (1982): 237-253.

Mintzberg, H. *The Nature of Managerial Work.* New York: Harper & Row, 1973.

Mintzberg, H. *The Structuring of Organizations.* Englewood Cliffs, NJ: Prentice-Hall, 1979.

Mintzberg, H. "Power and Organization Life Cycles." *Academy of Management Review* 9 (1984): 207-225.

Mintzberg, H., and Waters, J. "Tracking Strategy in an Entrepreneurial Firm." *Academy of Management Journal* 25 (1982): 465-499.

Negandhi, A. "Comparative Management and Organizational Theory: A Marriage Needed." *Academy of Management Journal* 18 (1975): 334-343.

Nonaka, D., and Okumura, A. "A Comparison of Management in American, Japanese and European Firms." *Management Japan* 17(1) (1984): 23-40.

Norburn, D. "GoGos, YoYos & DoDos: Company Directors and Industry Performance." *Strategic Management Journal* 7 (1986): 101-117.

Oka, T. "A Positive Management Style Takes Root in Japan." *Christian Science Monitor* 24 December 1982, pp. 11-13.

Ouchi, W. *Theory Z: How American Business Can Meet the Japanese Challenge.* Reading, MA: Addison-Wesley, 1981.

Pascale, R., and Athos, A. *The Art of Japanese Management.* New York: Warner, 1981.

"Patience, Restraint and a Sense of Danger: Six Profiles." *Dun's Review* July 1979, pp. 77-82.

"A Plastics Tycoon Builds a U.S. Empire." *Business Week* 1 August 1983, p. 37.

Porter, M.E. *Competitive Strategy: Techniques for Analyzing Industries and Competitors.* New York: Free Press, 1980.

"The Roadblocks Threatening Renault's Recovery." *Business Week* 8 October 1984, p. 60.

"Revolving Door." *Time* 4 February 1985, p. 45.

Richman, L. "Volkswagen Regains Some Beetle Magic." *Fortune* 21 March 1986, pp. 40-45.

Riesman, D., Glazer, N., and Denney, R. *The Lonely Crowd: A Study of Changing American Character.* New York: Doubleday, 1953.

Ronen, S., and Shenkar, O. "Clustering Countries on Attitudinal Dimensions: A Review and Synthesis." *Academy of Management Review* 10 (1985): 435-454.

Schein, E.H. *Organizational Culture and Leadership.* San Francisco, CA: Jossey-Bass, 1985.

Slocum, J.W., Jr., Cron, W., Hansen, R., and Rawlings, S. "Business Strategy and the Management of the Plateaued Performer." *Academy of Management Journal* 28 (1985): 133-154.

Smith, H. "Japan's Autocratic Managers." *Fortune* 25 January 1985, pp. 59-63.

Stewart, R. *Managers and Their Jobs.* London: Macmillan, 1967.

Sturm, P. "Arise: Ye Prisoners of Confiscation!" *Forbes* 5 March 1979, pp. 37-38.

"Sudden Growth." *Fortune* 11 September 1978, p. 14.

"Sweden's ASEA: Its Robots Reach for the U.S. as a High-Tech Drive Begins to Pay Off." *Business Week* 16 January 1984, pp. 104-105.

Tanzer, A. "Y.C. Wang Gets Up Very Early in the Morning." *Forbes* 15 July 1985, pp. 88-93.

Terpstra, V., and David, K. *The Cultural Environment of International Business.* Cincinnati, OH: Southwestern Publishing Co., 1985.

Tosi, H., and Slocum, J.W., Jr. "Contingency Approach: Some Suggested Revisions." *Journal of Management* 10 (1984): 9-26.

"Volvo's 'Emperor' Faces Rebellion in the Ranks." *Business Week* 31 March 1986, p. 45.

Ward's Business Directory of Major International Companies, 5th edition. Pelaluma, CA: Ward Publishing, 1985.

Whiting, J. "Methods and Problems in Cross-Cultural Research." In *Handbook of Social Psychology,* pp. 693-728. Edited by G. Lindzey and E. Aronson. Reading, MA: Addison-Wesley, 1968.

Whyte, W. *The Organization Man.* New York: Doubleday, 1956.

Williams, L., Whyte, W., and Green, C. "Do Cultural Differences Affect Workers' Attitudes?" *Industrial Relations* 5 (1966): 105-117.

Worrell, D., Davidson, W., Chandy, P., and Garrison, S. "Management Turnover Through Deaths of Key Executives: Effects on Investor Wealth." *Academy of Management Journal* 29 (1986): 674-694.

"A Young Outsider with Family Backing." *Fortune* 4 December 1978, pp. 120-124.

REWARDING CHIEF
EXECUTIVE OFFICERS

Gerardo R. Ungson and Richard M. Steers

Never before in the history of corporate management have executive rewards been as carefully scrutinized and as hotly contested. The magnitude and seeming inequity of executive compensation have provoked many stockholders, academicians, and the general public to raise disquieting questions: "Can anybody be worth that kind of money?" "Is there any limit to how much executives should be paid?" "What have executives done for their stockholders to deserve that kind of money?" Given the declining competitiveness of U.S. industries, there is even some question why U.S. executives are generally paid much more than their Japanese and European counterparts, whom many regard as being more successful. Reports of executive compensation, published annually in periodicals such as *Business Week* and *Forbes,* have intensified the controversy and have formalized the debate on these questions. With executive compensation on the rise, it is likely that this debate will continue for years to come.

The controversy revolves around three issues: (1) the magnitude of executive compensation which many regard as excessive; (2) the growing disparity between executive pay and the average pay of hourly workers; and

(3) the lack of consistency between executive compensation and measures of corporate performance.

A decade ago, executives for most of the 100 largest industrial organizations were paid an average of $300,000. In 1985, the figure has breached the $1 million mark ("Annual Survey. . .," 1985). Beyond figures and averages, salaries received by some top executives are simply staggering. In 1984, T. Boone Pickens, chairman of Mesa Petroleum Company, had a total compensation of $22.8 million. David Jones, chairman of Humana, took home $18.1 million. The rest of the top 20 executives for that year received anywhere from $2.3 million to $7.9 million.

Not only did executive compensation stay well ahead of the inflation rate, it also surpassed average pay increases for both white-collar workers, whose pay rose an average of 6.5 percent, and union officials, whose raises averaged 2.2 percent (Annual Suvery. . .," 1985). In a *Wall Street Journal* article, Peter Drucker suggested that "executive compensation is likely to become the biggest obstacle to management's attempts to limit wage and salary increases for the rank-and-file." Mindful of this emerging problem, he has proposed that CEO's pay be limited to no more than 20 times the average pay of hourly workers ("Executives Face. . .," 1986: 3).

Yet the most provocative issue that has been extensively examined over several decades is whether executives are deserving of such pay in terms of their performance. The apparent lack of consistency between executive compensation and corporate performance has prompted some writers to conclude that "pay for performance" is untenable in practice. For example, Augustine states: "There are many highly successful organizations in the United States. There are also many highly paid executives. The policy is not to intermingle the two" (Augustine, 1982: 1). A similar conclusion is made by Loomis who suggests that there is a relationship between executive pay and corporate performance, but in the reversed direction predicted by conventional expectations. She suggests that executives in large organizations are better rewarded than those in smaller firms which tend to have better corporate performance (Loomis, 1982).

It is this subject of executive compensation that constitutes the central focus of this paper. This chapter has three key objectives. It critically examines the empirical literature that relates executive compensation and corporate performance. Second, it reviews more recent attempts to evaluate the "fit" between pay and performance, including model-testing and variable specifications. A core argument is raised that better theoretical models of the pay for performance relationship are needed to explain patterns of empirical findings. Finally, it presents three theoretical perspectives—functional-rational, political, and attributional—as alternative ways to view the relationship and to shed more light on this controversial topic.

WHAT DETERMINES EXECUTIVE COMPENSATION?

Sales vs. Profit Maximization

Early research on the determinants of top executive compensation was undertaken by economists interested in examining hypotheses derived from the traditional theory of the firm that top managers operate to maximize profits. It was then argued that top management compensation, (i.e., salary and bonus) would be closely linked with profitability. This was generally held to be particularly true for managers who were also owners of the corporation (Baumol, 1958, 1967).

However, certain circumstances allow managers to pursue nonprofit goals of the firm. These occur when competition from other firms is low and when management control is independent from ownership control, thereby relieving the manager from market and stockholder pressures which are typically associated with profit maximization. Because these circumstances are most likely to occur in oligopolistic markets, an alternative hypothesis was that compensation would be more closely related to sales revenue subject to a minimum profit constraint (Masson, 1971).

Empirical studies of executive compensation have generally tested whether compensation is largely a function of profit or profitability, or some measure of size (sales, assets). While studies differ fundamentally in their use of samples, variables, and research methods, the underlying theories which motivated them are based on the "sales vs. profit maximization" hypothesis.

In an early study Roberts (1959) used a sample of 1,414 firms for the 1935-1950 period, and reported that CEO compensation (salary plus bonus) was primarily related to size (sales volume), and not profits. McGuire, Chiu, and Elbing (1962) conducted a follow-up study of 45 firms for each of the seven years, 1953-1959, and found that an expanded measure of CEO compensation (salary, bonus, and stock options) was also primarily related to sales rather than to profits. After testing for possible lagged relationships in which similar findings were observed, they interpreted their overall results as supporting Roberts' (1959) study.

Correcting for the Collinearity Between Sales and Profits

Noting the high colinearity between sales and profits, Lewellen and Huntsman (1970) measured compensation, sales, and profits relative to the firm's assets for 50 firms over a 21-year period, 1942-1963. Using this method, they reported that profitability had more significance for CEO compensation when compared to sales efficiency. Prasad (1974) utilized this same weighted index for analyzing 823 firms in different industries, and employed group rather than individual renumeration as a measure of compensation. His findings are supportive of Lewellen and Huntsman (1970)—that is, profitability emerged as a more potent influence on group executive compensation. Prasad did note, however, that sales efficiency also had a relevant degree of influence. Smyth, Boyes and Peseau (1975) replicated prior studies using executive compensation data for 1971 and reported that both sales efficiency and profitability impacted CEO compensation.

Deckop and Mahoney (1982) have argued that the measurement of sales, profits, and compensation relative to assets totally eliminates any size effect for compensation making interpretations about the relative effects of size and profits on compensation difficult. By dividing sales by assets, for example, the resulting measure is one of efficiency, e.g., the amount of sales generated for every dollar of assets, and not size. A later study by Ciscel and Carroll (1980) attempted to circumvent this problem by first regressing profits upon sales and calculating a residual profit score by subtracting predicted profits from observed profits. Then, they regressed CEO compensation against residual profit and sales. Using this method, they found that sales (or size effect) was predominant, although they also concluded that market variables (i.e., the size of their intercept variable) was a better predictor of CEO compensation.

Moderating Variables: Ownership Control and Strategy

Other studies have attempted to introduce variables that might moderate the relationship between CEO compensation and rewards. The first of these variables is the influence of owner control and the degree of oligopoly. Specifically, Wallace (1973) found that size (sales or assets) appeared to be the primary predictor of CEO compensation in general, but that profitability was a better predictor among owner controlled firms in unconcentrated industries.

The second moderating variable, studied by Murthy and Salter (1975), is that of diversification strategy. Their findings indicate that low correlations between CEO pay and financial performance are noticeable in companies with one dominant business, but that the link appears stronger in companies pursuing a variety of unrelated businesses. Murthy and Salter had interpreted this finding as arising from the changing role of the CEO. In particular, as the company's diversity increases (e.g., a firm moves to more unrelated businesses), the CEO role shifts from the details of managing individual businesses to allocating financial resources among them. In effect, the CEO's role tends to be similar to that of the divisional general manager whose compensation varies with divisional performance (Berg, 1969, 1973; Pitts, 1974).

Empirical work on the compensation of divisional general managers, while not focused directly at the CEO level, nonetheless provides some additional insights on the economics of CEO compensation. Berg's work (1969, 1973) on conglomerates and diversified firms suggests that differences in rewards systems can be explained in terms of the autonomy of divisional mangers. Following this line of reasoning, Pitts (1974) tested the hypothesis that reward structures, i.e., components of bonus programs, would differ significantly between firms that grew principally by internal expansion and those that grew principally by acquisitions. He noted that the characteristics of bonus systems for divisional managers in acquisitive conglomerates were more quantitative, more closely linked with divisional profitability (ROI), and had a wider range between the highest and the lowest paid divisional manager.

Pitts explained these differences in terms of the level of autonomy associated with growth strategies. Divisional managers in acquisitive conglomerates generally experience more autonomy than their counterparts in internally-grown conglomerates and consequently are better able to link their rewards (bonuses) to their own performance (ROI). As managers in internally-grown conglomerates have to depend more on each other for shared resources and technologies, their bonuses cannot be readily linked with individual performance. In addition, interdivisional boundary transactions that are essential to effective resource-sharing are not as easily quantified, thus partly explaining the prevalence of qualitative criteria in bonuses of these divisional managers.

A more recent study by Govindarajan and Gupta (1985) attempted to relate strategy, incentive bonus system, and effectiveness at the strategic business unit (SBU) level within diversified firms. Strategy was viewed as a continuous spectrum that ranges from increasing market share (usually resulting in low short term profitability and low or negative cash flow) to maximizing short term earnings and cash flow (usually resulting in decreasing market share). These two ends of the spectrum are commonly referred to as "pure build" and "pure harvest" strategies, respectively. The authors reported that, in terms of SBU effectiveness (i.e. self-reports of selected performance indices), incentive bonus systems depends on the strategy of the focal SBU. Specifically, greater reliance on long-run criteria and subjective (non-formula) approaches for determining the SBU general manager's bonus contribute to effectiveness in the case of "build" SBU's, hamper effectiveness of "harvest" SBUS's.

Cross Sectional vs. Time Series Analysis

Most studies that have tested the relationship between executive compensation and performance have been cross-sectional in nature. Murphy

(1985) has argued that cross-sectional studies are inherently limited in the specification of variables leading to serious interpretational problems, such as the effects of size.

In cross-sectional studies, it is not at all surprising that size (sales) explains the differences in CEO compensation. As CEO pay levels are based to a large extent on comparative pay surveys (Kraus, 1970), it is intuitively clear that CEO pay would covary to some extent with size, regardless of performance. Moreover, size also reflects the complexities and demands of the job, and it can be argued that CEOs in larger firms should be more substantially compensated. While it can be argued that CEO compensation is related to profitability for firms of a *given* size, it is more difficult to interpret the relative effects of size and profitability on CEO compensation (Deckop and Mahoney, 1982).

There is emerging evidence, however, that profitability can have significant impact on CEO compensation when size differences are controlled or when longitudinal analysis is performed (Deckop and Mahoney, 1982). The most compelling case for this argument is research by Murphy (1985) and his colleagues at the University of Rochester. He illustrates how a positive or a negative relationship between executive compensation and firm performance are artifacts of particular statistical techniques, if size differences between firms are ignored or not controlled.

Using 461 executives from 72 manufacturing firms for the period 1964-71, Murphy tested for the pay for performance hypotheses using both time series analysis and pooled cross-sectional regressions. He also refined measures from previous studies including salary, bonus, salary plus bonus, deferred compensation, and option values as individual measures of executive compensation; stock index as a cumulative measure of continuously accrued shareholder rate of return; and incorporated dummy variables (chairman, chief executive officer, president) to represent hierarchical levels; and corrected for executive transfers at turnover.

His principal findings were: (1) there is a close relationship between the shareholders' total return (including both price appreciation and dividends) and changes in executive compensation (salary and bonus); and (2) there is a close relationship between the shareholders' rate of return and the value of the executives' own stock. After dividing CEO pay into quintiles and ranking them according to total return to stockholders, Murphy was able to specify the dollar amounts (stock) that executives received commensurate to the rate of return. His findings indicate a clear correspondence between executive pay and firm performance. Finally, cross-sectional regression that did not control for size was similar to findings from previous studies (i.e., the dominance of sales over profits as a determinant of executive compensation). Murphy then concluded that specification errors were present in these analyses.

Refining Measures of Firm Performance

In general, studies of the pay-for-performance relationships have utilized different measures of firm performance. Of these measures, two are distinguished: earnings derived from accounting data and market returns based on stock prices. There is question as to the appropriateness of these measures for capturing short- and long-term performance.

Rappaport (1981, 1983) has presented the shortcomings of earnings and accounting performance standards. Specifically, earnings growth is achieved not only when management is investing at a rate of return above that demanded by the market, but also when it is investing below the market rate and thus decreasing the value of common shares. This is true because earnings do not reflect changes in risk, different expectations about inflation, or investment needed to enhance business value. During the 1970s, many companies, in fact, had impressive annual earnings per share growth rates, but provided their stockholders minimal or negative rates of return from dividends plus share price changes. Rappaport (1983) suggested that the issue might not be as much "pay for performance," as much as "pay for *what* performance."

While it is true that market returns realized by shareholders constitute the most direct means of linking top managements' interests with those of stockholders, they also have inherent limitations when used in incentive structures. First, a company's stock price can be greatly influenced by factors beyond management's control, e.g., inflation, recession, etc. Second, market returns can be influenced by optimistic and pessimistic expectations about the future. Finally, stock price cannot be directly linked to divisional performance.

Therefore, in contrast to stock price and stockholder return on investment, Rappaport (1981, 1983) has suggested a value contribution approach which estimates the future cash flows associated with particular strategies. Executives are then able to assess the economic value of alternative strategies to stockholders at both the business and corporate level of analysis. Since the value contribution approach incorporates both short- and long-term interests of the company, it maximizes strategic opportunities and provides a closer link between top management's motives and stockholders' interests. The use of cash flows as a measure of performance is also strongly endorsed by Rock (1984) who advocates these be adopted not only at the corporate level but at multiple levels of the organization.

Assessing the Research Evidence: Unresolved Issues

A systematic appraisal of this stream of research is difficult due to the diversity of samples, measures, time periods, and statistical methods used

Table 1.　A Framework for Analyzing Executive Compensation

Perspectives on Executive Behavior	Basis of Reward Allocation	Timing of Evaluation and Rewards	Nature of Rewards	Contextual Factors of Evaluation
Functional-rational				
Focus on bottom line results; assume purposeful choices of consistent actors	Emphasizes short-term and long-term financial measures (e.g., return on investment, net profits, successful acquisitions)	Typically considers CEO performance over 1 to 3 years as it relates to financial position of firm	Focuses on monetary rewards (e.g., salary, bonuses, stock options)	Focuses on compensation practices by types of industry or firm and by size of firm
Political				
Focus on political behavior; assumes that behavior reflects a diversity of goals based on pluralistic and political character of organization	Recognizes CEOs role as symbolic and political figurehead and effectiveness of CEO in using political process to facilitate organizational goals	Necessitates a more ambiguous time frame; looks for trends in performance based on political activity of CEO as it bears on financial performance	Focuses on both extrinsic monetary rewards and intrinsic rewards (e.g., prestige, recognition, challenge)	Recognizes industry and context but also considers nature of relationship between CEO and his or her evaluators (usually the board of directors)
Attributional				
Focus on symbolic activity and the process of legitimation	Emphasizes the accountability of CEOs to various constituencies within the organization; the CEO's ability to assure these constituencies that he/shre is in control becomes a basis for renumeration	Evaluation is tied to annual reports when the CEO formally takes account of his/her behavioral actions to constituenciess	Focuses on both extrinsic monetary rewards and intrinsic rewards (e.g., prestige, etc.)	Focuses on the process by which CEO activity is recognized and legitimized by the board of directors and other shareholders.

to examine the correlates of executive compensation (Table 1). Even so, some trends have begun to emerge.

There is some question regarding the adequacy and comprehensiveness of measures used. Most studies have emphasized the most visible form of executive renumeration, that is, bonus and salary, omitting other components such as stock options, deferred compensation, stock awards, performance bonus plans, etc. As many as 15 years ago, Lewellen and Huntsman (1972) noted the growing effects of stock options on total executive renumeration. In an extensive study of the top five executives of large industrial corporations, Lewellan and Huntsman estimated that, on average, only 50 percent of an executive's compensation is based on salary and bonus. They also found that the executives' after-tax earnings from company stock averaged three times the present value of their compensation packages. If such is generally true across executives, then most studies are seriously limited in their measure and inferences about compensation based on cash measures. Murphy's (1985) study which uses different measures of compensation, in fact, provides some indication that these different measures of compensation vary with firm performance.

While the importance of long-term incentives such as stock options have been noted (Poster, 1985), other studies have indicated that firms with long-term incentives were giving their stockholders an annual return no better than the return in companies without such incentives (Rich and Larson, 1984). Even so, nearly 40 percent of the Fortune 500 companies have now adopted some form of performance-based, long-term incentives, and it is estimated that aggregate payments to executives from these plans could exceed $1.5 billion over the next ten years (Rich and Larson, 1984). The efficacy of long-term incentives in motivating managers to improve company performance deserves more serious empirical attention in future studies.

A related problem is identifying measures of firm performance most appropriate for examining the relationship between pay and performance. The assessment of organizational effectiveness has been one of the more intractable problems in organizational theory (Steers, 1977; Goodman and Pennings, 1977). In both Murphy's (1985) and Rappaport's (1983) work, we see concerted attempts to define firm performance in the context of compensation structures. Despite these efforts, the inherent problems of measurement remain. Murphy's use of shareholders' return and stock indices are not under the complete control of the managers, thereby decreasing their effectiveness as motivational devices. Rappaport's use of value contribution is premised on one's ability to project future cash flows correctly for each alternative strategy—a situation that is not easily realized in uncertain environments. Since organizations tend to pursue many diverse goals, some favoring stockholders' interests and others meeting internal requirements for profitability, it is important to specify a priori what theory of effectiveness underlies the pay-for-performance relationship.

While it is generally agreed that CEO compensation is related to profitability for firms in a *given* size, it is still difficult to interpret the relative effects of size and profitability on CEO rewards. Murphy's use of time series vs. cross-sectional analysis is particularly noteworthy in establishing that CEO compensation is related to profitability measures depending on which statistical method is employed.

Due to a lack of empirical research, it is still not possible to evaluate whether CEO compensation is related to company strategy or strategic goals. With the growing popularity of performance unit plans-that is, incentive plans that directly link bonuses with the accomplishment of a predefined corporate goal—there is at least some anecdotal evidence that CEO compensation is partly related to strategic goals ("Annual Survey. . .," May 12, 1978).

Using a more restricted focus, Berg (1969, 1973) and Pitts (1974) have suggested that the level of managerial autonomy, as reflected in a firm's corporate strategy, might account for the differential components of a divisional manager's bonus. Whether this pattern is true for CEO's remains another question that has to be addressed in future studies. The possible parallels between the role of CEO's and divisional managers in diversified companies provide a point of departure for speculating on the lack of consistency between CEO rewards and performance, a subject of which the latter part of this paper is directed.

For the most part, researchers have studied the determinants of executive rewards for the purpose of inferring a decisional criterion or the motivational basis for executive decisions. Our assessment is that the field has advanced in refining study-measures and in developing more sophisticated analyses of the pay-for-performance relationship. Despite the flurry of studies, however, there is no clear consensus that executive compensation and firm performance are strongly related. Since many companies are just starting to incorporate long-term incentives into their overall compensation structures, there will be need for more empirical studies, and it is not likely that the pay-for-performance debate will be resolved in the near future.

We also believe that we have not progressed considerably in terms of developing cogent theories that explain the decision criteria or the motivation bases of executive compensation. Deckop and Mahoney's (1982) work based on agency theory is a promising approach to understanding decision criteria. At this time, however, the debate on the pay-for-performance issue is really one over measure or method, but not about theory. From our previous studies, we note particular circumstances under which CEO compensation and firm performance ought *not* to be related.

Accordingly, in the next section, we will present different perspectives that provide alternative explanations of extant empirical findings.

PERSPECTIVES FOR RE-EXAMINING THE PAY-FOR-PERFORMANCE RELATIONS

Functional-Rational Perspective

An implicit assumption underlying theories that prescribe a strong link between top executive rewards and performance is that of functional rationality, that is, the presumption that corporate events typically represent purposeful choices of consistent actors (Allison, 1971). As behavior is assumed to reflect purpose or intention, it is then presupposed that high rewards (such as bonuses or salaries) should be positively associated with the accomplishments of predefined goals (e.g., profitability). For example, most theories of motivation argue in favor of strong performance-reward contingencies. In cognitive theories such as expectancy/valence theory, it is suggested that performance is enhanced when employees see performance as leading to desired rewards. On the other hand, noncognitive theories, such as reinforcement theories, argue that rewards such as pay raises, bonuses, or even praise for a job well done often serve as conditioner reinforcers when tied to performance. Hence, whichever model is used, the motivational assumption underlying executive compensation is clear: tie rewards to desired performance in order to ensure maximum performance.

Theories of the firm that assert the maximization of the risk-adjusted stock value of the firm as reflecting the personal motives of managers also rely on the concept of functional rationality. The underlying assumption is that executives should work for stockholders, and that they should stress the present value of profits since the stock market can do a generally good job in capitalizing the value of the discounted future profits of the firm. Therefore, the link between executive rewards and firm performance is expected to be strong.

Political Perspective

Pfeffer (1981) has criticized models of rational choice as failing to take account of the diversity of goals and interests within organizations. The diversity of goals reflect the pluralistic nature of organizations, that is, organizational subunits, coalitions, and subcultures with different, if not conflicting, interests. Therefore, actions and decisions result from bargaining and compromise, with those units with the greatest power receiving the greatest rewards from the interplay of organizational politics.

To apply this perspective to CEO compensation, it is necessary to understand the complexities of the CEO role and how these complexities are related to CEO compensation.

Ungson and Steers (1984) suggested that the complexities in the CEO role are grounded in their activities as political figureheads to a wide array of constituents, and as political strategists in their dealings with the board of directors. As legal authorities of their firm, CEOs act as symbols and are obliged to perform symbolic activities such as attending ceremonial events, political functions, receiving important visitors, and so forth. In a broader context, the top manager acts as the boundary to the owners, government, employee groups, and the general public. They make their preferences known to him and he, in turn, is obliged to effectively transmit the company's position to them. Weick (1979) describes managerial work as managing myths, symbols, and images, and argues that managers should be viewed more as evangelists than accountants. Pondy (1978) also noted that a large part of leadership and power derives from the manager's ability to manage symbolic activity. These examples illustrate the importance of political figurehead roles and the symbolic functions to the CEO job. In terms of executive compensation, these political and symbolic activities are difficult to evaluate. They are not always clear, and the criteria for evaluating success in these activities are often equivocal.

In contrast to rational choice and bureaucratic models of organization, the political model emphasizes the role of political coalitions and interplays among coalitions (Cyert and March, 1963; Allison, 1971). In this context, the CEO assumes the role of a political actor who is active in managing not only political coalitions within the organization but external entities as well. Pfeffer's work on cooptation (1972, 1974) provides one example on how top managers operate to include external members (or adversaries) as part of the organizational boundaries in an effort to "win" these members to the company's position.

The political and strategic roles of the CEO are well dramatized in the maneuvering that characterizes mergers and acquisition. A case in point is the fast bid for the Martin Marietta Corporation made by the Chairman of the Bendix Corporation William Agee. After scores of moves and countermoves, Agee's company had to be rescued by Allied Corporation to prevent Bendix from losing a battle it had begun. There are those who have praised Agee's investment strategy but have questioned whether his actions were in the best interests of the company and stockholders. Evaluating his performance and an appropriate executive compensation package would be difficult when viewed in this political context.

A CEO's political acumen is also tested in his/her dealings with the board of directors. In fact, some writers (Williams, 1985; Patton, 1985) attribute escalating pay to internal boardroom dynamics. Board members, according to Williams, hardly make compensation decisions in an objective and independent manner. More frequently than not, the chief executive becomes involved in the pay-setting process by signalling the amount of compensation for subordinates below him. On occasion, the chief executive might approve of his/her compensation *before* it goes to the compensation committee.

The process is facilitated by compensation surveys made available by various compensation consultants. It is contended that companies avoid positioning themselves on the "average," and try to be "above average" in compensating their executives (Williams, 1985). Corporate performance might be considered, but such appears to be secondary compared to the board's desire to present a good image. Consultants enhance the process by recommending pay increases even when performance is below par, although they also raise corporate goals to justify their proposals.

Patton (1985) provides additional documentation on how relations between the CEO and the board of directors lead to escalating pay hikes. First, most board members are relatively unfamiliar with the industry in which to evaluate CEO performance, and consequently depend heavily on the CEO for guidance on compensation decisions. Relatedly, the board tends to rely on compensation surveys and consultants which, for reasons cited in the preceding paragraph, lead to high compensation, regardless of company performance. A second reason for the upward bias in executive compensation is that board members are themselves likely to be CEOs in other corporations. Patton (1985) notes that exchanges of board membership is often accompanied by membership on compensation committees. As a consequence, board members may be reluctant to rescind CEO pay (or give a lower bonus amount) even if so warranted, fearful that they might face similar circumstances in their own boards. Thus, the pressure to be mutually supportive is quite real.

The preceding examples provide graphic testimony to the complexities of the CEO role that result from political and strategic activities. These examples also suggest that other contextual factors, such as the relationship of the CEO with the board of directors, influence executive compensation decisions. Taken together, these observations suggest that the political and strategic activities of the CEO would provide a suitable context for understanding and explaining the ambiguous linkages between rewards and performance that have characterized previous research.

Attributional Perspectives

Evaluating performance involves examining the accountability of CEOs for their actions. Pfeffer (1981: 4) has suggested that the task of management is "to provide explanations, rationalizations, and legitimations for the activities undertaken in the organization." Through various mechanisms, such as annual reports, executives have attempted to restructure past events, frame present ones, and propagate their desired future-states. Implicit in these mechanisms are CEO causal reasonings or attributions of their own performance.

Staw (1980) has suggested that causal attributions either provide accurate explanation of events to enhance control of future outcomes, or provide justification for prior actions. Staw also hypothesized that the rationalizing of prior behavior in an attempt to make it seem rational occurs when there is strong need to defend one's ego. For example, it has been documented that individuals tend to attribute favorable outcomes to causes internal to themselves and to explain unfavorable outcomes to factors external to themselves. Self-serving attributions, as these are called, have been noted in both experimental studies as well as real settings (Miller and Ross, 1975; Zuckerman, 1979). Previous studies have tested whether self-serving attributions are caused by the nature of information or by motivational factors (Miller and Ross, 1975), while others have sought more specific contexts under which self-serving attributions are bound to occur (Snyder, Stephen, and Rosenfield, 1978; Bettman and Weitz, 1983).

While there are numerous media for the CEO to provide information that legitimizes his/her intentions and actions, the most prominent would be the company annual report, the "Letter to Stockholders" in particular. Typically, in such a letter, the CEO evaluates the firm's performance, justifies actions oriented at improving performance, and explains any performance downturns.

Those who have studied causal attributions from annual reports (Bettman and Weitz, 1983; Staw, McKechnie and Pfeffer, 1983; Salancik and Meindl, 1984) indicate that CEO explanations of performance are inextricably related to CEO attributions of causality. Bettman and Weitz (1983) noted the typical self-serving pattern of attributions (i.e., unfavorable outcomes were attributed more to external, unstable and uncontrollable causes than were favorable outcomes).

Staw and his colleagues (1983) also noted that self-serving attributions had consequential influences on the public, since these attributions were associated with subsequent improvements in stock price. Salancik and Meindl (1984) suggest that CEOs do not attempt to explain negative performance, but attempt to display it by providing an illusion that they are in control of the situation. Being in control conveys the impression that they are capable of rectifying the causes of any downturn, thereby justifying their positions as chief executive officers of the company. Salancik and Meindl argue that attributions are strategic biases used in proper contexts. They also noted that attributions are associated with subsequent improvements in performance.

These works provide direct documentation that attributions are important in managing organizations. In general, executives will assume responsibility for outcomes, whether good or bad, if they face the need to reassure their constituencies of their ability to direct corporate affairs. We then hypothesize that their ability to project control is tied to their compensation, as determined by the board of directors. That is, the more effective an executive is in accounting for his/her actions and performance, the greater the amount of compensation from the board.

These three perspectives yield different ways in which executive rewards and performance might be meaningfully related. In the functional-rational perspective, emphasis is placed on "hard" or "bottom-line" data. It is largely assumed that executive behavior represents purposeful choices of consistent actors. Discrepancies in the relationship are seen as arising from deficiencies within this instrumental relationship (i.e., the executive is not evaluated on financial performance), or inadequacies in measures (i.e., use of 'wrong' measures of bonus or performance) or methodology (i.e., limitations of cross-sectional methodology).

The political perspective, on the other hand, assumes that executive behavior reflects a diversity of goals representing both the pluralistic and the political character of the organization. In contrast to the functional-rational perspective, it sees any weak linkage between CEO rewards and performance as an outcome of the political and strategic roles of the CEO that are important but not easily quantified or formulated into some bonus formula.

Related to the political perspective, the attributional perspective emphasizes the role of CEO as managing symbolic activity and legitimizing actions and intentions. As such, any inconsistency between CEO rewards and performance is seen as a failure to account for the CEOs ability to legitimize performance to various constituencies, which, like political activities, are also difficult to quantify.

IMPLICATIONS FOR RESEARCH AND THEORY DEVELOPMENT

In an earlier paper (Ungson and Steers, 1984), we presented a number of research propositions about executive rewards and performance that were based on the political perspectives. These are discussed below, along with propositions regarding the rational and attributional perspectives (summarized in Exhibit 1).

P1.   CEO rewards may be more a function of political than of economic variables.

As noted above, previous studies that have examined the determinants of CEO compensation have used economic related criteria (sales, profitability, strategy) as predictors of CEO rewards. Although these variables can be justified for divisional general managers (and other managers in the lower echelons of the management hierarchy), they might not be as applicable to CEOs whose jobs tend to relate more to the political requirements of the corporation. Intuitively, it can be argued that political success eventually will be reflected in economic success. For instance, when Lee Iacocca was hired by Chrysler, there was an immediate increase in Chrysler's stock price. This was attributed, in part, to reports that Chrysler dealers and employees within the organization felt content with the change in leadership and the company's prospects under Iacocca's management (Pfeffer, 1981).

Unfortunately, a direct test of the relationship between Iacocca's reward and performance would obscure this particular context. In 1978 when he was hired, Iacocca received only $60,622 in salary and bonus. He did receive a $1.5 million recruitment bonus from Chrysler to be paid in 1979 and 1980 and approximately $400,000 for the settlement of matters relating to his termination at Ford ("Annual Survey. . .," 1980). With the salary reduction program in effect, however, he received a total of only $1 per year for 1980 and 1981. Meanwhile, it is commonly acknowledged that he was instrumental in a bail-out deal with the Congress and successfully negotiated a labor-cost advantage contract with the United Auto Workers (UAW). When viewed against Chrysler's continuing losses through 1980 alone, Iacocca's political contributions would be seriously understated.

Therefore, future research should be directed at developing political as well as economic factors that might account for variations in executive compensation. Traditional economic-related criteria of success such as profitability and sales maximization can be logically linked to special incentive programs such as performance achievement plans, but they do not adequately reflect the political skills of the CEO that may be crucial in accomplishing economic objectives in the long run. Political skills and contributions of CEOs are difficult to evaluate in quantitative terms because they seldom are clear or obvious. One approach would be to use, as a surrogate measure of political, attributions of political success by selected persons who are familiar with the CEO. In the case of Iacocca, such a measure would include attributions by persons inside and outside of Chrysler on Iacocca's effectiveness in dealing with Congress and the UAW. Reputational measures, however, are subject to various types of biases (Pfeffer, 1981). Clearly, this is one area that needs more serious empirical attention.

Parenthetically, it can be noted here that it is important to differentiate between CEO political skills that can be functionally related to a firm's long range performance and political qualifications that are serendipitously related to events surrounding executive succession. Iacocca's charm and charisma were important traits for managing Chrysler's problems, and a case can be made that these traits are related to the improvements of Chrysler's financial position. If, on the other hand, a person becomes CEO and is rewarded with a handsome bonus primarily because he or she happens to be the compromise candidate by two competing interests, then the justification of any huge bonus would be difficult.

P2. Change in CEO rewards are time-related and often difficult to quantify.

One issue that has not been as extensively examined in prior studies of CEO compensation is whether bonuses represent rewards for past actions or are made as an inducement for future contributions (Prasad, 1974). This raises the issue of time dimensionality, or the appropriate time frame in which to examine CEO performance-reward relationships.

Top executives are formally rewarded in terms of base salaries, bonuses, stock options, stock appreciation rights (SARs), performance achievement plans, and restricted stock options. Stock options, SARs and restricted stock options involve compensation that can be exercised within specified and nonspecified time periods. It is difficult, therefore, to relate these options to executive performance at any specified time period. Performance achievement plans (i.e., cash awards or shares that are earned for the achievement of predetermined financial targets) provide one exception, but such plans are still formative and constitute only a small fraction of CEO pay ("Annual Survey. . ., 1978).

Previous research on CEO compensation adds little to the understanding of which time frame to employ. In general, there is evidence from time-lagged regression utilizing one-to-two year differentials (Lewellen and Huntsman, 1972) that size (sales volume) and, to a lesser extent, profitability are significant predictors of CEO bonus and salary. The inclusion of political variables would tend to complicate further the question of what time frame to use; political transactions are not always compatible with time-period evaluations. For example, the success or failure of lobbying efforts by the automobile industry to obtain tariff concessions from Congress cannot be directly tied to specific years for evaluation. Even so, recognition of such efforts is essential if understanding of this important issue is to be furthered.

Future research and theory development, therefore, should closely examine the appropriateness of time frames selected for study. One procedure would be the use of longitudinal case studies in which the specific

mechanisms by which rewards are associated with overall CEO performance can be more directly examined.

P3. Studies of CEO compensation ignore important intangible features
of the job.

Most studies of CEO compensation focus on formal reward structures
(e.g., salary bonus, stock options) but place little attention on intrinsic
rewards and perquisites. A comprehensive examination of this subject
would include such variables. For instance, there is at least anecdotal
evidence that some executives take jobs as springboards to even more
prestigious and challenging jobs (Rowan, 1981), and that others accept jobs
either for the peace and tranquility or for the sense of challenge (Roche,
1975). The study of both the formal and informal reward structure of CEOs
would provide more latitude in explaining the gaps between CEO
compensation and performance.

Essentially, such a study would focus on what CEOs consider to be
significant outcomes resulting from their performance. With the increased
paychecks of CEOs, it is difficult to argue that money is not a major
influence on motivation. However, the magnitude of an executive's
compensation can also represent prestige and recognition from peer groups.
Hence, it is suggested that future research be directed at developing a more
comprehensive typology of the rewards that are made in recognition of
CEO's accomplishments (Kerr and Snow, 1980).

P4. CEO rewards might be better understood in the context of the CEO's
relationship with the board of directors.

Cross-sectional studies of the relationship between CEO compensation
and performance neglect the context of the CEO's relationship with the
board of directors. It is the board of directors that has the formal authority
to hire and fire CEOs as well as to decide on how much compensation ought
to be paid. As in the case of ITT, the chairman of the board (who also may
be the CEO of the company) may select other members of the board. There
are a number of ways, therefore, that resulting decisions on CEO
compensation might not result from CEO performance, as would be
predicted from motivational and normative decision making theories.
Members of the board of directors might be sympathetic with the CEO's
goals and programs, but they might not be entirely unbiased in evaluating
his/her performance. After all, to avoid giving a bonus would be an
acknowledgement by the board that it might have selected the wrong person.
Moreover, if CEO compensation is to impart an important symbolic
message to the general public that a good job is being done, the board may

elect to perpetuate this "myth" by giving a nice bonus even if such is not warranted in terms of company performance.

This practice is bound to be exacerbated as one considers the difficulties in hiring good CEOs. Meyers (1981) maintains that retaining the best executive will become a major corporate problem in the near future. He anticipates that the next decade will be characterized by increasing executive mobility as a result of: (1) greater demand for the fewer 40-to-60 year old executives available; and (2) increasing pressures that will restrict salaries, bonuses, and other management prerogatives. Consider, as one example, the turnover of executives at Pillsbury (Rowan, 1981). In 1980, the company experienced its fifth top executive turnover in 10 years when Vice Chairman Thomas Wyman left to become president of CBS. Chief financial officer Walter Scott also left to become president of Investors Diversified Services, and Donald Smith, a Pillsbury Vice President, left to become president of Pepsico's food service division. As the market for top executive talent becomes more competitive, boards of directors would be expected to attempt to retain executive talent even if the executives' performance falls short of expectation. Therefore it is not too surprising that firms seldom change their leadership except during times of crisis, or when it becomes painfully evident that the strategy associated with the incumbent CEO is no longer tenable (Starbuck and Hedberg, 1977; Starbuck, Greve, and Hedberg, 1978).

These observations suggest that future research direct closer attention to the role of the board of directors in determining CEO compensation, particularly in relation to the uncertainties of the CEO or top executive market. Summarizing some future research directions for boards of directors, Schendel and Hofer (1979) question whether boards in large well-established companies are captives of management until some crisis that requires them to challenge managerial leadership. If such is true, Schendel and Hofer also ask what might be done to establish the board's independence when crises are not present. One key toward unlocking these difficult questions would be to examine carefully how such interdependence is reflected in decisions involving CEO compensation.

P5. CEO rewards often depend on the ability of the CEO to justify prior actions and legitimize intentions to dif-ferent constituencies within the organization.

Most previous studies of CEO compensation have focused on the instrumental nature of the relationship between CEO rewards and firm performance, and have neglected the process by which the CEO accounts for his/her actions to various constituencies. Pfeffer (1981) and Staw (1980) have argued that some forms of justification are functions in persuading investors of the merits of one's company. Salancik and Meindl (1984) see attributions as resolving management's dilemma of promising organizational participants some outcomes that are contingent on the participation of others in the organization. By managing symbolically and reassuring various others that they have the ability to "control" the coalition, managers are able to effectively manage the coalition.

If management is persuasive in these efforts, then it is more than conceivable that they also get ably rewarded by the board of directors. Specifically, to the extent that managers are able to explain away unfavorable outcomes to external causes and attribute successful outcomes to themselves, then they are likely to be recognized as successful and duly compensated. Interestingly, actual firm performance may be parenthetical to such a decision. Salancik and Meindl (1984), for example, showed that executive causal attributions may not even reflect prior firm performance. Nonetheless, attributions do affect future performance, due to their consequential effects on external publics. This work provides some implications for rewarding executives. Even in the worst of economic times, the board of directors (and other) may view the CEO in control of events, and may reward him/her in anticipation of improved performance in the future. Even if performance does not improve, the CEO may continue to get ably rewarded if he/she is able to project an image that is reassuring to constituents.

IMPLICATIONS FOR MANAGEMENT PRACTICE

Numerous proposals have specified how top executive rewards might be better linked with performance. Aimed at both CEOs and divisional general managers, these proposals generally attempt to tie particular strategic goals to different types of executive compensation. An examination of the CEO compensation issue highlights several design considerations that explicitly recognize the political/strategic role and responsibilites of the CEO and complements current efforts to improve the practice of CEO compensation. In particular, the following implications for those concerned with CEO compensation are proposed.

1. *In many cases it may be appropriate to decouple rewards and performance.* The role of the divisional general manager, toward which various proposals have been directed, differs from the CEO office in fundamental ways. The divisional manager acts to meet predetermined goals, often times profitability, and develops boundary transactions that are needed to accomplish these goals. As such, bonuses at the divisional level generally are based on division profits (ROI), profit improvement, profits compared with the company's or division's industry, or the achievement of

the profit plan (Rappaport, 1978). Even in highly diversified organizations, in which divisional managers are fairly autonomous, the uniformity of direction is somewhat assured by linking divisional bonus to overall corporate profits (Pitts, 1974). The political activities of divisional managers, as exemplified in interdivisional transactions, can be accommodated within the company's reward structure.

On the other hand, the role of the CEO encompasses other boundary transactions that relate principally to the enhancement of the company's image over time. In effect, attempts to couple CEO bonus, for example, to ROI or other factors resembling those of the divisional general manager may prove to be illusory. At times, in fact, it might even be functional to couple loosely or even decouple rewards from performance to accommodate political/strategic activities of the CEO that are in the best interests of the company but are difficult to tie down to profitability measures in a given time period. Some examples of decoupling efforts would be the use of long term goals as surrogates for political success, the extension of the time period in which CEOs are to be evaluated for long term strategic efforts, and a more active role for boards in the planning and monitoring of CEO activities and performance.

2. *Long term strategic goals as a surrogate for political success should be used in conjunction with profitability measures.* Because businesses are subjected to quarterly evaluations by Wall Street, it is not likely that the present focus on profitability as a measure of performance will change substantially. It is possible, however, to emphasize the use of long run strategic goals in tandem with short term profitability measures. This is implicitly recognized in present efforts that call for an extended CEO evaluation period of up to three to five years (Rappaport, 1978). In a broad sense, the accomplishment of long term strategic goals would validate the success the CEO might have in his or her interorganizational and political transactions.

3. *The formalization of CEO compensation into a bonus formula may be untenable within a political context.* Several incentive programs are aimed at formalizing executive compensation through some form of bonus formula. This is possible with divisional general managers, but it is difficult to quantify or to relate to specific years. An alternative would be to involve more actively the board of directors in the planning and monitoring of CEO activities (Murthy and Salter, 1975), although the directors might not always be objective. On a somewhat wider scale, the use of outside review boards and panels that would be involved in appraisal and compensation decisions might be adopted. In any event, it is important to inform stockholders properly of such evaluations.

4. *The art of managing impressions, that is, presenting good and bad news, may be an important influence in decisions regarding executive compensation.* If executive attributions are indeed taken seriously by constituencies within the organization, then the art of managing impressions, or presenting good and bad news, would influence compensation decisions. Both Staw et al. (1983) and Salancik and Meindl (1984) are instructive on this point. Staw and his colleagues found that both high- and low-performing firms tend to accentuate positive events, although unsuccessful firms still need to explain their performance. By ending their letters in an upbeat note, these unsuccessful firms lessen the impact of their poor performance. Salancik and Meindl report that firms, particularly those with more variance in their performance, tend to take responsibility for outcomes, regardless of whether these were good or bad, to project the image that their management was in control. Those that do so tend to perform better in the future. Clearly, these are exploratory results that need to be examined more closely in future studies.

CONCLUSION

Given the magnitude of executive compensation, it is likely that the debate on whether executives are overpaid or whether they are rewarded based on performance will continue in the future. There is no clear consensus on whether executive compensation and performance are related, although a positive relationship between them has emerged in more recent studies. This chapter suggests three perspectives for reexamining the relationship. Recognizing these perspective may help us better understand some controversial issues that have characterized this debate.

ACKNOWLEDGMENTS

We would like to thank Margo Clausen, Chris Fisher, Jooyup Kim, and Dorothy Stauffer for their help in the literature review.

REFERENCES

Allison, G. T. *Essence of Decision.* Boston: Little, Brown, 1971.
Annual Survey of Executive Compensation. *Business Week* 11, May 1978, pp. 66-99.
Annual Survey of Executive Compensation. *Business Week* 12, May 1980, pp. 56-59.
Annual Survey of Executive Compensation. *Business Week* 6, May 1985, pp. 55-87.
Augustine, N. *Augustine's Laws.* New York: American Institute of Aeronautics and Astronautics" 1982.
Baumol, W.J. "On the Theory of Oligopoly." *Economica* 25 (1958): 187-198.

Baumol, W.J. *Business Behavior, Value and Growth.* New York: Harcourt, Brace and World, 1967.

Berg, N.A. "What's Different About Conglomerate Management?" *Harvard Business Review* 47(6) (1969): 112-120.

Berg, N.A. "Corporate Role in Diversified Companies." In *Business Policy: Teaching and Research,* pp. 298-347. Edited by B. Taylor and K. MacMillen. New York: Halstead, 1973.

Bettman, J.R., and Weitz, B.A. "Attribution in the Boardroom: Causal Reasoning in Corporate Annual Reports." *Administrative Science Quarterly* 28 (1983): 165-183.

Carlson, R.O. *Executive Succession and Organizational Change.* Danville, IL: Interstate Printers and Publishers, 1962.

Ciscel, D.H., and Carroll, T.M. "The Determinants of Executive Salaries: An Econometric Survey." *Review of Economics and Statistics* 62 (1980): 7-13.

Cyert, R.E., and March, J.G. *A Behavioral Theory of the Firm.* Englewood Cliffs, NJ: Prentice-Hall, 1983.

Dearden, J. "How to Make Incentive Plans Work." *Harvard Business Review* 50(4) (1972): 117-124.

Deckop, J.R., and Mahoney, T.A. "The Economics of Executive Compensation." Paper presented at the 42nd meeting of the National Academy of Management, New York, NY, 1982.

"Executives Face Change in Awarding of Pay, Stock Options." *Wall Street Journal* 28 February 1986, p. 33.

Goodman, P.S., and Pennings, J.M. *New Perspectives on Organizational Effectiveness.* San Francisco, CA: Jossey-Bass, 1977.

Govindarajan, V., and Gupta, A. "Linking Control Systems to Business Unit Strategy: Impact on Performance." *Accounting, Organization and Society* 10(1) (1985): 51-66.

Helmich, D.L., and Brown, W.B. "Successor Type and Organizational Change in the Corporate Enterprise." *Administrative Science Quarterly* 17 (1972): 371-381.

Kerr, J., and Snow, C.C. "Corporate Strategies and Rewards: A Conceptual Framework." Paper presented at the 40th meeting of the National Academy of Management, Detroit, MI, 1980.

Kraus, D. "The 'Devaluation' of the American Executive." *Harvard Business Review* 54(3) (1976): 84-94.

Lawler, E.E. *Motivation in Work Organizations.* Monterey, CA: Brooks-Cole, 1973.

Lewellen, W., and Huntsman, B. "Managerial Pay and Corporate Performance." *American Economic Review* 60 (1972): 710-720.

Loomis, C. "Archie McCardell's Absolution." *Fortune* 15 December 1980, pp. 85-94.

Loomis, C. "The Madness of Executive Compensation." *Fortune* 12 July 1982, pp. 42-52.

Masson, R.T. "Executive Motivations, Earnings, and Consequent Equity Performance." *Journal of Political Economy* 81 (1971): 1278-1292.

McGuire, J.W., Chiu, J.S.Y., and Elbing, A.O. "Executive Incomes, Sales, and Profits." *American Economic Review* 52 (1962): 753-761.

Metz, T., and Hughey, A. "Marietta and Bendix Reach New Accord." *Wall Street Journal* 24 September 1982, p. 3.

Meyers, K.A. "Why Companies Lose Their Best People—And What To Do About It." *Business Horizons* 24(2) (1981): 42-45.

Miller, D.T., and Ross, M. "Self-serving Biases in Attribution of Causality: Fact or Fiction?" *Psychological Bulletin* 82 (1975): 213-255.

Mintzberg, H. "A New Look at the Chief Execuitve's Job." *Organizational Dynamics* 1(3) (1983): 20-30.

Morrison, A. "Those Executive Bailout Deals." *Fortune* 13 December 1982, pp. 92-87.

Murphy, K.J. "Corporate Performance and Managerial Renumeration: An Empirical Analysis." *Journal of Accounting and Economics* 7(1) (1985): 1-32.

Murthy, K.R., and Salter, M. "Should CEO Pay Be Linked to Results?" *Harvard Business Review* 53(3) (1975): 66-73.

Patton, A. "Those Million-Dollar-a-Year Executives." *Harvard Business Review* 63(1) (1985): 56-62.

Pfeffer, J. "Size and Composition of Corporate Board of Directors: The Organization and Its Environment." *Administrative Science Quarterly* 17 (1972): 2181-228.

Pfeffer, J. "Cooptation and the Composition of Electrical Utility Boards of Directors." *Pacific Sociological Review* 17 (1974): 333-363.

Pfeffer, J. *Power in Organizations*. Marshfield, MA: Pitman, 1981.

Pitts, R.A. "Incentive Compensation and Organizational Design." *Personnel Journal* 53 (1974): 338-348.

Pondy, L. "Leadership Is a Language Game." In *Leadership: Where Else Can We Go?*, pp. 87-99. Edited by M.W. McCall, Jr. and M. Lombardo. Durham, N.C: Duke University Press, 1978.

Poster, C.Z. "Executive Compensation: Taking Long-Term Incentives Out of the Corporate Ivory Tower." *Compensation Review* 17(2) (1985): 20-31.

Prasad, S.B. "Top Management Compensation and Corporate Performance." *Academy of Management Journal* 17 (1974): 554-558.

Rappaport, A. "Executive Incentives vs. Corporate Growth." *Harvard Business Review* 59(3) (1981): 139-149.

Rappaport, A. "Selecting Strategies that Create Shareholder Value." *Harvard Business Review* 61(5) (1983): 49-62.

Rich, J.T., and Larson, J.A. "Why Some Long-Term Incentives Fail." *Compensation Review* 16(1) (1984): 26-37.

Roberts, D.R. *Executive Compensation*. Glencoe, IL: Free Press, 1959.

Roche, G. "Compensation and the Mobile Executive. *Harvard Business Review* 53(6) (1975): 53-62.

Rock, R. "Pay For Performance: Accent on Standards and Measures." *Compensation Review* 16(3) (1984): 15-36.

Rowan, R. "Rekindling Corporate Loyalty." *Fortune* 9 February 1981, pp. 54-58.

Rowan, R., and Moore, T. "Behind the Lines in the Bendix War." *Fortune* 18 October 1982, pp. 156-163.

Rumelt, R. *Strategy, Structure, and Economic Performance*. Boston, MA: Harvard Business School, 1974.

Salancik, G.R., and Meindl, J.R. "Corporate Attributions as Strategic Illusions of Management Control." *Administrative Science Quarterly* 29 (1984): 238-254.

Salter, M. "Tailor Incentive Compensation to Strategy." *Harvard Business Review* 51(2) (1973): 94-102.

Schendel, D.E., and Hofer, C.W. *Strategic Management*. Boston, MA: Little, Brown, 1979.

Smyth, D.J., Boyes, W.J., and Peseau, D.E. *Size, Growth, Profits, and Executive Compensation in the Large Corporation*. New York: Holmes and Meier, 1975.

Snyder, M.L., Stephen, W.G., and Rosenfield, D. "Attribtuional Egotism." In *New Directions in Attribtion Research*, pp. 91-117. Edited by J.H. Harvey, W.J. Ickes, and R.F. Kidd. Hillsdale, NJ: Lawrence Erlbaum, 1973.

Starbuck, W.H., Greve, A., and Hedberg, B.L.T. "Responding to Crises." *Journal Business Administration* 9 (1978): 111-137.

Starbuck, W.H., and Hedberg, B.L.T. "Saving an Organization from a Stagnating Environment." In *Strategy + Structure* = Performance, pp. 249-258. Edited by H.B. Thorelli. Bloomington, IN: Indiana University Press, 1977.

Stata, R., and Maidique, M.A. "Bonus System for a Balanced Strategy." *Harvard Business Review* 58(6) (1980): 156-163.

Staw, B.M. "Rationality and Justification in Organization Life." In *Research in Organizational Behavior*, pp. 2:45-80. Edited by B.M Staw and L.L. Cummings. Greenwich, CT: JAI Press, 1980.

Staw, B.M., McKechnie, P.I., and Puffer S.M. "The Justification of Organizational Performance." *Administrative Science Quarterly* 28 (1983): 582-600.

Steers, R.M. *Organizational Effectiveness.* Santa Monica, CA: Goodyear Publishing Company, 1977.

Steers, R.M., and Porter, L.W. *Motivation and Work Behavior.* New York: McGraw-Hill, 1983.

Stonich, P.J. "Using Rewards in Implementing Strategy." *Strategic Management Journal* 2 (1981): 345-352.

Ungson, G.R., and Steers, R.M. "Motivation and Politics in Executive Compensation." *Academy of Management Review* 9(2) (1984): 313-323.

Wallace, M.J. "Impact of Type of Control and Industrial Concentration on Size and Profitability in Determination of Executive Income." Ph.D. dissertation, University of Minnesota, 1973.

Weick, K.E. "Cognitive Processes in Organizations." In *Research in Organizational Behavior*, Vol. 1, pp. 41-74. Edited by B.M. Staw. Greenwich, CT: JAI Press, 1979.

Williams, M.J. "Why Chief Executives' Pay Keeps Rising." *Fortune* 1, April 1985, pp. 66-76.

Zuckerman, M. "Attribution of Success and Failure Revisited, or: The Motivational Bias is Alive and Well in Attribution Theory." *Journal of Personality* 47 (1979): 245-287.

PART II

EXECUTIVE BEHAVIOR IN CONTEXT

EXECUTIVE LEADERSHIP AND ORGANIZATIONAL OUTCOMES:
AN EVOLUTIONARY PERSPECTIVE

Elaine Romanelli and Michael L. Tushman

Macro organizational theory on organization performance increasingly emphasizes the dynamic character of evolving organization-environment fits. As discussed by Miles (1982), however, the field has split in its theoretical assessment of how ongoing alignments are accomplished—i.e., whether firms can adapt to changing environmental conditions through alteration of basic patterns in strategic, structural, and cultural activities (Child, 1972; Galbraith, 1977; Schendel and Hofer, 1979; Andrews, 1980) or whether inertial tendencies of organizations contribute to a primarily external control of outcomes (Hannan and Freeman, 1977; Pfeffer and Salancik, 1978; Aldrich, 1979).

One major point of theoretical controversy revolves around the extent to which leaders can influence performance outcomes. Traditional perspectives argue that leaders have significant impact on performance through influencing patterns in communication (Barnard, 1938), commitment (Selznick, 1957), and strategy and structure (Chandler, 1962; Child, 1972). More recent discussions emphasize the constraining properties of internal and external resource exchange activities (Hannan and Freeman, 1977; Pfeffer and Salancik, 1978; Pfeffer, 1981) and the power of institutionalized norms and values to sustain established activity patterns over time (Zucker, 1977; Hannan and Freeman, 1984). These factors inhibit the ability of executives to influence or alter the course of organization activity.

This chapter examines evidence from both perspectives to argue that executive leaders can and do implement decisions about the content and character of organizational activity, and that the nature and timing of these decisions have substantive consequences for performance outcomes. A dynamic perspective on processes of ongoing organization-environment alignments helps organize understanding of competing environmental and organizational pressures for change and inertia in organizations. A metamorphosis model of organization evolution (Starbuck, 1965; Miller and Friesen, 1984; Tushman and Romanelli, 1985) provides a basis for examining the role of executive leadership in mediating those pressures.

Specifically, we propose that, where environments are relatively constant and performance outcomes remain satisfactory, the core task of leadership is to sustain ideological commitment to established patterns of activity. Where environments are changing and/or performance outcomes are low or declining, leadership's primary task is to intervene on ongoing patterns of commitment and exchange to redirect the character of an organization's relationship with its environment. Performance consequences of attending or not attending appropriately to these different domains of organizational activity are discussed.

EXECUTIVE LEADERSHIP AND ORGANIZATIONAL OUTCOMES: A CRITICAL REVIEW

Executive leadership is one of the most intuitive and persistently researched of topics in organization theory and behavior. The majority of studies have been conducted at the small-group or subunit level of analysis and findings are inconsistent if not downright contradictory (Pfeffer, 1977). The situation is little better at the macro or total organization levels of analysis, though research is far less extensive (McCall and Lombardo, 1978).

This section reviews three bodies of literature that examine the relationship of executive leadership to organizational outcomes. Stewardship and succession studies shed light on the influence of leadership, on average, on performance outcomes. Case histories of organization creation and change reveal possible patterns in leader decisions and behaviors that affect systems of organization activity. Our review emphasizes differences in research questions across the research streams that variously illuminate when and how leaders may influence the course of organizational activity.

The Stewardship Studies

Stewardship studies seek to assess relative influences of external environments, organizational characteristics, and leadership on organizational performance outcomes. Leadership is measured as the period of incumbency of the top executive of a firm, thus the term stewardship. Researchers argue that if leaders are generally able to influence performance outcomes, then on average a significant relationship between the periods of their stewardship and performance outcomes should be found. Pfeffer (1977; 1981), along with others, cites results from these studies as evidence that leaders exercise relatively little influence over performance outcomes as compared with environmental and organizational conditions.

Lieberson and O'Connor (1972) conducted perhaps the seminal study of relative effects of leaders and environments on performance outcomes. Using a sample of 167 firms over a 20-year period, they apportioned variance in organizational performance to the effects of three criterion variables: *environments,* measured as year and industry to express differences in general economic and competitive conditions; *organizations,* using a dummy company variable to express differences in organizational size, location, supplier relationships, and so on; and *leadership,* measured as the period of an executive's tenure in the top managerial position. Profit, sales, and profit margin were used as measures of performance. Results showed contributions in the following ranges: 23 percent to 68 percent for company; 19 percent to 29 percent for industry: 7 percent to 15 percent for stewardship; and 2 percent to 3 percent for year. Salancik and Pfeffer (1977) conducted a similar analysis with respect to budget variance in 30 cities over 18 years and obtained similar results. Variance in the budget was accounted for 55 percent to 91 percent by city, 3 percent to 17 percent by year, and 7 percent to 15 percent by mayor. Pfeffer (1977; 1981) has argued that the findings indicate that environments, to a far greater extent than leaders, control the outcomes of organization activity.

Weiner (1978) conducted a replication of the Liberson and O'Connor study, arguing that predictor variables used in the analysis were not independent and that findings could thus be due merely to an order of entry effect. On a different sample, using precisely the same methodology as Lieberson and O'Connor, Weiner also found stewardship to account for only a small portion of variance in performance measures. However, when the order in which the criterion variables were entered was changed, stewardship jumped dramatically to account for 75 percent to 95 percent of variance across the three performance measures. In an effort to correct some of these problems, Weiner and Mahoney (1981) then developed specific measures of general economic and industrial conditions and assessed their effects on performance via multiple regression. Using a sample of 193 firms over a 19-year period, only organizational size was found to be significantly related to performance, and this only when performance was measured as absolute profit. Weiner and Mahoney had no data to specify any characteristics of leadership. However, when residuals from these regressions were analyzed with respect to stewardship, amount of variance explained jumped substantially.

Unfortunately, stewardship is correlated with other hypothesized influence variables and thus remains difficult to interpret. It coincides temporally with leadership tenure and thus *may* represent the effects of individual executives on performance. Tenure also corresponds, however, with particular periods of organizational history and environments. These studies do not sufficiently specify conditions of environment, characteristics of organizational activity, or decisions and behaviors of executives as they may affect these characteristics to distinguish among the various effects. We are left with an intriguing question regarding the origins of intercorrelation among these possible influences.

Succession Studies

Research on executive succession, in essence, constitutes the flip side of stewardship. Rather than assess the relationship of an executive's incumbency to performance, this research examines the influence of a change in executive on change in performance. Again, the key question centers on assessment of leaders' effects on performance on average. Though environment is less specified here than in the stewardship studies, effects of organizational history are much better indicated because of the longitudinal character of the analyses.

The majority of studies in this vein compare organizational performance outcomes during the period immediately prior to a succession event with those immediately following, usually one year in both cases. Results typically show little effect of a change in executive on performance outcomes, at least in the near term (Grusky, 1963; Gamson and Scotch, 1964; Eitzen and Yetman, 1972). Studies that have examined other potential explanatory variables—e.g., successor origin, personnel turnover—also consistently reveal prior term performance to be the best predictor of post-succession performance (Allen, Panian and Lotz, 1979; Brown, 1982). Additionally, the rate of succession in an organization over time has been found to be inversely related to performance (Helmich, 1978; Brown, 1982). Grusky (1963) has discussed the disruptive effects of executive succession on organizational activity patterns.

These findings, along with those from the stewardship studies, have contributed to current questioning of traditional assumptions regarding leader effects on organizational outcomes. Pfeffer (1981) has suggested that the predominant influence of leadership falls within the symbolic as opposed to substantive domain of organizational activity. Managers, he argues, play an important role of providing explanations that legitimate patterns of activity. Others suggest that leadership is largely an *attributed* cause of organizational outcomes deriving (1) from the needs of managers to demonstrate the efficacy of their actions and thus justify their incumbencies (Bettman and Weitz, 1983; Staw, McKechnie and Puffer, 1983) and (2) from a more general cognitive tendency of people to attribute causality to individuals where events are highly complex and relationships are very interdependent (Pfeffer, 1981; Salanick and Meindl, 1984; Meindl, Ehrlich and Dukerich, 1985).

These studies shed additional light on the process and meaning of leadership in organizations. Before we extrapolate from the research, however, that leaders in fact cannot influence substantive organizational outcomes, three additional factors must be considered.

First, the succession studies, like the stewardship studies, examine mainly performance as the organizational outcome against which leader effects should be observed. They do not specify decisions and policies of executives that may affect activity patterns or, through this effect, performance outcomes. If we assume simply that executives may rightly *or* wrongly attempt to intervene on ongoing activity patterns, and that their decisions about implementing either a change or sustainment are variably correct with respect to conditions of environments, then a finding of little leadership influence on performance outcomes, *on average,* should be expected.

Second, the studies usually examine post-succession performance at most one year following the succession event. Reasonably, we would expect decisions and policies of executives to take time to influence either activity patterns or performance. Studies of senior executive time in office and organization performance indicate the relationship to be positive (Eitzen and Yetman, 1972; Salancik and Pfeffer, 1980). Though this result might be explained by a general regression to the mean effect (Gamson and Scotch, 1974), other investigators have found the relationship to be significantly moderated by conditions of environment and distributions of ownership (Pfeffer and Salancik, 1977; Salancik and Pfeffer, 1980). Apparently, different conditions of environments and organizational history influence the extent to which executives may be able to influence a change over time.

A final stream of succession research examines how differences in successor characteristics may be related to different degrees and kinds of post-succession organizational change. Helmich and Brown (1972) found outsider successors far more likely to implement changes in organizational activity patterns than insiders. Helmich (1977) has discussed the greater need of outsider successors to establish a quick and firm impression of authority. Staw, Sandelands, and Dutton (1981) point out how the commitments of insider successors to policies and politics of the ongoing organization inhibit their engaging in major change or even perceiving the need for it. Pfeffer and Salancik (1977) and Virany, Tushman and Romanelli (1985) have shown how different characteristics of pre-succession organization moderate the type of successor most likely to be installed.

Studies of succession, to a far greater extent than studies of stewardship, indicate that executive leaders on average exercise little direct influence over performance outcomes of organization. The succession literature also indicates, however, that conditions of succession—both environmental and organizational—seem to moderate the extent to which successors are likely or able to intervene on ongoing activity patterns. Before we conclude that the concept of leadership is primarily a "romance" (Meindl et al., 1985) engaged in by researchers and managers to explain what is complex, research must examine whether and how executive leaders may influence patterns of activity through decisions, policies, and behaviors, and when different kinds of decisions and behaviors will be most appropriate.

Case Histories

Case histories of organizations have been conducted to expose the workings of many organizational processes, including commitment (Selznick, 1949), power and politics (Pettigrew, 1973), creation (Kimberly, 1980), and decline (Harrigan, 1980). Research questions typically center on how and whether organizations respond to changing environmental conditions or, in the case of creation, to conditions for the first time. Like the stewardship and succession literatures, case studies consider that environments play a key role in signalling some need for activity by organizations. In this research, however, investigators focus on specific conditions of environments and specific responses of organizations, particularly as they are guided by the decisions and behaviors of executive leaders.

A note on the case history method and our treatment of this literature is warranted. Though the histories we review below typically attribute an effect of leadership on performance outcomes, and cases may even be chosen on the basis of this attribution, we review it here only for its evidence that executives may, under some circumstances, affect activity patterns. The problems of generalizing from case literature are well known. We believe, however, that this literature currently stands as the sole body of research that has examined the relationship of executive leader behaviors and decisions to characteristics of organizational activity. We review it here for what it may tell us about directions for more rigorous research.

Studies by Selznick (1949) on the formation and early development of the Tennessee Valley Authority and by Kimberly (1980) on the establishment of a new and innovative medical school provide rich data for examining the influence of founding executive leadership on organizational activity patterns. In each instance, the authors offer extensive detail on the contexts of these foundations. Creation of the TVA occurred in the midst of strong political pressures to decentralize government provision of services. Kimberly's medical school was founded amid apprehensions about a shortage of doctors in the mid-1970s and concerns about public dissatisfaction with trends toward specialization in modern medicine.

Against these backgrounds, the authors examine the backgrounds of founders—how their particular experiences and peculiaristic world views combined to make them both the chosen and the choosers of organizational innovation—as well as the specific set of activities these men pursued to get their organizations underway. A.E. Morgan was selected by Franklin Roosevelt as the first chairman of the TVA board precisely because he symbolized an autonomy from government processes that was to characterize this organizational experiment. Once in place as Chairman, however, Morgan personally established TVA policies of local governance and small administration and selected other members of the governing board (most particularly, H.A. Morgan). These substantive activities at once directed the conduct of TVA administration and symbolized the innovative character of the enterprise. H.A. Morgan, because of his political ties to the land grant college system, established a network of relationships with these entities that further defined the structural design of the TVA administration. The founder of Kimberly's medical school was selected for somewhat similar reasons: he symbolized, by his background and well-known aversion to current medical education practices, that a new thing was to be tried. Again, however, his personal decisions about how to accomplish the innovation— e.g., apprenticeship for students, minimal bureaucracy, involvement of local doctors in college administration—established the course of substantive activity for the school.

Studies of organization creation raise two points about the effects of executive leadership on organizational outcomes. First, while conditions of environments influence both the fact and nature of organizational foundations (Carroll and Delacroix, 1983), founders retain significant choice regarding specific strategic and structural attributes of the new ventures. Apprenticeship was not the only model of innovation that Kimberly's medical school founder could have followed. A.E. Morgan was in no way restricted to establishment of a small group administrative structure, and indeed he faced considerable resistance to its implementation. Decisions by these executives substantively governed the kind of organization that was to be founded and thus affected organizational abilities to cope with conditions of environments.

Second, the studies indicate that effects of founders' decisions and behaviors extended far into the organizations' lives. TVA has retained its small group administrative structure as well as its close ties with local land grant colleges. Kimberly describes how the medical school retained its emphasis on apprenticeship as the model of innovative medical education despite pressures from external environments toward greater bureaucratization over time. The values and visions of the founding executives established a system of beliefs and norms that guided hiring, training and socialization of employees into the future.

This major effect of original, creating decisions on later patterns of organizational activity testifies to the influence that leaders can have on organizational outcomes and underscores the role of organizational history in influencing the degree of effect that executives can have later in an organization's life. Numerous authors have described how this influence of early history constrains patterns in organizational activity over time even as major changes in strategy and structure are implemented (Miles and Snow, 1978; Brittain and Freeman, 1980; McKelvey, 1982; Miles, 1982). Case histories of change help specify the nature of this role, as well as characteristics of leader decisions and behaviors that may best cope with this constraining influence.

Countless researchers have chronicled processes of organizational change (or absence of change) and the role of leadership in influencing change. Possibly best known is Chandler's (1962) analysis of the transitions of four firms from single to multiproduct businesses through implementation of multidivisionalized forms. Though cited primarily for his finding of "structure follows strategy," Chandler's explicit intent was to conduct a comparative analysis of administrative innovation in response to changing environmental conditions. For each duPont, Sears, General Motors, and Standard Oil, Chandler describes how environmental conditions rendered ongoing systems and strategies of these companies increasingly ineffective and how executives translated their "visions" for the future (Pettigrew, 1979) into major strategic and structural reorientations. For example, Pierre duPont (an insider successor) and his executive committee explicitly recognized that the conclusion of World War I would cause a dramatic decline in demand for explosives, the company's principal product line. Funds were allocated to develop new product lines and the company was radically reorganized to support these basic diversifications. Chandler's work on Sears, which is paralleled by a study by Stryker (1961), describes that company's fairly fast shift from primary activity in the mail order catalog business to establishment of a chain of department stores. Though the need for this change was signalled by declines in the mail order business, the substantive activities of the organization were altered according to the vision and policies of an executive.

Miles' (1982) analysis of cigarette manufacturers' diversification responses to publicity about the cancer-causing effects of tobacco shows as well how the perceptions and decisions of senior executives affect substantive characteristics of organization. In comparing acquisition, divestiture and performance outcomes of the six major tobacco firms over time, however, he also reveals how executives were constrained by earlier functional competences of the firms and how adherence to those competences affected later performance outcomes (see also Rumelt, 1974). Previously developed competences were tied, in Miles' analysis, to characteristics and decisions of earlier executives. Clark's (1970) analysis of the origins and evolution of Reed, Antioch, and Swarthmore liberal arts colleges similarly attests to the constraining influence of organizational pasts and attributes major changes in the character of those colleges to periodic interventions by executives.

These histories emphasize largely substantive interventions by executives on ongoing organizational activity patterns. Others have emphasized executive influence on symbolic outcomes as critical supports to substantive intervention. Kaufman (1960) has described how Gifford Pinchot, "father" of the U.S. Forest Service, radically altered the character of the organization by supporting major interventions on ongoing activity patterns with massive programs of training and socialization. Sills (1980) describes how executives at the YMCA and the American National Red Cross implemented basic changes in the activities of those organizations by communicating that the superordinate goals of the associations were unchanged. The YMCA replaced Christian evangelism with betterment in the health, morals, and social affiliation of young adults as the mission of the organization. At the Red Cross, a blood donor program was initiated and sustained on the premise that the principles and satisfactions of volunteerism easily encompassed far more than war and disaster relief. Clark (1972) and Sayles (1979) discuss the power of substantive decisions and interventions to symbolize the advent of a new order.

These few case histories of creation and change indicate that executive leaders can, under some conditions, powerfully direct or redirect the course of an organization's activity. Though environments pose threats to organizational existence that should signal some response by organizations, they do not dictate the response. Though characteristics of organizations constrain the form of activity or intervention that can perform well, they do not preclude change. The perceptions and responses of executives in firms influence what the course of an organization's activity will be.

CONDITIONS AND CHARACTERISTICS
OF EXECUTIVE INFLUENCE

Research on executive leadership and organizational outcomes indicates three factors to be critical to understanding how and under what conditions executives may effectively disrupt or sustain a course of organizational activity. First, environments pose critical contingencies that control the performance outcomes of organizations, *given* a pattern of organizational activity. Second, established patterns of activity constrain the nature of activity that can be accomplished feasibly in the future. Third, the decisions, backgrounds, and policies of executives influence patterns of activities under some conditions. Both the nature and timing of executive influence are important.

The metamorphosis model of organization evolution (Starbuck, 1965; Miller and Friesen, 1980; Tushman and Romanelli, 1985) helps organize understanding of how these complex factors interact over the course of an organization's history to create conditions that are more or less appropriate to executive intervention, and that are more or less constraining. Pfeffer's (1981) general classification of organizational outcomes into substantive and symbolic domains of activity suggests how we may characterize leader decisions and policies to examine different processes of influence on maintenance or change of activity patterns. Each of these are briefly reviewed here.

The Metamorphosis Model

As outlined by Miller and Friesen (1984) and Tushman and Romanelli (1985), the metamorphosis model of organization evolution attends simultaneously to dynamics of inertia and processes of change that influence the course of an organization's development over time. Organizations establish, during creation, a basic orientation toward the conduct of internal and external, political and economic exchanges that is revealed in patterns in strategic, structural, and normative activity (Zald, 1970). Negotiation of critical exchange relationships establishes a system of interdependencies and related power distributions that inhibit flexibility in decision-making and response patterns (Pfeffer and Salancik, 1978; Pfeffer, 1980). As organizations develop socially constructed understandings about appropriate behaviors in a context, and as valuations of established responses become institutionalized, the extent to which organizational members will even perceive a need for flexibility or change is reduced (Zucker, 1977; Staw et al., 1981). So long as performance remains high or acceptable to organization members, and so long as environments continue to select the established pattern of activities, convergent processes are expected to feed and build toward ever tighter systems of support for the developed orientation.

Should the established activity pattern be revealed to be ineffective, however, whether due to sustained low performance or major change in environmental conditions, a pressure for change emerges. As a consequence of exchange dependencies and power distributions that inhibit alteration of established relationships, and depending on the degree to which these have become institutionalized, change in the activity patterns must be of a radical and discontinuous nature, i.e., metamorphic. Only through the rapid disruption of ongoing relationships, across many or all levels and domains of activity, can inertia be mitigated.

Empirical evidence in support of the metamorphosis model is beginning to mount. Miller and Friesen (1984) show that change attempts are more successful where more rapid and radical interventions occur. Tushman and Romanelli (1985) find that major reorientations in fact do occur where performance outcomes are low or environments change drastically. These findings are independent of whether the content or direction of change is subsequently successful. However, preliminary evidence suggests that firms that are more successful over long time periods restrict their major reorientations to responding to environmental change. Lower performing firms appear to disrupt activity patterns frequently or only in response to performance crisis (Tushman and Romanelli, 1985).

The metamorphosis model describes an empirically observable pattern of progress or evolution at the macro-organizational level of analysis. The model's focus on inertia-producing factors in organizations and environments and its consequent proposal for change of a metamorphic nature directs attention to questions of how interruptions on ongoing patterns can be accomplished.

Substantive and Symbolic Domains of Activity

As discussed throughout the above reviews, if we are to separate out relative influences of environments, organizations, and leadership on organizational outcomes, direct research attention must be paid to the content of leader decision behaviors and to the relationship of these decisions and behaviors to characteristics of organizational activity. Pfeffer (1981) has usefully characterized domains of organizational activity in terms of substantive and symbolic. Substantive refers to those outcomes of organizational activity that have physical referents. These include such characteristics as performance, budget allocations, and the distribution of personnel across functional areas. Symbolic refers to outcomes pertaining to beliefs, attitudes, and values of organizational members.

Fairly straightforwardly, executive decisions and behaviors can be categorized as attempting to influence substantive and/or symbolic outcomes, keeping in mind only that substantive decisions and behaviors often carry strong symbolic overtones. Though little empirical work has been conducted to classify formal types or domains of leader activities, these categories map nicely onto those suggested by Thompson (1967), Mintzberg (1973), and Tsui and Karwan (1985). Each of these authors describes patterns of behavior that either direct the content of organizational activities or support the attitudes and values of organizational members. The parsimony of the substantive/symbolic scheme for classifying domains of activity and outcomes leaves open the way for generalization across companies and time periods where the specific content of activities and decisions will vary. The nature and timing of leadership influence can be examined against the backdrop of evolving organizational and environmental pressures.

EXECUTIVES LEADERSHIP AND ORGANIZATION EVOLUTION

This section builds on the metamorphosis model of organization evolution to consider how the decisions and behaviors of executive leaders may serve either to sustain or reorient patterns in organization activity, and the conditions under which different types of behaviors will be more or less appropriate.

Leadership Influence on Convergence

As described above, periods of convergence in organizations are those in which previously initiated strategies, structures, processes and core values are refined and institutionalized. Strategies and structures already in place possess a distinct dynamism that propels the organization forward largely of its own accord. Rules, hierarchy, and tradition, established earlier in the organization's life, serve to ensure that the substantive work of the organization gets done within a set of guidelines embodied in strategies and structures (see Downs' [1967] discussion of dynamic conservatism). To the extent that executive leadership is complacent about the effectiveness of ongoing activity systems, they need not (and typically will not) engage directly in substantive behaviors to control them.

The same is not true of symbolic behaviors. During convergent periods, relative to periods of reorientation, effective leader decisions and behaviors will be directed primarily toward the symbolic outcomes of organization existence. Because new persons are constantly entering the organization and because people already participating are exposed to more diverse stimuli than those provided by the organization alone, the leader cannot relax vigilance with respect to symbolic outcomes. Legitimation, explanation, and rationalization, as well as incremental substantive decisions, are constant requirements of executive leadership during convergent periods (Barnard, 1938; Kaufman, 1960; Neustadt, 1980).

Note that as described by the metamorphosis model, convergent periods are much longer than reorientations. Where successful, symbolic supports for activity will be embodied throughout systems of organizational activity and belief, which themselves reinforce socially-constructed understandings. These factors may partially account for findings of little leader effect on organizational outcomes, attributed or otherwise.

Primary attention to symbolism when the organization fits well with its environment may affect performance outcomes on several counts. First, smooth organizational functioning requires a fair degree of consensus about legitimate goals, values, and resource allocations as well as widespread adherence to norms governing outlooks and behaviors (March and Simon, 1958). Consensus, while it reduces the potential for disruptive conflict, also serves as an efficient and unobtrusive socializing mechanism that reinforces policies and communications from executives (Katz, 1980). Second, commitment of employees to continued participation in the firm ensures that the firm can retain investments in and dependencies on training and skills. Finally, though reorientations may sometimes be successful under these conditions, radical disruption of ongoing systems is difficult and risky even during the worst of times. Where commitments to old and apparently effective patterns are well-entrenched, rationalization and legitimation of major changes in those patterns may be impossible. The result of an attempt may be no reorientation and a substantial decline in commitment to previous patterns.

Leadership Influence on Reorientation

Should environments change so as to threaten the efficacy of established alignments, or should performance be deemed generally inadequate, the organization must alter its pattern of activity or fail. Leaders have their most profound and important influence on organizational outcomes where pressures for change emerge. First, a perception of current or impending difficulty is necessary. Second, some substantive intervention on ongoing activity patterns will have to occur.

Inertial processes operate to reduce the probability that problems will be accurately perceived and/or acted upon (Staw et al., 1981; Kiesler and Sproull, 1982). The longer the prior convergent period, and the more successful and older the organization, the more these inertial processes operate to insulate and uncouple executive leadership from the organization's competitive environment (Boswell, 1973; Hall, 1976). We expect, in most cases, that executives will institute a reorientation when events have already transpired to reveal the need for change. Performance declines constitute strong signals of organizationenvironment misalignment. It is the mark of inspired executive leadership to recognize *impending* need for change. Regardless, because of inertial properties of organization, direct intervention is necessary if change is to occur.

In order to implement a major change, executive leadership must engage actively in *both* substantive and symbolic behaviors. Existing distributions of power that support ongoing exchange relationships must be disrupted and new exchange patterns must be implemented. Commitments to previous ways of doing things must be replaced with newly rationalized objectives. These not only legitimate the particular changes being implemented but also the need for change in the first place (Normann, 1977).

Executive intervention on ongoing activity systems, where signals indicate that the basic character of an organization's relationship to its environment is changing for the worse, also relate to performance in several ways. First and most simply, failure to initiate either substantive or symbolic changes in organization activity patterns will result ultimately in an overall failure of the organization. It is problematic whether or how long organizations can survive with essentially ineffective patterns of activity for a context (Aldrich, 1979). Organizations may possess sufficient slack resources to "fund" a decline in performance for indefinite periods. Some organizations, like elementary schools, may be so imbued with value in the general society that any level of performance is accepted over no performance. Regardless, sustained lack of response to changing environmental conditions should lead to the final demise and death of an organization.

More interesting to our argument here is examination of performance outcomes arising from a failure to attend *simultaneously* to both substantive and symbolic domains. We argued above that to attempt a reorientation where conditions of environment are stable and performance outcomes are acceptable leads to a fundamental break in trust between executives and organizational members. Rationalizations are tougher to sell when performance signals the efficacy on ongoing systems. Here we argue that not to institute some basic changes in activity patterns leads to a decline in the commitment of employees to ongoing systems and a failure of old or makeshift rationalizations. Performance declines can be dismissed as temporary only for so long.

Substantive intervention on existing patterns of organizational activity makes an attempt to establish a new basis of alignment with environments and, at the same time, signals to employees and external parties that the organization possesses some basic viability. Simply, employees, stockholders, and external exchange partners can rationalize that some action, possibly any action, is better than continued decline in performance. Action alone should generate at least some commitment to continued participation in the firm and to "trying" this new way. As discussed earlier in this chapter, substantive actions carry symbolic content.

Because the new way is untested, however, and because some factions of the organization will seek to sustain old patterns of activity, it is essential that new rationales for the new behaviors be promoted. Though performance decline may generate some commitment to attempt a change, it will not produce commitment to specific patterns in activity. Attention to symbolic outcomes that are specific to the new patterns in activity is required to develop consensus about the basic legitimacy and efficacy of the new patterns and to foster adherence to norms of behavior in the new situation. Failure to rationalize the activities will result in conflict among employees and subunits of the organization that inhibits any re-establishment of normal activity.

Regardless of whether the character of the reorientation is "correct" with respect to environmental conditions, and we do not argue that it will be, failure to act and failure to legitimate actions, at the same time, will lead to a prolonged period of organizational disruption. Disruptions produce uncertainties about the core coherency and legitimacy of organizational activity. These themselves will ultimately generate a performance decline. A vicious circle emerges (Masuch, 1985).

CONCLUSION

This chapter has examined literature on the relationship of executive leadership to organizational outcomes to argue that senior managers can and do substantively affect the content and character of organization activity. Conditions of environment govern the nature of organizational activity pattern that will prove most effective. Characteristics of organizations constrain the form of new activity pattern than can feasibly be adopted. Executive leaders, however, determine whether a new pattern will be attempted and what the nature of the pattern will be. Performance accrues as a result of the timing of these decisions as well as their content. Building on a metamorphosis model of organization evolution, we have proposed a pattern in decisions and behaviors of executives that can mediate conflicting pressures in organizations for inertia and change.

We would like to close with two points regarding directions for future research and implications for managers. First, nothing is guaranteed in our arguments that executives will necessarily behave appropriately to sustain or reorient patterns in organizational activity. Research that specifies characteristics of leader behavior and relates them systematically to conditions faced by a firm and to performance outcomes remains to be conducted. We have tried to suggest an approach that is consistent with existing theory and research.

Second, nothing is guaranteed that substantive reorientations will necessarily succeed. The large and growing body of research that examines the content of relationships between conditions of environments and characteristics of organizational activity sheds light on performance consequences of activity patterns. We have emphasized here the general nature and timing of executive leader influence on organizational activities.

ACKNOWLEDGMENTS

The authors would like to thank several anonymous reviewers for critical comments on an earlier draft of this paper, as well as the Strategy Research Center, Columbia University, for assistance and support.

REFERENCES

Aldrich, H.E. *Organizations and Environments.* Englewood Cliffs, NJ: Prentice-Hall, 1979.
Allen, M.P., Panian, S.K., and Lotz, R.E. "Managerial Succession and Organizational Performance: A Recalcitrant Problem Revisited." *Administrative Science Quarterly* 24 (1979): 167-180.
Andrews, K.R. *The Concept of Corporate Strategy.* Homewood, IL: Richard D. Irwin, 1980.
Barnard, C.I. *The Functions of the Executive.* Cambridge, MA: Harvard University Press, 1938.
Bettman, J. and Weitz, B.A. "Attributions in the Board Room: Causal Reasoning in Corporate Annual Reports." *Administrative Science Quarterly* 28 (1983): 165-183.
Boswell, J. *The Rise and Fall of Small Firms.* London: Allen & Unwin, 1973.
Brittain, J., and Freeman, J.H. "Organizational Proliferation and Density Dependent Selection." In *The Organizational Life Cycle,* pp. 291-338. Edited by J.R. Kimberly and R.H. Miles. San Francisco, CA: Jossey-Bass, 1980.
Brown, M.C. "Administrative Succession and Organizational Performance: The Succession Effect." *Administrative Science Quarterly* 27 (1982): 1-16.
Carroll, G.R., and Delacroix, J. "Organizational Foundings: An Ecological Study of the Newspaper Industries of Argentina and Ireland." *Administrative Science Quarterly* 28 (1983): 274-291.
Chandler, A.D. *Strategy and Structure: Chapters in the History of American Industrial Enterprise.* Cambridge, MA: MIT Press, 1962.
Child, J. "Organization Structure, Environment and Performance: The Role of Strategic Choice." *Sociology* 6 (1972): 2-21.
Clark, B.R. *The Distinctive College: Antioch, Reed, and Swarthmore.* Chicago, IL: Aldine, 1970.
Clark, B.R. "The Organizational Saga in Higher Education." *Administrative Science Quarterly* 17 (1972): 178-184.
Downs, A. *Inside Bureaucracy.* Boston, MA: Little Brown, 1967.
Eitzen, R., and Yetman, N. "Managerial Change, Longevity, and Organizational Effectiveness." *Administrative Science Quarterly* 17 (1972): 110-116.
Galbraith, J.R. *Organization Design.* Reading, MA: Addison-Wesley Publishing Co., 1977.
Gamson, W.A., and Scotch, N.A. "Scapegoating in Baseball." *American Journal of Sociology* 70 (1964): 69-72.
Grusky, O. "Managerial Succession." *American Journal of Sociology* 49 (1963): 21-31.

Hall, R.H. "A System Pathology of an Organization: The Rise and Fall of the Old *Saturday Evening Post.*" *Administrative Science Quarterly* 21 (1976): 185-211.

Hannan, M.T., and Freeman, J.H. "The Population Ecology of Organizations." *American Journal of Sociology* 82 (1977): 929-64.

Hannan, M.T., and Freeman, J.H. "Structural Inertia and Organizational Change." *American Journal of Sociology* 49 (1984): 149-164.

Harrigan, K.R. *Strategies for Declining Businesses.* Lexington, MA: D.C. Heath, 1980.

Helmich, D.L. "Leader Flows and Organizational Process." *Academy of Management Journal* 21 (1978): 463-478.

Helmich, D.L., and Brown, W.B. "Successor Type and Organizational Change in the Corporate Enterprise." *Administrative Science Quarterly* 17 (1972): 371-381.

Katz, R. "Time and Work: Toward an Integrative Perspective." In *Research in Organizational Behavior,* Vol. 2, pp. 81-127. Edited by B. Staw. Greenwich, CT: JAI Press, 1980.

Kaufman, H. *The Forest Ranger: A Study in Administrative Behavior.* Baltimore, MD: The John Hopkins University Press, 1960.

Kiesler, S., and Sproull, L. "Managerial Response to Changing Environments: Perspectives on Problem Sensing from Social Cognition." *Administrative Science Quarterly* 27 (1982): 548-570.

Kimberly, J.R. "Initiation, Innovation and Institutionalization in the Creation Process." In *The Organizational Life Cycle,* pp. 18-43. Edited by J.R. Kimberly and R.H. Miles. San Francisco, CA: Jossey-Bass, 1980.

Lieberman, S. and O'Connor, J.F. "Leadership and Organizational Performance: A Study of Large Corporations." *American Sociological Review* 37 (1972): 117-130.

March, J.G. and Simon, H.A. *Organizations.* New York: John Wiley, 1958.

Masuch, M. "Vicious Circles in Organizations." *Administrative Science Quarterly* 30 (1985): 14-33.

McCall, M.W., Jr., and Lombardo, M.M. *Leadership: Where Else Can We Go?* Durham, NC: Duke University Press, 1978.

McKelvey, B. *Organizational Systematics.* Berkeley, CA: University of California Press, 1982.

Meindl, J.R., Ehrlich, S.B., and Dukerich, J.M. "The Romance of Leadership." *Administrative Science Quarterly* 30 (1985): 78-102.

Miles, R.F., and Snow, C.C. *Organizational Strategy, Structure and Process.* New York: McGraw Hill, 1978.

Miles, R.H. *Coffin Nails and Corporate Strategies.* Englewood Cliffs, NJ: Prentice-Hall, 1982.

Miller, D., and Friesen, P.H. *Organizations: A Quantum View.* Englewood Cliffs, NJ: Prentice-Hall, 1984.

Mintzberg, H. *The Nature of Managerial Work.* New York: Harper and Row, 1973.

Neustadt, R.E. *Presidential Power.* New York: John Wiley & Sons, 1980.

Normann, R. *Management for Growth.* New York: John Wiley & Sons, 1977.

Pettigrew, A.M. *The Politics of Organizational Decision Making.* London: Tavistock, 1973.

Pettigrew, A.M. "On Studying Organizational Cultures." *Administrative Science Quarterly* 24 (1979): 570-581.

Pfeffer, J. "The Ambiguity of Leadership." *Academy of Management Review* 2 (1977): 104-112.

Pfeffer, J. *Power in Organizations.* Marshfield, MA: Pitman Publishing, 1980.

Pfeffer, J. "Management as Symbolic Action: The Creation and Maintenance of Organizational Paradigms." In *Research in Organizational Behavior,* Vol. 3, pp. 1-52. Edited by L.L. Cummings and B.M. Staw. Greenwich, CT: JAI Press, 1981.

Pfeffer, J., and Salancik, G.R. "Organizational Context and the Characteristics and Tenures of Hospital Administrators." *Academy of Management Journal* 20 (1977): 74-88.

Pfeffer, J., and Salancik, G.R. *The External Control of Organizations: A Resource Dependence Perspective.* New York: Harper & Row, 1978.

Rumelt, R.P. *Strategy, Structure and Economic Performance*. Cambridge, MA: Harvard University Press, 1974.

Salancik, G.R., and Pfeffer, J. "Constraints on Administrator Discretion: The Limited Influence of Mayors on City Budgets." *Urban Affairs Quarterly* 12 (1977): 475-498.

Salancik, G.R., and Pfeffer, J. "Effects of Ownership and Performance on Executive Tenure in U.S. Corporations." *Academy of Management Journal* 23 (1980): 653-664.

Salancik, G.R., and Meindl, J.R. "Corporate Attributions as Strategic Illusions of Management Control." *Administrative Science Quarterly*, 29 (1984): 238-254.

Sayles, L.R. *Leadership: What Effective Managers Really Do—And How They Do It*. New York: McGraw-Hill, 1979.

Schendel, D.E., and Hofer, C.W. *Strategic Management*. Boston, MA: Little Brown, 1979.

Selznick, P. *TVA and the Grass Roots*. Berkeley, CA: University of California Press, 1949.

Selznick, P. *Leadership in Administration*. New York: Harper & Row, 1957.

Sills, D.L. *The Volunteers*. Glencoe, IL: The Free Press, 1980.

Starbuck, W.H. "Organizational Growth and Development." In *Handbook of Organizations*, pp. 451-533. Edited by J.G. March. Chicago, IL: Rand-McNally, 1965.

Staw, B.M., Sandelands, L.E., and Dutton, J.E. "Threat-Rigidity Effects in Organizational Behavior: A Multilevel Analysis." *Administrative Science Quarterly* 26 (1981): 501-524.

Staw, B.M., McKechnie, P.I., and Puffer, S.M. "The Justification of Organizational Performance." *Administrative Science Quarterly* 28 (1983): 582-600.

Stryker, P. *The Character of the Executive*. New York: Harper & Row, 1961.

Thompson, J.D. *Organizations in Action*. New York: McGraw-Hill, 1967.

Tsui, A.S., and Karwan, K.R. "Leadership Effects on Organizational Outcomes: A Simulation Study." Working paper, Duke University, 1985.

Tushman, M.L., and Romanelli, E. "Organization Evolution: A Metamorphosis Model of Convergence and Reorientation." In *Research in Organizational Behavior*, Vol. 7, pp. 171-222. Edited by L.L. Cummings and B.M. Staw. Greenwich, CT: JAI Press, 1985.

Tushman, M.L., and Romanelli, E. "Reorientation and Long Term Organizational Performance: An Empirical Study." Unpublished manuscript, Columbia University, 1985.

Virany, B., Tushman, M.L., and Romanelli, E. "A Longitudinal Study on the Determinants of Executive Succession." Working paper, Columbia University, 1985.

Weiner, N. "Situational and Leadership Influence on Organizational Performance." *Proceedings of the Academy of Management*, 1978, pp. 230-234.

Weiner, N., and Mahoney, T.A. "A Model of Corporate Performance as a Function of Environmental, Organizational, and Leadership Influences." *Academy of Management Journal* 24 (1981): 453-470.

Zald, M.N. "Political Economy: A Framework for Comparative Analysis." In *Power in Organizations*, pp. 221-261. Edited by M.N. Zald. Nashville, TN: Vanderbilt University Press, 1970.

Zucker, L.G. "The Role of Institutionalization in Cultural Persistence." *American Sociological Review* 42 (1977): 726-742.

CONTINGENCY PERSPECTIVES ON STRATEGIC LEADERSHIP:
CURRENT KNOWLEDGE AND FUTURE RESEARCH DIRECTIONS

Anil K. Gupta

The last few years have seen the accumulation of considerable research and some insights into questions such as: "What are the backgrounds from which chief executives emerge?" (Gupta, 1985); "How do chief executives come to be where they are?" (Pfeffer, 1977); "What are the demographic and personality characteristics of chief executives?" (Gupta and Govindarajan, 1984a; Miller, Kets de Vries, and Toulouse, 1982; Miller and Toulouse, 1986); "How do chief executives think?" (Isenberg, 1986); "How do chief executives go about doing their daily work?" (Kotter, 1982; Mintzberg, 1973; Peters, 1979); and "What impact do chief executives have on organizational performance?" (Lieberson and O'Connor, 1972; Weiner and Mahoney, 1981). As one outcome of this research, it is now widely accepted that the differences among chief executive officers (CEOs)—including general managers of strategic business units (SBUs) within the corporation—are at least as profound as the similarities among them. For instance, important differences have been hypothesized or discovered between public sector versus business executives (Brown, 1970), entrepreneurs versus professional managers (Schere, 1982), and transactional versus transformational leaders (Burns, 1978; Tichy and Ulrich, 1984).

An emerging theoretical perspective is that these executive differences play a substantial role in the functioning of organizations (Hambrick and Mason, 1984). In specific terms, the emergent paradigm argues that because different organizations generally pursue different strategies (Henderson, 1970; Miles and Snow, 1978; Porter, 1980; Rumelt, 1974), and because the implementation of different strategies requires differing skills, values, and knowledge on the part of chief executives (Leontiades, 1982; Stybel, 1982; Szilagyi & Schweiger, 1984; Tichy, Fombrun, and Devanna, 1982), a systematic alignment of executive leadership to organizational strategies is likely to yield superior performance (Gupta, 1984). This "strategic contingencies" paradigm is noteworthy not only for its intuitive and logical appeal but also for the fact that its validity has received empirical support (Gupta and Govindarajan, 1984a; Govindarajan, 1985; Miller and Toulouse, 1986).

Against this background, the primary objective of this paper is to shed new light on and delineate some new research directions on linkages between organizational strategies and executive leaders. The logical approach underlying this analysis is as follows: first, some key assumptions implicit in the currently prevailing strategic contingencies paradigm are identified; second, the validity of each assumption is examined critically in the belief that, like all theories, all assumptions are only partially true; finally, the implications of this critical examination for future research within this broad area are delineated and discussed. As a precursor to this "meta-contingency" analysis, the next section reviews briefly the current status of the strategic contingencies perspective and the knowledge and insights that this perspective has so far yielded.

STRATEGIC CONTINGENCIES RESEARCH ON EXECUTIVE LEADERSHIP

In the context of the very long history of research on leadership (Bass, 1981), the *strategic* contingencies perspective is of relatively recent origin dating perhaps to the mid-1970s when the General Electric Company implemented the concept of "strategic business units" and initiated systematic attempts to integrate the strategic and the executive manpower planning processes (Aguilar and Hamermesh, 1981). Several factors seem to account for this recency of the strategic contingencies perspective. One, with the emergence of strategic management as a field of study, it is only recently that researchers have begun to focus systematically and explicitly on leadership at the level of chief executives and general managers. In contrast, virtually all "traditional" leadership research had tended to focus either on leaders in nonwork settings (e.g., street gangs, school children) or on leaders operating at much lower levels in the organizational hierarchy (e.g., shop-floor supervisors). Thus, excluding biographical studies, leaders so far have been studied almost exclusively in their "interpersonal" roles as the heads of small groups rather than in their "institutional" roles as the heads of large business enterprises (Selznick, 1957).

Two, recent socioeconomic developments seem to have elevated the CEO's role as the central figure in the functioning of corporations. For instance, capital markets now increasingly expect the corporate CEO and his/her staff to "add value." One potentially effective way for the CEO to do this is by attempting to realize potential synergies, such as the sharing of facilities and skills, among different SBUs (Gupta and Govindarajan, 1986a; Porter, 1985; Vancil, 1980). The concomitant need for managing inter-SBU coordination and conflict resolution would seem to have created a trend toward greater centralization and more hands-on management on the part of corporate CEOs. Additionally, owing to stiffening foreign competition and the emergence of "corporate raiders," companies appear to have begun facing substantially greater external threats in their product and capital markets. The resulting crises in many companies have often required drastic action—elevating the substantive as well as the symbolic roles of CEOs. Finally, because of the vastly increased insurance premiums for corporate directors, the composition of boards seems now to be shifting towards company insiders. Since inside board members are "usually senior managers who are dependent on the boss for their livelihood and less likely to challenge him" ("The Job Nobody Wants," 1986: 56), the typical corporate CEO's latitude for action would seem to have increased over the past decade.

Three, in the early stages of the strategic management field, the predominant concern of scholars seemed to be with strategy formulation, in terms of both how strategies should be formulated and what the strategic choices should be (Henderson, 1970; Hofer, 1975; Kiechel, 1982; Schendel and Hofer, 1979). The recent increase in research emphasis on issues of strategy implementation (Bourgeois and Brodwin, 1984; Galbraith and Kazanjian, 1986; Gupta and Govindarajan, 1984b; Hamermesh, 1986a; Stonich, 1982) also seems to have added momentum to an examination of the impact that general managers' demographic and personality backgrounds have on the execution of different organizational strategies.

Given this evolutionary background, it is not surprising that the emerging strategic contingencies perspective differs from traditional leadership research in terms of both what types of leaders are being studied and the conceptual lenses through which they are being studied. In specific terms, the conceptual arguments underlying the strategic contingencies perspective are: (1) required strategic competences differ across organizations and over time; (2) managers differ in the educational, experience, and personality makeups—and, thus, the competences—they bring to their positions; and (3) matching managers to strategies leads to improved performance. Since the vast majority of large industrial firms in many countries are diversified into more than one business (Scott, 1973), these strategic contingency arguments have been extended and tested at both the overall corporation as well as the individual business unit levels.

Strategic Contingencies at the Corporate Level

At the corporate level, strategic differences have been conceptualized primarily in terms of the extent and type of diversification undertaken by different firms. Following Rumelt (1974), extent of diversification refers to the multiplicity of businesses in which the firm operates, and type of diversification refers to the nature of linkages—vertical, horizontal, or none—between these businesses. Thus, Lotus Development, operating only in the software market, exemplifies a nondiversified "single business" firm. Texas Instruments, with businesses ranging from semiconductor components to completely assembled computer systems, illustrates a "vertically integrated" firm. Procter & Gamble, operating in the horizontally-linked detergents, health and beauty aids, and food products markets, typifies a "related diversified" firm. Finally, ITT, operating in businesses as diverse as hotels, insurance, and telecommunications, epitomizes the "unrelated diversified" conglomerate.

Berg (1969), Gupta (1984), Leontiades (1982), Scott (1973), and Vancil (1980) have argued that different points along the spectrum from single business to unrelated diversified firms require different priorities and perspectives on the part of the CEO. At the single business end, the number of profit centers is limited—often just one—and the boundaries of the external environment are relatively well defined. Thus, the locus of responsibility and initiative regarding decisions about how to compete within the particular industry and which functional strategies to pursue (in R&D, manufacturing, marketing, etc.) rests appropriately with the firm's CEO. In contrast, at the unrelated diversified end, given the large number of businesses, the CEO's primary task becomes portfolio management, i.e., the addition or deletion of businesses and the allocation of resources to the different businesses. Vancil and Lorange (1975) have argued that, in such a firm, the locus of responsibility for decisions regarding how to compete and what functional strategies to pursue within particular markets can and should rest primarily with the various SBU-level general managers and not with the corporate CEO.

Following these arguments, at the single business end, some of the more critical skills for the CEO are argued to be familiarity with the particular firm and industry, expertise in R&D, manufacturing, or marketing, as well as high interpersonal orientation. In contrast, at the unrelated diversified end, it is skills relating to financial management and *im*personal financial control that become more useful. These and other related hypotheses pertaining to the contingency impact of variations in corporate-level strategy have been discussed in detail in Gupta (1984) and Leontiades (1982).

In terms of empirical evidence linking corporate-level strategies to characteristics of corporate CEOs, the only study to have undertaken such an investigation has indeed yielded supportive results. Based on a study of 53 *Fortune* 500 companies in 1980, Song (1982) concluded that whereas CEOs of internal diversifiers (essentially related diversified firms) came from primarily production and marketing backgrounds, those of acquisitive diversifiers (essentially unrelated diversified firms) came from primarily finance, accounting, and legal backgrounds. A similar study on differences in strategic leadership (albeit with a focus on boards of directors rather than CEOs) has also yielded positive results. Based on a comparison of 50 single business and 50 diversified firms, Baysinger and Zeithaml (1985) concluded that boards of diversified firms tended to be comprised of proportionately more outside directors than those of single business firms. These findings provide encouragement for further empirical investigations within this broad area.

Strategic Contingencies at the SBU-level

Unlike corporate-level strategy, existing conceptualizations of SBU-level strategy are considerably more complex and there exists less consensus regarding how best to differentiate one SBU's strategic context from another's. Nonetheless, there exist at least three conceptualizations of SBU-level strategy that have been used widely in theoretical and empirical research: (1) the SBU's "strategic mission" in the corporate portfolio (Abell and Hammond, 1979; Henderson, 1970; Larreche and Srinivasan, 1982); (2) the SBU's "competitive strategy" vis-à-vis other firms in its industry (Porter, 1980); and (3) the extent of the SBU's emphasis on product-market innovation (Miles and Snow, 1978). Since the last two strategic dimensions, competitive strategy and emphasis on product-market innovation, seem to be tapping the same underlying construct (Hambrick, 1983), the following review will focus on only the first two strategic dimensions, *strategic mission* and *competitive strategy*.

The concept of "strategic mission" derives from the basic premise that, because of variance in markets' attractiveness and businesses' competitive positions, at any point in time, all businesses are unlikely to be equally attractive candidates for capital investment. Along this dimension, the two most prominent archetypes are argued to be "build" and "harvest" (Buzzell and Wiersema, 1981; Gupta and Govindarajan, 1984b). A "build" mission, exemplified by AT&T in its computer business, signifies an intent to invest capital in the SBU in order to increase market share and competitive position even at the risk of some reduction in short-term earnings. In contrast, a "harvest" mission, exemplified by General Electric in its light bulb business, signifies an intent to maximize short-term cash flow and earnings even at the risk of some reduction in market share. The proponents of the strategic contingencies perspective have argued that, for "build" SBUs, given their longer time horizon, earlier stages in the product life cycle, and the need to battle for market share, the following general management characteristics are related to effectiveness: risk-taking propensity, tolerance for ambiguity, internal locus of control, marketing and/or R&D backgrounds, and greater industry familiarity (Gupta, 1984; Leontiades, 1982; Strategic Planning Institute, 1981; Wissema, Van der Pol, and Messer, 1980; Wright, 1974). The opposite personality characteristics and functional backgrounds in production and/or accounting-finance have been hypothesized for effective general managers of "harvest" SBUs.

The concept of "competitive strategy" refers to a business' intended basis for the achievement of some market advantage over competitors. Along this dimension, Porter (1985) has identified "differentiation" and "cost leadership" as the two most prominent archetypes. A strategy of differentiation, exemplified by Sony and JVC in consumer electronics, indicates a preference for superior product or service attributes even at the risk of higher costs and prices. In contrast, a strategy of cost leadership, exemplified by Sharp and Emerson in consumer electronics, signifies just the opposite kinds of preferences, i.e., an intention to be the lowest cost provider of the product/service even at the risk of some sacrifice in quality and/or features. The proponents of the strategic contingencies perspective have argued that, for a differentiation strategy, the ability to foster creativity through a willingness to depart from previous practices, stronger interpersonal orientation, greater tolerance for ambiguity, higher industry familiarity, and strong marketing or product R&D skills are likely to be more effective. In contrast, for the implementation of cost leadership strategies, it is the ability to maximize internal throughput efficiency through tight operational and financial controls and the avoidance of new product initiatives that are argued to be more critical (Gupta, 1984).

Several empirical studies have yielded positive results supporting the hypothesized contingency linkages between SBU strategies and characteristics of SBU general managers. Gupta and Govindarajan (1984a) found not only that build SBUs were headed by general managers with greater risk-taking propensity and greater tolerance for ambiguity but also that the theorized matching of managerial characteristics with SBU strategy was associated with greater effectiveness. In three separate studies, Govindarajan (1985), Miller, Kets de Vries, and Toulouse (1982), and Miller and Toulouse (1986) have also demonstrated that general managers heading business units pursuing strategies of differentiation and/or product innovation tended to be more internal in their locus of control (Rotter, 1966) relative to their counterparts heading business units pursuing strategies of cost leadership and/or little product innovation. The first of these studies also found a positive association between the predicted strategy-locus of control linkages and SBU performance. Three other studies (Hambrick, 1981; Hitt, Ireland, and Stadter, 1982; Snow and Hrebiniak, 1980), while not focusing explicitly on the characteristics of the general manager, have also reported either that the predominance of different functional areas (R&D, production, etc.) or that the power of managers heading different functions tended to vary systematically with differences in business unit strategies.

As the above review indicates, the strategic contingencies perspective has received support at the business unit level also. Further reinforcement, at least in terms of face validity, might derive from the fact that several corporations have reportedly been engaged in linking executive selection with strategic requirements at the SBU level for several years ("Wanted: A Manager. . .," 1980). To sum up, given the consistency of supportive empirical results at both the corporate and the SBU levels, it might not be inaccurate to claim that the strategic contingencies perspective on executive leadership is making steady progress towards becoming a well-established paradigm.

TOWARDS META-CONTINGENCY ANALYSIS OF STRATEGY-LEADERSHIP LINKAGES

Despite the progress of the strategic contingencies perspective, our understanding of the general phenomenon of "strategic leadership" is still meager. At a broad level, two major paths seem to exist for the researcher interested in pursuing this subject further. One would be to continue investigations along the currently established avenue by focusing on contingency linkages between as-yet-unexamined dimensions of strategy (e.g., corporate-wide functional strategies, international competitive posture, form and extent of external strategic alliances, interlinkages with other business units, etc.) and as-yet-unexamined CEO characteristics (e.g., decision-making style, interpersonal orientation, inter-industry mobility, etc.). Such investigations would need to be carried out not only in terms of uncovering direct linkages between strategy and CEO characteristics (easier, more often attempted, but less interesting) but also in terms of examining the interactive effect of these linkages on organizational performance (more difficult to do, less often attempted, but more interesting). A second approach would be to look for loopholes in the basic strategic contingencies paradigm itself as it currently stands. As Popper (1972) has argued, such a negativist approach can greatly propel the continuing evolution of knowledge. This is because the potential outcomes of a negativist approach will inevitably be useful: either the current theory will emerge stronger for having withstood the search for loopholes, or it will get subsumed in a broader, more powerful theory of which it is merely a special case.

Taking the latter of these two approaches, the rest of this paper critically examines the validity of some key assumptions implicit in the extant strategic contingencies research and speculates on new insights and research directions that are yielded by an explicit recognition of the only partial validity of each assumption. The issues and prevailing assumptions subjected to this analysis are:

1. *Constraints on the CEO's power.* Prevailing assumption: CEOs, including general managers of SBUs, have a free rein.
2. *Individual CEO versus the executive team.* Prevailing assumption: The characteristics of the individual CEO are far more critical than those of the top executive team.
3. *CEOs: strategy formulators or strategy implementers?* Prevailing assumption: The primary task of CEOs is the implementation rather than the formulation of strategies; in other words, selection of strategies precedes the selection of CEOs.
4. *Sources of contingencies—strategy versus environment.* Prevailing assumption: The appropriateness of CEO characteristics depends more strongly on contingencies imposed by organizational strategies than on those imposed by the environmental contexts of organizations.
5. *Simple versus complex notions of "fit."* Prevailing assumption: For every strategic context, there exists, at least in theory, an "ideal" profile of CEO characteristics. Further, contingency linkages between the strategic context and any particular CEO characteristic operate independently of those between the strategic context and any other CEO characteristic.
6. *Demographic characteristics versus personality versus behavior.* Prevailing assumption: Strategic contingencies research on CEO characteristics should precede that on CEO behavior.

Constraints on the CEO's Power

The assumption that CEOs matter rests on two premises: one, that CEOs differ from each other; and two, that the individual CEO's decisions and actions have a significant impact on organizational activities and performance. Given the weight of substantial scientific and anecdotal evidence as well as its obvious face validity, the first of these premises must be regarded as essentially indisputable. Concerns such as Pfeffer's (1977) regarding the likely "homogeneity of leaders" are easily countered by direct empirical evidence pertaining to significant CEO differences along important dimensions such as age, educational background, and functional experience (Grimm and Smith, 1985; Gupta, 1985; Song, 1982), willingness to take risk (Brockhaus, 1980; Gupta and Govindarajan, 1984a), tolerance for ambiguity (Gupta and Govindarajan, 1984a; Schere, 1982), locus of control (Govindarajan, 1985; Miller, Kets de Vries, and Toulouse, 1982), decision-making style (Slocum and Hellriegel, 1983), flexibility (Miller and Toulouse, 1986), and need for achievement (McClelland, 1961; Miller and Toulouse, 1986). However, since the second premise has engendered considerably greater controversy, it needs to be examined in greater detail.

It is true that few chief executives have either the time or the expertise to exert a *direct* influence over the daily minutiae of research, purchasing, manufacturing, marketing, sales, distribution, and other decisions through which strategies get realized. However, there exist at least five arguments in support of the premise that they do have considerable opportunities to influence these decisions *indirectly* by shaping the "context" within which they are made.

First, while CEOs may not make routine or even many strategic decisions themselves, they often select the key executives who are much closer to the taking of concrete and important organizational actions. For instance, the CEO of General Electric has noted in a recent videotaped interview that he himself is the key decision-maker in the selection/promotion of over 100 senior executives and is involved on a "pass off" basis in the selection/ promotion of some 600 other executives.

Second, as illustrated by the well-known case of General Motors under Alfred Sloan, CEOs often use their power to reshape the organizational structure to influence lower-level decision-making. Cyert and March (1963), Allison (1971), and Arrow (1974) have argued that each structure operates as a unique channel for the collection and processing of information. Thus, ceteris paribus, different structural arrangements tend to yield different decisions and actions. For instance, "an SBU whose scope is defined as X-ray machines is likely to compete more narrowly. . .than an SBU whose scope is defined as diagnostic imaging equipment" (Hamermesh, 1986b).

Third, CEOs control the dispensing of organizational rewards at least for the key executives. As Barnard (1938) and Simon (1947) argued, the personal values and norms of individuals do not fully determine what they might be willing to do; accordingly, for every individual, there exists a "zone of indifference" within which the organization may specify any of several modes of behavior and, in personal value terms, the individual would be indifferent as to which. Aware of this reality, CEOs use the dispensing of rewards to channel organizational decisions and actions within these "zones of indifference."

Fourth, CEOs control the allocation of scarce resources. It is true that most strategic initiatives originate from lower levels in the hierarchy rather than from the chief executive's office (Bower, 1970; Burgelman, 1983); however, in order to succeed, these initiatives must be provided with the needed resources. Thus, even if the only real option for the CEO is to make "Go/No Go" types of decisions, the typical scarcity of resources (Arrow, 1974) dictates that he/she must choose among the various initiatives, thereby exercising considerable influence over the organization's strategic direction.

Fifth, aside from control over resource allocation, many CEOs also have a major impact on the form and scale of resources that the organization is able to attract from the external environment. Pfeffer and Salancik (1978) have argued that CEOs are often selected because of their contacts and credibility. As Lee Iacocca demonstrated persuasively in his turnaround of Chrysler, these contacts and credibility can enable CEOs to personally influence the generation of external resources thereby reinforcing their power over resource allocation.

Notwithstanding these multiple channels of influence for the CEO, research support for the extent of CEO impact on organizational performance has been decidedly mixed (Brown, 1982). Lieberson and O'Connor (1971), in their study of chief executives' influence over corporate performance, as well as Salancik and Pfeffer (1977) in their study of mayors' influence on city budgets, reported that, after controlling for the effect of external factors (such as the economy, the industry, etc.), chief executives' impact on organizational outcomes was relatively minor. These findings led Pfeffer (1977) to posit that the selection of organizational leaders (such as general managers or CEOs) was largely a symbolic ritual without much substantive import and led Pfeffer and Salancik (1978: 19) to conclude starkly that:

> studies estimating the effect of administrators. . .have found them to account for about ten percent of the variance in organizational performance, a striking contrast to the 90 percent of the intellectual effort that has been devoted to developing theories of individual action.

Despite these findings, more recent investigations on the impact of CEOs have tended to be considerably more supportive. Thus, in a replication of Lieberson and O'Connor's (1972) study with an improved statistical analysis, Weiner and Mahoney (1981) reported that changes in CEOs accounted for approximately 44 percent and 47 percent of the variance in corporate profitability and stock prices, respectively. Similarly, on the basis of a 20-year longitudinal study, Smith, Carson, and Alexander (1984) concluded that leadership did make a significant difference when one's focus was not on the mere event of a change in leadership but on *who* the new leader was. Nearly identical results have been reported also by Pfeffer and Davis-Blake (1986: 72) in a recent study on CEO succession in sports teams:

> Succession has no effect on subsequent team performance when prior performance is controlled, a result consistent with those of other studies. However, when the competence of new coaches is included in the analysis, it appears that succession affects subsequent performance. . . .The results suggest that attempts to estimate succession effects need to consider the competence of successors.

On balance, it would seem that CEOs are neither omnipotent nor impotent (Gupta, 1984). Their discretion (i.e., latitude for action) varies across situational contexts and across outcome dimensions, an often overlooked conclusion that even Lieberson and O'Connor (1972: 124) seemed to share:

> In short, all three performance variables are affected by forces beyond a leader's immediate control, but the bounds on a leader's impact may vary between goals. Leaders' options within an organization may vary widely depending on the goals or activities involved.

Along these lines, Hambrick and Finkelstein (1987) have theorized that managerial discretion is a function of environmental (e.g., market growth rates, quasi-legal constraints), organizational (e.g., resource availability, internal political conditions), as well as individual (e.g., external contacts, credibility) characteristics. If managerial discretion indeed varies across contexts, then the salience of contingency linkages between organizational strategies and executive leaders should also be expected to vary across contexts, tending to be stronger in high discretion contexts. In a more formal sense, the following meta-contingency proposition can now be extended: *Theories positing contingency relationships between organizational strategies and executive leadership will find stronger support in those environmental and organizational contexts which afford the CEO greater discretion than in those contexts that severely restrict the CEO's discretion.*

Several new investigations are suggested by this broad proposition. For instance, it should be useful to compare the strength of strategy-leadership linkages between contexts where, on a prima-facie basis, managerial discretion differs significantly. By way of example, this might be done: (1) between SBU and corporate levels of analysis; (2) between autonomous and highly interlinked SBUs; (3) between small versus large organizations; (4) between organizations operating in stable and dynamic environments; (5) between heavily regulated and less regulated private sector businesses; and (6) between private and public sector organizations.

The Individual CEO Versus The Executive Team

Barring rare exceptions (Hambrick, 1981; Romanelli and Tushman, 1983), virtually all empirical studies on executive leadership have focused on the individual chief executive rather than the top executive team (e.g., Gupta and Govindarajan, 1984a; Lieberson and O'Connor, 1972; Miller and Toulouse, 1986; Salancik and Pfeffer, 1977 and 1980). At least implicitly, scholars seem to have assumed that, in terms of impact on organizational activities and performance, the individual CEO or general manager is far more important than the top management team. Support for this assumption would seem to derive from both the formal as well as the symbolic power of the chief executive. As stated earlier, in most private enterprises, the CEO has the formal power not only to dictate the substance of strategic decisions but also to appoint or remove other executives who might propose or review strategic initiatives. Since the proverbial "buck" does indeed stop at the CEO's desk, he/she is rightly held responsible for the actions or inertia of other executives. Thus, it would seem appropriate to view the chief executive as also the architect of his/her executive team thereby making a research focus on the CEO a parsimonius way of studying executive leadership. Apart from formal power, the "symbolic" role of the CEO also has the potential to serve as a source of real power to shape corporate behavior. For instance, the media focuses far more on the chief executive than it does on other members of the exceutive team. By way of partial evidence, it might be noted that, while the media frequently conducts peer group surveys to determine "the most admired CEOs," there are almost no surveys conducted to determine "the most admired executive teams." This visibility provides CEOs with an almost unique power to personally shape the expectations and values of individuals both inside and outside the organization. Some scholars have argued that the power to shape values might even be more important than formal power (Peters, 1979). Thus, on this account also, it seems justified to view the CEO as the preeminent executive leader.

Without disputing the preeminent role of the CEO, it can be argued that a CEO's intentions regarding the composition of the executive team need not match the actual composition or the real power of other executives in that team. While this is obviously possible in the case of SBUs, whose general managers typically must seek corporate approval for their top appointees, such situations can occur frequently at the corporate level also. As Hambrick (1981) and Pfeffer and Salancik (1978) argued, the real power of any manager is a function not of formal membership in the top management team but of the extent to which the individual helps the organization cope with strategic or environmental contingencies. Thus, analogous to Mintzberg's (1978) conceptualization of strategy, it should be useful to take cognizance of both "intended" and "realized" top management teams; in fact, it was the latter perspective that Thompson (1967) seemed to have in mind when he theorized about the "dominant coalitions" of organizations.

To the extent that the composite characteristics of top executive teams may not mirror the CEO's personality, several arguments exist in support of the expectation that observed linkages between organizational strategies and characteristics of the executive team are likely to be stronger than those between organizational strategies and characteristics of the individual CEO: (1) In the universe of all CEO succession contexts, there are bound to be some where an individual with the desired "ideal" profile of characteristics is simply not available. Under norms of rationality, in such contexts, the CEO or those who appointed him/her may decide to compensate for the CEO's weaknesses with an appropriate "supporting cast." (2) In the case of SBU-level general managers, exposure to and experience at managing different kinds of strategies and businesses is often viewed as an essential component of managerial development. As part of this developmental process, "fast track" middle-level general managers may deliberately be given charge of even those SBUs to which they are, in a theoretical sense, mismatched. Such lateral rotation of SBU general managers may serve also to help ease inter-SBU coordination and conflict resolution (Galbraith, 1973; Porter, 1985). To the extent that such lateral transfers leave SBUs with at least partially mismatched general managers, it may again be necessary to compensate for the general managers' weaknesses with appropriately composed top management teams. (3) As Lamont and Anderson (1985) demonstrated, not all organizations pursue pure strategies e.g., "pure internal diversification," "pure acquisitive diversification," "pure build," or "pure harvest" and so on. In such situations also, the appointment of an appropriately diverse top management team, with different executives taking primary responsibility for different elements of the organization's "mixed" strategy, might be the most effective way to align executive leadership with organizational strategies.

A focus on the executive team, unlike that on just the CEO, can also enable an exploration of how diversity within the team influences organizational behavior and performance. As Pfeffer and Salancik (1978) argued, the appointment of different individuals—who can credibly represent the interests of different constituencies—can be very instrumental in ensuring the political survival of organizations. Similarly, focusing on environmental monitoring rather than political cooptation, Arrow (1974) as well as Lawrence and Lorsch (1967) argued that, the more diverse an organization's environment, the more necessary it becomes to have a differentiated top management team in order to appropriate monitor the diversity of the environment. Research on strategic-decision making processes provides yet additional evidence supporting the importance of studying executive teams. Building on Janis' (1972) concerns regarding the dangers of "groupthink," several studies have demonstrated that, as long as mechanisms for conflict resolution exist, the presence of conflict and diversity in strategic viewpoints, as well as in the set of strategic options considered, contributes positively to the quality of the final strategic decisions (Bourgeois, 1985; Cosier, 1982; Schweiger, Sandberg, and Ragan, 1986; Wanous and Youtz, 1986).

To sum up, the following broad propositions can now be advanced: (1) Contingency linkages between organizational strategies and characteristics of the top executive team will find stronger support than those between organizational strategies and characteristics of the individual CEO. (2) The contingency impact of organizational strategies on executive teams will be reflected in the relative power of the different executives comprising the team. (3) There will be a positive correlation between the rate of change in an organization's strategy and the rate of change in the composition of its top executive team. (4) Internal diversity within the top executive team is likely to be more useful to organizations undergoing strategic reorientation than to those pursuing strategic stability. (5) Internal diversity within the top executive team is likely to be more useful for organizations operating in complex and uncertain environments than for those operating in simple and more predictable environments. (6) Independent of the strategic context, there will also be a positive correlation between executive team diversity and organizational performance.

CEOs: Strategy Formulators or Strategy Implementers?

By definition, the notion that matching executives to organizational strategies enhances organizational performance assumes that strategies get specified *prior* to executive selection; in other words, for most CEOs, strategies are assumed to be a given and the CEO's primary task is assumed to consist of the implementation rather than the formulation of strategies.

Strong empirical support for this position derives from observational studies of what chief executives/general managers "really" do (Carlson, 1951; Kotter, 1982; Mintzberg, 1973; Sayles, 1964; Stewart, 1967). As Mintzberg (1973: 5) observed, given the unrelenting nature of the executive's work pace and the brevity, variety, and fragmentation of his/her work activities, "the job of managing does not develop reflective planners." Fresh evidence has continued to support these observations. Note, for instance, Isenberg's (1984: 84) conclusions from a recent study of 12 division heads in six corporations:

> Of course, senior managers do think about the content of their businesses, particularly during crises and periodic business reviews. But this thinking is always in close conjunction with thinking about the process for getting *others* to think about the business. In other words, even very senior managers devote most of their attention to the tactics of implementation rather than the formulation of strategy.

Notwithstanding these observations, it is also true that organizational strategies do change over time (Chandler, 1962; Mintzberg, 1978). Thus, dissociating the CEO from a major role in strategy formulation runs the risk either of accepting environmental determinism as the process by which organizational strategies come to be or of viewing the CEO as a rather impotent observer of strategic changes initiated by others. Since, at a general level, both of these positions are invalid (Bourgeois, 1984; Hambrick and Finkelstein, 1987), one must accept the CEO's primary task as encompassing not just the implementation but also the (re)formulation of organizational strategies. Going one step further, if one notes that most CEOs do not get involved deeply in operational decisions, the valid perspective might even be that the CEO is the prime architect of the company's strategy. If so, then what does one make of the strategic contingencies notion that executive selection must be tailored to pre-specified strategies?

On balance, it would seem that the "strategist" is just as likely to precede "strategies" as the reverse, or that the causality runs both ways, a conclusion that Virany, Tushman, and Romanelli (1985: 20) also seem to share:

> (Strategic) reorientations and CEO change are strongly related. The causal linkage between these two events is not clear. (Our) data indicate that CEO change and reorientations occur during the same time period. Most likely, causality can run in either direction. Sometimes a new CEO will initiate a reorientation; while other times existing executives or board members initiate strategic reorientations which, in turn, require a new CEO. . . .Future research must more clearly untangle the linkages between CEO succession and reorientations.

A partial untangling of the CEO's formulation and implementation roles is suggested by research on organizational evolution. Several recent studies have indicated that strategic evolution in most organizations occurs not through a slow accretion of steady change but through a process more akin to what has been termed "punctuated equilibria" in evolutionary biology i.e., the evolutionary history of organizations can be seen as consisting of long periods of relative strategic stability punctuated by short periods of major, often drastic, strategic change (Greiner, 1972; Miller and Friesen, 1984; Tushman and Romanelli, 1985). If we accept this perspective, then we would conclude that, although, in a strict sense, formulation and implementation are intertwined processes that are constantly operative in all organizations, the relative prominence of the two processes ebb and flow. In other words, there are periods in organizational histories when the then-CEO's primary concern is with the establishment of a new strategy, just as there are other periods when the then-CEO's primary concern is with "making the current strategy work." Note, for instance, the following anecdotal observation regarding the 3M Corporation:

> Unlike retired Chairman Lewis W. Lehr, who mapped broad directions for 3M, (new Chairman Allen F.) Jacobson plans to concentrate more on the nuts-and-bolts of implementing strategies and reaping the rewards of rising research and development spending ("How Jake Jacobson. . .," 1986: 106).

It can now be concluded that, in studying linkages between organizational strategies and executive leaders, researchers need to discriminate between three types of CEO tenures: those associated primarily with strategic reorientations (Type I), those associated primarily with strategic stability (Type II), and those encompassing both strategic reorientations and strategic stability (Type III). In Type I scenarios, CEOs would be studied primarily as strategy formulators. Analytically, this would imply treating CEO characteristics (and even organizational performance) as independent variables and organizational strategies as the dependent variables—this is the approach taken by Hambrick and Mason (1984) as well as by Miller and Toulouse (1986). In Type II scenarios, CEOs would be studied primarily as strategy implementers. Analytically, this would imply treating organizational strategies, CEO characteristics, and contingency interactions between the two as independent variables and organizational performance as the dependent variable—this is the approach taken by Gupta and Govindarajan (1984a). In Type III scenarios, as illustrated by the celebrated case of John Connelly at Crown Cork & Seal (Bower, 1973), CEOs would appropriately be studied as both strategy formulators and strategy implementers; in such cases, both forms of analyses just outlined would need to be undertaken. The advantage of such a tailored approach would seem to lie in providing us with a clearer interpretation of empirical findings and in reducing the likelihood of drawing spurious conclusions—potential problems that could occur if Type I analyses are undertaken unknowingly in what are truly Type II contexts, or vice versa. It might be noted that no previous research seems to have made this form of needed discrimination.

A discrimination between the three types of contexts outlined above might also permit an examination of whether different skills or personality characteristics are associated with strategic reorientations as contrasted with stability. While no empirical examination along these lines has yet been attempted, such an expectation is consistent with Leontiades' (1982) conceptualization, as well as with Tichy and Ulrich's (1984) distinction between transactional and transformational leaders. There also exists at least some anecdotal evidence in support of this broad expectation. Note, for instance, the recent case of CEO succession at AM International:

> Joe B. Freeman may have done so well turning around AM International Inc. that he worked himself right out of a job. . . .Internal documents and interviews with current and former executives show that Mr. Freeman was at least in part a victim of his own success: While directors credit him with an excellent job of reviving AM, they believe that the rejuvenated company needs a different kind of manager (Cox, 1984: 33).

In short, some CEOs might be particularly good at managing strategic change but not strategic stability, others at managing strategic stability but not strategic change, while a few rare ones might be good at managing both strategic change and strategic stability. An examination of why this is so would also be a valuable contribution to our understanding of strategic leadership.

Sources of Contingencies: Strategy Versus Environment

Closely related to the question of whether executive leaders operate as formulators and/or as implementers is the issue of whether executive characteristics are (and should be) contingent on organizational strategies as distinct from organizational environments. The distinction between the two perspectives has not always been recognized; thus, the notion of "matching managers to strategies" has at times been incorrectly equated with that of "assigning managers on the basis of product life cycles." Since we do know that quite different strategic options can be pursued by businesses operating within the *same* product life cycle stage within the *same* industry (Harrigan, 1981; Porter, 1980), the distinction between the two perspectives is very real and must be recognized as such.

Consistent with the arguments of Child (1972), it is now well accepted that while the environment imposes constraints and presents opportunities, it does not determine organizational strategies in any definitive sense (Bourgeois, 1984). In most industry environments, multiple viable strategic options exist, the choice among which is dictated by nonenvironmental factors including organizational capabilities, executive values, and even bureaucratic inertia (Andrews, 1971; Henderson, 1970; Miles and Snow, 1978; Porter, 1980). In fact, for most corporations, there would seem to be no logical basis even for viewing the boundaries of the task environment as a given. This is illustrated by examples such as National Steel or Greyhound Corporation, companies that have decided to move out altogether from their original steel and bus transportation businesses. A major outcome of strategic decisions to merge, acquire, or divest businesses is to alter the boundaries of the organization's task environment. Even without altering the boundaries of their task environments by navigating within and across industries and countries, organizations are sometimes able to alter in major ways the salient features of the very environments to which they are assumed to adapt. This was the key argument behind Galbraith's (1967) theorization of "the new industrial state." There also exist concrete examples in the form of what Sony, Yamaha, and Kawasaki have done to alter the basic structures of their supposedly mature radio, musical instrument, and motorcycle markets, respectively.

The appropriate conclusion to draw from the above discussion would be not that strategic choices are independent of organizational environments, but that strategies are linked only partially to organizational environments. Competitive, macroeconomic, and sociopolitical factors do constrain mobility within and across industries (Porter, 1976). Similarly, while multiple viable strategic options exist in most industries, not all strategic options are equally viable in all industries (Porter, 1985). To illustrate, while both differentiation and cost leadership might appear as equally viable strategic options for a computer manufacturer, the same is unlikely to be true for a food grain trader. Thus, strategic choices are neither independent of nor determined by environmental contexts; in other words, the organizational environment acts as *a* but not as *the* constraint on strategic choice.

The looseness of the linkage between environments and strategies also implies that "environmental contingencies" are not likely to be isomorphic with "strategic contingencies." Accordingly, an organization's environmental context has the potential to exert a direct contingency impact on the composition and characteristics of executive leadership in addition to an indirect impact via the imposition of constraints on strategic choice. Thus, notions such as "match managers to strategic missions" and "assign managers on the basis of product life cycles" might both be partly true— but for *different* reasons.

The possibility of environmental contingencies in addition to those imposed by organizational strategies raises several important questions that future research might pursue: First, How do environmental contingencies operate? A useful approach here would be to begin by differentiating among environments first by level of analysis and then cross-sectionally. Take the robotics business of General Motors. Totally aside from GM's strategy in this business, one can view this business' environment at different levels of analysis: "growth" stage in product life cycle, the "robotics" industry, the "U.S." economy, the set of "western industrialised countries," the whole "world," and so on. It is not inconceivable that these different slices of environment, like layers of an onion's skin, may impose independent contingencies on executive leadership.

Second, are environmental contingencies less, equally, or more important than strategic contingencies? Answers to this question can be pursued in the context of specific industry environments as well as globally. As discussed earlier, potential strategic variety can vary across industry contexts. In the theoretically extreme case where only one viable strategic option exists, environmental contingencies might be viewed as completely overshadowing strategic contingencies. At the other extreme, perhaps in highly fragmented industries such as restaurants, potential strategic variety may be huge and strategic contingencies might tend to overshadow environmental contingencies. However, it would seem that, in the vast majority of industry contexts, available strategic variety is likely to be at an intermediate level. Thus, the following broad proposition can now be advanced: The relative strengths of strategies and enivronments as sources of contingency for executive leadership vary across contexts; generally, however, the utility of executive leadership characteristics is likely to be equally contingent on organizational environments and organizational strategies.

Third, when is the impact of strategic and environmental contingencies additive and when is it interactive? Since the answer to this important question would need to be pursued in the context of specific managerial characteristics, specific environmental contingencies, and specific strategic contingencies, no attempt will be made here to develop detailed hypotheses. However, it might be noted that this question would be relevant for every managerial characteristic that is significantly contingent on both strategies and environments. For illustrative purposes, let us consider the characteristic "industry familiarity." It can be argued that the utility of industry familiarity would be greater in industries that are competitively and technologically more complex. It has also been argued that the utility of industry familiarity is likely to be greater for SBUs pursuing build and/or differentiation strategies than for those pursuing harvest and/or cost leadership strategies (Gupta, 1984). In addition to testing these hypotheses independently, a further and very interesting question to pursue would be whether (and, if so, why) the impact of industry complexity, strategic mission, and competitive strategy on the utility of industry familiarity is additive or interactive. Similar questions need be raised and pursued for other managerial characteristics whose effects are found to depend on both strategies and environments.

Simple Versus Complex Notions of Fit

A common tendency in virtually all contingency research in the organizational sciences has been to hypothesize contingency linkages almost solely in "isomorphic" terms i.e., for every value of each contextual variable, there is presumed to exist a uniquely matched "ideal" value of each design variable; as values for the design variable exceed or fall below this uniquely matched value, performance is presumed to be suboptimal (Schoonhoven, 1981). As a substream within the organizational sciences, strategic contingencies research on executive leadership has also shared in this tendency. In fact, the whole notion of "matching" managers to strategies implies that, for each strategic context, there exists a unique "ideal" profile of managerial characteristics.

The notion of different strategic contexts requiring different profiles of CEO characteristics is certainly an improvement over the earlier perspectives that a good general manager can be a good general manager in any organization. However, if research were to stay at the level of testing only isomorphic contingency relationships, and analysing each leadership characteristic separately, there is a risk of at least two oversimplifications. One, executive characteristics that have either a "strict universalistic" or a "simultaneously universalistic and contingency" effect on organizational performance are likely to get deemphasized. Two, potential interactions among multiple characteristics—in the form of substitution effects, infeasible combinations, or negative joint effects—are likely to get ignored. Accordingly, as discussed below, there is need to move from simple to more complex notions of fit.

Notwithstanding differences in the strategic contexts of organizations, there is much in common among most general management positions-one example being the need to manage interrelationships with a wide variety of people (Kotter, 1982; Mintzberg, 1973). To the extent that commonalities exist, there are bound to be leadership characteristics that contribute positively to organizational performance irrespective of strategic context, a conclusion similar to that drawn by House and Baetz (1979: 352): "We speculate that there are certain properties of all leadership situations that are present to a significant degree and relatively invariant, and that there are likely to be somewhat specific traits required in most if not all leadership situations." Some illustrative examples of such universally beneficial characteristics for CEOs might be: willingness and ability to work hard, industry familiarity, and interpersonal competence (Peters and Waterman, 1982). True, successful CEOs who do not appear to work very hard, have short industry tenures, and/or are not very skillful interpersonally can be located; however, the theoretical argument here is that, even in these cases, irrespective of strategic context, working harder, developing greater industry familiarity and becoming more skillful interpersonally can only improve, not worsen, organizational performance. Accordingly, for every executive characteristic, there is need to view both universalistic and contingency perspectives as potentially valid unless conceptual arguments or empirical data persuade us otherwise (Dewar and Werbel, 1979).

Along these lines, it is important to note further that there may well be leadership characteristics that are universally useful at the same time that their utility is *also* a function of context. Let us consider the case of interpersonal competence again. In the absence of any large scale study on this characteristic at the level of chief executives, we might accept Argyris' (1962) arguments that interpersonal competence has a positive utility for all CEOs. Even so, it is entirely plausible that the *positive* utility of interpersonal competence for CEOs of unrelated diversified firms may be *less* than its *positive* utility for CEOs of related diversified firms, a major reason being that the latter set of CEOs would be called upon to manage inter-SBU coordination and conflict resolution on a far more frequent basis than the former set of CEOs. Similarly, at the SBU level, one might hypothesize that, while the utility of interpersonal competence would always be *positive*, it is likely to be *greater* in the case of general managers heading SBUs pursuing differentiation rather than cost leadership strategies (Gupta, 1984). In situations such as these, if the hypotheses are valid, tests of isomorphic contingency relationships between strategy and interpersonal competence would yield negative results whereas those for the universalistic impact of interpersonal competence on performance would yield positive results. Because virtually all extant contingency research, including that on leadership, has viewed universalistic and contingency relationships as mutually exclusive, the traditional approach would suggest that the analysis of CEO interpersonal competence be stopped here. However, as discussed above, this would be clearly premature. *The following broad proposition can now be extended: Every executive leadership characteristic can be classified as being one of the following four types, none of which is an empty set:* (1) those that have little impact on organization performance, irrespective of strategic or environmental context; these might be called *"irrelevant"* characteristics; (2) those that have a significant effect on organizational performance, but due solely to strategic and/or environmental contingencies; these might be termed *"strictly contingent"* characteristics; (3) those that have a significant impact on organizational performance; however, the impact on performance is universalistic and not contingent on either strategic or environmental context; these might be termed *"strictly universalistic"* characteristics; (4) those that have a universalistic impact on organizational performance; however, the strength of this universalistic

Figure 1. Impact of Executive Characteristics on
Organizational Performance: Some Alternative Scenarios

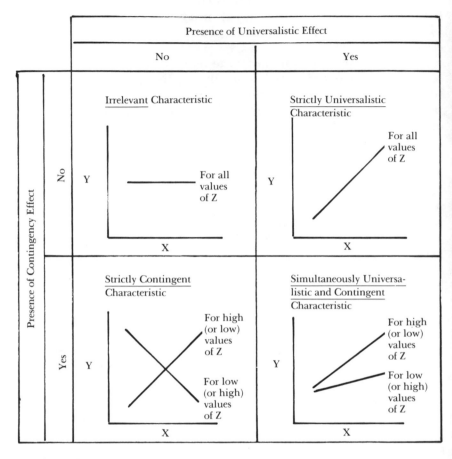

Legend: Y = Organizational Performance
X = Executive Characteristic
Z = Strategy and/or Environmental Context

impact is contingent on strategic and/or environmental factors; these
might be termed as *"simultaneously universalistic and contingent"*
characteristics. A graphical depiction of these alternative scenarios is
contained in Figure 1.

A discrimination of executive characteristics along, as well as an analysis
of the overall relative importance of, these four types of characteristics
would seem to add substantially to our knowledge of strategic leadership.
Analytic approaches for undertaking such discrimination have been

presented and discussed in Gupta and Govindarajan (1986b) and Schoonhoven (1981).

In addition to bivariate analyses along the lines just discussed, there is need also to undertake multivariate analyses that examine the *joint* linkage between a set of multiple executive characteristics and one or more strategic variables. The necessity of conducting such multivariate contingency analyses has been discussed more generally by Van de Ven and Drazin (1985) and can be illustrated here through an example. Consider the case of managerial characteristics needed for effectively implementing various types of strategic missions. Bivariate empirical research has already indicated that each of the following characteristics—greater marketing experience, greater risk-taking propensity, greater tolerance for ambiguity, and a more internal locus of control—improves SBU effectiveness at the "build" end of the strategic mission spectrum and hampers it at the "harvest" end (Govindarajan, 1985; Gupta and Govindarajan, 1984). Notwithstanding the validity of these findings, it is entirely conceivable that the following forms of interactions among characteristics might exist, interactions that are currently not being tapped by the more restricted bivariate analyses: (1) For any particular strategic mission, the "ideal" combination of executive characteristics—as predicted by the bivariate analyses—may be simply infeasible. (2) Two of these characteristics may, in reality, be substitutes for each other so that, once an optimal value on one characteristic has been achieved, the value of the other characteristic becomes irrelevant. (3) The joint presence of particular values on these characteristics (such as all high or all low) may have negative consequences not predicted by the bivariate analyses: for example, excessive dynamism if all of the values are high and excessive rigidity if all of the values are low. Thus, at least theoretically, it is possible that the "ideal" profiles of CEO characteristics yielded by multivariate contingency analyses may differ from those yielded by bivariate analyses. In fact, for the same strategic context, multivariate contingency analysis may even yield multiple "ideal" profiles thus signalling the presence of equifinality (Van de Ven and Drazin, 1985). The implication of this discussion for future research on strategic leadership would seem to be that, while it should begin with bivariate analyses, it should strive to evolve to multivariate ones.

Demographics versus Personality versus Behavior

Barring observational studies of executive behavior (Isenberg, 1984; Kotter, 1982; Mintzberg, 1973)—none of which examined linkages between executive behavior and the content of organizational strategies—all studies on strategic leadership have focused on executive *characteristics* rather than executive *behavior* (Govindarajan, 1985; Gupta and Govindarajan, 1984;

Hambrick and Mason, 1984; Miller and Toulouse, 1986; Song, 1982). One possible reason for this might be "do-ability." Executive characteristics can be studied relatively less expensively, faster, and comparatively easily either through surveys (if the focus is on personality characteristics) or through secondary data (if the focus is on demographic characteristics). In contrast, a study of behavior usually requires direct observation which is not only more expensive and time consuming but also needs deeper and more difficult-to-obtain access to the participating executives. Notwithstanding these constraints on the study of behavior, it should be useful to compare and contrast the relative pros and cons of studying executive demographics versus personality versus behavior. At least three important criteria can be utilized to undertake such comparative assessments: closeness of impact on organizational actions and performance, ease of research replication, and practical utility of research results (see Figure 2).

In terms of closeness of impact, it would seem that executive behavior has the most, and executive demographics the least, direct impact on organizational actions and performance, with personality characteristics falling somewhere in between. In fact, all models or theories focusing on executive characteristics have viewed behavior as the mediating variable through which demographic or personality variables influence organizational actions and performance. Of course, if demographic or personality characteristics could accurately and comprehensively predict behavior, this distinction would not be very meaningful. In reality, however, this is rarely so: demographic variables such as age, education, and work experience account only partially for individual personality, and the combination of demographic and personality variables accounts only partially for individual behavior (Argyris, 1976; House and Baetz, 1979; Maddi, 1972). It follows that studies of executive behavior that utilize the methodologies adopted by Kotter (1982) and Mintzberg (1973) and that aim explicitly to examine linkages between executive behavior and the content of organizational strategies should pay rich dividends. Given positive results from studies on executive characteristics, the odds of obtaining positive results from studies on executive behavior would seem to be extremely favorable. More importantly, one is likely also to uncover the strategic salience of those executive behaviors that might be linked more strongly to factors other than personality—one example being the reward systems under which chief executives, including SBU general managers, operate (Govindarajan and Gupta, 1985; Kerr, 1982). Thus, the issue of equifinality might be relevant not just within a set of executive characteristics but also across executive characteristics versus other administrative mechanisms.

In terms of ease of research replication, the preferred rank ordering would seem to be exactly the reverse. Demographic characteristics can be measured objectively and unambiguously; further, research on demographic

Figure 2.   A Comparative Assessment of Research on Executive Demographics, Executive Personality, and Executive Behavior

		Focus of Study	
Assessment Criteria	Executive Demographics	Executive Personality	Executive Behavior
Closeness of impact on organizational actions and performance	• Least direct impact	• Moderately direct impact	• Most direct impact
Ease of data collection and research replication	• Easiest • Data collection through secondary sources • Least constrained by access and resource problems	• Moderately difficult • Data collection through survey instruments • Moderately constrained by access and resource problems	• Most difficult • Data collection through survey instruments and direct observation • Most constrained by access and resource problems
Utility of research results	• Most useful to securities analysts and managers concerned with predicting competitors' actions • Moderately useful to directors and senior corporate executives concerned with executive selection	• Most useful to directors and senior corporate executives concerned with executive selection • Also useful to the focal managers themselves in terms of helping them make better self-selection decisions when evaluating future career moves	• Most useful to the focal managers themselves in terms of helping them to improve their own effectiveness • Also useful to directors and senior corporate executives in terms of helping them to design compensation systems aimed at encouraging the "desired" behavior

characteristics can often be done through secondary sources making access barriers to very senior executives a nonissue. Thus, notwithstanding their indirect impact on organizational strategies and performance, in the case of demographic characteristics, the prospects of building a cumulative body of knowledge would seem to be high; in comparison, given the constraints on do-ability discussed earlier, one may have to wait much longer for a cumulation of knowledge on executive behavior. In terms of ease of research replication, personality characteristics would seem to fall in between demographic characteristics and executive behavior.

Finally, on the criteria of practical utility, all three factors seem to be quite important—but for different reasons. Depending upon the vantage point, the nature of practical concerns can be expected to vary. Securities analysts concerned with predicting the future actions of a large number of firms and corporate executives concerned with predicting competitors' behavior are likely to have access only to demographic data and thus should find studies focusing on demographic characteristics most helpful. In comparison, both demographic and personality-based studies are likely to be most helpful to boards of directors and other individuals concerned with executive selection, partly because they are likely to desire greater accuracy in predicting future executive behavior and partly because they would often have access to data on both demographic and personality characteristics. Even if potential chief executives and general managers were reluctant to take standard personality tests, experienced executive recruiters have argued that accurate personality assessments can be made either by abstracting from observations of candidates in non-traditional interview settings (Reynolds, 1986) or by analysing available or extractable data on how the executives managed critical situations on earlier occasions (Gerstein and Reisman, 1983). Finally, behavioral studies are likely to be of most relevance to the focal executives themselves because of their desire to improve their own effectiveness in their current jobs; since these executives have to regard their own demographic and personality characteristics as "givens," they are likely to find insights on how to tailor their behaviors to strategic requirements to be of greatest relevance. Nonetheless, demographic and personality characteristics should also be of help to these executives because they must make self-selection decisions when evaluating career moves.

To sum up, as outlined in Figure 2, there appear to exist sufficient (although, in each case, different) grounds to support "full steam ahead" research investigations on all three types of factors—demographic, personality, as well as behavior.

CONCLUSIONS

A recent reviewer of several biographies of corporate CEOs commenced his review with the following observation:

> CEOs are hot, their biographies and autobiographies a growth industry. Just take a look at the shelves in any reasonably well-stocked bookstore, and you will find an assortment of CEOgraphy unmatched since the so-called Gilded Age 100 years ago, when newspapers and magazines routinely carried admiring portraits of captains of industry and commercial tycoons (Webber, 1986: 114).

It would seem that the present paper and the book of which it is a part are themselves contributors to and reflections of strategic leadership as a currently "growth" industry. In such a context, I believe that future reviews on this subject are likely to judge the present research emphasis on executive leaders as representing not a fad but a justified recognition of their tremendous ability to either improve or worsen organizational performance.

Reflecting this belief, it is argued here that current research efforts within this broad area must continue to maintain their momentum. In this endeavor, the central premise of this paper has been that the payoffs from a gradual shift in emphasis from simple to more complex frameworks of strategic leadership are likely to be high. Executive leaders need to be studied (1) comparatively in high versus low discretion settings; (2) both as individual CEOs and as executive teams; (3) both as strategy formulators and as strategy implementers; (4) in terms of linkages not only with organizational strategies but also with organizational environments; (5) in terms of not only demographic or personality characteristics but also in terms of behavior; and (6) with the a priori expectation that different executive characteristics or behaviors are likely to have differing forms of influence on organizational strategies and performance. It is hoped that the ideas presented in this paper will serve as helpful conceptual and methodological guides in this endeavor.

ACKNOWLEDGMENTS

Many of the ideas in this paper were presented earlier at faculty research seminars held at Dartmouth College and at the University of Maryland at College Park. The author is grateful to numerous colleagues at both of these institutions for their helpful comments and suggestions. Special thanks are due also to Ming-Jer Chen, Don Hambrick, Ed Locke, Lee Preston, Ken Smith, and N. Venkatraman for their detailed comments on earlier drafts of this paper.

NOTES

1. In the context of this paper, unless otherwise stated, the term "chief executive officer" is intended to refer to corporate-level chief executive officers as well as to general managers or presidents of strategic business units within corporations. This is so because the arguments advanced in this chapter are seen as being fully valid across both levels of analysis.

REFERENCES

Abell, D.F., and Hammond, J.S. *Strategic Market Planning*. Englewood Cliffs, NJ: Prentice Hall, 1979.

Aguilar, F.J., and Hamermesh, R.G. *General Electric: Strategic Position—1981*. Boston, MA: Graduate School of Business Administration, Harvard University, Case Monograph No. 9-381-174, 1981.

Allison, G.T. *Essence of Decision*. Boston, MA: Little, Brown, 1971.

Andrews, K.R. *The Concept of Corporate Strategy*. Homewood, IL: Dow Jones-Irwin, 1971.

Argyris, C. *Interpersonal Competence and Organizational Effectiveness*. Homewood, IL: The Dorsey Press, 1962.

Argyris, C. *Increasing Leadership Effectiveness*. New York: John Wiley, 1976.

Arrow, K.J. *The Limits of Organization*. New York: W.W. Norton & Co., 1974.

Barnard, C.I. *The Functions of the Executive*. Cambridge, MA: Harvard University Press, 1938.

Bass, B.M. *Stogdill's Handbook of Leadership*. New York: The Free Press, 1981.

Baysinger, B.D., and Zeithaml, C.P. "A Contingency Approach to Diversification and Board Composition: Theory and Empirical Evidence." Working paper, College of Business Administration, Texas A&M University, 1985.

Berg, N.A. "What's Different about Conglomerate Management." *Harvard Business Review* 45 (1969): 112-120.

Bourgeois, L.J., III. "Strategic Management and Determinism." *Academy of Management Journal* 9 (1984): 586-596.

Bourgeois, L.J., III. "Strategic Goals, Perceived Uncertainty, and Economic Performance in Volatile Environments." *Academy of Management Journal* 28 (1985): 548-573.

Bourgeois, L.J., III, and Brodwin, D.R. "Strategic Implementation." *Strategic Management Journal* 5 (1984): 241-264.

Bower, J.L. *Managing the Resouce Allocation Process*. Boston, MA: Division of Research, Graduate School of Business Administration, Harvard University, 1970.

Bower, J.L. *Crown Cork and Seal and the Metal Container Industry*. Boston, MA: Graduate School of Business Administration, Harvard University, Case Monograph No. 9-373-077, 1973.

Brockhaus, R.H., Sr. "Risk-Taking Propensity of Entrepreneurs." *Academy of Management Journal* 23 (1980): 509-520.

Brown, J.S. "Risk-Propensity in Decision-Making: A Comparison of Business and Public School Administrators." *Administrative Science Quarterly* 15 (1970): 473-481.

Brown, M.C. "Administrative Succession and Organizational Performance: The Succession Effect." *Administrative Science Quarterly* 27 (1982): 1-16.

Burgelman, R.A. "A Model of the Interaction of Strategic Behavior, Corporate Context, and the Concept of Strategy." *Academy of Management Review* 8 (1983): 61-70.

Burns, J.M. *Leadership*. New York: Harper and Row Publishers, 1978.

Buzzell, R.D., and Wiersema, F.D. "Modelling Changes in Market Share: A Cross-sectional Analysis." *Strategic Management Journal* 2 (1981): 27-42.

Carlson, S. *Executive Behavior: A Study of the Work Load and the Working Methods of Managing Directors.* Stockholm: Strombergs, 1951.

Child, J. "Organization Structure, Environment, and Performance: The Role of Strategic Choice." *Sociology* 6 (1972): 1-22.

Cosier, R.A. "Methods for Improving the Strategic Decision Dialectic Versus the Devil's Advocate." *Strategic Management Journal* 3 (1982): 373-384.

Cox, M. "Ex-Chief of Recovering AM International Appears to Be a Victim of His Own Success." *The Wall Street Journal* 27 January 1984, p. 33.

Cyert, R.E., and March, J.G. *A Behavioral Theory of the Firm.* Englewood Cliffs, NJ: Prentice Hall, 1963.

Dewar, R., and Werbel, J. "Universalistic and Contingency Predictions of Employee Satisfaction and Conflict." *Administrative Science Quarterly* 24 (1979): 426-448.

Galbraith, J.K. *The New Industrial State.* Boston, MA: Houghton Mifflin, 1967.

Galbraith, J.R. *Designing Complex Organizations.* Reading, MA: Addison Wesley, 1973.

Galbraith, J.R., and Kazanjian, R.K. *Strategy Implementation: Structure, Systems and Process.* St. Paul, MN: West Publishing Co., 1986.

Gerstein, M., and Reisman, H. "Strategic Selection: Matching Executives to Business Conditions." *Sloan Management Review* 19(1) (Winter 1983): 33-49.

Govindarajan, V. "Matching Business Unit General Manager's Locus of Control with Business Unit Strategy: Impact on Performance." Working paper, The Amos Tuck School of Business Administration, Dartmouth College, 1985.

Govindarajan, V., and Gupta, A.K. "Linking Control Systems to Business Unit Strategy: Impact on Performance." *Accounting, Organizations, and Society* 10 (1985): 51-66.

Greiner, L.E. "Evolution and Revolution as Organizations Grow." *Harvard Business Review* 52(4) (1972): 37-45.

Grimm, C.M., and Smith, K.G. "Management Characteristics, Strategy, and Strategic Change." Paper presented at the 5th annual meeting of the Strategic Management Society, Barcelona, Spain, 1985.

Gupta, A.K. "Contingency Linkages Between Strategy and General Manager Characteristics: A Conceptual Examination." *Academy of Management Review* 9 (1984): 399-412.

Gupta, A.K. *Top Management Background: A Study of the Fortune 75.* Special report prepared at the request of Monsanto Company. Boston, MA: School of Management, Boston University, 1985.

Gupta, A.K. "Matching Managers to Strategies: Point and Counterpoint." *Human Resouce Management* 25 (1986): 215-234.

Gupta, A.K., and Govindarajan, V. "Business Unit Strategy, Managerial Characteristics, and Business Unit Effectiveness at Strategy Implementation." *Academy of Management Journal* 27 (1984a): 25-41.

Gupta, A.K., and Govindarajan, V. "Build, Hold, Harvest: Converting Strategic Intentions Into Reality." *Journal of Business Strategy* 4(3) (1984b): 34-47.

Gupta, A.K., and Govindarajan, V. "Resource Sharing Among SBUs: Strategic Antecedents and Administrative Implications." *Academy of Management Journal* 29 (1986a): 695-714.

Gupta, A.K., and Govindarajan, V. "Testing for Interaction in Contingency Research: Conceptual and Methodological Issues." Working paper, College of Business and Management, The University of Maryland, 1986b.

Hambrick, D.C. "Environment, Strategy, and Power Within Top Management Teams." *Administrative Science Quarterly* 26 (1981): 253-275.

Hambrick, D.C. "High Profit Strategies in Mature Capital Goods Industries." *Academy of Management Journal* 26 (1983): 687-707.

Hambrick, D.C., and Finkelstein, S. "Managerial Discretion: A Bridge Between Polar Views of Organizational Outcomes." In *Research in Organizational Behavior*, Vol. 9, pp. 396-406. Edited by L.L. Cummings and B.M. Staw, Greenwich, CT: JAI Press, 1987.

Hambrick, D.C., and Mason, P.A. "Upper Echelons: The Organization as a Reflection of Its Top Managers." *Academy of Management Review* 9 (1984): 193-206.

Hamermesh, R.G. *Making Strategy Work*. New York: John Wiley & Sons, 1986a.

Hamermesh, R.G. "Making Planning Strategic." *Harvard Business Review* 64(4) (1986b): 115-120.

Harrigan, K.R. *Strategies for Declining Industries*. Lexington, MA: Lexington Books, 1981.

Henderson, B.D. *Perspectives on the Product Portfolio*. Boston, MA: Boston Consulting Group, 1970.

Hitt, M.A., Ireland, R.D., and Stadter, G. "Functional Importance and Company Performance: Moderating Effects of Grand Strategy and Industry Type." *Strategic Management Journal* 3 (1982): 315-330.

Hofer, C.W. "Toward a Contingency Theory of Business Strategy." *Academy of Management Journal* 18 (1975): 784-810.

House, R.J., and Baetz, M.L. "Leadership: Some Empirical Generalizations and New Research Directions." *Research in Organizational Behavior* 1 (1979): 341-423.

"How Jake Jacobson is Lighting a Fire Under 3M." *Business Week* 21 July 1986, p. 106.

Isenberg, D.J. "How Senior Managers Think." *Harvard Business Review* 62(6) (1979): 80-90.

Janis, I.L. *Victims of Groupthink: Psychological Studies of Foreign Policy Decisions and Fiascoes*. Boston: Houghton Mifflin, 1972.

"The Job Nobody Wants." *Business Week* 8 September 1986, p. 56.

Kerr, J. "Assigning Managers on the Basis of the Life Cycle." *Journal of Business Strategy* 2(4) (1982): 58-65.

Kiechel, W., III. "Corporate Strategies Under Fire." *Fortune* 27 December 1982, pp. 34-39.

Kotter, J.P. *The General Managers*. New York: The Free Press, 1982.

Lamont, B.T., and Anderson, C.R. "Mode of Economic Diversification and Economic Performance." *Academy of Management Journal* 28 (1985): 926-933.

Larreche, J., and Srinivasan, V. "Stratport: A Model for the Evaluation and Formulation of Business Portfolio Strategies." *Management Science* 28 (1982): 979-1001.

Lawrence, P.R., and Lorsch, J.W. *Organization and Environment*. Boston, MA: Division of Research, Graduate School of Business Administration, Harvard University, 1967.

Leontiades, M. "Choosing the Right Manager to Fit the Strategy." *Journal of Business Strategy* 3(2) (1982): 58-69.

Lieberson, S., and O'Connor, J.F. "Leadership and Organizational Performance: A Study of Large Corporations." *American Sociological Review* 37 (1972): 117-130.

Maddi, S.R. *Personality Theories; A Comparative Analysis*. Homewood, IL: The Dorsey Press, 1972.

McClelland, D.C. *The Achieving Society*. Princeton, NJ: Van Nostrand, 1961.

Miles, R.E., and Snow, C.C. *Organizational Strategy, Structure, and Process*. New York: McGraw-Hill, 1978.

Miller, D., and Friesen, H. *Organizations: A Quantum View*. Englewood Cliffs, NJ: Prentice Hall, 1984.

Miller, D., Kets de Vries, M.F., and Toulouse, J.M. "Top Executive Locus of Control and Its Relationship to Strategy-making, Structure, and Environment." *Academy of Management Journal* 25 (1982): 237-253.

Miller, D., and Toulouse, J.M. "Chief Executive Personality and Corporate Strategy and Structure in Small Firms." *Management Science* 32 (1986): 1389-1409.

Mintzberg, H. *The Nature of Managerial Work*. New York: Harper & Row, 1973.

Mintzberg, H. "Patterns in Strategy Formation." *Management Science* 24 (1978): 934-948.

Peters, T.J. "Leadership: Sad Facts and Silver Linings." *Harvard Business Review* 57(6) (1979): 164-172.

Peters, T.J., and Waterman, R.H., Jr. *In Search of Excellence.* New York: Harper & Row, 1982.

Pfeffer, J. "The Ambiguity of Leadership." *Academy of Management Review* 2 (1977): 104-112.

Pfeffer, J., and Davis-Blake, A. "Administrative Succession and Organizational Performance: How Administrator Experience Mediates the Succession Effect." *Academy of Management Journal* 29 (1986): 72-83.

Pfeffer, J., and Salancik, G.R. *The External Control of Organizations.* New York: Harper & Row, 1978.

Popper, K.R. *Objective Knowledge.* London: Oxford University Press, 1972.

Porter, M.E. "Please Note Location of Nearest Exit: Exit Barriers and Planning." *California Management Review* 19(2) (1976): 21-33.

Porter, M.E. *Competitive Strategy.* New York: The Free Press, 1980.

Porter, M.E. *Competitive Advantage.* New York: The Free Press, 1985.

Reynolds, R.S., Jr. "How to Pick a New Chief Executive." *Fortune* 1 September 1986, p. 113.

The Right Manager for the Strategic Mission. Cambridge, MA: Strategic Planning Institute, 1981.

Rotter, J.B. "Generalized Expectancies for Internal Versus External Control of Reinforcement." *Psychological Monographs* 80, No. 609, 1966.

Rumelt, R.P. *Strategy, Structure, and Economic Performances.* Boston, MA: Graduate School of Business Administration, Harvard University, 1974.

Salancik, G.R., and Pfeffer, J. "Constraints on Administrative Discretion: The Limited Influence of Mayors on City Budgets." *Urban Affairs Quarterly* 12 (1977): 475-498.

Salancik, G.R., and Pfeffer, J. "Effects of Ownership and Performance on Executive Tenure in U.S. Corporations." *Academy of Management Journal* 23 (1980): 653-664.

Sayles, L. *Managerial Behavior.* New York: McGraw-Hill, 1964.

Schere, J.L. "Tolerance of Ambiguity as a Discriminating Variable Between Entrepreneurs and Managers." *Proceedings of the 42nd Annual Meeting of the Academy of Management*, New York, 1982, pp. 404-408.

Schendel, D.E., and Hofer, C.W. *Strategic Management.* Boston, MA: Little Brown, 1979.

Schoonhoven, C.B. "Problems with Contingency Theory: Testing Assumptions Hidden Within the Language of Contingency Theory." *Administrative Science Quarterly* 26 (1981): 349-377.

Schweiger, D.M., Sandberg, W.R., and Ragan, J.W. "Group Approaches for Improving Strategic Decision-Making." *Academy of Management Journal* 29 (1986): 51-71.

Scott, B.R. "The Industrial State: Old Myths and New Realities." *Harvard Business Review* 51(2) (1973): 133-148.

Selznick, P. *Leadership in Administration.* New York: Harper & Row, 1957.

Simon, H.A. *Administrative Behavior.* New York: Free Press, 1947.

Slocum, J.W. Jr., and Hellriegel, D. "A Look at How Managers' Minds Work." *Business Horizons.* July-August (1983): 58-68.

Smith, J.E., Carson, K.P., and Alexander, R.A. "Leadership: It Can Make a Difference." *Academy of Management Journal* 27 (1984): 765-776.

Snow, C.C., and Hrebiniak, L.G. "Strategy, Distinctive Competence, and Organizational Performance." *Administrative Science Quarterly* 25 (1980): 307-335.

Song, J.H. "Diversification Strategies and the Experience of Top Executives of Large Firms." *Strategic Management Journal* 3 (1982): 377-380.

Stewart, R. *Managers and Their Jobs.* New York: Macmillan, 1967.

Stonich, P.J. *Implementing Strategy.* Cambridge, MA: Ballinger Publishing, 1982.

Stybel, L.J. "Linking Strategic Planning and Management Manpower Planning." *California Management Review* 25(1) (1982): 48-56.

Szilagyi, A.D., Jr., and Schweiger, D.M. "Matching Managers to Strategies: A Review and Suggested Framework." *Academy of Management Review* 9 (1984): 623-637.

Thompson, J.D. *Organization in Action.* New York: McGraw-Hill, 1967.

Tichy, N.M., Fombrun, C.J., and Devanna, M.A. "Strategic Human Resource Management." *Sloan Management Review* 23(2) (1982): 47-61.

Tichy, N.M., and Ulrich, D.O. "The Leadership Challenge: A Call For the Transformational Leader." *Sloan Management Review* 25(3) (1984): 59-68.

Tushman, M.L., and Romanelli, E. "Organizational Evolution: A Metamorphic Model of Inertia and Reorientation." In *Research in Organizational Behavior,* Vol. 7, pp. 171-222. Edited by B. Staw and L.L. Cummings. Greenwich, CT: JAI Press, 1985.

Van de Ven, A.H., and Drazin, R. "The Concept of Fit in Contingency Theory." *Research in Organizational Behavior,* Vol. 7, pp. 333-365. Edited by L.L. Cummings and B.M. Staw. Greenwich, CT: JAI Press, 1985.

Vancil, R.F. *Decentralization: Managerial Ambiguity by Design.* New York: Financial Executives Research Foundation, 1980.

Vancil, R.F., and Lorange, P. "Strategic Planning in Diversified Companies." *Harvard Business Review* 53(1) (1975): 81-93.

Virany, B., Tushman, M.L., and Romanelli, E. "A Longitudinal Study on Determinants of Executive Succession." Working paper, Columbia University, 1985.

Wanous, J.P., and Youtz, M.A. "Solution Diversity and the Quality of Group Decisions." *Academy of Management Journal* 29 (1986): 149-158.

"Wanted: A Manager to Fit Each Strategy," *Business Week* 25 February 1980, p. 166.

Webber, A.M. "The CEO Is the Company." *Harvard Business Review* 65(1) (1986): 114-123.

Weiner, N., and Mahoney, T.A. "A Model of Corporate Performance as a Function of Environmental, Organizational, and Leadership Influences." *Academy of Management Journal* 24 (1981): 453-470.

Wissema, J.G., Van der Pol, H.W., and Messer, H.M. "Strategic Management Archetypes." *Strategic Management Journal* 1 (1980): 37-47.

Wright, R.V.L. "A System for Managing Diversity." Cambridge, MA: Arthur D. Little, 1974.

THE DYNAMICS OF CEO/BOARD RELATIONSHIPS

John R. Kimberly and Edward J. Zajac

INTRODUCTION

Why do some firms perform better than others? This question dates from the founding of the second firm in history. The comparative analysis of performance has intrigued researchers, bedeviled investors, and engaged managers for generations. Answers have proved elusive, particularly in contemporary conditions with rapidly changing technologies, uncertainty in global markets, and increasing skepticism about the efficiency of large corporations.

Accelerating rates of change in the environments that most firms face have led to a virtual explosion in research on corporate strategy. The conventional wisdom emerging from this research is that those firms most likely to perform well under such conditions have clearly articulated strategies, and structures which are carefully designed to support those strategies (Chandler, 1962; Miller and Friesen, 1984.) However, while the strategy, structure, performance theme is very strong in contemporary research, empirical evidence is mixed. There appears to be either more to the story or the need for a somewhat different story. The model, in other words, is either incomplete or inappropriate.

A second theme in research on corporate performance is that of leadership. The American public has always been fascinated by corporate power and its most concrete manifestation, the men and women who sit at the apex of the corporate pyramid. These people represent the ultimate in personal and professional achievement, and all manner of intellect, skill, and insight is attributed to them. The three letters CEO have come to symbolize what many aspire to but few achieve, the position of final authority, the place where the buck stops, the last word in career progression.

Biographies and autobiographies of those who have been particularly visible in their roles as CEOs abound, a testimony to the fantasy of every person that, were it not for the fickle finger of fate, there (s)he would be too.

In view of the widespread fascination with the CEO as role and with the personal lives of many of those who have been in the role, there has been surprisingly little serious analysis of executive leadership as a social phenomenon to be understood as such. Studies of "leadership," of course, are plentiful. It turns out, however, that the vast majority of these are really studies of supervisor/subordinate relationships, not of top executives. The general literature on leadership, therefore, reveals much more about first line supervisors and middle managers than it does about CEOs.

The work by Peters and Waterman (1982) carried a strong message of empowerment to managers, and the level of interest in the chief executive officer and his or her role in shaping corporate performance has been heightened by this message. Lee Iacocca's autobiography is but one example. The underlying argument is that the CEO with vision and charisma can both develop and articulate the appropriate strategy and engage the loyalty and productivity of corporate employees in ways that will assure extraordinary performance.

Attribution of such impact to CEOs has been controversial, and debates about the effects of executive leadership on corporate performance abound. Do leaders make a difference? Can effective leaders influence corporate performance? While only the most doctrinaire population ecologist would take the extreme negative position, how much of a difference leaders make, and under what conditions, is certainly not obvious. Ralph Stogdill, an eminent and long-time student of leadership, produced a handbook on the subject (Stogdill, 1974), which noted literally thousands of studies of the phenomenon. While there appears to be some agreement that some combination of personal attributes, leader-follower relations, and environmental forces accounts for the apparent impact of particular leaders at given moments in time, there is little consistent empirical evidence supporting the relative causal priority of these three clusters of variables.

The concept of "transformational leadership" (Tichy and Devanna, 1986) helps to bridge research on strategy and research on leadership. Effective transformational leaders combine both symbol and substance in ways which engage their followers in meaningful commitment to a vision of the future. There is some anecdotal evidence about effective transformational leaders and their behavior; yet this evidence is almost always retrospective—that is, exploits become visible and researchers then try to reconstruct what the leaders have done in an effort to account for the exploits. Furthermore, rarely do we glimpse the failures. Transformational leaders are "successful" by definition. What about the myriad flawed efforts? How are they to be understood? Can one really have a theory of leadership and performance based only on "successes?"

It is not our purpose in this paper to review the literature extensively or to become involved in debates about the symbolic versus operational effects of senior executives (Beatty and Zajac, 1987). We come to the analysis of the problem of executive leadership with the perspective that leaders can and generally do have an impact on the organizations for which they have responsiblity. We believe that the more exceptional case is the one in which the CEO has no impact, and our purpose in this paper is to suggest that an interesting and significant, though largely unresearched, domain of impact is in the kinds and quality of relations that are created and maintained between the CEO and the board of directors.

Almost without exception (e.g., Donaldson and Lorsch, 1983), research on corporate strategy, executive leadership and performance neglects the issue of corporate governance. Yet boards of directors and boards of trustees are by definition responsible for the overall conduct of the corporation. Their legal and fiduciary responsibilites at least imply some interest in corporate strategy and in executive leadership. The CEO serves at the pleasure of the board; it is the board's responsibility to hire, evaluate, and fire the CEO. While it is certainly true that some boards discharge these responsibilities with more dispatch and more competence than others, it is also true that the responsibilities are theoretically as great in one corporation as in another.

What do we know about the structure and behavior of boards and about their impact on performance? The answer is surprisingly little. We do know something about the connectedness of firms through overlapping board memberships. This tradition of research on "interlocking directorates" (e.g., Pennings, 1980; Schoorman et al., 1981) is oriented more toward the issue of the concentration of corporate control than toward the issue of performance at the level of the firm. We also know something about board size and composition, with some attempts to relate these to other variables such as performance (e.g., Baysinger and Butler, 1985; Pfeffer, 1972). This type of research typically avails itself of publicly available data on characteristics of board members, such as sex, age, and employer. While these dimensions may be relevant in adding to our understanding of boards, the studies often appear to be framed as much by available data as by theory

(Zajac, 1988). A third line of research, more germane to our concerns, has focused on the problem of internal control (e.g., Mizruchi, 1983) and has inquired into the balance of power between executives and boards. This work is promising, but appears to rely too heavily on the proportion of outside directors as the determinant of the balance of power.

There are far fewer studies which refer to the behavioral aspects of the board's functioning and provide insights which go beyond size and composition. Alderfer (1986) has conducted one such study in which he observes the impact of group dynamics on boards and CEO/board relations. Chitayat (1985: 69) has also investigated the relationship between board chairmen and CEOs, and finds that the board chairman "seems to be relatively inactive while the CEO's have assumed. . .the responsibility and power necessary to manage the business." These studies, however, do not explicitly deal with performance outcomes.

Thus, we conclude that while conceptually it appears reasonable to argue that performance depends on the articulation and implementation of appropriate strategies, on the symbolic and substantive contributions of executive leadership, and on the informed and competent exercise of corporate governance, there are significant gaps in research. Figure 1 highlights the traditional research emphases in these areas, and suggests several potentially fruitful research agendas.

Figure 1

.... Very little research

– – –· Some research

————— Relatively large amounts of research

As noted in this figure, research on governance and its relationship both to leadership and to corporate strategy is relatively sparse. In this paper we argue that the nature of the relationships between the CEO and the board is both a significant gap in and a particularly fertile domain for research on corporate performance.

STRATEGY, LEADERSHIP, GOVERNANCE AND PERFORMANCE

The recent wave of corporate mergers and acquisitions and of corporate efforts to diversify or consolidate provide an unusually good opportunity to examine the interplay between chief executives and boards. Generally, these relationships are hidden from public view, coming to public attention only when there is the hint of scandal or extraordinary (usually extraordinarily poor) performance. However, several recently publicized instances of changes in corporate strategy, when viewed collectively, are highly suggestive of a number of questions that researchers interested in corporate performance should ask about the dynamics of CEO/board relationships.

Most important, these instances reveal that much might be learned about performance by focusing on the *relationship* between the CEO and the board. At the very least, the public accounts suggest wide differences on numerous dimensions along which the relationship might vary. The remainder of this paper develops this possibility in detail. First, we present summaries of four widely-reported corporate transitions, identifying some common themes and generating a set of questions for researchers to investigate in greater depth. Then we suggest two theoretical perspectives that might help order the phenomena. And finally, we sketch out an agenda for researchers interested in the issues.

THE DYNAMICS OF CEO-BOARD RELATIONS: FOUR CASES

The four cases discussed below—BankAmerica, CBS, Union Carbide, and Allegheny International—were chosen for three principal reasons. First, each involved an instance in which corporate governance was implicated in a significant way in the strategic decision-making process. Second, each occurred within a roughly comparable time span of 12 months, so it might be argued that each was subject, at the most general level, to a common set of social, political, and economic forces. And, finally, each received a good deal of attention in the media, thus providing unusual accessibility to governance issues.

Our accounts are based entirely on secondary sources, but even these data, removed as they are from the actual decision-making process, are richly suggestive of a set of questions which might usefully be pursued in establishing the linkages among corporate strategy, leadership, governance and performance.

BankAmerica

The story of CEO/board relations at BankAmerica is particularly interesting in its complexity, involving initial board support for the incumbent CEO, criticism of this support from outside parties, the granting of golden parachutes to top management, the need to respond repeatedly to takeover attempts, pressure for changes from federal banking regulators, and finally, the decision to replace the CEO, Samuel Armacost.

Armacost was named as the successor to A.W. Clausen as President and CEO of BankAmerica, effective April 1981. In early 1981, it became clear that the prior successful expansion of BankAmerica was producing sizable loan losses. The problems continued through the early 1980s and federal regulators forced the company to increase its loan-loss reserves in 1984 and 1985. By mid-1985, the unfavorable sequence of events forced the firm to begin the first layoffs in its 81 year history, cut its dividend for the first time in 53 years, and sell its headquarters building. In early 1986, the company reported a $337 million loss for 1985.

Out of these events emerged, not surprisingly, some board discontentment with Armacost's performance. On February 20, 1986, Sanford Weill, former president of American Express Company, offered to infuse the ailing company with $1 billion in new equity—under the condition that he replace Armacost as CEO. The board's response was harsh: "We have no interest in considering you as a candidate," wrote board member Franklin D. Murphy, described as "an ardent Armacost supporter" ("BofA Isn't Ready . . .," 1986: 53). The board's rejection of Weill and his proposal was unanimous, with two directors reportedly abstaining. According to the *Economist* ("Board Repels Boarder," 1986: 78), the decision was reached "against the opposition of at least four of Bank of America's 21-member board (including Charles Schwab, who encouraged Weill to make the offer)." The same report also stated that Armacost had told the board that the company did not need the $1 billion, even though Armacost himself was believed to have explored a similar option with an investment banking firm.

Several days after the board's decision, BankAmerica received an informal merger offer from First Interstate Bancorp. At the urging of Armacost, the Board announced that it was "not negotiating a merger with First Interstate or anyone else" ("Armacost Wins. . .," 1986: 17). During the first half of 1986, the bank lost $577 million. During the August 1986 board meeting, the board approved generous severance packages ("golden parachutes") for Armacost and seven other top managers. Armacost's maximum special severance benefits were as much as $1.7 million ("BankAmerica Gave Severance. . .," 1987).

In September 1986, Charles Schwab, who had sold his discount brokerage to BankAmerica in 1983, quit the board. One article describes him as "tired of challenging Chief Executive Samuel Armacost and the other directors to cut costs," and notes that Armacost had been holding Sunday dinner meetings with outside directors since March. Schwab was technically an insider and therefore was not invited ("Schwab Gives Up. . .," 1987).

In September, board members Beckett and Grey (outside directors) were believed to have met with federal banking regulators to discuss the problems facing BankAmerica and the presence of a series of rumors regarding the health of the company. In early October, First Interstate returned with a $2.78 billion bid for the company. On October 12, 1986, Armacost was replaced as President and CEO of BankAmerica by his predecessor, A.W. Clausen. Board members Beckett and Grey were thought to be the engineers of the request for Armacost's resignation. Of the 11 outside directors on the board, eight had been originally appointed by Clausen. An unnamed source close to the bank was quoted as saying: "The board has panicked and in a panic situation you go with the guy you know" ("BankAmerica Board . . .," 1987: 3).

CBS

The CEO/board relationship at CBS resembles the BankAmerica case in some respects. The board of directors at CBS was also confronted with a merger proposal and a dramatic increase in the publicity of their actions, and the board also ultimately forced the CEO, Thomas Wyman, from his position at CBS. This case, however, involves a different set of dynamics, as the following description suggests.

CBS's performance had begun to slip in the last few years. Combined advertising revenues for the three major networks had dropped for the first time in almost 15 years, and the decreases were expected to continue. CBS faced a declining share of this shrinking market, having dropped to No. 2 in the Nielsen ratings, behind NBC. *Business Week* ("The Bad Days. . .," 1986) reported that advertising executives viewed CBS's lineup of new shows as fairly weak and that its mainstays were showing signs of age. The previously unthinkable—a drop to the No. 3 position—was now considered possible.

These ominous trends did not go unnoticed in the media. On the contrary, CBS, which had always "enjoyed" more media attention than its two major competitors, began to receive a great deal of negative publicity about its difficulties. This culminated in September 1986 with a *Newsweek* cover story entitled: "Civil War at CBS—The Struggle for the Soul of a Legendary Network" (1986). The September board meeting, reported the *Wall Street Journal*, "took place under intense media scrutiny and in a carnival-like atmosphere," with "about a dozen teams of television news crews . . . outside the ground-floor entrance" ("CBS's Wyman. . .," 1987: 29).

CEO Wyman had enjoyed the support of the majority of the board up to this point. One board member particularly vocal in his opposition to Wyman's leadership, however, was Laurence Tisch, chairman of Loews Corp., which held a 24.9 percent of CBS's shares outstanding. Tisch, who had been invited by Wyman to join CBS's board in November 1985 (after Loews had initially purchased an 11.9 percent stake in the company), was viewed as a stabilizing influence for CBS, insulating the company from future hostile takeover attempts through his large holdings ("CBS's Wyman . . .," 1987). Tisch, however, had also declined the board's suggestion that he sign a contract limiting his purchases to 25 percent. The support for Mr. Wyman, one might argue, was in part strengthened by the board's wariness of Tisch's potential actions. Tisch's brother, a former president at Loews, had in fact publicly stated that it was Loews' intention to control CBS someday. On the eve of the board's scheduled September meeting, the entire CBS Board, with the exception of Wyman and Tisch, met during a private dinner meeting, apparently to agree on a way of resolving the conflict between the two men. An unidentified director arranged the meeting, and Wyman and Tisch were informed that the meeting was taking place.

These issues provided the context under which the board met on the morning of September 10, 1986. The first item discussed was the projections for the third and fourth fiscal quarters, which predicted continued decline in profits. The board's already sober mood was not helped by the news. Wyman then apparently told the board of his plan "that could 'get more money for shareholders,' in the words of a participant" ("How The CBS . . .," 1986: 11). This plan was Coca-Cola's friendly offer to pay a substantial premium for CBS's shares. Wyman also mentioned a second possible buyer, also ready to pay a generous amount for CBS. The board, and Tisch in particular, was stunned; an official present at the meeting noted that "there was deadly silence," although it has since been speculated that some of the directors were aware of the offer. Wyman, Tisch, and William Paley, founder and retired chairman of CBS, were then asked to leave the room. A six hour debate ensued, with Paley and Tisch occasionally returning to the boardroom, and finally concluded with the naming of Tisch as interim CEO, Paley as acting chairman, and Wyman as the executive without portfolio—but with roughly $2 million in severance pay.

As one director commented about the ouster of Wyman: "He misread the board . . . if Tom hadn't taken his position (i.e., suggested the merger),

nothing would have happened at that meeting" ("How The CBS . . .,"
986: 11).

Union Carbide

While the relationship between the CEO and the board at Union Carbide
is not filled with the same complexity found in the other cases illustrated
here, it is highly significant in providing an interesting example of the
special role outside directors can play in a major corporation. The example
is drawn from an experience which boards are encountering with increasing
frequency; namely, an organization's attempt to resist a hostile takeover
attempt.

From December 9, 1985 to January 8, 1986, Union Carbide was engaged
in a dramatic takeover defense against a hostile suitor, GAF Corp. The
successful defense represented the first time that a major company had
defeated an all-cash offer for its shares. More important for this discussion,
it is perhaps the first time that a major corporation's independent, outside
directors engineered the defense, to the overall benefit of shareholder value.
Given the rising numbers of all-cash, hostile takeover offers, and the increase
in board sensitivity to the legal implications of their actions, the Union
Carbide case "is expected to become a model takeover defense for years to
come," and "a landmark in the history of takeover battles" ("Outside
Directors. . .," 1986: 1).

An important precursor to the takeover confrontation was, of course, the
Bhopal tragedy, where an estimated 2,000 people died as a result of a poison
gas leak from one of Union Carbide's Indian plants. The wave of lawsuits
stemming from this accident forced the stock price of the company
drastically downward. With this depressed stock price, the company was
vulnerable to takeovers from a wide range of possible buyers.

In September 1985, GAF disclosed that it had acquired nearly 10 percent
of Union Carbide's shares outstanding. Union Carbide's board met with
legal advisors shortly thereafter, largely for the purpose of establishing the
rights and obligations of the board in the event of a takeover fight. The
board's concern was heightened by the fact that, as a result of the Bhopal
tragedy, Union Carbide had lost practically all of its directors' liability
insurance. Theoretically, if the board were to be proven negligent in their
duties to the shareholders, the directors' personal wealth might be
jeopardized.

While it is difficult to infer how the board's behavior might be affected
by such circumstances, it is noteworthy that the board's reaction to the first
proposed defense strategy, a "poison pill" was negative and that the
proposal was strongly rejected by the board, despite some management
support. A task force, comprised of investment bank advisors, four

management representatives, and three outside directors, was formed to consider other defense strategies. Union Carbide fully expected GAF to make an offer. Alternative defense strategies such as taking the company private through a leveraged buyout, finding a more friendly suitor, and even buying the hostile suitor were considered. On December 9, 1985, the anticipated GAF bid was announced.

Later that week, the board met at the offices of Union Carbide's legal advisors, and the various possible courses of action were discussed. The company was unwilling to accept GAF's offer, and GAF's own shares were too expensive for Union Carbide to purchase. The leveraged buyout was considered, as was an exchange offer recommended by Union Carbide's legal advisors and investment officers, in which the company would buy back 35 percent of its shares, using cash and debt securities, from existing shareholders—at a generous price, higher than GAF's per share offer.

At this point in the debate, management members of the board, including the Chairman, Walter Anderson, were asked to leave the room ("Outside Directors...," 1987). The remaining directors then asked the lawyers if there were any other issues not raised while management had been present in the meeting. Satisfied that all issues had been discussed, the outside directors quickly agreed against a leveraged buyout, and for the exchange of cash and debt for outstanding stock. The management directors returned to the meeting, were informed of the preferences of the outside directors, and a unanimous vote in support of the proposal was reached. The board viewed the exchange proposal as directly benefiting shareholders.

However, GAF then sweetened its offer on December 26, leading Union Carbide's board to convene once again to consider it. They again rejected the GAF offer, but decided that it was necessary to improve the exchange offer to shareholders. To pay for this new offer (involving 55 percent of all shares), it was necessary to sell the profitable and growing consumer products division. Initial management opposition was stilled when it became clear that GAF had also intended to sell the division. A legal advisor for Union Carbide commented that "for management, this was painful... it wanted to develop this area. But if it (the division) was going to be sold anyway (if GAF won), then the value might as well go to Carbide's shareholders." ("Outside Directors...," 1986: 12). Several days later, GAF abandoned its bid for Union Carbide. The board was elated and celebrated with champagne. The elation of top management was less visible.

Allegheny International

Robert J. Buckley, former Chairman of Allegheny International, Inc., submitted his resignation to the Board on August 17, 1986. Turnover in executive leadership is not unusual; it happens all the time. In many cases, turnover is the result of a planned transition at the top. In this case, however, it came about as the result of increasingly poor financial performance by the company, increasing discontent on the part of the shareholders, and unusual public visibility of the company's situation, the most damaging being a cover story in *Business Week* the previous week titled "Trouble!" ("Big Trouble. . .," 1986).

From what can be pieced together from publicly available materials, Mr. Buckley began his employment at Allegheny in 1972 when the company was called Allegheny Ludlum Industries and was a specialty-steel producer. He had previously been employed at General Electric, Standard Steel, and Ingersoll Milling Machine Co. In 1975, he became CEO of Allegheny, and over the course of the next eleven years moved the company out of the steel business and into a variety of consumer businesses. The company was renamed to reflect this change in strategy, and its sales volume increased rapidly, passing the $2.5 billion mark in 1982.

During this period, Mr. Buckley became actively involved in the cultural life of Pittsburgh, site of the corporation's headquarters, becoming president of the Pittsburgh Symphony Society. The corporation made generous donations to various arts organizations and became viewed as a good citizen of the community.

After 1981, however, financial performance worsened. Profits declined steadily through 1985, when there was a large loss. Long-term debt increased, and the corporation's stock price fluctuated in a downward trend, moving from a high of 55 in 1981 to a low of 15 in July of 1986.

As performance indicators worsened, questions arose about certain aspects of the company's conduct. Three areas, in particular, received attention in the media. First, there were allegations that a number of management expenses were unusually and unnecessarily high, especially in a time of deteriorating performance. Examples cited were the maintenance of a number of corporate jets, the purchase of a large and expensive house in Pittsburgh to entertain clients, reimbursement to senior management for expenses whose relevance to the conduct of corporate business was questionable, and a substantial number of personal loans to executives at very low rates of interest. None of these actions in and of itself is necessarily an indicator of questionable practice or executive judgment; each can be found elsewhere is in the corporate world. But taken together, and in the context of worsening performance, they raised questions about control.

Second, there were questions about how important strategic decisions involving investments in certain real estate and oil and gas ventures were made. These investments did not appear closely related to Allegheny's core businesses, and there was some implication that poor business judgment at best and conflict of interest between executives and shareholders at worst was involved. Again, although the specific issues are different, the question raised has to do with control.

In addition, questions were raised about whether the company provided enough information to its shareholders about various aspects of its operations. Here again, there is room for legitimate debate about how much information is enough, but there are statutory requirements which specify minimum reporting standards. There have been allegations that the company may have failed to comply with one or more of these requirements.

Finally, and perhaps most importantly for our purposes, much public discussion ensued in the wake of the previous disclosures and questions about why the AI board had apparently failed to take any action to address any of the issues. The board was composed of experienced and distinguished individuals, many of whom had considerable experience on other boards. Their low profile struck many as surprising. As the *Business Week* article put it, "Management theory has it that strong outside directors are the best protection shareholders have. AI's deterioration, though, has taken place despite a board that included prestigious outsiders" ("Big Trouble. . .," 1986: 57).

Obviously, there is a great deal more to the story of the relationship between the CEOs and the boards in these four cases than has been revealed in public accounts. Our intent, however, is not to ferret out all of the details in any particular case but rather to argue that even these brief accounts are suggestive of a series of questions about the relationships between CEOs and boards to which researchers interested in the relationship among corporate strategy, executive leadership and corporate performance ought to pay more attention. Most prominent among these questions are the following:

BankAmerica

- Why did the board and the CEO refuse the offer of Sanford Weill to infuse the company with one billion dollars in new equity?
- Why did the board announce it was not interested in a merger with anyone else?
- Why did the board approve generous golden parachutes for the CEO and other top managers?
- Why did Charles Schwab quit the board?
- What was the purpose of CEO's private dinner meetings with outside directors?
- Why did the board wait so long before removing CEO Armacost?
- Why did the board then hire the previous CEO once again?

CBS

- Why did the CEO misjudge the opinion of the board regarding possible merger partners?
- What was the function of the private board dinner, which excluded the CEO and his most vocal critics?
- How did the heightened publicity surrounding the company affect CEO/board relations?
- Why was the board opposed to a merger which, in the words of the CEO, could "get more money for shareholders?"

Union Carbide

- Did the absence of director liability insurance affect the board's actions?
- Why did the board and the CEO favor different responses to the hostile takeover threat?
- How did the board's outside directors gain what appeared to be such a powerful role?
- How was the board able to institute the procedure by which the CEO and other inside board members are asked to leave during board discussions?

Allegheny International

- How did Mr. Buckley achieve the extensive amount of influence he apparently had in the corporate decision-making process?
- What measures did the board use to judge Mr. Buckley's performance, and how rigorously were they applied?
- Why did the board, composed of nine distinguished outsiders and five insiders, not exercise more control over the conduct of AI's affairs?
- How much information did the board actually have, and how was the amount of information controlled and monitored?

General Questions

Looking across the four cases collectively, there are a number of more general questions which emerge:

- How do CEOs obtain and exercise a degree of influence vis-à-vis the board which apparently goes beyond that inherent in the role?
- How do boards evaluate CEO performance, and with what degree of stringency?

- What factors influence the role that boards actually play in the life of a given company as opposed to the role they are formally ascribed?
- What are the dynamics of information gathering and dissemination in the conduct of corporate affairs at the very highest echelons? What do boards demand, what does the senior leadership provide, where are the conflicts, and how are they resolved? How might the styles of the CEO and the board be characterized with respect to degree of closed or openness in information requested and/or disseminated?
- What connections are there between board/CEO relations and corporate performance?

CEO/BOARD RELATIONS AS AN AGENCY PROBLEM

The general questions emerging from the four cases suggest the need for a framework for analyzing systematically the relationship between a CEO and the board. In considering the types of theoretical approaches that would be useful for an analysis of CEO/board relations, one important desideratum would be that the theory itself be relational, i.e., that it address issues which are particularly relevant for interactions between individuals, groups, or organizations. Agency theory (Jensen and Meckling, 1976) represents one such approach. Originally developed in the economics literature, agency theory examines the relationship between a principal (a person interested in delegating responsibility for a set of decision problems) and an agent (a person acting on behalf of the principal, for which he is paid a fee). This agency relationship is one of the oldest and most common codified modes of social interaction (Ross, 1973).

Chakravarthy and Zajac (1984), who use the agency approach in analyzing the strategic relationship between CEOs and their business unit managers, offer a framework for analysis which isolates two underlying dimensions implicit in the classic agency problem: information asymmetry and lack of goal congruence. The first dimension refers to the extent to which the agent, by virtue of his knowledge of the local environment and the principal's inability to easily monitor the agent's activity, typically enjoys an informational advantage vis-à-vis the principal. The dimension of goal congruence refers to the extent to which the agent, in acting in his own interest, is likely to seek outcomes which are different from those desired by the principal. This is not to say that the agent is maliciously subversive, but to suggest that it is unreasonable to expect that the agent will consistently act contrary to his own interest.

While Chakravarthy and Zajac focused on the utility of agency theory in constructing a normative framework linking a firm's strategic context to its control and incentive system design, the agency model can also be usefully

Figure 2.   An Agency Approach to CEO/Board Relations

GOAL CONGRUENCE

		High	Low
INFORMATION	High	BankAmerica	Union Carbide
SYMMETRY	Low	CBS	Allegheny International

(adapted from Chakravarthy and Zajac, 1984)

applied to the study of CEO/board relations. Indeed, as will be shown, the four case studies of relationships between CEOs and boards has implicitly described issues surrounding agency problems and their consequences.

The following section examines how the four cases of CEO/board relations exhibit variation with respect to the two dimensions of the agency problem discussed above. While the four cases are diverse examples of CEO/board interactions, and suggest that there is no "typical" CEO/board relationship, the agency framework in Figure 2 does represent one way in which the four cases can be meaningfully compared and contrasted.

We view the framework as suggesting that the courses of events described in the cases were often unsurprising and predictable, given the characteristics of the agency relationship between each company's board and CEO. The location of the cases in the framework is intended to facilitate comparison along a common basis, not to suggest any overall assessment of the relative severity of CEO/board relational problems for the cases (other, nonagency problems are not captured in the framework, and are discussed in a later section).

Case 1: Allegheny International

If the published accounts represent an accurate picture of the CEO/board relationship at AI, it would appear that Allegheny's CEO was engaged in a variety of activities which seemed not to be in the interest of the firm. In terms of the agency relationship, there was low congruence between the actions of the CEO and the actions that the board would have desired. In addition, the board appeared to be unaware of the sometimes questionable activities of the CEO leading up to the *Business Week* cover story: in other words, information symmetry was very low. This might explain the fact that, despite the undesirable situation at AI, the ongoing relationship between the board and CEO could be characterized as one with no apparent conflict. It was only after the intense publicity generated by the embarrassing national magazine cover story, i.e., the information asymmetry was lessened, that CEO Buckley submitted his resignation.

This situation represents the classic agency problem: the combination of low goal congruence and low information symmetry. It is thus interesting to note that the expected actions of an agent in this setting, according to agency theorists, is an excessive consumption of perquisites, which precisely depicts the publicly reported actions of the CEO at AI. As an agent, the CEO enjoyed full consumption of perquisites (e.g., private jets, lavish parties, etc.).

Case 2: Union Carbide

The Union Carbide case suggests similarities and differences with that of Allegheny International. The major difference was that the board played an influential role in the strategic decision facing the firm (how to respond to GAF's takeover offer), with the outside board members, in particular, taking the initiative in obtaining the information needed (using legal and investment banking consultants) to respond quickly and decisively to the GAF offer. The information asymmetry problem present in the AI case was not present in the Union Carbide case.

Of particular interest here is the issue of goal congruence between the CEO and the board. After exploring a wide range of alternatives, Union Carbide's board chose the alternative which was most favorable to shareholders; top management, however, preferred another alternative less attractive to shareholders (a leveraged management buyout). In other words, the goal congruence between CEO and board was low, as in the AI case. The well-informedness of the board, however, was sufficient to overcome potential CEO resistance to the board's decision. Thus, the difference in outcome of the Union Carbide case relative to the Allegheny International case can be traced to the ability of the board to overcome the information asymmetry problem.

Case 3: CBS

The main feature in public accounts of the CBS case is the CEO's failure to inform the board of his intentions regarding a proposal for CBS to be acquired. This information asymmetry ultimately led to the CEO's demise, as the shocked board, upon hearing of the CEO's actions for the first time, reacted in a predictable way in asking for his resignation. While the typical agency scenario depicts the agent as exploiting his informational advantage, the CBS case suggests that some agents may find it in their interest to reduce the information asymmetry themselves.

This, of course, is not consistent with the usual agency approach. We argue, however, that the situation at CBS is dissimilar to the AI case in an important respect; namely, the high level of goal congruence in the CBS case. In broad terms, both the CBS board and the CBS CEO were interested in a financial solution to the company's financial problems which would have benefited shareholders. It was the fact that the board was uninformed about the CEO's actions which was ultimately the problem.

This is not to suggest that agency theory is less useful in gaining insights in this case. On the contrary, the theory is useful in indicating that the CBS case is not a full-fledged agency problem, but one which economists have analyzed in terms of team theory (Marschak and Radner, 1972). Standard team theory assumes goal congruence, and the team—in this case, the CEO and the board—tries to make joint policy decisions using different sets of expert information. Team theorists identify the key problem as how best to encourage information exchange among team members. Clearly, this was the problem which CBS was unable to solve.

Case 4: BankAmerica

The BankAmerica case is particularly interesting in that public accounts do not show the CEO/board relationship as characterized by information asymmetry or lack of goal congruence. Neither the agency nor the team theory problems appear to be present in this case. The board continued publicly to support the CEO, suggesting that goal congruence was not an issue, and the board appeared to be well-informed.

Nonetheless, the absence of an agency problem between the board and the CEO does not automatically ensure an organizationally beneficial relationship, as the BankAmerica case indicates. This suggests that the economic agency framework might be usefully complemented by an approach which is more sociopolitical in nature; namely, an approach which deals with power and influence. The next section offers a framework for analyzing the power relationships which arise from the relative level of involvement of the board and the CEO in organizational decisions.[1]

A BEHAVIORAL FRAMEWORK FOR ANALYZING CEO-BOARD RELATIONS

The inclusion here of a theoretical approach which is more behavioral in nature does not imply that the agency framework is inappropriate, but that it is incomplete as an explanatory framework for understanding CEO/board relations. Figure 3 suggests a categorization of the CEO/board relations in the four cases discussed earlier which offers a perspective complementary to the agency approach.

The term "intensity of involvement" refers to the degree of the CEO's or the board's involvement in the decisions affecting the strategic direction of the firm, i.e., decisions which would normally involve the board and the CEO. It is only a subjective assessment of involvement, not a statement as to the quality of the board's or the CEO's abilities. Defined in this way, it becomes clear that it is possible, for example, to have both a highly involved board and a highly involved CEO, i.e., the two dimensions are independent. It is also possible that intensity of board and CEO involvement may vary across major decisions and over time.

The discussion will begin with the off-diagonal quadrants, representing imbalanced levels of "involvement intensity" of the board and the CEO. In the case of low board involvement and high CEO involvement, Allegheny International, from all reports, appears to be a classic example of the underinformed board, unable or unwilling to ask the CEO critical questions about important decisions. If one believes published accounts, Allegheny's CEO was engaged in a variety of activities which should have been the subject of the board's attention. Clearly, the company as a whole did not benefit, financially or otherwise, from many of the CEO's decisions and actions leading up to the *Business Week* cover story.

Despite the undesirable situation, the ongoing relationship between the board and CEO could be characterized as one with no apparent conflict. It was only after the intense publicity generated by the embarrassing national magazine cover story that pressure mounted and CEO Buckley submitted his resignation. The fact that the board was not an initiator of actions against Buckley suggests that the board's involvement intensity in the strategic direction of Allegheny International was not strong.

In the other off-diagonal quadrant, the Union Carbide case suggests a very different type of CEO/board relationship. In the strategic decision facing the firm (how to respond to GAF's takeover offer), the board's role

Figure 3.   A Behavioral Approach to CEO/Board Relations

		INTENSITY OF CEO INVOLVEMENT	
		Low	High
INTENSITY OF BOARD INVOLVEMENT	Low	BankAmerica	Allegheny International
	High	Union Carbide	CBS

was highly influential in the final outcome. The outside board members, in particular, took the initiative of gaining the information needed (using legal and investment banking consultants) to respond quickly and decisively to the GAF offer. A wide range of alternatives was explored, and the board chose the alternative which they believed was most favorable to shareholders, despite the fact that management preferred another alternative. Warren Anderson's top management position was undoubtedly somewhat weakened by the recent tragic events at Bhopal; indeed, he had previously submitted his resignation to the board, which the board refused.[2]His deference to the board, one could argue, was not unpredictable. In any event, the lack of conflict between the board and the CEO allowed Union Carbide to meet the threat of a GAF takeover with a unified response. Thus, the Union Carbide case demonstrated the same absence of conflict as observed in the Allegheny International case; the implications, however, differ substantially depending on whether the CEO or the board is more strongly involved.

Characterizing the relationship between the CEO and the board at BankAmerica as low involvement intensity for both parties requires further explanation. The justification for this labeling is based on the observation that neither the BankAmerica board nor the CEO seemed willing to deviate substantially from the status quo, despite a host of indicators suggesting that fundamental changes were needed. The board seemed to spend a great deal of energy reaffirming its support for CEO Armacost, even as pressures for his removal mounted. Proposals which could have infused the company with $1 billion of needed capital were quickly dismissed by the board, due largely, perhaps, to the fact that the proposals were made conditional on Armacost's resignation. One might therefore be tempted to conclude that the CEO was strongly involved in BankAmerica's strategic decisions. But aside from his defensive attempts to resist losing his job, he was unable or unwilling to steer a new course for the firm. In this sense, neither he nor the board aggressively assumed the leadership role for the organization. Instead, BankAmerica suffered through several years of huge financial setbacks.

In finally replacing Armacost, after reported banking regulator pressures and amid rumors that the firm was failing, the board emerged from its pattern of inertia only to reinstate Armacost's predecessor, who some had viewed as partially responsible for the dramatic losses incurred by the company. As noted earlier, the board's action was described by a close observer in the following way: "The board has panicked and in a panic situation you go with the guy you know" (BankAmerica Board. . .," 1986: 3). Such behavior suggests that, absent a major reorientation, the board is unlikely to be intensely involved in reshaping the strategic direction of the firm in the near future.

Finally, labeling the CBS case as one with high board and CEO involvement intensity can be explained by way of contrast with the BankAmerica case. Whereas BankAmerica's board suffered from what appeared to be an unwillingness to change either strategic direction or the CEO (this was one of reasons Charles Schwab resigned in frustration from the board), the CBS situation involved a board with very strong, if implicit, ideas on the strategic direction of CBS, and a CEO with equally strong views on that direction. Unfortunately for the CEO, these views did not converge. While CBS's declining performance was perhaps a contributing factor to the decision to ask for CEO Wyman's resignation, apparently the most powerful factor was Wyman's inability to sense the board's fervent desire for CBS to remain independent. In the board's eyes, CBS was not simply an organization; it was an institution.

According to published reports, in raising the issue of a possible takeover by Coca-Cola, CEO Wyman may have been seeking a direct confrontation with board member Laurence Tisch, chairman of Loews Corp., which owned 24.9 percent of CBS's shares outstanding. Wyman felt that Tisch was undercutting his leadership and actually attempting to gradually take control of CBS. However, Wyman's choice of using a takeover as the method of forcing Tisch's hand (thereby gaining the Board's support) was disastrous. Wyman's strong move met with equally strong resistance, as he had totally misjudged the board's aversion to selling the firm.

In examining the symmetrical cases, the BankAmerica situation did not necessitate an open conflict between board and CEO. It would appear that the increased media attention, combined with bank regulator pressure and bankruptcy rumors, ultimately led to the decision to replace Armacost. As for CBS, while Wyman might have survived the September board meeting had he not raised the issue of a takeover, his confrontational approach and his inability to understand the board's view on the strategic direction of the firm would likely have led to an open conflict at some later point in time.

AN AGENDA FOR RESEARCH

Both the agency approach and the behavioral approach are useful in suggesting how the CEO/board relationship (and its potential effects on organizational performance) can be better understood. Of course, our emphasis on relational issues such as goal congruence, information asymmetry, and intensity of CEO and board involvement in organizational decision-making does not fully capture the dynamics of the CEO/board relationship. In this final section, we identify a number of additional variables which may help to illuminate the connections between CEO/board relations and performance.

The Impact of Past Performance

In general, we would argue that to understand the current character of CEO/board relations and their implications for performance, one needs to understand a good deal about the past. In particular, one needs to understand the performance climate. The relationships between CEO and board are likely to differ depending upon whether this climate is relatively benign or contentious. If corporate performance is falling, levels of contention are likely to be higher than if performance is steady or moving in a positive direction. Here, of course, the issue of information asymmetry comes into play. CEOs may vary with respect to whether they wish to bring potential performance problems to the attention of the board early or to keep the visibility of these potential problems low, hoping that improvements will occur soon. A CEO's assumptions about the expectations of the board for performance may be an important moderator of the effect of performance climate on the relationship. Thus, we would argue that past performance influences the present character of interaction, thereby influencing decisions and, unavoidably, future performance.

The Role of History

It is important to know what the history of the relationships between the CEO and the board has been in any particular firm in order to understand the current relationship. If this past history has typical patterns, such as a strong CEO and a less strong board, or strong board involvement in operational decisions, or high degrees of conflict between board and CEO, these will inevitably color the current relationship. Past history is not deterministic; however, it does give shape to the way in which current actors think about their roles.

The extent to which the past history of the relationship affects the current CEO/board relationship is an important research question in itself. The influence of history can manifest itself (1) in the development of norms and "signals" between CEO and board; (2) in the prior experience that either the CEO or the board members have had in their respective roles; (3) in personal ties between the CEO and the board and among board members themselves; and (4) in perpetuating concentration of power by allowing the CEO also to occupy the position of Chairman of the Board.

Norms and Signals

To understand CEO/board relations and their implications for performance at a given moment in time, it is necessary to have an appreciation for how these relations have developed over time. As Alderfer (1986) argues, they are influenced by the same dynamics which influence any social unit: implicit and explicit norms develop which shape the behavior of relevant actors in powerful and predictable ways. Without understanding these norms, one can hardly understand the nature of the relationship.

As in any group, board members signal each other in a variety of obvious and subtle ways about what behavior is appropriate. Although each board member is fully capable of making individual, automomous decisions, there is undoubtedly a certain "group effect" operating at any given time which influences how a board member behaves. There will almost always be an informal hierachy of influence within the board, sometimes reinforced by the formal structure of board committees. The flow of influence in the decision making process is both interesting and subject to intervention and manipulation.

Just as board members signal one another about appropriate behavior, so the CEO signals or attempts to signal board members about what he or she wants from them. Again, this refers to the exercise of influence over the decision-making process. To what extent, and under what conditions, are board members likely to respond positively to the signals they get from the CEO, and when are they likely to resist?

Prior Experience in Similar Roles

Although it may be obvious, an important influence on a board member's behavior will be the nature and extent of his or her previous experience as a board member. This previous experience will condition the member's expectations about appropriate behaviors and may cause the member to be sensitive to some issues and insensitive to others. The person joining a board with no previous experience is most likely to be the most open to influence both by other board members and by the CEO.

Previous experience as a CEO enables the board member to put himself or herself in the CEO's position and to be sensitive to issues from that perspective. Furthermore, knowing something about the nature of the relationship between the individual's own experience as CEO and the relationship that person had with his or her own board might help predict how that person would respond in the current situation.

A CEO's previous experience with boards is likely to shape present behavior. CEOs tend to develop particular styles toward and expectations of boards, and these will unavoidably influence behavior in the present context. Of great interest, of course, is the case when a new CEO is hired from outside the focal company. In this situation, the board has one set of expectations and the CEO may have a very different set. How they begin to work together in the absence of previous contacts, and how each develops information on the other prior to the hiring decision, is of great interest, both theoretical and practical.

Just as board members may have had previous experience or current experience as CEO, so may the CEO sit on one or more boards in other companies. The nature of these experience may influence how the CEO views boards as operating, and may help him or her to deal effectively with the board.

Personal Ties

The nature and depth of connections between any one board member and any other board member are potentially important influences on behavior. Kinship ties, friendship ties, and professional ties all potentially bind one board member to another and provide potential channels of influence in the decision-making process. To understand the way in which board members behave individually and collectively, one needs to know the nature of the connectedness among them.

In the same way, connections between the CEO and the individual board members may influence the way in which board members behave in the decision-making process. Kinship, friendship, and professional ties between board members and the CEO may be important determinants of how a board member behaves vis-à-vis the CEO in any particular situation. To the extent that the CEO has influenced the board recruitment process, we may expect the number and strength of these ties to be high. Connectedness to the board may provide the CEO with an opportunity to exercise significant influence in the decision-making process. CEOs who have been characterized as extremely powerful have been able to exert extraordinary amounts of influence over their boards. Personal and professional connections are one vehicle for achieving such influence.

The Concentration of Power

Although it is relatively common for the CEO also to occupy the position of Chairman of the Board and thereby to exert extraordinary influence over the board, this concentration of power may not be ideal from the standpoint of performance. A recent survey (Heidrick and Struggles, 1982) found that the CEO is also chairman of the board in over three fourths of the largest corporations in the country. Somewhat surprisingly, this tendency is greater the larger the enterprise. On the other hand, a poll of over one thousand graduates of six leading business schools found that nearly half of the respondents opposed having the CEO serve as board chairman (Clymer, 1987).

From our point of view, having the same individual fill both positions clearly affects the nature of the relationship between the CEO and the board. It gives the CEO more formal control and the opportunity to exert more influence over the decision process, both directly and indirectly. By making dissent more difficult, it has the potential to be detrimental to corporate performance, irrespective of the capabilities of the individual filling the positions.

Because of the pervasiveness of the practice, however, it may be difficult to justify doing otherwise in any particular instance. The CEO may feel that to keep the positions separate would reflect a lack of confidence in his or her abilities. Thus, the practice may be continued for historical and contextual reasons, despite what appears to be compelling performance-related reasons for doing otherwise.

CONCLUSION

In a volume concerned with executive leadership, we wish to make the point forcefully that the traditional metaphor of the organizational pyramid, with the CEO at the apex, omits consideration of the governance function in corporate life. Executive leaders are not autonomous decision-makers. Technically, they serve at the pleasure of their boards. Because both CEOs and boards may define and enact their roles differently from one case to the next, and because decisions taken at the top may have profound consequences for corporate performance, the interplay between CEOs and boards warrants careful research attention.

We have suggested a number of questions which one might ask about the dynamics of this relationship, using publicly available descriptions of four cases of corporate transitions, and we have suggested two perspectives and a number of variables which promise to illuminate the relationship. These suggestions represent an agenda for research which is admittedly ambitious and fraught with methodological complexity. But serious work in this area will help place the role of executive leadership in its proper context.

NOTES

1. One could, of course, argue that the BankAmerica case involved an agency problem between shareholders and the board. However, as the following discussion suggests, an alternative perspective may shed more light on this issue.
2. Anderson has since left Union Carbide.

REFERENCES

Alderfer, C.P. "The Invisible Director on Corporate Boards." *Harvard Business Review* 64 (1986): 38-52.

"Armacost Wins Vote of Confidence." *The Business Month,* April 1986, p. 17.

"The Bad Days at Black Rock Aren't Over Yet." *Business Week* September 20, 1986, p. 36-37.

"BankAmerica Gave Severance Packages to Top Officials in August, Sources Say." *Wall Street Journal* October 6, 1986, p. 2.

"BankAmerica's Board to Request That Armacost Quit, Sources Say." *Wall Street Journal* October 10, 1986, p. 3, 20.

"BankAmerica Asks Suiter to Withdraw." *Wall Street Journal* November 4, 1986, p. 2.

Baysinger, B.D., and Butler, H.N. "Corporate Governance and the Board of Directors: Performance Effects of Changes in Board Composition." *Journal of Law, Economics and Organization* 1 (1985): 101-124.

Beatty, R, and Zajac, E.J. "CEO Change and Firm Performance in Large Corporation: Succession Effects and Manager Effects." *Strategic Management Journal* 8 (1987): 305-318.

"Big Trouble at Allegheny." *Business Week* August 11, 1986, pp. 56-61.

"Board Repels Boarder." *The Economist* March 11, 1986, p. 78.

"BofA Isn't Ready to Give Up On Armacost Yet." *Business Week* March 17, 1986, p. 53.

"CBS Shake-Up: Wyman Out, Tisch In, Paley Back." *Broadcasting* September 15, 1986, pp. 39-41.

"CBS's Wyman Forced to Quit, Sources Assert." *Wall Street Journal* September 11, 1986, pp. 3 and 29.

Chakravarthy, B., and Zajac, E.J. "Tailoring Incentive Systems to a Strategic Context." *Planning Review* 12 (1984): 30-35.

Chandler, A.D. *Strategy and Structure*. Cambridge, MA: MIT Press, 1962.

Chitayat, G. "Working Relationships Between the Chairman of the Board of Directors and the CEO." *Management International Review* 25 (1985): 65-70.

"Civil War at CBS." *Newsweek* September 18, 1986, pp. 46-50.

"Clausen May be the Safe Choice, But Is He the Right One?" *Business Week* October 27, 1986, pp. 108-110.

Clymer, A. "A Times Poll of MBA's." *New York Times Magazine,* May 3, 1987, pp. 58-59.

Donaldson, G., and Lorsch, J.W. *Decision-Making at the Top*. New York: Basic Books, 1983.

Heidrick and Struggles, Inc. *The Changing Board*. Chicago, IL: Heidrick and Struggles, Inc., 1982.

"How the CBS Board Decided Chief Wyman Should Leave His Job." *Wall Street Journal* September 12, 1986, pp. 1 and 11.

Jensen, M.C., and Meckling, W.H. "Theory of the Firm: Managerial Behavior, Agency Costs, and Ownership Structure." *Journal of Financial Economics,* 3 (1976): 305-360.

Marschak, J., and Radner, R. *Economic Theory of Teams*. New Haven, CT: Yale University Press, 1972.

Miller, D., and Friesen, P.H. *Organizations: A Quantum View*. Englewood Cliffs, NJ: Prentice Hall, 1984.

Mizruchi, M.S. "Who Controls Whom? An Examination of the Relation Between Management and Boards of Directors in Large American Corporations." *Academy of Management Review* 3 (1983): 426-435.

"Outside Directors Led the Carbide Defense that Fended Off GAF." *Wall Street Journal* January 13, 1986, pp. 1 and 12.

Pennings, J.M. *Interlocking Directorates*. San Francisco, CA: Jossey- Bass, 1980.

Peters, T.J., and Waterman, R.H., Jr. *In Search of Excellence: Lessons from America's Best-Run Companies*. New York: Harper & Row, 1982.

Pfeffer, J. "Size and Composition of Corporate Boards of Directors: The Organization and Its Environment." *Administrative Science Quarterly* 17 (1972): 218-227.

Ross, S. "The Economic Theory of Agency: The Principal's Problem." *American Economic Review* 63 (1973): 134-139.

Schoorman, F.D., Bazerman, M.H., and Atkin, R.S. "Interlocking Directorates: A Strategy for Reducing Environmental Uncertainty." *Academy of Management Review* 6 (1981): 243-251.

"Schwab Gives Up on BankAmerica." *Fortune* September 15, 1986, p. 14.

Stogdill, R.M. *Handbook of Leadership*. New York: Free Press, 1974.

Tichy, N.M., and Devanna, M.A. *Transformational Leadership*. New York: Wiley, 1986.

"Unfurl the Golden Parachutes at Bank of America." *The Economist* October 11, 1986, pp. 87-88.

Zajac, E.J. "Interlocking Directorates Research: A Critique and Redirection." Working paper, Northwestern University, 1988.

THE ROLE OF THE CEO AND TOP MANAGEMENT IN THE CREATION AND IMPLEMENTATION OF STRATEGIC VISION

Shelley R. Robbins and Robert B. Duncan

The major challenge facing organizations today is to develop the capability to anticipate and influence the changes affecting them in their markets. As their markets change and become increasingly competitive, organizations need to reevaluate and change their strategies. The organizational changes which are now occurring are typically major reorientations to the marketplace, such as those in the automotive, computer, and airline industries. These changes typically require comprehensive alterations in the organizations's strategy, structure, decision support systems, reward systems, human resource systems and culture, in order to redirect the organization toward a new strategic thrust. Given the comprehensiveness of these types of organizational changes, the CEO and top management play a more major role in their initiation and implementation than in smaller, internal changes. During these major shifts in the marketplace, the vision of the CEO and top management is a critical tool by which change is initiated and sustained. Bennis and Nanus (1985) and Tichy and Ulrich (1984) have suggested that the leader uses vision as a tool for initiating and implementing change. They have defined vision as a future state for the organization, which serves as a "target that beckons" for the direction of organizational activity. A vision reflects the organizations's basic beliefs and values, its priorities regarding objectives, and specifies the means by which objectives will be pursued.

Early management writers (Selznick, 1957) and scholars of political leadership (Burns, 1978) have suggested that top leaders transform organizations through the introduction of new goals and values. According to James McGregor Burns (1978: 43-44):

> The essence of leadership. . .is the recognition of real need, the uncovering and exploiting of contradictions among values and between values and practice, the realigning of values, the reorganization of institutions where necessary, and the governance of change. Essentially, the leader's task is consciousness-raising on a wide plane.

There has been a great deal of discussion in the business press recently regarding the importance of corporate values and visions and the key role that CEOs like Roger Smith of General Motors and Jack Welch of General Electric play in creating and reshaping their corporation's vision. In the management literature, however, there has been very little systematic discussion regarding the concept of vision, how leaders use vision, and the process of vision creation. Recently, Leavitt (1986) addressed the concept in his formulation of pathfinding. Vision was identified as a component of pathfinding that looked to the future in a creative way to make the organization more proactive.

In this chapter, vision is defined as the shared, aspired future state for the organization which identifies the organization's values, sets priorities for goals and objectives, and sets the guidelines by which these goals and objectives will be pursued. Organizational visions are different from their resulting strategies in that visions represent a shared set of beliefs about the organization's aspired role in the market place. On the other hand an organization's strategy is a much more specific statement regarding the present and future resource deployments and environmental interactions that indicate how the organization will achieve its objectives (Hofer and Schendel, 1978). Organizational vision drives strategy, and an organization may have multiple strategies as it implements its vision.

The basic premise of this chapter is that *envisioning,* or the process by which the CEO and top management create and utilize visions for the future to initiate change is the key to the initiation and implementation of a major reorientation for an organization.

However, despite the recent flood of literature on visions, most of it has been normative. While a large body of multidisciplinary leadership literature exists, it only remotely addresses how leaders initiate and manage change. Further, while the literature on strategic adaptation suggests what the role of the leader should be, there has been no effort to integrate the two. Undertaking this task will allow researchers to develop a comprehensive theory of how organizational change is initiated; how organizational visions are created or modified; and the role of vision in the change process.

The objective of this chapter is to examine the role of the chief executive officer (CEO) and top management team in the initiation of change and development of organizational visions. Rather than following the normative path of the current executive leadership literature, it is our intent to develop a model of change leadership which is both theory *based* as well as *linked* to theoretical models of leadership and of change. In order to accomplish this objective, this chapter will include: (1) a review of the literature on strategic adaptation to determine what these theories indicate regarding the behavior of top management in the strategic change process; (2) a review of the leadership literature to determine what leadership theories indicate about top management's role in the organization; and (3) a new model of the process by which the CEO and top management develop and initiate organizational vision, or the envisioning process.

STRATEGIC ADAPTATION THEORIES AND TOP MANAGEMENT IMPLICATIONS

Within the literature on organizations and change, theories of strategic adaptation address how organizations change either by adapting to meet environmental contingencies, or by choice processes of top managers. This section will review the literature on strategic adaptation with an analysis of the implications regarding top management's behavior and role in the strategic change process. In order to analyze current perspectives on strategic adaptation, we have classified the various perspectives into those dealing primarily with the relative effects of contextual and organizational variables on the organization's ability to change, and those dealing with the actual processes of how those changes occur.

Tables 1, 2, and 3 present each of the models described below and the implications of each theory for the behaviors of top managers in the organization, as well as limitations of the theories for explaining top management behavior with respect to the process of envisioning.

Table 1.   Contextual Theories of Strategic Change:
Implications for Top Management Behavior

Theory	Theory Implies	Theory Does Not Specify
1. Natural Selection	• Environment determines organizational outcomes • Top managers can determine: — goals and niche — structural arrangements — market strategy • Despite availability of choices, managerial impact is limited due to environmental influence and structural inertia	• How top management has an impact • What the process is by which choices are made • Does not address the issue of vision
2. Resource Dependence	• Environment exerts influence on organizational activities • Managers can influence: — managing interdependencies — allocating resources — establishing negotiated environment — managing political coalitions	• What determines how resources are allocated, interdependencies are managed, what kind environment is negative • Around what issues are coalitions built • Does not address the issue of vision
3. Strategic Choice	Managers can exercise strategic choice with regard to: — selecting strategies — determining organizational design — selecting performance criteria	• What determines and drives strategy selection • What determines performance criteria • Does not address the issue of vision
4. Hybrid a. Lawrence and Dyer	• Industry and market structure present organizational constraints with regard to information complexity and resource scarcity • Top managers can determine organizational mechanisms for handling environmental constraints • Managers must simultaneously manage innovation and efficiency	• What drives strategic choice • Does not address the issue of vision
b. Hrebiniak and Joyce	• Strategic choice and environmental determinism are not mutually exclusive	• What drives strategic choice • Does not address the issue of vision

Table 2. Process Theories of Strategic Change:
Implications for Top Management Behavior

Theory	Theory Implies	Theory Does Not Specify
1. Decision-Making Process	• Change is a result of the decision process of top managers	• How priorities for decisions are set • Does not address the issue of vision
2. Cognitive Process	• Top managers initiate the need for change through a cognitive problem sensing process	• What are the implications for vision formulation process • Does not address the issue of vision
3. Political and Social Process	• Top managers exert influence over the social and political arena in organizations • The greatest area for influence is through changing organization members' perceptions of critical strategic issues	• How visions are determined and negotiated • Does not address the issue of vision

Table 3. Leadership Theories:
Implications for Top Management Behavior

Theory	Theory Implies	Theory Does Not Specify
1. Psychological	Top managers enhance: — individual commitment to the organization — individual motivation to attain goals — individual satisfaction and performance	• How goes are set, values are determined, priorities across goals, or selection of means to attain goal • How political or group related behaviors effect leader behavior • Does not address the issue of vision
2. Sociological	Top managers can influence organizational structure and performance in a limited manner	• How the leadership process impacts structure and performance • Does not address the issue of vision

Table 3 (continued)

Theory	Theory Implies	Theory Does Not Specify
3. Symbolic	Top managers interpret organization events by creating symbols and managing meaning	• What the process is by which this occurs • What the outcome of symbolic management is • Does not address the issue of vision
4. Fit	Characteristics of top management will impact strategic outcomes	• What the process is by which this occurs • Does not address the issue of vision
5. Normative Roles	Top managers have a specific repetoire of tasks and roles	• What the process is by which this occurs • Does not address the issue of vision

Contextual and Organizational Characteristics Theories

In order to develop our analysis, we have classified the literature which deals with the impacts of contextual and organizational variables into five major categories: (1) natural selection; (2) resource dependency; (3) strategic choice; (4) hybrid; and (5) random theories. These categories are concerned with the extent to which managers or environments exercise predominant influence over organizational outcomes and the ability of organizations to adapt to environmental changes (Child, 1972; Miles and Cameron, 1982).

Natural Selection. The natural selection perspective (Hannan and Freeman, 1977) assumes that organizations are captives of a specific environment which is immutable with respect to influence attempts by the organizations it contains. Organizations are also characterized by inertia, and possess little slack for coping with proposed change (Miles and Cameron, 1982). Thus the environment is extremely deterministic with regard to organizational outcomes and activities.

Even within the population ecology framework, Hannan and Freeman do not deny that top managers in organizations have some choice of behaviors with which they can manipulate organizational activities, even though those activities may not affect the ultimate survival of the organization. Rather, they suggest that because of structural inertia, managers are more likely to be able to effect changes in the more peripheral layers of the organization's structure. The core aspects of an organization, which are viewed in hierarchical order with regard to top management's ability to change them, are: (1) its stated goals; (2) its forms of authority; (3) its core technology; and (4) its marketing strategy. At the top of the hierarchy, publicly stated goals are subject to the strongest constraints with regard to managers' ability to make structural changes, while marketing strategies are seen as subject to lesser inertial forces.

Additionally, the strength of inertial forces, or the ability to change, may also vary with life-cycle phase, size, the market structure of the industry, and complexity of the organization, so they may be less strong in a particular organization, and thus more discretion exists for top managers. For example, in the late 1960s the Japanese auto producers developed a strategy that emphasized small, fuel efficient, high quality cars that clearly differentiated them from the way American producers chose to position themselves in the market. The result was that the Japanese developed a niche that had not existed earlier (Sobel, 1984).

While the natural selection perspective suggests that managers can to some extent determine organizational goals, structure, and strategies, it fails to include the means by which top management has an impact on the organization, or the process by which top managers select those goals and strategies.

Resource Dependence. The resource dependence perspective (Pfeffer and Salancik, 1978) suggests that organizations: (1) are dependent on resources in the environment in order to survive; (2) are more likely to survive when they can control those resources on which they are dependent; and (3) may need to transact with other organizations for the necessary resources. Because survival is partially explained by the ability to cope with these environmental contingencies, the negotiation of exchanges to ensure the continuation of these needed resources is the focus of much of organizational action (Pfeffer and Salancik, 1978). Thus, the key problem for the survival of an organization is its ability to manage the interdependencies between itself and its environment. Top managers have the potential capability to alter these interdependencies through such proactive behaviors as merging with or entering into a joint venture with another organization. However, the occurrence of these behaviors will depend on the degree of influence which the environment exerts over the organization.

In situations where environmental dependencies are very high, the organization's outcomes are determined primarily by its context, thus, administrative action is largely symbolic. Where the demands from the environment are great, managerial action will be geared toward managing the interdependencies they confront. In situations where the organization exerts less influence over the interests of the organization, management's function is to direct the organization toward more favorable environments and to manage and establish negotiated environments favorable to the organization (Pfeffer and Salancik, 1978).

The resource dependence theory implies that managers can exert influence with regard to such activities as managing organizational interdependencies, allocating resources, establishing a negotiated environment, and building political coalitions. However, it does not suggest the process by which resources are allocated, how interdependencies with the environment are managed, how top managers decide what kind of negotiated environment will be sought, or around what issues coalitions are built.

Strategic Choice.   In contrast to the more deterministic perspectives of natural selection and resource dependence is the strategic-choice perspective (Child, 1972). This perspective assumes that managers can exercise considerable choice concerning what environments they will operate in and how they will relate to those environments. It also emphasizes that organizations may profoundly influence environments and that organizations are capable of learning and changing under the guidance of executive leaders (Miles and Cameron, 1982). In order to accomplish these aims, executives have at their disposal three sets of options and choices: (1) strategic options, which include the choice of organizational purposes, operations and domains; (2) structural options, which include the choices of organizational designs and structures which in turn, influence the internal political and cultural context of decision making; and (3) performance options, which includes the choice of which performance dimensions which will be emphasized and where slack resources will be used. From this perspective, an organization's inability to adapt is a function of executive leadership and top-management decision making (Miles and Cameron, 1982). Child (1972) also suggests that organizational variables may also affect top managers decision-making capabilities. For example, declining performance may cause decision makers to alter structural arrangements in order to simplify administrative tasks, or eliminate staff functions, or alter the way the organization deals with the external environment. While this perspective suggests that all organizational events are driven by the choices of top management, it fails to address the key issues of exactly what determines and drives strategy selection, what determines the performance criteria which will be used, who initiates strategic choices, and how they are implemented in the organization.

Hybrid Perspectives.   The hybrid perspectives include those which suggest that both organizational and environmental variables will impact the degree of strategic choice available to managers in organizations. Lawrence and Dyer (1983), in an attempt to synthesize the environmental determinism and organizational choice approaches, suggest that an organization's adaptive capability is a function of the relationship between the complexity of its information requirements and the scarcity of resources in the environment. They see the relationship between the organization and its environment as one in which the environment sets conditions that help shape the organization, as well as one in which the organization can shape and influence its environment. They define "readaptation" as a continuous process,

> a form of organizational adaptation in which the organization and its relevant environment interact and evolve toward exchanges that are more acceptable to the internal and external stakeholders as evidenced by continuing high levels of innovation, efficiency, and member involvement (Lawrence and Dyer, 1983: 295).

The main tasks for management, then, are to develop organizational mechanisms for dealing with information complexity and resource scarcity, which are determined for a specific organization by its industry and the market structure of that industry. Thus, the industry and the environment set limits and constraints in which managers can exercise choice.

This theory also suggests that stakeholders both internal and external to the organization may be able to exert influence depending on the nature of the organization and the social system in which it operates. Depending on the relationship between information complexity and resource scarcity, different stakeholders will be able to exert more or less control over the organization and its relationship to the environment. They suggest that in situations where information complexity is high, and resource scarcity is low, professionals will be more likely to dominate the organization and its available choices.

In a second type of hybrid theory, Hrebiniak and Joyce (1985) have criticized the conceptualization of strategic choice versus environmental determinism as an either/or issue, and have presented an alternative conceptualization of these issues by suggesting that strategic choice and environmental determinism are not mutually exclusive, competing explanations of organizational adaptation. Rather, they are independent variables which can interact, thus presenting four main types of adaptation processes, depending on the levels of environmental or managerial influence. They suggest that organizations may be more likely to fall into one of four quadrants, dependent on the type of organization and the degree to which the environment or managers can impact its performance and survival.

While the hybrid theories do provide a richer perspective than the either/or focus of single focus theories, they still fail to explain how choices occur and what is the driving mechanism behind them.

Loosely Coupled/Random Theories.   One additional alternative to the dichotomy of natural selection versus strategic choice is random transformation theory, in which internal organizational changes are only loosely coupled with the desires of organizational leaders and with the demands of the environment (March and Olsen, 1976; Weick, 1979). Generally, within this perspective, top managers can exercise choices, but the consequences of choice may result in unrelated decisions, no clear strategy, and thus, any adaptation which occurs is a chance process. There is little indication of what drives these choices and no indication as to what holds the organization together in any cohesive manner. Perhaps the vision of the leader is the element that holds the organization together. The concept of vision as it will be developed in this paper will address this issue.

Process Theories

The preceding section has attempted to show the weaknesses in the contextual and organizational characteristics theories of adaptation with regard to explaining top management behavior. In general, these theories do not tell us (1) what it is that drives the strategic decision-making process; (2) what the organizational decision-making priorities should be; and (3) what the process is by which this occurs.

While the contextual theories may be useful for suggesting the extent to which managerial choice versus environmental determinism impact organizational outcomes, these macro level theories and classifications of strategic choice and organizational change fail to take into account the more micro-level processes within each theory. Within the strategic choice perspective, these predominant theories and research on change and choice focus on organizational outcomes, such as survival, and fail to reflect the actual process of change and the dynamics of changing. Pettigrew (1986) suggests that the theories of strategic choice and change can be categorized into three general perspectives: (1) a decision-making process; (2) a cognitive sense-making process; and (3) a political and social process.

Decision-Making Process Theories.   The decision making process theories (Allison, 1971; Pettigrew, 1973; March and Olsen, 1976; Quinn, 1980; Burgelman, 1983) view organizational efforts as a result of a series of decisions made within the organization, and they focus on the decision process as the unit of analysis. These theories include those which view the decision process as rational or bounded rational (March and Simon, 1958), as well as those which view decision making as an incremental, non-linear process (Quinn, 1980), or even a totally non-rational process (Cohen, March and Olsen, 1972).

Cognitive Process Theories. These theories (Kiesler and Sproull, 1982; Daft and Weick, 1984; Dutton and Duncan, 1987) view the organizational change process as a cognitive sensemaking and problem-solving process. Kiesler and Sproull (1982) suggest that problem sensing is composed of three cognitive processes: noticing, interpreting, and incorporating stimuli. Noticing will be dependent on organizational structures and environmental scanning procedures, as well as certain characteristics of the environment. Leaders must then construct or assign meaning to the stimuli, and then their interpretations are influenced both by individual characteristics as well as by organizational variables, such as culture. Finally, incorporating the stimuli involves memory and information storage processes, which will be influenced by variables such as organizational age and size, belief systems, and information systems.

Dutton and Duncan (1987) describe the sense-making process which occurs in the minds of organizational decision makers as an iterative, cyclical process which is triggered by some type of performance disturbance, such as a discrepancy between actual and expected performance. The sensemaking process consists of three stages: (1) activation, or triggering; (2) an assessment of urgency; and (3) an assessment of feasibility, which leads both to changes in vision and strategy, as well as providing a momentum for change. The process of sense making helps to explain why organizations respond differently to similar changes in the environment.

Political and Social Process Theories. Pettigrew (1986) has examined top management from the perspective of the dynamics of power as well as focusing on the areas in an organization where top management exerts influence. Strategic change represents a challenge to the core system of meaning for the organization. Change involves questioning and ultimately displacing the organizations's existing ideology.

The main task of strategic change for Pettigrew (1985), is for top managers to develop new perceptions of the environment and thus create new issues for the organization to address. Top management, then, exerts its greatest influence by interpreting and defining the relevant environment and identifying the critical strategic issues facing the organization. Once a new set of strategic issues are identified and these are labeled as urgent, a new set of values and beliefs emerge to create a modified ideology. Thus, for Pettigrew, the key activities for top management in the strategic change process are interpretation, sense-making, and strategic issue identification.

Implications of Process Theories. The process theories provide an improvement over the contextual theories in explicating the strategic change and adaptation process. They imply that top management processes can be interpretive, and are catalysts for the organization and its members to begin to define and redefine the environment. These theories also suggest that the change process involves some sorts of values, goals and ideologies, and it is around these goals and ideologies that decision-making, sensemaking, and political activities take place. Further, they suggest that organizational events and decisions are a collection of social activities, and that top managers do not act alone.

However, these theories still fail to provide us with certain critical concepts. First, they suggest that these processes are either cognitive or political, but the two perspectives are rarely integrated. Second, these theories also fail to tell us what it is that drives the processes, or what the triggers are for sensemaking, decision-making, and political behaviors. Understanding these processes is critical, because it is the vision of top management which is the impetus for change and the catalyst for the strategic change process. Vision can be viewed as the missing link in that process, and it is vision and the process of vision making which must be further understood in order to fully understand leadership and strategic change.

Leadership Theories and Top Management Implications

The other body of literature which requires analysis is the multi-disciplinary leadership literature. While the strategic adaptation literature is directed mainly at organizational level phenomenon, we anticipated that the leadership literature would provide us with a theoretical basis for understanding individual top management behavior and its role in the envisioning process. In order to provide a systematic analysis, we have classified the leadership literature into the following categories: (1) psychological theories; (2) sociological theories; (3) symbolic management theories; (4) fit theories; and (5) normative role theories. Table 3 presents a summary of the theories and their implications for top management behavior in the change process.

Psychological Theories. From the psychological and social-psychological perspective, the focus of leadership theory and research has been the social influence process between leader and follower. House and Baetz (1979) define leadership as the degree to which the behavior of a work group member is perceived as an acceptable attempt to influence the perceiver regarding his or her activity as a member of a particular group, or the activity of other group members. Research in this area has addressed which behaviors or characteristics of a leader of a work group or an organization will promote higher levels of effort and performance in subordinates. Multiple competing theories have addressed leader traits (Stogdill, 1974), behavioral and situational characteristics (House and Mitchell, 1974), and contingency theories (Fiedler, 1970) as determinants of subordinate behavior. The outcome variables which have been studied have been primarily the subordinate's compliance with leader influence attempts, employee motivation and satisfaction, and individual and group productivity. Based on these outcome measures, specific leadership styles, or combinations of leader behaviors, have been identified as causing significant amounts of variance in: (1) the effort level of subordinates when not under direct surveillance; (2) the adaptability to change; (3) levels of follower's turnover; (4) absences; (5) subordinate productivity; (6) the degree of subordinates' learning from supervisory training efforts; (7) the quality of decisions; (8) the degree to which subordinates accept these decisions; and (9) subordinates' motivation (House and Baetz, 1979).

The psychological literature implies that leaders can enhance the motivation for organizational members to attain goals and improve the satisfaction and performance of members. Further, specific traits, such as intelligence, dominance, self-confidence, and task-relevant knowledge are found to differentiate effective from ineffective leaders (Stogdill, 1974).

Bass (1985) and House (1977) have suggested that the leadership process has an emotional, or charismatic component which will cause extra follower effort, and thus yield greater organizational performance through enhanced individual effort. Charismatic leaders are thought to be transformational leaders for organizations in that they can arouse and articulate feelings of need among followers, and have the ability to build on these needs and values through drama and persuasion.

Despite the abundance of literature in this area, the psychological leadership literature fails to address the process by which goals are set by the leader, how values are determined, and how the means to attain the goals are selected. It also fails to address the political or group-related aspects of leader behavior.

Sociological Theories. The sociological perspective is concerned with the impact of the leader on organizational structures and performance. In direct contrast to psychological theories of leadership, these theories suggest that individual influences cannot counteract the influences of organizational structure and environmental influences on organizational outcomes (Pfeffer and Salancik, 1978). Two predominant bodies of leadership research have come out of the sociological perspective: (1) the structural literature which deals with the effect of administrative characteristics on organizational performance; and (2) the literature on executive succession, which looks at the effect of a change in top leadership on organizational outcomes.

The literature which addresses the effects of leadership on structure (Lieberson and O'Connor, 1972; Pfeffer and Salancik, 1977; Weiner and Mahoney, 1981) has been inconclusive regarding the extent to which top managers can influence organizational outcomes, but suggests that environmental and organizational factors explain a greater portion of the variance in organizational performance than leadership does.

Research on executive succession is concerned with the impact of the transfer of authority on organizational performance, and has looked at the impact of succession on performance, top management changes, and organizational death rates (Gouldner, 1952; Grusky, 1963; Gamson and Scotch, 1964; Helmich and Brown, 1972; Pfeffer, 1981b; Reinganum, 1985). Results of these studies have been mixed. Carroll (1984) has reviewed the mixed results of the succession studies and attributes these results to differences in organizational context (such as type of organization and ownership), the timing of the succession relative to the organizational life cycle, and the type of transfer in control.

The sociological perspective on leadership suggests that leaders may have some impact on the structure and performance of organizations. However, it does not provide us with data on the process by which the leader impacts organizational variables.

Symbolic Management Theories. The previous studies are often cited as supportive of the evidence that organizational outcomes are so greatly influenced and constrained by environmental and organizational factors, that the role of the leader is seen as primarily symbolic (Pondy, 1978; Pfeffer, 1977, 1981a; Pfeffer and Salancik, 1978; Meindl et al., 1985). Because organizational decisions are constrained by the environmental context of the organization, the principal role of top management is symbolic, by providing "rationalizations or reasons that make sense of and thereby explain the organization's activities" (Pfeffer, 1981b: 9). Pfeffer asserts that the four general forms of symbolic action are language, ceremonies, the use of symbols, and settings.

Related to the view of management as symbolic activity are studies which link management behavior to organizational culture. Schein (1985) views culture as the unifying force which can support or hinder an organization's ability to undergo change, and suggests that the organizational leader has the major responsibility for guiding the survival and integration of the organization, primarily through the leader's impact on the creation and maintenance of organizational cultures. Siehl and Martin (1984) suggest that top management uses symbolism, in the form of jargon and stories, to transmit and institutionalize organizational values and culture.

Meindl, Ehrlich, and Dukerich (1985), suggest that leadership is a socially constructed explanatory concept used to make sense of organizational systems, and that individuals have developed romanticized views of what leaders do and what they are able to accomplish. Because of our need to make sense out of organizational phenomenon, attributions are made toward the leader with regard to helping account for organizational activities and outcomes. The romance and mystery surrounding the concept of leadership are critical for sustaining "followership" within an organization. Similarly, Staw and Ross (1980) found that subjects rated administrators highest when they followed a consistent course of action, allocated minimum resources, and were ultimately successful, thus suggesting that attributions of leadership success are made based on perceptions of what it means to the follower or observer to be a successful leader or administrator.

The symbolic and attributional perspectives are an important contribution in that they add richness to the sociological and psychological perspectives by suggesting that not all leader behavior is substantive or leads to substantive organizational outcomes. As such, these views do not negate the importance of organizational leadership; rather, they attribute the success of the leader to the perceptions of the followers, and to the ability of the leader to imbed values in the organization. Perceptions, beliefs and values are a critical part of organizational life, and the ability of the leader to influence these should be seen as one part of the leadership process, and not as a negation of the value of leadership for an organization.

Fit Theories.   Fit theories are concerned with demonstrating relationships between CEO characteristics, organizational characteristics, and organizational strategies. Hambrick and Mason (1984) have proposed that observable managerial background characteristics, such as age, tenure, functional specialty, education, and socio-economic roots act as filters through which members of the dominant coalition perceive the environment. These characteristics cause the leaders to attend selectively to the environment, and through the process of differentially interpreting the environment, organizational strategies and performance will reflect the characteristics of the dominant coalition. Similarly, Gupta (1984) has developed a series of propositions which specify the relationships between certain generic strategies and the types of general managers required for each strategy. The assumptions underlying both these approaches are that a strong correlational relationship exists between types and styles of leaders, and types of strategy.

Normative Role Theories.   Normative role theories include theories of leadership which specify from a normative standpoint the types of functions which leaders should serve for organizations. Chester Barnard (1938), one of the earliest management theorists to specify the role of the executive, suggested that the executive fulfilled three main functions for the organization: (1) the maintenance of organizational communications; (2) the securing of essential services from individuals in the organization; and (3) the formalization of the purposes and objectives of the organization, all of which maintain organizational equilibrium.

Selznick (1957) sought to develop a goal-oriented, structural functionalist theory of organization. He further distinguished between the functions of administrative management (Barnard's focus) and actual leadership. He believed that the "executive becomes a statesman as he makes the transition from administrative management to institutional leadership" (1957: 4). The institutional leader has a primary role of setting policies, and is seen as an expert in the promotion and protection of values of the organization. The interpersonal leader, on the other hand, smooths the path of interaction, eases communications, evokes personal devotion, and allays anxiety for members of the organization.

Mintzberg's (1973) analysis of CEOs led him to suggest that the CEO has a multitude of roles which he occupies in an organization, which include: figurehead, leader, liaison, monitor, disseminator, spokesman, entrepreneur, disturbance handler, resource allocator, and negotiator.

Bennis and Nanus (1985) suggest that the effective leader has a unique dream or vision, which articulates a view of a realistic, credible, attractive future for the organization, a condition which is better in some important ways than what now exists. This vision can be used by members of the organization as a motivational tool. The vision and its supporting ideologies must then be communicated to members of the organization and positioned throughout the organization, in order to change internal structures and external linkages. The leader must also establish trust with members of the organization by developing effective linkages between the external environment and internal organizational administration. Finally, the leader must be able to learn from multiple sources and to provide the proper organizational setting for innovative learning by members of the organization.

Levinson and Rosenthal (1984), in their study of six CEOs, determined that none of the CEOs started with a vision. Each one had diagnosed the organization by using an internal model that they had, and a vision then emerged from interactions between the CEO and senior management regarding how to resolve the strategic issues that were identified in the diagnosis. Second, each CEO had a strong self image and some ideal that they were striving for. For example, Reginald Jones of General Electric wanted to turn over to his successor a stronger organization, Walter Wriston of CitiCorp wanted to demonstrate the effectiveness of his consumer banking perspective. Finally, these CEOs had a number of traits in common. They were persuasive and had good interpersonal skills, were characterized by restless dissatisfaction with the organization's performance, provided a climate for risk taking, had good conceptual skills to make sense out of the messy, uncertain environments in which they worked, and were good at interpreted what was going on within their organizations and thus helped define reality.

Tichy and Ulrich (1984) have extended Burns' concept of the transformational leader and developed a theory of the role of this type of leadership in organizational transitions. First, the transformational leader provides the organization with a vision of some desired future state. This vision must give direction to the organization and at the same time be congruent with the leader's philosophy. Next, the leader must be able to mobilize commitment to that vision and transmit his or her vision into reality. In order to achieve this transformation, the transformational leader must understand the environment, the organization, and the motivational needs of members of the organization. Additional skills include the ability of the leader to understand, analyze, and manage the requirements of various stakeholders who play major roles in organizational success. The leader must also manage the culture, human resource systems, reward systems, and structure so that these systems are in line with the desired changes. Finally, changes must be accepted and institutionalized in the organization through the use of symbols and ceremonies.

Leavitt (1986) has identified pathfinding, problem solving and implementing as the three components in the top management process. Pathfinding is like Bennis and Nanus's (1985) vision creation process. Pathfinding is concerned with mission, purpose, and asking the right questions, rather than with generating the right answers. Problem solving is concerned with generating solutions to complex problems by means of logical analysis of all the facts. Implementing is then concerned with getting solutions integrated into the routine functioning of the organization. Leavitt indicates that these three management processes may be incompatible with one another. It may be difficult for an individual to have the creativity and openness of a pathfinder and at the same time be disciplined to the analytic rigor of a problem solver, or the teamwork, consensus-oriented concern that the implementer needs.

While the normative role theories extend the conceptualization of leadership by covering the complexities of the leader's role, these theories are largely descriptive and do not provide us with an explanation of the processes which the leader goes through in his or her attempt to guide the organization through a strategic transition.

ENVISIONING

This section presents a theoretical framework for looking at the leadership process from the standpoint of "envisioning." In this section we will develop a model of the envisioning process, or the process by which the CEO and members of top management create visions for the organization's future.

Vision Defined

Organizational vision is defined as the *shared aspired future state for the organization which identifies the organization's values, sets priorities for goals and objectives, and sets the guidelines or roadmap by which these goals and objectives will be pursued.* Organizational visions have three components. A vision is an aspired future state and thus it identifies the *values and beliefs,* or what the organization stands for and believes in, and the goals it will pursue. Visions also *set priorities* for the organization, indicating to organizational members which goals and values should be important to achieve. Finally, a vision lays out the *means* that will be used to accomplish organizational objectives, or determine how priorities will be accomplished. A central element of a vision is that it is shared by members of the organization.

Organizational visions can serve several different *functions* for the organization and its members. A vision can serve a *motivational function* in that by targeting the organization's future, it can serve as a rallying point for organizational members. General Electric's CEO, Jack Welch, used technological innovation and market leadership as motivational elements of his vision, elements which he believed would be inspirational to GE employees. A vision can also serve a *roadmap function* in that it is a bridge between the present and the future, which indicates how the organization is going to pursue its objectives. A vision also serves a *control function* in that it can act as a benchmark whereby individual and organizational performance can be evaluated. At General Electric each business unit had to be first or second in its market or it was seriously examined as a candidate for divestiture.

Finally, an organizational vision can serve a *change function* as it points to an anticipated state that the organization is striving for. Thus the vision serves as a change goal. General Motor's vision for its Saturn Corporation emphasizes a paperless organization. This provides a change function in that every task associated with the development of the Saturn project is directed at using direct computer console communication and instant retrieval of information.

In examining the three components of vision—values, priorities for objectives, and means for achieving these objectives—the leader has a tremendous potential for affecting each component. However, the leader probably has the greatest opportunity to impact the values/beliefs component. As Bennis and Nanus (1985) indicate, the leader is the emotional and spiritual resource for the organization. The initial task that the leader performs in taking charge is to pay attention to and make sense out of what is going on in the environment and determine what part of the environmental events are important for the organization's future. The leader thus sorts out for the organization the things to which it should pay attention. It is here that the leader's personal values begin to shape the organization's vision, since the leader's values influence what he/she thinks is an important organizational focus. For instance, GE's Welch had values regarding organizational excellence that emphasized technological innovation and being first or second in each market.

However, while a leader like Welch helped to focus attention on these values, the leader does not do this in isolation from the rest of the organization. The leader articulates these values and these are then developed in more detail within the dominant coalition. The leader is a catalyst here but not the sole source of the organization's basic underlying values.

Attributes of Vision

Corporate visions vary by content and also can vary according to other attributes that may affect their implementation potential. In examining how organizations create visions, we must be concerned then with not only the vision-making process but also the potential for any given vision to be implemented. In this discussion we will examine three attributes of visions: (1) *clear/ambiguous;* (2) *simple/complex;* and (3) *consensus/lack of consensus.* Obviously, there are other attributes of corporate visions. However, these three were picked for this initial development of the concept of the corporate vision-making process as they were expected to provide the greatest contributions to our ability to differentiate visions and to assess their potential for implementation.

Visions can differ widely as to their *degree of clarity* regarding the organization's values, priorities of objectives, and the means by which these objectives will be pursued. At IBM there is absolute clarity as to the values of excellence, a continual striving to be better, and customer orientation. These values then set clear priorities for individual and organizational objectives. There is also no ambiguity regarding the means to be used. Respect for the individual, excellence and constant focus on the customer dominates all behavior in pursuing organizational objectives (Rodgers, 1986).

Other organizations may lack this clarity across the components of corporate vision. Currently at General Motors there is clarity regarding the values of customer focus, innovation and cost containment. However, there is confusion as to priorities—is it customer focus, innovation or cost containment first and foremost? There is also confusion over the means. Will cost cutting be the major factor in leading GM to be more competitive or will more creative, differentiated high quality cars be more effective? It is not clear to organization members which goals they are really supposed to emphasize to make the organization more competitive.

The *degree of complexity* can also differentiate visions. Complexity refers to the number of values, objectives and means identified to attain those objectives that are specified in a corporate vision. IBM's vision is relatively simple in that it emphasizes the individual, excellence, and customer orientation (Rodgers, 1986). Other organizations may develop long laundry lists of values, objectives and means that become overwhelming for the individual and the organization when it comes time to try and implement the vision.

The *degree of consensus* within the organization regarding the vision is a crucial attribute. Bennis and Nanus underscore the importance of consensus and identify such factors as diversity in values, rapid technological innovation, and more willingness to experiment as reasons why it's difficult to reach consensus (Bennis and Nanus, 1985). The greater the consensus on the values, objectives and means for achieving these objectives the more likely is the overall vision to be accepted and implemented.

The Envisioning Process

Within each individual organization, the vision will take on a unique form and set of characteristics because the envisioning process is one in which top decision makers interpret and make sense of environmental and organizational contingencies and translate those characteristics into a strategic vision which is specific and makes sense for that particular organization. The concept of strategic vision is a way of explaining why two similar organizations in the same industry may take different strategic directions.

Daft and Weick (1984) suggest that the process of creating and accumulating interpretations about the environment are, in addition to being influenced by characteristics of the environment, also influenced by the nature of the answer sought, the previous experience of the questioner, and the method used to acquire it. They suggest that within organizations, individuals come and go, but organizations preserve knowledge, behaviors, mental maps, norms, and values over time. Reaching convergence of interpretations among members characterizes the act of organizing (Weick, 1979) and enables the organization to interpret as a system. The authors suggest that differences in interpretation are due to both management's beliefs about the analyzability of the external environment, and the extent to which the organization intrudes into its environment in either an active or passive way.

Thus, while the envisioning process is one in the minds of top decision makers, and draws on organizational knowledge, previous patterns of making sense of organizational events, and negotiated decisions among members of top management, the leader still has the potential to play a

Figure 1

**Sensemaking
Phase**

Context
Industry
Culture
Structure
Leader Behavior

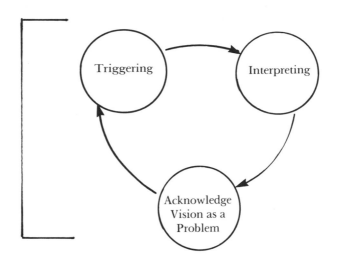

**Vision Creation
Phase**

Context
Industry
Culture
Structure
Leader Behavior

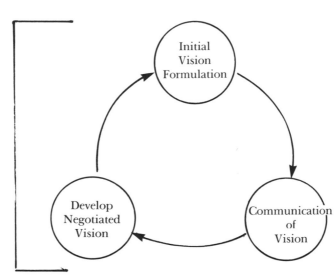

dominant role. By means of developing strategic vision, the leader stimulates the organization to identify what it stands for and what its priorities should be. John Sculley's arrival at Apple helped that organization to sort out what it truly stood for and what its priorities were going to be for the 1980s as a computer company. Sculley helped Apple to identify market focus as being just as important a value as was innovation ("Apple Regroups," 1985). In this case, Sculley worked with top management at Apple to modify the corporate values and then set priorities for objectives which emphasized the importance of profits and market share as well as innovation as corporate objectives. Finally, Sculley helped to modify the means component of vision by emphasizing the importance of competitive analysis and marketing as important mechanisms for achieving corporate objectives.

The envisioning process will now be discussed in detail. As Figure 1 indicates, there are two phases in the envisioning process. The first phase is the individual sensemaking process. The second phase is the process of vision creation.

Phase I: Individual Sensemaking. Sensemaking is an iterative, cyclical, interpretive process which occurs in the minds of decision makers, in which they interpret and make sense of environmental and organizational contingencies (Dutton and Duncan, 1987). Kiesler and Sproull (1982) suggest that problem sensing is composed of three cognitive processes: noticing, interpreting, and incorporating stimuli. The sensemaking process that occurs as part of the creation of vision also consists of three stages. First, noticing, which here involves the activation, or *triggering* of the need for action; second, *interpreting,* in which decision makers interpret the contingencies facing the organization, and third, *incorporating stimuli,* or the *acknowledgment and recognition of the need for change,* in the form of a new vision for the organization.

The *trigger phase* initiates the sensemaking phase. This phase is most likely to be activated by some type of performance gap or disturbance. These triggers can be either internal or external to the organization. External triggers can consist of such things as changes in the market place that impact the organization's performance, changes in customer preferences, changes in the regulatory structure of the industry, or scarcity of resources available to the organization. For example, the market place may become more competitive with the result that the organization may have to take action. During the trigger phase, an organizational or environmental event comes to the forefront, so that the leader can begin to notice discrepancies in them.

For example, as competition with the established air carriers heated up at People's Express, the organization needed to begin to respond and make changes in its strategy. Burr did not pay attention to the changes in customer travel preferences soon enough, and subsequently, was unable to modify the vision of his organization to deal with the increased competition from established carriers like American and United.

There are also a number of triggers internal to the organization that may initiate the first stage of the vision-making process. Changes in top management may initiate reconsideration of the organization's position by the CEO or board of directors. Recent changes in top management at CBS have caused much speculation that the network will go through some rather substantial reassessment of its vision and resulting strategy. A change in the power structure within the organization can also launch this process. Top management may change and bring individuals with different perspectives into power who may then cause the organization to re-evaluate how it is doing. A conflict in goals could also emerge that could cause top management to reassess how it is performing. The specific stimuli in the organization or in the environment which the leader will attend to may depend on background characteristics such as age, experience, education, or technical specialty (Hambrick and Mason, 1984).

Once some strategic issue has been triggered, top management then must *interpret,* or assign meaning to it. Here issue diagnosis becomes important. The approach that decision makers use in diagnosis usually has two components: (1) a model that guides information search; and (2) a process.

The specific model which is used is important in that it determines the kind of information that is sought out to interpret the issue, and becomes a radar screen that decision makers scan to obtain key information. For example, if a model is used that is complete in that it focuses on strategy, structure, decision support systems, reward systems, human resource systems, culture, performance effectiveness, as well as the external environment, there is a greater potential for an accurate understanding of the problem. On the other hand, if a more narrow model is used, it is more likely that a narrow incomplete diagnosis of the triggered issue will exist. For example, if just a financial perspective is used, every issue will be viewed as financial. An organization may be so consumed with cutting costs that it loses sight of how excessive cost cutting may impact the quality of the organization's product or service.

The process used in problem diagnosis is also important. If the CEO and top management unilaterally diagnose the problem, there may be less commitment in the organization to dealing with the triggered problem than if there was more widespread participation in the diagnostic stage.

This problem diagnosis may then result in the realization of a specific problem area within the organization which must be adjusted, or it may result in the realization that ambiguity, confusion, and conflict exist with regard to organizational values, beliefs, and goals. Whether this diagnosis is considered problematic or not is in part dependent on the culture of the industry and the organization.

For example, in the past the organization may not have had a clear vision, but that may not have been significant or problematic because the environment was fairly placid and stable. If the world or marketplace suddenly changes, the lack of clear goals suddenly becomes a problem. The American automobile industry provides an excellent example here. During the 1960s and early 1970s, the industry rested on its past accomplishments and had no clear vision for the future other than more of the same—i.e., big cars, bulky styling, cushy soft ride, etc. The initial entry of the Japanese into the small car market in the mid-1960s was not perceived as a threat. In fact, the Japanese were dismissed as not being significant competitors, as Americans would not give up their long love affair with the large car (Yates, 1983; Sobel, 1984). It was not until the mid-1970s that the American producers began to take the rise in Japanese market share as a long term serious threat to American producer survival.

Once the CEO and top management realizes that there is some performance problem, the question becomes what determines if this "problem" is recognized as a vision problem or not. It is predicted that certain kinds of performance problems are more likely to be labeled as vision problems. Those kinds of problems that lead to confusion or questioning the organization's values and beliefs are likely to be labeled vision problems. When there is confusion over priorities for the organization, there is a greater likelihood that vision will be defined as the real problem. Finally, when there is confusion or disagreement regarding the means to use in pursuing organizational objectives, vision again is likely to be defined as the underlying problem.

Phase II: The Vision Creation Process. The second phase of the envisioning process is the vision creation process, which consists of three phases: first, the initial formulation of an image or vision for the organization; second, the communication of that vision to top management; and third, the refinement of a negotiated organizational vision. The result of this process is a completed vision statement for the organization.

The initial process of *vision formulation* is largely an individual process in the minds of the CEO and top management. It is at this point, as well as during the sense-making process, that personal characteristics will affect the creative process, and in which leadership skills will be evident. The personal characteristics which will separate the visionary leader from one who adheres to a less creative vision during these stages include the following: the ability to tolerate ambiguity, visualize new patterns in old information, and integrate multiple, complex components of an organization's strategy (Quinn, 1980). Other important personal characteristics may include creativity and its related characteristics of cognitive flexibility, originality, independence, inquiringness, and a sense of personal identity (MacKinnon, 1978); intelligence, dominance, self-confidence, energy, and task-relevant knowledge (Stogdill, 1974); and personal values and beliefs.

In addition to personal characteristics, the leader will also be influenced in this process by his or her network of social and business contacts, both internal and external to the organization. If the leader is a member of other boards of directors or clubs, these social networks may influence perceptions of the environment accordingly. One of the explanations offered for the American auto industry being so slow in recognizing the Japanese threat is that auto executives lived in cultural isolation in Detroit from the nonautomotive society (Yates 1983). Executives worked, played and lived together with little input of ideas from outside the Detroit industrial community. As a result, they had a very narrow understanding of the reality of the marketplace.

Once the leader has formulated his/her interpretations of the environment by listening and interacting with those around, the leader can create the initial vision for the organization. However, the next step is to *communicate* the vision to top management and the rest of the organization. The task for the leader here is to make the vision meaningful to other members of the organization so that they can identify with it and become committed to it. This is the management of meaning stage, as Bennis and Nanus (1985) have described it. The task is to make the vision tangible and real for members of the organization. It is here that the leader's skill as communicator and persuader become important.

Because of the prevalence of multiple decision makers with multiple interests, strategic decision making in organizations has been considered a political process (Narayanan and Fahey, 1982; Gray and Ariss, 1985). A political view of decision making implies that the initial vision of the leader may not be automatically transformed into the organization's vision. Rather, political processes will intrude. Political processes may also have differential effects in different stages of the organizational lifecycle (Gray and Ariss, 1985). Differences between organizational priorities during early and more mature stages of organizational growth will result in both a political focus on different priorities, as well as differing strengths of political forces.

The implications of this view for developing a theory of leadership is that despite the ideal view that the leader's vision is the impetus for strategic change, organizational forces may intervene such that the resulting vision may not be that of the leader, but rather a *negotiated* vision arising from political activity among members of the top management team. This negotiated "organizational" vision may in fact be more important to the organization than the singular "leader" vision, because the process of politics, coalition building, and decision making involves the strengthening of beliefs regarding the nature and importance of the vision, and hence builds commitment to the ultimate vision that emerges. For instance, John Young, the head of Hewlett-Packard, has suggested that "successful companies have a consensus from top to bottom on a set of overall goals. The most brilliant management strategy will fail if that consensus is missing" (Carr, 1984).

CONCLUSION

The objective of this chapter has been to develop a framework for understanding the role of the CEO and top management in setting the basic strategies and direction of the organization. In reviewing the strategic adaptation and leadership literature, we determined that these theories explained some of the behavior of senior managers that ranged from making choices regarding strategy and structure to their leadership styles in certain situations. However, neither of these bodies of literature addresses the fundamental issue of what drives strategic choice in organizations.

The envisioning process is offered here as a means for explaining the process which fundamentally determines strategic choice. Vision, as we define it, is the shared aspired future state for the organization which identifies the organization's values, sets priorities for goals and objectives, and sets the guidelines or roadmap by which these goals and objectives will be pursued. Our model of the envisioning process, which consists of individual sensemaking and vision creation, needs to be tested directly, but can also be drawn upon by researchers who wish to refine theoretical models of the effects of executives on organizations.

This framework also has some direct implications for the executive practitioner, in that it clarifies the concept of vision and its components as well as lays out a sequence of events that the leader might follow as he/she attempts to create or implement a new or modified vision for the organization.

ACKNOWLEDGMENT

The authors wish to acknowledge the support of the James C. Allen Chair in Strategy and Organizations at Kellogg.

REFERENCES

Allison, G.T. *Essence of Decision*. Boston, MA: Little Brown, 1971.
"Apple Regroups." *Microtimes*, July 1985.

Barnard, C.I. *The Functions of the Executive.* Cambridge, MA: Harvard University Press, 1938.

Bass, B.M. *Leadership and Performance Beyond Expectations.* New York: The Free Press, 1985.

Bennis, W.G., and Nanus, B. *Leaders: The Strategies for Taking Charge.* New York: Harper & Row, 1985.

Burgelman, R.A. "Toward a Model of Internal Corporate Venturing in the Diversified Major Firm." *Administrative Science Quarterly* 28 (1983): 223-244.

Burns, J.M. *Leadership.* New York: Harper & Row, 1978.

Carr, J. "Success as a State of Mind." *Financial Times* 13 February 1984.

Carroll, G.R. "Dynamics of Publisher Succession in Newspaper Organizations." *Administrative Science Quarterly* 29 (1984): 93-113.

Child, J. "Organizational Structure Environment and Performance: The Role of Strategic Choice." *Sociology* 6 (1972): 1-22.

Cohen, M.D., March, J.G., and Olsen, J.P. "A Garbage Can Model of Organizational Choice." *Administrative Science Quarterly* 17 (1972): 1-25.

Daft, R.L., and Weick, K.E. "Toward a Model of Organizations as Interpretation Systems." *Academy of Management Review* 2 (1984): 284-295.

Dutton, J.E., and Duncan, R.B. "The Creation of Momentum for Change Through the Process of Strategic Issue Diagnosis." *Strategic Management Journal* 8 (1987): 279-296.

Fiedler, F.E. *A Theory of Leadership Effectiveness.* New York: McGraw-Hill, 1970.

Gamson, W.A., and Scotch, N.A. "Scapegoating in Baseball." *American Journal of Sociology* 70 (1964): 69-72.

Gouldner, A. "The Problem of Succession in Bureaucracy." In *Reader in Bureaucracy.* Edited by R. Merton. Glencoe, IL: Free Press, 1952.

Gray, B., and Ariss, S.S. "Politics and Strategic Change Across Organizational Life Cycles." *Academy of Management Review* 4 (1985): 707-723.

Grusky, O. "Managerial Succession and Organizational Effectiveness." *American Journal of Sociology* 69 (1963): 21-31.

Gupta, A.K. "Contingency Linkages Between Strategy and General Manager Characteristics: A Conceptual Examination." *Academy of Management Review* 9 (1984): 399-412.

Hambrick, D.C., and Mason, P.A. "Upper Echelons: The Organization as a Reflection of Its Top Managers." *Academy of Management Journal* 9 (1984): 193-206.

Hannan, M.T., and Freeman, J.H. "The Population Ecology of Organizations." *American Journal of Sociology* 82 (1977): 929-964.

Helmich, D.L., and Brown, W.B. "Successor Type and Organizational Change in the Corporate Enterprise." *Administrative Science Quarterly* 17 (1972): 371-381.

Hofer, C.W., and Schendel, D.E. *Strategy Formulation: Analytical Concepts.* St. Paul, MN: West Publishing, 1978.

House, R.J. "A 1976 Theory of Charismatic Leadership." In *Leadership: The Cutting Edge,* pp. 189-207. Edited by J.G. Hunt and L.L. Larson. Carbondale, IL: Southern Illinois University Press, 1977.

House, R.J., and Baetz, M.L. "Leadership: Some Empirical Generalizations and New Research Directions." In *Research in Organizational Behavior,* pp. 341-423. Edited by B.M. Staw. Greenwich, CT: JAI Press, 1979.

House, R.J., and Mitchell, T.T. "Path-Goal Theory of Leadership." *Journal of Contemporary Business* (1974): 81-94.

Hrebiniak, L.G., and Joyce, W.F. "Organizational Adaptation: Strategic Choice and Environmental Determinism." *Administrative Science Quarterly* 30 (1985): 336-349.

Kiesler, C.A., and Sproull, L.S. "Managerial Response to Changing Environments: Perspectives on Problem Sensing from Social Cognition." *Administrative Science Quarterly* 27 (1982): 548-570.

Lawrence, P.R., and Dyer, D. *Renewing American Industry.* New York: The Free Press, 1983.

Leavitt, H.J. *Corporate Pathfinders*. Homewood, IL: Dow Jones-Irwin, 1986.

Levinson, H., and Rosenthal, S. *CEO: Corporate Leadership in Action*. New York: Basic Books, 1984.

Lieberson, S., and O'Connor, J.F. "Leadership and Organizational Performance: A Study of Large Corporations." *American Sociological Review* 37 (1972): 117-130.

Mackinnon, D.W. *In Search of Human Effectiveness*. Buffalo, NY: Creative Education Foundation, 1978.

March, J.G., and Olsen, J.P. *Ambiguity and Choice in Organizations*. Bergen, Norway: Universtesforlaget, 1976.

March, J.G., and Simon, H.A. *Organizations*. New York: Wiley, 1958.

Meindl, J.R., Ehrlich, S.B., and Dukerich, J.M. "The Romance of Leadership." *Administrative Science Quarterly* 30 (1985): 78-102.

Miles, R.H., and Cameron, K. *Coffin Nails and Corporate Strategy*. Englewood Cliffs, NJ: Prentice Hall, 1982.

Mintzberg, H. *The Nature of Managerial Work*. New York: Harper & Row, 1973.

Narayanan, V.K., and Fahey, L. "The Micro-Politics of Strategy Formulation." *Academy of Management Review* 7 (1982): 25-34.

Pettigrew, A.M. *The Politics of Organizational Decision Making*. London: Tavistock, 1973.

Pettigrew, A.M. "Examining Change in the Long-Term Context of Culture and Politics." In *Organizational Strategy and Change*, pp. 269-318. Edited by J.M. Pennings. San Francisco, CA: Jossey-Bass, 1985.

Pettigrew, A.M. "Some Limits of Executive Power in Creating Strategic Change." In *Executive Power*, pp. 132-154. Edited by S. Srivastva and Associates. San Francisco, CA: Jossey-Bass, 1986.

Pfeffer, J. "The Ambiguity of Leadership." *Academy of Management Review* 2 (1977): 104-112.

Pfeffer, J. "Management as Symbolic Action: The Creation and Maintenance of Organizational Paradigms." In *Research in Organizational Behavior*, Vol. 3, pp. 1-52. Edited by L.L. Cummings and B.M. Staw. Greenwich, CT: JAI Press, 1981a.

Pfeffer, J. *Power in Organizations*. Boston, MA: Pitman, 1981b.

Pfeffer, J., and Salancik, J.P. "Organizational Context and the Characteristics and Tenure of Hospital Administrators." *Academy of Management Journal* 20 (1977): 74-88.

Pfeffer, J., and Salancik, J.P. *The External Control of Organizations: A Resource Dependence Perspective*. New York: Harper & Row, 1978.

Pondy, L. "Leadership is a Language Game." In *Leadership: Where Else Can We Go?*, pp. 87-99. Edited by M.W. McCall, Jr. and M.M. Lombardo. Durham, NC: Duke University Press, 1978.

Quinn, J.B. *Strategies for Change: Logical Incrementalism*. Homewood, IL: Richard D. Irwin, 1980.

Reinganum, M.R. "The Effect of Executive Succession on Stockholder Wealth." *Administrative Science Quarterly* 30 (1985): 46-60.

Rodgers, F.G. *The IBM Way*. New York: Harper & Row, 1986.

Salancik, G.R., and Pfeffer, J. "Constraints on Administrative Discretion: The Limited Influence of Mayors on City Budgets." *Urban Affairs Quarterly* 12 (1977): 475-498.

Schein, E.H. *Organizational Culture and Leadership*. San Francisco, CA: Jossey-Bass, 1985.

Selznick, P. *Leadership in Administration: A Sociological Interpretation*. Evanston, IL: Row, Peterson, and Co., 1957.

Siehl, C., and Martin, J. "The Role of Symbolic Management: How Can Managers Effectively Transmit Organizational Culture?" In *Leaders and Managers: International Perspectives on Managerial Behavior and Leadership*, pp. 227-239. Edited by J.G. Hunt, D. Hosking, et al. New York: Pergamon Press, 1984.

Sobel, R. *Car Wars: The Untold Story*. New York: E.P. Dutton, 1984.

Staw, B.M., and Ross, J. "Commitment in a Experimenting Society: An Experiment on the Attribution of Leadership from Administrative Scenarios." *Journal of Applied Psychology* 65 (1980): 249-260.

Stogdill, R.M. *Handbook of Leadership: A Survey of Theory and Research*. New York: The Free Press, 1974.

Tichy, N.M., and Ulrich, D.). "Revitalizing Organizations: The Leadership Role." In *Managing Organizational Transitions*, pp. 240-264. Edited by J.R. Kimberly and R.E. Quinn. Homewood, IL: Richard D. Irwin, Inc., 1984.

Weick, K.E. *The Social Psychology of Organizing*. Reading, MA: Addison-Wesley, 1979.

Weiner, N., and Mahoney, T.A. "A Model of Corporate Performance as a Function of Environmental, Organizational, and Leadership Influences." *Academy of Management Journal* 3 (1981): 453-470.

Yates, B. *The Decline and Fall of the American Automobile Industry*. New York: Random House, 1984.

PART III

EXECUTIVE TRANSITIONS

EXECUTIVE LEADERSHIP AND SUCCESSION:

THE PROCESS OF TAKING CHARGE

John J. Gabarro

Dramatic examples of executive succession capture the public's attention and often make headlines in the business and popular press. These often involve colorful figures in large corporations—often companies in trouble. Yet executive succession is a fairly commonplace event in organizational life; managers take charge of new assignments every day at every level. A recent study of general managers by Kotter (1982) showed that the managers in his sample (average age 47) had taken charge of new management jobs anywhere from three to nine times during their careers, with the sample's average being between five and six such changes.

Despite its common occurrence, the process of taking charge is one of the least understood activities in management. As a topic it has not been explicitly or systematically studied by either management theorists or organizational psychologists. Although a great deal of research has been done on the broader topic of management succession, and especially on factors leading to succession, very little has focused on the activities and problems faced by the new manager after he or she actually takes charge.

It is this gap in the succession process—what executives do to take charge and what factors influence that process—that this chapter addresses.

More specifically, this chapter presents a descriptive framework of the taking charge process, the succession factors that influence it and the implications of this framework for succession planning and leadership development. Before proceeding, however, it is useful to be explicit about what is meant by "taking charge." Taking charge, as the term is used here, refers to the process by which a newly appointed manager: (1) gains understanding and mastery of a situation; (2) develops a sufficient power base and credibility to gain acceptance as an organization's leader;[1] and (3) has an impact on the performance and processes of the organization. The process begins when a manager starts a new assignment and ends when he or she has mastered it in sufficient depth to have the organization running as well as resources, constraints and his or her own ability allow. Implicit in this definition is the premise that a new manager has not fully taken charge until he or she understands the situation in depth, has gained acceptance as its leader, *and* has had an effect on it.

PUTTING THE TOPIC IN PERSPECTIVE

The process of taking charge of a new assignment is an integral aspect of executive succession. In pragmatic terms it can be considered the last phase of an executive succession. Prior activities leading to it include deciding that a change in leadership is needed, choosing a new leader, planning the transition, and briefing and otherwise preparing the new manager prior to his actual assumption of the assignment. One can argue that in terms of closure, a management succession is not fully realized or completed until the new manager has actually taken charge of the organization.

As such, the taking charge process is deeply imbedded in the larger process of management succession. Unlike the larger topic of management succession, however, very little empirical work has been done on the actual activities and processes by which managers take charge. A review of the literature shows that relatively few field studies have set out to examine how new managers actually take charge of their assignments. The few exceptions include two landmark field studies of successions: Gouldner's (1954) study of a new manager of a gypsum plant; and Guest's (1962a) study of a new manager of an automobile plant. Gouldner's study focused on the bureaucratic patterns initiated by the new manager as a result of institutional pressures and on the consequences of his actions. Guest's study focused on changes in leadership patterns and their consequences for plant morale and productivity. Both studies, despite their age, remain robustly descriptive and are still rich with insights about the dynamics of taking charge.

Since then, most work on the taking charge process (as compared to succession) has tended to be prescriptive rather than descriptive and has tended to be based on either anecdotal evidence or personal experience rather than on empirical research (e.g., Bibeault, 1982; Goodman, 1982; Whitney, 1987). Recent work on taking charge by Bennis and Nanus (1985) has focused on broad leadership processes such as the leader's vision, his ability to empower an organization, and his creation of meaning (see Bennis and Nanus, pp. 26-84, 89-109; and 215-226, in particular). Other work such as Steiner (1983) has focused on formulating public policy, dealing with constituent interest groups, and the social performance and responsibility issues facing the new CEO. With the exception of these and a small number of other studies, which I will review, very little empirical work has focused on the taking charge process explicitly.

In contrast, a great deal of research has been done on the conditions leading to successions and the situational, background and personal factors influencing them. Although these studies have not focused on the taking charge process per se, they have considerable relevance for understanding the factors bearing on how managers take charge, the problems they are likely to face and their eventual success. The process of taking charge must therefore be approached in a fashion that considers other succession variables and factors.

Because the taking charge process is an integral part of management succession, it is useful to conceptualize it as occurring within the context of a set of succession characteristics, as shown in Figure 1, such as the successor himself, his background, the situation he is facing and why he was chosen. With this approach, a process model of leadership succession can be developed to describe both the activities that comprise the taking charge process, as well as the factors that influence a manager's execution of these activities.

In developing a process model of leadership succession I will first describe the taking charge process and the generic tasks that comprise it as well as its temporal dimensions. Then I will examine more closely those succession factors which research suggests have a situational bearing on how managers take charge. This will enable us to understand more systematically the taking charge process and the issues a manager is likely to face in a given situation. The purpose in using this approach is that it will result in a process model which is both descriptive and predictive: descriptive in terms of highlighting the kinds and degrees of work needed for a manager to take change in a given situation; and predictive in terms of gauging the relative difficulty which a manager is likely to encounter in performing this work.

Figure 1. Taking Charge in Context

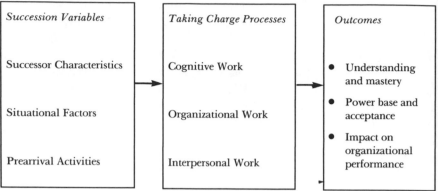

THE TAKING CHARGE PROCESS

As described earlier, the taking charge process is completed when the new manager has: (1) gained an understanding and mastery of the situation; (2) developed a power base in the position and sufficient credibility to be accepted as the organization's leader; and (3) had an impact on the organization's performance and processes. This definition presumes that understanding an organization's business and organizational issues at a substantive level is necessary for a new manager to be effective and that this process of familiarization is an essential component of taking charge. It also assumes that taking charge of an organization requires that its members acknowledge that the new manager is, in fact, in charge. This acceptance requires that the new manager establish a power base that goes beyond "headship" status (Gibb, 1969) or the legitimate authority that goes with the position (Kotter, 1977, 1985). Finally, the definition also presumes that the new manager has had a substantive effect on the organization's performance and processes. All three of these assumptions go beyond the act of succession as an event which simply marks a change in command. It is for this reason that the taking charge process can be seen as the logical culmination of the succession process.

With this three-fold definition of the desired outcomes of taking charge, it is possible to bracket what the taking charge process entails. At the most general level, the taking charge process can be conceived of as entailing a number of activities that can be grouped into (1) cognitive work, (2) organizational work, and (3) interpersonal work. Although these activities are obviously interrelated, I will discuss them separately.

Cognitive Work

Learning about and understanding a new situation requires cognitive work. The nature of this work includes learning, developing or enhancing one's cognitive map, and diagnosing current problems. The formulation or review of an organization's strategy which often accompanies a change in leadership also requires cognitive work. Much of this work may occur inside a manager's head, but it is nonetheless an important aspect of the process.

Indeed, McGivern (1978) in a study of successions in small firms in the United Kingdom identifies the tasks of acquiring relevant knowledge and a grasp of the technical issues facing the organization as critical to a manager's success in taking charge. Morrison (1975) also identifies the acquisition of situation-specific technical and management knowledge as a central aspect of the post-arrival stage of management succession.

Similarly, Gabarro (1987) in a comparative field study of 17 executive successions, found that the initial evaluative and orientational learning, assessment, and diagnostic work of taking charge occupied a great deal of the attention of the managers he studied during their first six months on the job. Taking-charge work figured as a major theme in his interviews with them at the three- and six-month periods of time. Its prevalence as a theme did not diminish until after the 18-month period. Not surprisingly, the cognitive tasks of learning and orienting oneself to the situation were particularly strong preoccupations of managers who were industry outsiders and of those involved in turnarounds.

Organizational Work

The development of credibility and acceptance as a leader as well as actually influencing organizational performance require a great deal of organizational work. The term organizational work is used here to include developing a set of shared expectations among followers, resolving and mediating conflict and building a cohesive management team.

A critical task identified by McGivern (1978), Gordon and Rosen (1981), Gilmore and McCann (1983), and Gabarro (1987) is the development of a set of shared expectations within the organization's management group. In their excellent discussions of the post-arrival factors of a succession, Gordon and Rosen (1981) highlight the importance of this task as part of a new manager's need to cope with discrepancies between his "path-goal" perception and those of the organization's members. The developing of shared expectations is also implicit in their discussion of the "sending, receiving and evaluating of role expectations for both sides that will set the stage for future action." (Gordon and Rosen, 1981: 246.) They point out that this is particularly important if the new manager is known to the group (an insider) since old role expectations are likely to be incompatible with the new role.

Gilmore and McCann (1983), in a study of leadership successions in correctional institutions, also discuss this activity as part of a "contracting process" in which expectations, values and perceptions are worked out between the new manager and organizational members. Their treatment of the expectations issue also includes the need to consider shareholder expectancies and situational pressures. Gabarro (1987) also describes the process of working through a set of shared expectations as a central aspect of the organizational work of taking charge. He found that a failure to do so was one of the factors that distinguished between successful successions and those that failed (a failed succession was defined as one in which the new manager was terminated within three years of assuming the assignment).

Closely related to the task of developing a set of shared expectations is the need to resolve and mediate conflict. In a study of leadership succession in a mental health organization, Redlich (1977) found that the working through of differences, particularly with key norm-setting individuals, was an important aspect of the new leader's succession work. He also postulates that this working-through phase of activity has to take place before the reestablishment of equilibrium and the setting of new norms can occur. McGivern (1978) and Greenblatt (1983) also describe the resolving of differences as a critical task of taking charge, and Gabarro (1987) identifies the failure to resolve differences as one of the patterns that distinguishes failed from successful transitions.

Both the processes of developing a set of shared expectations and effectively resolving conflicts are implicit in the task of developing a cohesive management team. In comparing failed successions with successful ones, Gabarro (1987) found that one of the patterns that characterized unsuccessful managers was that they chose not to work with their new subordinates as a group and preferred to work with them on a one-on-one basis. Unsuccessful managers tended to avoid meeting with their staffs in group settings and preferred written communications. A comparison of the activity chronologies of managers in successions that failed with those that succeeded also showed that unsuccessful managers used regularly scheduled staff meetings and problem-focused task forces to a significantly lesser degree than managers who succeeded. Gabarro described this preference for working alone or on a one-on-one basis with key subordinates as a "lone ranger" syndrome and argued that it contributed to a sense of lack of direction as well as problems of communication and lack of cohesion.

Interpersonal Work

Closely related to the organizational work just described are the interpersonal tasks of developing effective working relationships with key subordinates, peers and one's superiors so that a basis of mutual expectations and influence exists. The development of effective working relationships is identified as a critical aspect of taking charge by both McGivern (1978) and Morrison (1975). Gabarro (1985, 1987) goes so far as to identify the quality of a manager's working relationships at the end of his first 12 months as the single factor which discriminates most saliently between those transitions that succeeded and those which ultimately failed (a poor working relationship was defined as one which either the new manager or his subordinate described as being ineffective or dissatisfying). As a group, managers in the failed successions had a significantly greater number of ineffective relationships with key subordinates, peers and superiors at the end of their first 12 months than did managers in the transitions that succeeded. Although many reasons were given for these relationship problems, Gabarro concluded that the underlying theme was the new manager's inability or unwillingness to work out a set of mutual expectations among key subordinates or to develop a foundation of trust or influence in these relationships.

Similarly, Sathe (1985) describes the need to develop credibility as one of the central tasks facing a newcomer in establishing him or herself in a new setting. Sathe defines credibility as a relational attribute which develops as an interaction of trust and influence. In these terms, he conceptualizes credibility as an attribution that results from the development of both influence and trust in a relationship.

Sathe's conclusions about the importance to a newcomer of developing credibility are consistent with Gordon and Rosen's (1981) reference to the development of sources of power and influence as a key postarrival factor and McGivern's (1978) description of the need to establish control.

STAGES IN THE TAKING CHARGE PROCESS

In terms of how managers engage in these tasks over time, several authors have postulated that management successions occur in stages. Gordon and Rosen's (1981) conception of prearrival and postarrival factors can be construed as a stage paradigm, although they do not present these factors as such. Greenblatt (1983) has described a fairly simple model in which he identifies two postarrival phases which he describes as an *Assertion Phase* in which the new leader presents his personality, style and programs and a *Working Through Phase* in which differences are resolved leading to change.

A more elaborate stage description has been developed by Redlich (1977) based on the temporal sequencing of archetype issues that the new leader and his organization need to work through. Redlich defines them as follows: (1) An *Anticipatory Stage* which he describes as a period of uncertainty and anxiety that lasts until a new manager is chosen; (2) An *Appointment Stage* in which the successor is announced, thereby relieving some of the anxiety; information is exchanged about him and the reality of the succession sets in; (3) An *Inauguration Stage* in which the task is for superiors to assure constituents and to create a sense of solidarity and optimism; (4) A *Honeymoon Stage* which consists of a period of sizing up, testing and learning (similar to the mutual observation activities described by Gordon and Rosen); (5) An *Assertion Stage* (similar to Greenblatt's Assertion Phase) in which the new leader's task is to present his personality, style and programs thereby creating a period of discomfort in which disagreements and differences emerge; (6) A *Working Through Stage* (also similar to Greenblatt's) which he describes as a period of resolution of differences and a time for stabilizing relationships; and finally (7) An *Equilibrium Stage* in which a new equilibrium is established and new norms are set. One of the underlying themes in Redlich's post-arrival stages is that the new leader's succession and initiatives will create a period of destabilization which needs to be followed up with activities which result in a new equilibrium.

Gabarro (1983, 1985, 1987) has postulated a stage paradigm of the learning and action involved in the taking charge process. The stages are based on prevalent themes that emerged from time-staggered interviews with new managers and their key subordinates during their first three years in the assignment and on case chronologies developed for each of these successions. The cases summarized the new manager's major areas of involvement and the organizational and policy changes they implemented by three month periods for their first three years on the job (or in the case of failed successions until such time as the manager was terminated). Gabarro described these stages as follows: (1) A *Taking Hold Stage,* typically lasting from three to six months, which is characterized by a great deal of learning of an evaluative and orientational nature, culminating with a burst of organizational changes of a corrective nature; (2) An *Immersion Stage,* a period of relatively little change activity, lasting from 4 to 11 months, in which the manager immerses himself in managing the business in a more informed fashion as well as in acquiring a deeper and finer-grained understanding of the situation, culminating in the manager developing a new or a greatly revised concept of how to improve performance; (3) A *Reshaping Stage,* typically lasting from three to six months, which is characterized by a great deal of organizational change activity that is triggered by the concept developed during the Immersion change, involving changes of a more basic nature than those made during the Taking Hold stage; (4) A *Consolidation Stage,* typically lasting from three to nine months, in which both learning and change activity focus on consolidating and following through on the changes implemented during the prior stage; and finally, (5) A *Refinement Stage* in which most of the manager's learning is routine and incremental. The underlying theme in Gabarro's stages is the developing nature of the learning and action-taking involved in taking charge, beginning with learning and diagnostic work of an orientational and evaluative nature leading to corrective actions, followed by a period of relatively little change but deeper and finer-grained learning which is then followed by change of a more basic nature, consolidation, and finally a gradual diminishing of change activity.

Gabarro found that this pattern of three waves of change occurred in all of the successions he studied, regardless of whether they were turnarounds or normal successions, industry-insider or industry-outsider successions. Figure 2 presents a plotting of these data disaggregated by type of succession. Gabarro found relatively little organizational change activity from the 30th month through the 42nd month, the last period for which data were gathered.

Based on analysis of top management changes in correctional institutions, Gilmore and McCann (1983) have also developed a four-phase model of the leadership succession process using a stakeholder analysis approach. Their first stage deals with selection and contracting issues in which initial expectations are negotiated between the new leader and the institution. Their second stage, Entry, is a period of further testing of expectations and negotiation of differences during which the new manager's actions are the subject of considerable scrutiny by the organization as it attempts to discern his intentions. In this regard, this stage is very similar to Gordon and Rosen's "mutual observation" activity and Redlich's Honeymoon Stage. The resolution of this stage is influenced by a number of situational factors including problem urgency. Their third stage, Initial Initiatives, is characterized by a great deal of action-taking, including program changes, personnel actions and organizational changes and is directly analogous to Redlich's Assertion Stage and Gabarro's Taking Hold Stage. The final stage, Pattern Setting, grows out of the prior stage and involves the reestablishment of organizational stability in terms of greater predictability in processes, norms and routines. In this regard this stage is similar to Redlich's Equilibrium Stage and Gabarro's Refinement Stage.

Although the Redlich, Gilmore and McCann, and Gabarro stages focus on different aspects of the taking charge process, they share several temporal commonalities. All of them describe periods of initial learning and testing, followed by periods of destabilizing change. All three of the stage paradigms also culminate with a period of re-equilibrating activities (Redlich's Working Through and Equilibrium Stages, Gilmore and McCann's Pattern

Figure 2.   Average Number of Organizational Changes Per Six Month Period, Categorized.

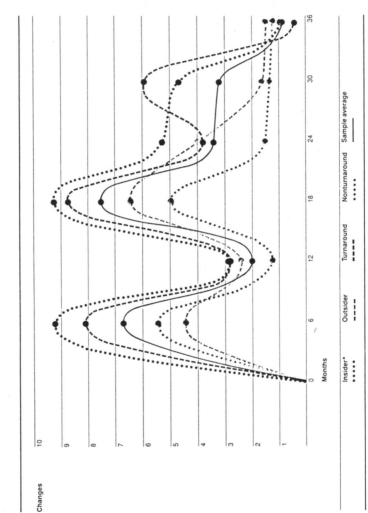

Reproduced with permission: Gabarro, J.J. *The Dynamics of Taking Charge.*
(Boston: Harvard Business School Press, 1987, p. 16.)

Setting Stage and Gabarro's Refinement Stage). Another characteristic of the Gilmore and McCann and the Redlich stages is a movement from the initial surfacing and testing of differences to a process of resolution of differences through a tacit or explicit renegotiating a new social order.

In summary, the empirical work on the topic suggests a number of commonalities in the activities involved in taking charge of an organization as well as in the way in which these activities are implemented over time. Let me now turn to the question of what factors influence these processes.

SUCCESSOR CHARACTERISTICS AS FACTORS

The management succession literature is relatively rich in research on the effects of prior background and contextual variables on succession outcomes and on the problems managers are likely to face in taking charge. The most salient of these factors include successor characteristics, situational favorableness and "prearrival factors" (Gordon and Rosen, 1981; Brady and Helmich, 1984).

Successor Origin: Organizational Insiders vs. Outsiders

Most empirical work on the effects of a new manager's background has focused on differences between managers promoted from within (organizational insiders), and those brought in from outside (organizational outsiders). The findings concerning successions at the CEO level are quite consistent: organizational outsiders tend to replace more subordinates and make more changes as they take charge than do insiders. In a frequently cited study of school system superintendents, Carlson (1962) found that organizational outsiders, whom he characterized as career bound and mobile, instituted more organizational changes than organizational insiders, whom he described as place bound and long-tenured. Carlson argued that organizational outsiders (because of their orientations and predispositions) are more task-oriented than insiders. Carlson also argued that outsiders, because they are not part of the previously existing political system, face more neutral and cooperative staffs than insiders. This enables them to expand their staffs, building a base of "beholden" supporters, thereby enabling them to retool the organization for a new direction. Carlson also theorized that an outsider effectively suspends the social system of interest groups and cliques and this suspension gives the outsider greater flexibility and latitude in ameliorating internal conflict and in redirecting the organization's course.

Studies by Grusky (1960) and Helmich (1971) support the presence of this pattern among U.S. CEO successions. An important study by Helmich and

Brown (1972) tested the hypothesis that inside successions (in their case to corporate presidencies) resulted in fewer replacements of subordinates than outsider successions. In this major study of 208 chemical and allied product companies, they found that organizational outsiders made more personnel changes among their "executive role constellations" (Hodgson, Levinson, and Zaleznik, 1965) than insiders. Helmich and Brown found this pattern to persist, even when controlled for successor style, firm performance, size, growth, and base technology. Helmich (1975b) also found that older firms tended to promote insiders more often than outsiders. Later studies by Helmich (1977a, 1977b) supported his earlier findings and also showed that outsider CEOs were more likely to expand the size of their boards concurrent with their replacement of vice presidents. He also found, however, that rapid rates of turnover at the top tend to slow the pace of organizational growth.

The implication of this persistent theme in the literature seems clear: organizational outsiders are more likely to make changes as they take charge than insiders. However, these implications have to be tempered by several caveats. The first is that most of these studies pertain to CEO successions rather than senior level executive successions and the resulting dynamics may not be the same. In appointing a new CEO, the decision to search outside the firm is very likely a reflection of an explicit desire by a board to bring about change. Thus, we would expect outsider CEOs to actively initiate more change than insiders. Brady and Helmich (1984) make this point in discussing Carlson's earlier research: "In extrapolating this theory to general organizational situations we might conclude that outside-elected successors are typically brought in because of the need for substantial change." They make the same point in reference to CEO aspirations following succession: "The outside CEO successor is typically brought in with a mandate for change and this invariably entails firing or pressuring members of the executive staff into leaving" (p. 50).

A second caveat is that the appointment of an outsider is not necessarily correlated with improved future organizational performance (Grusky, 1963) even though, as Brady and Helmich suggest, the outside appointment may be in response to past poor performance. In an extensive longitudinal study of CEO and senior level successions in the microcomputer industry, Virany and Tushman (1987) found that high performing firms made significantly fewer external promotions than less successful organizations. Moreover, several studies suggest that the appointment of outsiders increases the degree of dislocation that is typically involved in successions (Brady and Helmich, 1984) as well as the difficulties faced by the new manager as he takes charge (Gabarro, 1987).

Industry-Relevant Experience and Transferability of Skills

Unfortunately, relatively little research has been done on the effects of industry-specific experience per se on either the degree of change a new manager makes or on the success of that change. The little research that has been done on the transferability of an executive's skills across industries suggests that transferability is limited and that industry insiders are more likely to take charge effectively than outsiders. In one of the few studies on this topic, Peery and Shetty (1976) found that of 270 corporations in 26 different industry groups only 29 had gone outside of their firms for executives in the top level category and only 14 of these were industry outsiders. Brady and Helmich (1984) cite this study in describing the costs to industry outsiders in taking charge, underscoring the difficulty and amount of time needed for an industry outsider to acquire the "organizational and institutional skills (knowledge of the intricate pattern of interaction of the firm with key elements of the environment)" that are needed to take charge (1984: 107-108).

Their conclusions are very consistent with Kotter's research on general managers and the importance of industry and institutional knowledge to their effectiveness (Kotter, 1982, 1985). Elsewhere, Brady and Helmich also discuss some of the problems faced by industry outsiders as including difficulties in overcoming opposition and gaining acceptance which are critical aspects of the organizational and interpersonal work of taking change. They also point out that industry outsiders report more problems than insiders in being unprepared in terms of lack of knowledge about the firm or industry (Brady and Helmich, 1984). The lack of this background cannot help but make the cognitive work of taking charge more difficult. Brady and Helmich's conclusions are also consistent with more recent research by Virany and Tushman (1987) indicating that high performing firms in the microcomputer industry had executive teams that were comprised significantly more of managers with previous experience in the electronics industry than less successful firms. These findings are also supported by a comparative study of industry-insider and industry-outsider successions by Gabarro (1983, 1987) which showed that industry insiders experience fewer difficulties than outsiders, take hold of their assignments more quickly and make on average twice as many changes during their first three years on the job as industry outsiders.

Thus the findings on the effects of prior industry-specific experience are fairly consistent. Lack of industry specific experience is likely to make the taking charge process more difficult and is likely to require more learning and assimilation on the part of the new manager.

Prior Functional Experience

Unfortunately, very little research within the management succession literature has focused on the effects of prior functional experience. The only study cited in Brady and Helmich's exhaustive review of this literature concerns differences in the leadership style tendencies of young managers with different functional backgrounds. In another study, Hall (1976) found that companies generally had CEOs who had functional backgrounds in the company's general category of technology. Firms in technologically sophisticated industries tended to have CEOs with technical backgrounds, while those involved in technologically unsophisticated industries tended to draw CEOs with marketing and sales experience. The inference is that firms choose CEOs with functional backgrounds appropriate to their firms' needs, but the study did not describe how this prior experience influenced the actions taken by CEOs as they took charge.

In a field study of 17 management successions of senior level executives described earlier, Gabarro (1983, 1987) found that previous functional experience has a profound influence on the actions the new managers took, as well as the areas and problems they focused on, especially during their first three to six months. Gabarro found that this effect continued, although in diminished fashion, even after 27 months in the job (Gabarro, 1987). Using a detailed chronology of changes made by the new managers and the areas they focused on by one-month periods, Gabarro found that with very few exceptions, new executives' initial actions, as well as the major changes they made during their first three years on the job, tended to involve those areas in which they had the greatest previous functional experience. He cautioned, however, that care should be used in drawing cause-effect conclusions, as it was likely that these managers were chosen for these assignments because top management believed that their prior experience was relevant to the new assignment.

Even with these caveats in mind, the existing research suggests that (1) a manager's prior functional experience is likely to influence the areas he focuses on as well as the actions he takes as he takes charge; and (2) if the functional experience is relevant, it is likely to make the transition smoother. On the other hand, it is also possible to speculate that if a manager's prior experience is not relevant or constitutes a bad "fit" with the job's requirements it could put the manager at a significant disadvantage.

Other Situationally Relevant Successor Characteristics

Although organizational origin, prior industry-specific experience and functional background cover much of what is relevant to successor characteristics, evidence exists that other background factors can also be salient. In a now classic study, Salancik and Pfeffer (1977) found that candidates with backgrounds which enabled them to deal with an organization's critical contingencies were more likely to be chosen for important posts than those who lacked these competencies. In this study of hospital administrators, they confirmed Thompson's (1967) earlier work on the relationship between succession to leadership and a candidate's ability to cope with organizational uncertainties. They conclude that managers "are selected to cope with the organization's critical contingencies, and. . .these contingencies are related to organizational context" (p. 75). One of the inferences of this study is that some backgrounds will be seen as more salient than others depending on the particular problems or challenges an organization faces. One would also expect that new managers who possess the skills needed to deal with critical contingencies would begin the taking charge process with stronger power bases as well as stronger mandates for change (Pfeffer, 1981).

The Salancik and Pfeffer findings are supported by Virany and Tushman's (1987) work on the microcomputer industry, in which they found that as the industry matured, the historically high performing firms showed a decrease in the percentage of their top management groups with backgrounds in engineering and an increase in the percentage of those with backgrounds in marketing and sales. In contrast, top management groups in the lower performing firms showed a significantly lesser rate of change over time. Virany and Tushman propose that this difference reflects a greater capacity on the part of the high performers to adapt to changing environmental requirements through management succession.

In the study cited earlier, Gabarro (1987) also found that background factors other than prior functional and industry experience could influence the problems faced by managers as they took charge, including such factors as whether a manager had experience in a large or a small company, an entrepreneurial setting or a stable one. He cites one case in which a manager whose entire career had been in large stable organizations who had serious problems taking charge of an entrepreneurial organization. In another case a manager who had extensive previous experience managing within a large sophisticated firm was unable to cope with the hands-on requirements of a small company. Gabarro attributed part of the failure of these two executives to their lack of situationally-relevant experience. Thus it is clear that a number of succession characteristics, such as those related to critical contingencies and type of institutional experience, can also influence a manager's ability to take charge effectively.

Effects of Management Style and Predispositions

Although less easily documented than other successor characteristics, considerable evidence exists that management style can influence the taking charge process. The effects of a new manager's style on the actions he takes are well documented in two of the earliest case studies of leadership successions. Gouldner (1954) described in detail the consequences of the impersonal and bureaucratic style of the new plant manager he studied, including noncooperation and a "lionizing" of his predecessor who had not been particularly liked while he was in command (which Gouldner labeled the "Rebecca Myth" after the lamented, eponymous figure in Daphne Du Maurier's novel). This resulted in the new manager's strategic replacement of key people as a means of reducing this resistance and further bureaucratizing the organization. Gouldner's findings were consistent with an earlier study by Argyris (1952) cited in Brady and Helmich (1984). Argyris found that within five months of succession, new managers with bureaucratic styles caused greater turnover in lower supervisory ranks than those with participative styles.

Guest (1962a, 1962b) also stressed the effects of a new plant manager's leadership style on the actions and their consequences. In contrast to Gouldner's study, the new plant manager in Guest's study formed informal personal ties with subordinates and, ignoring the bureaucratic procedures and powers vested in his office, elicited workers' views on how to improve performance through informal networks. Guest (1962b) outlined the parallels and differences between the managers he and Gouldner studied and attributed the success of the manager in his study to his more open, informal, people-centered leadership style. Koch (1962) studied the adaptation of plant supervisors to a new head of operations whose style was highly structured and found patterns of dissatisfaction similar to Gouldner's (1954), supporting Guest's (1962b) conclusions.

Subsequent work, however, has not supported the clear dichotomy between the Gouldner and Guest studies in terms of the effects of task-centered styles versus people-centered styles on either subordinate reactions or on performance. Kotin and Sharaf (1967), for example, have characterized the advantages and disadvantages of these two styles in terms of "tight" and "loose" approaches to taking charge. A "tight" style is desirable when it enables an administrator to impose order and controls on a situation that is dysfunctionally ambiguous or chaotic. They argue that a "loose" style is effective when it is desirable to maintain flexibility, such as when the organization's work requires creativity or when it is desirable for the new manager to leave the situation intentionally ambiguous such as, for example, when a manager wishes to temporarily avoid confronting conflict or to buy time as he establishes himself. Kotin and Sharaf also argue that these stylistic predispositions will influence the nature of the actions a new manager takes in terms of both structural changes and direct influence attempts.

Kotin and Sharaf's conclusions are quite consistent with the findings of the longitudinal field study by Gabarro (1987) in which he found that the styles of new managers influenced both subordinate's expectations and reactions during their first six months on the job. The study also showed that managers' personal preferences for control or delegation reflected themselves in the structural and personnel changes they made. Several of the general managers whom he studied had changed their organization's structures to accommodate their preferences for either greater control or for delegation. Gabarro found that differences in management style along with the hands-on vs. delegation continuum were a frequent source of conflict between new managers and their subordinates. When this occurred, it increased the interpersonal problems facing the new managers as they took charge, often resulting in the termination of subordinates. Gabarro also found that those mangers who had strong hands-on styles tended to have prior experience in either small firms or entrepreneurial settings. From this, Gabarro surmised that their management styles had been shaped by their previous experiences as managers.

A discussion of the potential effects of management style would not be complete without reference to extensive work on the topic by Helmich. Several of his surveys and actuarial studies have focused explicitly on this question. In developing a model of presidential succession, Helmich (1975a) concludes that a new manager's "need deficiency" is the most important variable influencing his actions, including how task-oriented he is likely to be (consistent with earlier work by Carlson, 1962). He also predicts that task-oriented leaders will deemphasize interpersonal relationships and induce or create subordinate turnover. On the other hand, Helmich also found evidence in another study that the more employee-centered the new CEO, the more he tended to make changes in executive staff positions (Helmich, 1975c). Less clear, however, is the relationship between leadership style and performance. Although an earlier study by Helmich (1971) found that an employee-centered style on the part of CEOs was somewhat associated with profitability, he was reluctant to generalize from these findings because of the low degree of association.

Based on this and other research, Brady and Helmich (1984) make several conjectures about the effects of leadership style but conclude that the advantages of one style over another are highly situational, depending on the need for creativity and the maturity of an organization, and that success or failure is not as much dependent on style as it is on the appropriateness of the style to the context.

In summary, a number of studies on the effects of a new manager's preferences and style on a management succession suggest that these variables can have an influence on a new manager's actions in taking charge, and that, depending on the situation, a possibility exists that management style can be a source of difficulty or problems.

SITUATIONAL FACTORS

A number of situational factors of both an internal and external nature can potentially influence the issues and problems a manager faces as he or she takes charge. The two most extensive reviews of situational and contextual factors bearing on successions are given by Gordon and Rosen (1981), and Brady and Helmich (1984).

Performance Problems as a Source of Situational Adversity

There is considerable evidence that the degree to which an assignment is a "turnaround" situation will influence the difficulty a new manager faces in taking charge. Brady and Helmich (1984), for example, cite work by Grusky (1961), and Ginzberg and Reilly (1961), showing that managers taking charge of organizations that are experiencing performance problems will face a high degree of instability and unrest among their executive ranks. This cannot help but make the team-building and relationship development tasks of taking charge both more critical and more difficult. In discussing "successions in rough times" they argue that it is difficult to change CEOs in the midst of organizational problems and that the break in leadership involved in management change is likely to exacerbate these problems, especially if the new CEO is an outsider.

Although Brady and Helmich's arguments are not directly based on empirical work, they are very consistent with the results of Gabarro's field studies, cited earlier, in which he found that turnaround managers were under much more pressure to improve performance and felt a greater sense of urgency to act on the situation. He also found that managers in turnarounds implemented nearly 50 percent more organizational and personnel changes during their first six months than non-turnaround managers, and nearly double the number of changes as non-turnaround managers during their second year in office.

Another pattern identified by Gabarro was that turnaround managers made a number of changes in their early stages of taking charge that they recognized as being suboptimal and which would have to be expanded on or corrected later. The reasons managers gave in these instances were that they did not have the time to "do it right" the first time because of the pressure to stop the losses. Gabarro also found that subordinates in turnarounds reported much more fear than in non-turnarounds and that this fear put additional pressure on their new managers to gain control of the situation and develop credibility. The study also found, however, that managers taking charge of turnarounds benefited from a number of advantages in taking charge compared to their non-turnaround counterparts: they were given much more latitude and discretion by their superiors, received approvals for changes more quickly, and generally began the process with larger power bases and mandates for radical change. He also found that they faced less resentment from subordinates who had been passed over for the job than managers in non-turnarounds.

On the basis of these studies, it seems apparent that managers in turnaround situations or in situations where performance problems exist will face discernibly more difficult challenges in taking charge. The diagnostic and assessment work of taking charge is likely to be laced with a great sense of urgency, as is the organizational work of developing a cohesive management team and a sense of shared expectations.

Internal Situational Factors

In a detailed synthesis of the post-Weber literature on succession, Gordon and Rosen (1981) posit a situational favorableness model that is particularly exhaustive in terms of internal contextual factors bearing on a succession. Their model consists of some 20 organizational factors that can be inventoried to predict the difficulties facing a successor as he takes charge. These include the goal motivation of the group to be led, the legacy of the predecessor, flexibility of the group's role structure, cohesion and conformity within the group, level of democratization within it, and the existence of irreversible policies that may be in the newcomer's path.

The factors identified by Gordon and Rosen largely focus on the firm's internal context rather than external contingencies, but they provide a means for gauging how difficult an internal situation a new manager is likely to face as well as the amount of organizational and interpersonal work needed to take charge.

One of the factors described by Gordon and Rosen as being a salient contextual variable (which is also referred to by Brady and Helmich) is the contrast effect that occurs between a new manager and his predecessor, that is, subordinates naturally compare the new manager with their former superior (a phenomenon also found by Gabarro (1987) in the early stages of a new manager's taking charge). Gordon and Rosen point out that this can be particularly troublesome if the predecessor's role and strategy was different from the successor's. McGivern (1978) also identifies the potential danger to a newcomer of a predecessor attempting to impede changes the newcomer initiates. Christensen (1953) found that predecessor resistance was particularly a problem in small but growing firms when predecessors remained as major shareholders.

Concerning the potentially subversive effects of one's predecessor, Levinson (1974) goes so far as to warn incumbent CEOs against handpicking their successors. Using a psychoanalytic framework he argues that unconsciously CEOs wish to prove that no one can fill their shoes and therefore they will choose replacements who are likely to fail or, at a minimum, perform less well than they had. Based on these studies and others reviewed earlier, it seems that if a new manager's predecessor remains in the organization as the new manager's boss, the situation could become potentially problematic. In terms of the taking charge process it would suggest that it is especially important for the new manager to gain his predecessor's support and commitment to changes he wishes to make as he takes charge.

Presuccession Activities

An important part of the context in which a new manager takes charge is the preparatory activity that has taken place prior to his or her assumption of the assignment. Gordon and Rosen, cited earlier, identify the screening and selection procedure and the new leader's mandate as two important "prearrival" factors. Holmberg (1986) in a study of Swedish CEOs found that the new CEO's mandate was a critical and determining factor influencing the succession and the changes in strategies, structure and systems implemented by new CEOs. Gabarro's studies also bear out the importance of this presuccession work, especially in regard to developing a "going-in mandate." Gabarro found that problems encountered by several of the managers he studied could be traced back to a lack of a going-in mandate or a failure to negotiate expectations carefully enough (Gabarro, 1987: 94-97). Gabarro also found that a new manager's superior could defuse a great deal of hostility on the part of people who had seen themselves as candidates for the new manager's job by explaining to them why they were not chosen. In cases where this did not occur, it took longer for the new managers to establish credibility. Gordon and Rosen also describe this disappointment as a potential source of problems.

Succession Itself as a Source of Disruption

Before ending the review of contextual factors bearing on the taking charge process, it is important to note that considerable evidence exists that the succession event is, in and of itself, a source of contextual instability. Whatever the longer-term consequences of a succession, a change in leadership is a source of destabilization and disruption, at least in the short term. This observation was first made by Gouldner and Grusky (1959), and again by Grusky (1960) building on the work of Gouldner (1954), Weber (1946), and Newcomer (1955). Gouldner and Grusky argued that successions are sources of major disruptions in the organization as a whole and in the executive role system in particular. A field experiment by Jackson (1953) also confirms the disruptive consequences of changes in leadership. More recently, Brady and Helmich (1984) have described successions as destroying group cohesiveness and engendering conflict. They cite early studies by Whyte (1949), Dale (1957), and others which document increased levels of tension, resignations and other dramatic events (including arson) as negative consequences of successions.

Although successions will vary in their degree of disruptiveness, it is clear that the instability and uncertainty they create are part of the reality that new managers face as they take charge of a new assignment. This is no doubt one of the reasons why the organizational work of developing a cohesive management team and a shared set of expectations is such an important aspect of the taking charge process (McGivern, 1978; Gilmore and McCann, 1983; Gabarro, 1987). One can also hypothesize that the more disruptive the succession, the more critical will be the task of rebuilding an organization and developing a coherent sense of direction.

In summary, a number of situational factors can have a bearing on the work of taking charge. These include situational adversity, especially performance problems, the degree to which a perception exists that there is a need for change, the new manager's power base and credibility within the organization, the strength of the management team and their expectations of the new manager. Relevant situational factors also include support form superiors, the presence of allies within the organization (particularly those who can bridge the transition from the predecessor to the new manager as pointed out by Brady and Helmich) and the favorableness of the situation in terms of receptivity to the new manager (as defined, for example, in Gordon and Rosen's situational favorableness model).

A PROCESS MODEL OF LEADERSHIP SUCCESSION

Having described the activities that constitute the taking charge process and the succession factors that have a bearing on it, it is possible to develop a process model of succession which relates these variables to outcomes. Figure 3 summarizes the constellation of successor and contextual factors just reviewed as well as the cognitive, organizational and interpersonal work described earlier. The number of potential relationships among these factors, activities and outcomes are too numerous to summarize in a simple schematic such as that shown in Figure 3. Nonetheless, the model can serve as a broad descriptive framework which can be used to anticipate those taking charge tasks which are likely to be critical in a given situation. For example, one can expect that for a manager who lacks situationally relevant experience, the cognitive work of taking charge will be particularly critical. Similarly, a lack of power base or the absence of a strong going-in mandate

Figure 3. A Process Model of Succession to Leadership

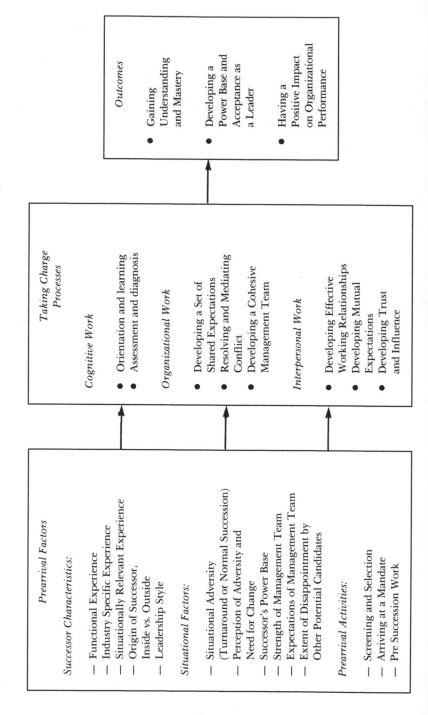

will make the organizational work especially critical. The process model outlined in Figure 3 can also be used as a predictive inventory of the difficulties a manager is likely to face in a given situation.

One can predict for instance, that the more relevant a successor's background characteristics to an assignment, the easier will be the cognitive, organizational and interpersonal work of taking charge and the more likely that the manager will succeed in gaining mastery, developing a power base and having a positive impact on performance. Conversely, the greater the disjuncture between these factors and the situation at hand, the more difficult it will be to take charge effectively. One can safely surmise, for example, that a new manager lacking relevant industry, functional or other situationally relevant experience will have a much greater learning task and more cognitive work to do than one who is not lacking this background. This cognitive work takes time and energy. Furthermore, it is likely that a manager in such a situation will find that his or her lack of relevant background makes it more difficult to accomplish some of the organizational work of taking charge, such as mediating conflict and developing shared expectations. Moreover, this lack of relevant experience is also likely to make the interpersonal work of establishing credibility more difficult. If we add to this scenario the additional information that the situation is a turnaround with a weak management team, it should be quite clear that to expect rapid results is foolhardy. Once laid out, these potential problems become apparent. The contextual factors described in this example would indicate that a considerable amount of time, native ability and effort would be needed before the manager could master the situation, develop acceptance and have a lasting impact on performance.

Let me point out, however, that the successor factors listed in Figure 3 are not monotonic as a group, and herein lies the potential value of considering the implications of each of these factors individually. For example, assume a hypothetical situation in which the new manager has relevant functional and industry experience, but comes from a smaller and more entrepreneurial setting than that of his new organization. If we add to this the assumption that he also has a more hands-on and interventionary leadership style than that to which his new subordinates are accustomed, we can expect that although he is likely to have only moderate difficulty in the cognitive work of taking charge, he is apt to have greater difficulty with some of the organizational and interpersonal work involved. Similarly, a new manager may be chosen from outside of the industry because he brings a new and needed skills base to the organization. It is reasonable to expect that he will bring new insights to the cognitive work of taking charge but that this may come at a price in terms of greater front-end learning and orientation.

In the same vein, the situational factors described in Figure 3 can also be used in a predictive fashion. The research reviewed earlier shows that the presence of performance problems clearly makes the taking charge process more difficult. However, the organizational and interpersonal work needed to take charge may be greatly moderated by the extent to which an a priori perception exists within the organization that change is needed. If this is a widely shared perception, especially among the new manager's key subordinates and superiors, the organizational work of developing a common set of expectations, resolving conflict and developing a cohesive management group may be easier than in a normal succession. This is because people feel the need for direction more keenly since the urgency of the situation is so apparent. One can also anticipate that the organization may be more receptive to new strategic or program initiatives under these circumstances than might typically be the case.

Similarly, one can expect that the power base a new manager brings to an assignment will bear directly on the ease or difficulty of the organizational work of taking charge. A manager who has previously developed a high degree of credibility within the organization will find both the organizational and interpersonal work of taking charge easier than one who does not have such a base. Unless, of course, the credible manager dissipates this asset through ill informed actions or offensive behavior. A new manager with strong, manifest support from top management and a clear change mandate will also begin the process with an advantage.

The strength and expectations of the management team in place can also be expected to influence the nature and extent of organizational and interpersonal work needed. A highly competent and cohesive group can either make these tasks easier (if their expectations and those of the new leader are congruent) or problematic (if the new manager discerns a need for change in priorities, practices or policies). In the latter case, one can expect that the tasks of developing shared expectations, resolving emergent conflicts and developing credibility will not only be more difficult but also critical to the new leader's success.

In addition to serving as a vehicle for identifying how various succession factors can influence the difficulty and criticality of taking charge, the process model can also be used to gauge potential interactive effects, not only among situational factors but also between situational contingencies and the new manager's abilities. For example, it is likely that a manager who is relatively unskilled interpersonally and who also lacks a power base or a strong mandate will have considerable difficulty in a situation that is conflict-ridden and in need of change. This is because the manager lacks the skills and influence necessary to do the organizational and interpersonal work needed to master the situation, regardless of how effective he is at the cognitive work of diagnosing the situation.

One of the findings of the Gabarro studies, cited earlier, provides a good illustration of this type of interaction effect. In comparing failed succession with those that succeeded, Gabarro found that the managers who failed were, as a group, more often industry-outsiders who had difficulties with the organizational and interpersonal work of taking charge than those who succeeded. As compared to the rest of the sample, they had a greater number of relationships with key subordinates which were described as being ineffective at the end of their first year and they also used group-based vehicles for diagnostic and problem solving work to a significantly lesser degree (1987). Gabarro describes this pattern of being an industry-outsider and being poor at the organizational work of taking charge as particularly lethal. Although one can argue that developing effective working relationships and a focused management group are important in all successions they are particularly important to industry outsiders who begin their successions with a number of disadvantages in term of their knowledge base. Thus it is understandable that the combination of being an industry outsider and failing to develop effective working relationships emerges as a lethal combination. An industry outsider needs both cooperation and counsel in the early stages of taking charge or he runs the risk of making poor decisions and ill-informed changes. More than other managers, he also needs input in performing the cognitive work of assessment and diagnosis.

IMPLICATIONS FOR SUCCESSION PLANNING

Using the process model as a framework, a number of implications can be drawn for succession planning, transition management and career development.

Selection

At the most basic level, the relationships between successor characteristics and the work of taking charge has direct implications for leadership selection. The research reviewed in this chapter makes it clear that a successor's previous experience—functional, industry specific and other situationally relevant background factors—influences his or her ability to take charge effectively. They influence the actions managers take to master an assignment, the problems they are likely to face and ultimately—if too large a gap exists between the successor's background and the situation's requirements—their relative success.

The importance of these successor factors challenges the myth of the all-purpose professional manager who, regardless of previous experience, can step into any job in any industry and immediately have an impact. The amount of time and difficulty experienced by John Sculley in taking charge of Apple (Uttal, 1985) is a good contemporary example of the importance of industry specific experience (as well as other succession factors such as power base and the predecessor effects described earlier). Despite his in-depth prior experience as a general manager and his stellar track record as a leader, it took Sculley nearly three years to master the situation in terms of the criteria described at the outset of this chapter. Prior experience and specific industry knowledge do matter, and they influence not only what a manager brings to the assignment but also the amount of work needed to take charge. All other things being equal, the research reviewed in this chapter suggests that an industry insider with relevant functional experience is likely to take charge more effectively than an outsider without industry specific experience.

Although some managers become "turnaround" specialists, they are the exception and not the rule, and it can be argued that they are themselves specialists of a kind. They have in-depth experience in going into difficult situations and identifying those factors that provide greatest leverage in improving performance. Indeed, extensive experience in turnaround situations constitutes a background factor which is, in Salancik and Pfeffer's terms, relevant to the organization's critical contingencies.

The situational factors described in Figure 3 also have implications for successor selection. The most salient of these include a candidate's power base (particularly in terms of his or her credibility and the extent to which it is transferable to the new assignment). A manager's power base will obviously influence his or her ability to perform the organizational and interpersonal work of taking charge. Also salient are situational adversity and the strength of the management team in place. Performance problems call for a seasoned manager, and if the stakes are high enough, one who has previously been through a turnaround. Similarly, a weak management team will require not only a seasoned manager but one who also brings organizational skills and developmental abilities to the assignment.

Finally other, more subjective factors, such as leadership style, can make a difference and should be considered in succession planning. The potential for conflicts in management styles, though less discernible than other factors, can influence not only the new manager's problems but the ease and success with which he or she takes charge. These are "softer" and more subjective factors than those just described and are therefore seldom considered as explicitly as background factors in succession planning. Only the savviest planners give them the full weight they deserve in making selection decisions, yet the research reviewed earlier shows that they can have a major influence on how effectively a manager takes charge.

Transition Management

As the preceding discussion suggests, there are a number of actions that top management can take to minimize potential problems for managers taking charge of new assignments. The most obvious of these is to make the new manager's going-in mandate as explicit as possible, and where it is not possible (because top management simply doesn't understand the unit's business or the unit's industry is in a state of turmoil) to make that fact known to the new manager and to arrive at some general parameters and priorities.

Similarly, top management can also anticipate and minimize the potential problems that a new manager may face because of lack of relevant background, particularly during early stages, by ensuring that there is adequate back-up support that the new manager can tap into, either in subordinates or in corporate staffs. If there are obvious voids in a new manager's prior experience, such as those referred to earlier, it is foolhardy to ignore them. It is far better to assess them realistically and to work with the new manager in figuring out how to close them.

More subtle contingencies, such as predictable conflicts with key subordinates or potential clashes in management style, are more difficult to deal with. Nonetheless, ignoring them as potential problems will serve neither the new manager nor his organization. At a minimum, they deserve to be flagged and discussed as possibilities and, to the extent possible, action-planned. If the stakes are high enough to the organization, outside help may be appropriate.

Another area in which a new manager's superior can facilitate the taking charge process concerns the disappointment that may be experienced by subordinates of the new manager who saw themselves as potential candidates for the new manager's job. This problem exists at all levels, but is particularly acute in upper-level successions. There is always the risk that a valuable subordinate who was passed over for the job will not only resist or impede the new manager but may also leave. Ultimately, it is up to the new manager himself to establish credibility with disappointed rivals and no one can do that for him. However, the research reviewed earlier as well as common sense suggests that the task will be made easier for the new manager if whoever makes the succession decision takes the time to explain to other candidates why the new manager was chosen. This cannot help but make the organizational and interpersonal work of taking charge less difficult, especially in the early stages of the transition.

Finally, it is possible to take the transition management process one step further by making professional resources available to the new manager that can help him or her accelerate the initial work of mutual assessment and setting expectations. Some companies such as General Electric and Exxon have developed a process called "assimilation meetings" through which initial expectations are worked out between the new manager and his direct reports early in the succession. The assimilation meetings are conducted by human resources staff or consultants and can serve as vehicles by which the new manager and his subordinates can raise initial expectations, questions and concerns early in the new manager's tenure (Donnelly, 1985). If well managed, such vehicles can hasten the process by which initial information and expectations are communicated.

In the assimilation process a consultant or a human resource professional meets with the new manager's subordinates as a group during the new manager's first three weeks on the job (but without the new manager present). The purpose of the first meeting is for the new manager's subordinates to surface their concerns, expectations and problems areas they feel are critical and to raise whatever questions they have about the new manager, his background, style or intentions. The professional resource person then summarizes these issues and reports them to the new manager. An important aspect of this process is that anonymity is maintained so that the manager's new subordinates do not have to censor their concerns. The resource person may also serve as a sounding board if the manager wishes. Very shortly after this second meeting—usually within days—the new manager meets with his direct reports as a group to discuss these issues and describe his own expectations (Donnelly, 1985).

Interventions like assimilation meetings can shorten substantially the amount of time and effort needed to surface and address differences in expectations about roles, motives, directions and priorities, which might otherwise take months to discover and deal with. In this respect they can accelerate the cognitive and organizational work of taking charge. However, as the research reviewed in this chapter indicates, the taking charge process is too multifaceted to view such devices as panaceas and they should be seen as tools rather than solutions.

Career Development

The implications of the process model described in Figure 3 highlight some difficult trade-offs for career development in terms of what is good for an individual manager, his or her unit and the corporation as a whole. If a corporation's objective is to develop a well-trained pool of managerial and leadership talent, then it must make succession decisions which put executives in assignments which stretch them by broadening their experience base. This will inevitably mean putting them in charge of organizations for which they have less than optimal experience. Predictably, this will make the taking charge work more difficult in these instances, and a danger exists that the performance of the new manager's unit may suffer as a result, at least in the short term. In cases like these, the question is whether the benefits to the new manager (in terms of his or her development) and to the larger corporation (in terms of developing managerial breadth) are worth the costs to the unit involved and to the new manager himself in terms of poor initial performance.

This trade-off is further sharpened by the reality that executives (like all human beings) learn as a result of feedback from unsuccessful experiences, as well as successful ones. Recent research by McCall and Lombardo (in press) suggests that executives may learn even more from failures and difficult assignments than they do from successful or routine ones. The development of executive leadership requires assignments that broaden a manager and add to his or her skills base and repertoire as a leader (Kotter, 1985). These are the very assignments that the research reviewed in this chapter suggests will make the cognitive, organizational and interpersonal work of taking charge difficult. Mastering these assignments takes time and may involve the new manager making mistakes.

On the other hand, if a corporation always makes succession decisions that err on the side of maximizing the efficacy with which managers take charge, another kind of cost is paid in the long run: A lack of breadth in executive ranks that becomes increasingly noticeable at middle and upper levels. Thus a "safe" adherence to the implications of Figure 3 can exact a price in terms of executive development. The way out of this dilemma is to provide developmental assignments that will stretch managers but are not so out of line in terms of successor characteristics and situational factors that they result in failure. In this respect, the kind of systematic, a priori, examination of the variables summarized in Figure 3 can help inform succession decisions that involve these kinds of executive development trade-offs.

CONCLUSION: EXECUTIVE LEADERSHIP AND SUCCESSION

The major purpose of this chapter has been to develop a framework for describing the taking charge process and its relation to succession factors of a situational and background nature. Although its principal focus has not been on leadership per se, either as a process or as an attribute, the research reviewed here is relevant to the topic and particularly to the question of what constitutes executive leadership. In a very direct way, a manager's ability to take charge of an organization is a test of his or her executive leadership, at least insofar as it pertains to success in a given situation. The studies reviewed in this chapter suggest that leadership style (and conflicts in style) play an important role in taking charge. But so do a number of other factors including background and experience, successor origin, situational adversity, other contextual factors and prearrival activities.

Many of these variables figure prominently in the literature on leadership, particularly situational adversity and power base. Other variables, however, such as functional and industry-specific experience and other situationally relevant background factors do not. Yet on close inspection they make a difference to a leader's success in taking charge and underscore the extent to which effective leadership is contingent on background and context. One of the consequences of looking at leadership through a succession lens is that these other variables emerge more sharply in their importance. In developing a process model of executive succession, my purpose has been to relate the cognitive, organizational and interpersonal work of taking charge to these contextual variables. My hope is that making these relationships explicit will inform both the dynamics of management succession and the requisites of executive leadership.

NOTES

1.   Here I am drawing on Gibb's (1969) distinction between "headship" status which organizational members may grant a new manager upon appointment and "leadership" which implies acceptance and commonality of goals and aspirations.

REFERENCES

Argyris, C. *Executive Leadership*. New York: Harper and Brothers, 1952.
Bennis, W.G., and Nanus, B. *Leaders: The Strategies for Taking Charge*. New York: Harper and Row, 1985.
Bibeault, D. *Corporate Turnaround*. New York: McGraw Hill, 1982.
Brady, G. F., and Helmich, D. L. *Executive Succession Toward Excellence in Corporate Leadership*. Englewood Cliffs, NJ: Prentice-Hall, 1984.
Carlson, R.D. *Executive Succession and Organizational Change*. Danville, IL: Interstate Printers and Publishers, 1962.
Christensen, C.R. *Management Succession in Small and Growing Enterprises*. Boston: Division of Research, Harvard Business School, 1953.
Dale, E. "DuPont: Pioneer in Systematic Management." *Administrative Science Quarterly* 2(I) (1957): 25-59.
Donnelly, K.J. "The Assimilation Process at General Electric." Paper presented at the Annual Meeting, Academy of Management, San Diego, CA: 1985.
Gabarro, J. "Stages in Management Succession: The Process of Taking Charge." *Research and Course Development Profile*, pp. 193-215. Boston: Harvard Business School, 1983.
Gabarro, J. "When A New Manager Takes Charge." *Harvard Business Review* 63(3) (1985): 110-123.
Gabarro, J. *The Dynamics of Taking Charge*. Boston, MA: Harvard Business School Press, 1987.
Gibb, C. "Leadership." In *Handbook of Social Psychology*, 2nd. ed. Vol. 4, pp. 205-282. Edited by G. Lindzey and A. Aronson. Reading, MA: Addison-Wesley, 1969.

Gilmore, T., and McCann, J. "Designing Effective Transitions for New Correctional Leaders." In *Criminal Corrections: Ideals and Realities*, pp. 125-138. Edited by J. Dorg. Lexington, MA: Lexington Books, 1983.

Ginzburg, E., and Reilly, E. *Effecting Change in Large Organizations.* New York: Columbia University Press, 1961.

Goodman, S.J. *How to Manage a Turnaround.* New York: Free Press, 1982.

Gordon, G.E., and Rosen, N. "Critical Factors in Leadership Succession." *Organizational Behavior and Human Performance* 27 (1981): 227-254.

Gouldner, A.W. "The Problem of Succession in Bureaucracy." In *Reader in Bureaucracy*, pp. 339-351. Edited by R. Merton. Glencoe, IL.: Free Press, 1952.

Gouldner, A.W. *Patterns of Industrial Bureaucracy.* Glencoe, IL: Free Press, 1954.

Gouldner, A.W., and Grusky, O. "Role Conflict in Organizations: A Study of Prison Officials." *Administrative Science Quarterly* 3(4) (1959): 463-467.

Greenblatt, M. "Management Succession: Some Major Parameters." *Administration in Mental Health* II(1) (1983): 3-10.

Grusky, O. "Administrative Succession in Formal Organizations." *Social Forces* 39(2) (1960): 105.

Grusky, O. "Corporate Size, Bureaucratization, and Managerial Succession." *American Journal of Sociology* 67 (1961): 263-269.

Grusky, O. "Effects of Inside vs. Outside Succession on Communication Patterns." *Proceedings of the 77th Annual Convention of the American Psychological Association*, pp. 451-452, 1969.

Grusky, 0. "The Effects of Succession: A Comparative Study of Military and Business Organizations." In *The New Military*, pp. 83-117. Edited by M. Janowitz, New York: Russell Sage Foundation, 1964.

Grusky, 0. "Managerial Succession and Organizational Effectiveness." *American Journal of Sociology* 69 (1963): 21-31.

Guest, R.H. *Organizational Change: The Effect of Successful Leadership.* Homewood, IL: Irwin-Dorsey, 1962a.

Guest, R.H. "Managerial Succession in Complex Organizations." *American Journal of Sociology* 62 (1962b): 47-54.

Hall, J.L. "Organizational Technology and Executive Succession." *California Management Review* 19(1) (1976): 35-39.

Helmich, D.L. "The Impact of Administrative Succession on the Executive Role Constellation." Ph.D. dissertation, University of Oregon, 1971.

Helmich, D.L. "Organizational Growth and Succession Patterns." *Academy of Management Journal* 17 (1974a): 771-775.

Helmich, D.L. "Predecessor Turnover and Successor Characteristics." *Cornell Journal of Social Relations* (1974b): 249-260.

Helmich, D.L. "The Executive Interface and President's Leadership Behavior." *Journal of Business Research* 3(1) (1975a): 43-52.

Helmich, D.L. "Corporate Succession: An Examination." *Academy of Management Journal* 3 (1975b): 429-441.

Helmich, D.L. "Succession: A Longitudinal Look." *Journal of Business Research* 4 (1975c): 355-364.

Helmich, D.L. "Executive Succession in the Corporate Organization: A Current Integration." *American Management Review* 2(1) (1977a): 252-266.

Helmich, D.L. "The President's Position: Successor Characteristics and the Organizational Process." *University of Michigan Business Review* 29(1) (1977b): 11-14.

Helmich, D.L., and Brown, W.B. "Successor Type and Organizational Change in the Corporate Enterprise." *Administrative Science Quarterly* 17 (1972): 371-381.

Hodgson, R.C., Levinson, D.J., and Zaleznik, A. *The Executive Role Constellation: An Analysis of Personality and Role Relations in Management.* Boston, MA: Division of Research, Harvard Business School, 1965.

Holmberg, I. *Förtagsledares Mandat.* Lund: Studentlitteratur, 1986.

Jackson, J. "The Effects of Changing the Leadership of Small Work Groups." *Human Relations* 6 (1953): 25-44.

Koch, J.L. "Managerial Succession in a Factory and Changes in Supervisory Leadership: A Field Study." *Human Relations* 31(1) (1978): 49-58.

Kotin, J., and Sharaf, M. "Management Succession and Administrative Style." *Psychiatry* 30(3) (1967): 237-248.

Kotter, J.P. "Power, Dependence and Effective Management." *Harvard Business Review* 57(4) (1977): 125-136.

Kotter, J.P. *The General Managers.* New York: Free Press, 1982.

Kotter, J.P. *Power and Influence.* New York: Free Press, 1985.

Levinson, H. "Don't Choose Your Own Successor." *Harvard Business Review* 52(6) (1974): 53-62.

McCall, M.W., Jr., and Lombardo, M.M. *The Lessons of Experience.* New York: Harper and Row, In Press.

McGivern, C. "The Dynamics of Management Succession." *Management Decision-U.K.* 16(1) (1978): 32-42.

Morrison, P. *Chief Succession in the Small Business.* Ph.D. dissertation, University of Durham (England), 1975.

Peery, N.S., and Shetty, Y.K. "An Empirical Study of Executive Transferability and Organizational Performance." *Academy of Management Proceedings,* University of Colorado. (1976): 145-149.

Pfeffer, J. *Power in Organizations.* Marshfield, MA: Pitman, 1981.

Newcomer, M. *The Big Business Executive: Factors that Made Him, 1900-1950.* New York: Columbia University Press, 1955.

Redlich, F.C. "Problems of Succession." Paper presented at Annual Meeting of American Psychiatric Association, Toronto, ONT, 1977.

Salancik, G.R., and Pfeffer, J. "Organizational Context and the Characteristics and Tenure of Hospital Administrators." *Academy of Management Journal* 20(1) (1977): 74-88.

Sathe, V. *Managerial Action and Corporate Culture.* Homewood, IL: Richard D. Irwin, 1985.

Steiner, G. *The New CEO.* New York: Macmillan, 1983.

Thompson, J.D. *Organizations in Action.* New York: McGraw-Hill, 1967.

Uttal, B. "Behind the Fall of Steve Jobs." *Fortune,* August 1985.

Virany, B., and Tushmann, M.L. "Executive Success. The Changing Characteristics of Top Management Teams." *Journal of Business Venturing,* in press.

Weber, M. *From Max Weber: Essays in Sociology.* Edited by H.H. Gerth and C.W. Mills. New York: Oxford University Press, 1946.

Whitney, J. *Taking Charge.* Homewood, IL: Dow Jones-Irwin, 1987.

Whyte, W.F. "The Social Structure of the Restaurant Industry." *American Journal of Sociology* 54(4) (1949): 320-330.

CHIEF EXECUTIVE EXIT:
THE HERO'S RELUCTANT RETIREMENT

Jeffrey A. Sonnenfeld

The public cares a great deal about the careers of rising leaders. The public cares even more about the style of management of reigning leaders. But it is not until there is already a succession crisis that there is concern about the difficulties of the aging incumbents and their retirement from top office. The key to understanding the retirement of leaders is their heroic self image.

Consider the following examples of late career chief executive officers. Armand Hammer, who has run Occidental Petroleum for 30 years, is 90 years old. 74-year-old William Norris had run Control Data for 29 years. J. Peter Grace, 73 years old, has lead W.R. Grace for 41 years, and the late Florence Eiseman, at age 85, continued to oversee the manufacture of stylish clothing bearing her name since 1931.

Perhaps more noteworthy was the Cleveland industrial empire builder Cyrus Eaton who died at age 95 as chairman of the Chesapeake and Ohio Railroad and a director of Detroit Steep Rock Iron Mines, The Baltimore and Ohio Railroad, Cleveland-Cliffes Iron Co., Kansas City Power and Light Company, and the Sherwin Williams Company; as owner and operator of two large cattle farms; as trustee of eight institutions including the University of Chicago and Denison University, and as a fellow of the

American Academy of Arts and Sciences. Another long-tenured chief executive, Justin W. Dart, built Dart Industries, a diversified consumer products and chemical company out of a struggling drugstore chain called United-Rexall Drugs. Dart had announced at age 72, "I want my death and my retirement to be simultaneous " (Hollie, 1979: H-1). Three years later, having merged his company with Kraft Inc. and subsequently serving as chairman of the new corporation's executive committee, he died. At age 70, Ben W. Heineman, the chairman of Northwest Industries shelved his initial retirement plans to perform a major corporate over-haul. In accepting a three year extension, he explained "I'm not ready to retire from life. I'm not going to sit around with a blanket over my knees" (Johnson, 1983: 31).

What drives these individuals to continue to work? Why do they push themselves to continue to produce? Why is retirement a concept which is anathema to them? In this article, possible responses to these questions will be explored. In particular, I discuss why some chief executive officers remain in office until the end of their days, while others graciously step down years before retirement deadlines. The discussion begins with an examination of the arguments of the cynics who gainsay the heroic role of corporate leaders. I challenge this cynicism with a discussion of the many types of activities of chief executives and discuss their significance to substantive decision making as well as to symbolic comprehension of corporate life. After establishing that chief executives may, at the least, serve heroic roles within the cultures of their own firms, I discuss five personal qualities common to American business heroes and how they quench society's thirst for such heroism. Next I examine the key barriers to exit which heroes face. Then I propose four distinctive patterns of departure from the executive suite. Finally, I consider why some chief executives follow one pattern and others follow another.

CORPORATE FOLK HEROES: LIVING LEGENDS OF BUSINESS CHEERLEADERS?

The great folk heroes rarely retired when they grew older. The novel *Lonesome Dove* described two retired Texan rangers of the late 1870s as forgotten cowboy heroes in search of a purpose as the frontier became more settled (McMurty, 1984). They drifted, lost through the plains, vacillating between honest and dishonest work. At last they were saved, when they led an epic trail drive of cattle to Montana. Their public and personal pride were jointly restored. They rediscovered lost values of courage, loyalty, and strength needed to survive the trip and regain their heroic valor. Across cultures, Beowulf and Odysseus avoided such dangers by their perpetual search for new adventure.

In many ways, Henry Ford was an authentic folk hero who held tightly to the reins of power to the end. He presented himself as a self-made success born into the modest home of Irish immigrant farmers. A relentless efficiency expert, he used mass production techniques to bring automobiles within reach of the average American. With the encouragement of his employer, Thomas Edison, another folk hero, Ford brought America into a new age. The Model A automobile in 1903, the Model T automobile in 1908, the moving assembly line in 1913, and seemingly paternalistic labor practices made this industrialist a national legend. An image of benevolence and innovation smothered a reality of later labor abuse, personal viciousness, and bigotry. After the death of his only son Edsel, Ford wrote out a codicil that would have passed his power after death to a board of trustees rather than to a single individual, such as his grandson Henry Ford II. Only through the intervention of Henry II's mother and wife was a succession plan to Henry II mapped out (Lacy, 1986). Is it fair, however, to consider that those who lead private businesses are truly heroic? If so, what do they have in common in facing retirement?

CORPORATE HEROES OR EMPTY LEGENDS?: THE SIGNIFICANCE OF CEOS

Before discussing their difficulties in exiting, we should first consider why we should even care about who fills the chief executive's office. Reports of corporate events and even political histories of nations often portray complex systemic phenomena as the consequence of individual decisions. According to Ralph Waldo Emerson, "An institution is the lengthened shadow of one man" (Emerson, 1841: 35-73). Certainly the "great man" view of history has been applied to the corporate world by recent writings of management enthusiasts. Perhaps the accumulated power of a single person, whether a corporate chieftain or national leader is overstated. It has been suggested that we over-simplify the true underlying institutional complexities which shape our society and create the myth of powerful individuals to provide us with the illusion that we can fully understand and influence abstract forces.

This point was made in an especially articulate attack upon such record setting best selling management books as *Iacocca* by Lee Iacocca; *Managing* by Harold Geneen; *In Search of Excellence* by Thomas J. Peters and Robert H. Waterman, Jr.; and *CEO: Corporate Leadership in Action* by Harry Levinson and Stuart Rosenthal. This attack appeared in a New Republic article entitled "The Executive's New Clothes." The author, Robert Reich (1985), charged that these books presented strong-willed, colorful, hands-on missionaries with the evangelical message that anyone, with tenacity and charisma, can be a captain of industry as well. The creation of these "cowboy capitalists," he suggested, brings comfort to Americans who fear the "faceless oligarchs" truly running corporate bureaucracies. In his words,

> There is an overwhelming tendency in American life either to lionize or pillory the people who stand at the helms of our large institutions—to offer praise or level blame for outcomes over which they may have little control. This tendency is particularly apparent in regard to the performance of large corporations, whose legitimacy in our political and economic system continues to be an open question. The current infatuation with successful CEOs offers an illustration. The unfortunate result is that we are distracted from deeper questions about the organization of our economic system. In personalizing these exciting tales, we overlook much bigger stories (Reich, 1985: 22-28).

These chief executive profiles, Reich argued, preach simplistic atmospherics about motivating team spirit, while the success of which they boast is at best narrow and short-lived. He portrayed chief executives as dull, hardworking negotiators—whose public pronouncements are largely ignored.

Similar points were made a year later in an article by economist John Kenneth Galbraith. He argued that the leaders of today's corporations are anonymous bureaucrats. He doubted whether anyone outside the executive suite could name the heads of any major U.S. corporation. With the disappearance of charismatic tycoons, Galbraith (1986a) claimed that "the stock market reacts with refined indifference to the passage of command in the great corporation" (1986a: 3). According to Galbraith's description of the demise of the creative entrepreneurs of the turn-of-the-century and the rise of the managerial technocrat, the modern business executive makes speeches to a wide variety of groups, but they are rarely quoted. Their noncontroversial, bland speeches do not represent the views of any individual leader, but rather the entire organization. The measured words are written by the organization, not its leader. Galbraith suggested that the concept of powerful individual executives is a social invention.

This spirit can be traced back to economist Joseph Schumpeter's 1942 prediction that capitalism's very success creates the seeds of its own destruction. The growth of innovative entrepreneurships into stable bureaucracies, he argued, would reduce innovation to routine, as the irresistible drift towards bureaucracy bulldozed through individual initiative and destinies. The German sociologist Max Weber (1947) welcomed this process whereby executive charisma would be routinized into rational economic organization. These scholars of political economy claim that the once influential masters would depart and leave their servants in charge adorned with only the trappings of power.

Such skepticism over the impact of top executives can even be found among management theorists. Two schools of thought now in vogue overtly minimize the role of executive discretion. One, the "population ecology" school suggests that organizations survive due to the process of random natural selection by the environment (Aldrich, 1979). The current character of firms is thought to represent the conditions existing at the time of their inception which have survived trials for fitness. A second group of management scholars, the "resource dependence school" suggests that firms do change over time, but again not as a result of management initiative. The firm's changing strategies are largely a response to external forces such as the availability of supplies, changes in markets, and legal regulation (Pfeffer and Salancik, 1977).

Perhaps, however, this reminder, like those of the more recent political economists, neglected the significance of the leader as a force of inspiration to the anonymous warriors and a catalyst for societal change through symbolic as well as real attributes.

Entrepreneurial Leaders or Bureaucratic Managers?

The Schumpeter thesis and later versions by Galbraith and Reich overlooked important factors. Capitalism has not been destroyed by its own success in the form of strangling bureaucracies. New enterprises continue to appear and challenge the dominance of existing bureaucracies. Furthermore, even older atrophying bureaucracies are often capable of renewal through innovative turnaround management. Many firms such as IBM, Xerox, and Polaroid have made disproportionately large contributions to the development of new technology. These were led by men who had not yet attracted the attention of scholars while they built their enterprises.

Furthermore, we could readily look at *Fortune* 500 manufacturing and service firms such as Digital Equipment, Wang Laboratories, Hewlett Packard, Apple Computer, Control Data, Intel, McDonald's, Dunkin Donuts, Texas Air, Hospital Corporation of America, Capital Cities Broadcasting, Wal-Mart, and the Limited to appreciate that new enterprise can still join the ranks of major U.S. firms within the reign of the founders. In 1986, *Fortune* anointed Digital Equipment founder Ken Olsen, "the most successful entrepreneur in the history of American business" (Petric, 1986: 24-32) for having taken his firm from nothing to $7.6 billion in three decades. The magazine claimed that even controlling for inflation, this is far greater growth than even achieved by: Henry Ford in his automobile company; Andrew Carnegie in his steel company; and John D. Rockefeller in his oil company.

Olsen, along with Edwin Land of Polaroid, H. Ross Perot of Electronic Data Systems, Frank Lorenzo of Texas Air, and Steve Jobs of Apple Computer, serve as ready reminders of the inaccuracy of Schumpeter's prediction of the death of entrepreneurship. Over half of the MBA student body at the Harvard Business School fights to enroll in courses with entrepreneurship in the course title. By midcareer, almost a quarter of each class has become self-employed. The dream of creating a new business is still very much in the nation's mythology as well as its reality.

Furthermore, we can critique the cynics of executive heroism beyond this appreciation of new entrepreneurs. Innovative leaders do not appear only outside of large bureaucracies. Those whom Galbraith has characterized as colorless organization men are what historian Alfred D. Chandler, Jr. (1977) labelled "managerial capitalists." These managerial capitalists, in contrast to the financial capitalists who preceded them, did not have controlling ownership in the institutions which they led. The imaginative and successful overhaul of General Motors in the 1920s brought this firm to industrial dominance. Alfred P. Sloan, Jr.'s transformation of GM was a model for many other firms even though he was never an entrepreneur with controlling interest. Although William C. Durant formed the company in 1908, he provided little central control over his sprawling auto empire and lost control of it to debt holders such as Pierre duPont. Sloan, an engineer, was made president in 1924.

Great industrial enterprises such as IBM, AT&T, Sears and General Motors have all suffered difficulties over the years, but some of their days of greatest glory were not under the reign of the founding entrepreneurs. Rather, these days were under the rule of the professional manager disparaged by Schumpeter, Galbraith, and Reich. Theodore Vail as a salaried manager created the novel strategic vision for AT&T which guided it from early in the century through to the mid-1970s. Robert Wood as a salaried top executive of Sears brought this catalogue house into the newly emerging business of suburban retail stores. Neither Thomas Watson, Sr. nor Thomas Watson, Jr. ever held controlling ownership of IBM, but they transformed this firm from the old Computing-Tabulating-Recording Company into one of the most admired industrial firms in the world. By the mid-twentieth century, salaried top managers of large mass retailing, manufacturing, and transportation enterprises led bureaucracies which more efficiently coordinated the flow of goods and services from production to the consumers. New technologies and expanding product markets called for enhanced administrative expertise and leadership (Chandler, 1977). The research of Rosabeth Kanter (1983) and the observations of Peter Drucker (1985) indicate that innovation and dynamism are possible in virtually all large modern enterprise. It is possible for individual leaders to harness and direct the might of large bureaucracy so that it is a vehicle for enhancing rather than smothering individual will.

Furthermore, Galbraith was recently challenged on his unsupported assertion that "the stock market reacts with refined indifference to the passage of command in the great corporation" (Galbraith, 1986: 69). Stewart

Friedman and Harbir Singh (1986a, 1986b) of Wharton challenged Galbraith's pronouncements based upon their own study of successions at 235 Fortune 500 firms. They studied stock market prices 400 days before each succession announcement through to 800 days afterwards along with published indications of the reasons for the chief executive's departure, later contact between the firm and the outgoing chief executive, and the source of the new chief executive. When a chief executive was forced out of office due to poor firm performance, the stock rose at the time of his exit. Stock price was not affected, however, when the succession was a routine, planned retirement. Thus the information over the change of individuals in command evidently was sufficiently salient to influence investor decisions. We can look at the impact of actual decisions of chief executives in certain firms which caused them to stand apart from their competitors in the same industry.

Political Leadership and the Management of Symbols

Thus we have now addressed those suspicious that individual chief executives no longer matter as much as they did in some mystical prior entrepreneural period. A second charge of the skeptics remains. This is that the chief executive, much like the manager of a professional sports team, is really a symbolic scapegoat. Thus some try to minimize the role of management by suggesting that it is largely symbolic. Chief executives, it is implied, deal with meaning and sentiments rather than substance. Such management writers suggest that substantive corporate actions are principally the consequence of external interdependencies and threats rather than a product of executive vision.

The appreciation of the symbolic aspects of leadership, however, in no way diminishes the actual power of the chief executive. In his pathbreaking thesis *Presidential Power*, Richard Neustadt (1960) compared the methods of influence used by several U.S. presidents including Woodrow Wilson, Franklin D. Roosevelt, Harry Truman, and Dwight Eisenhower. Neustadt noted the imposing constraints upon the chief executive and suggested that the president is both a leader and a clerk. Neustadt quoted Truman in office, "I sit here all day long trying to persuade people to do the things they ought to have sense enough to do without my persuading them. . .that's all the power of the President amounts to" (Neustadt, 1960: 9-10).

By contrast, Neustadt relayed Eisenhower's exasperation through the comments of a top White House aide, "The President still feels that when he's decided something—that ought to be the end of it and when it bounces back undone or done wrong, he tends to react with shocked surprise" (Neustadt, 1960: 9-10). Neustadt's review of these leadership styles of U.S. Presidents concluded that power through the use of symbols and persuasion was at least as important as power through overt command for getting things done. Management scholar Joseph L. Bower (1983) has extended this power through symbols and persuasion to the private sector chief executive. Bower has shown how private sector leaders have needed to manage an internal political economy of self-interested coalitions as well as the expected external constituencies of the firm. According to former Schlumberger chief executive Jean Riboud, "running a company is like politics, you are always balancing interests and personalities and trying to keep people motivated" (Auletta, 1984: 123). Decades earlier, management scholar Philip Selznik (1957) labelled this symbolic leadership function that of "institutionalization" whereby a firm's values are infused through the leader's efforts to navigate the firm beyond immediate tasks towards larger common purposes.

Symbolism versus "Substance?"

Despite the cynical belief that a chief executive's symbolic influence is merely decorative, a large body of research findings support the argument that the truly powerful leaders are those who rule more than by decree. For over 50 years, academicians and chief executives have emphasized the importance of the symbolic functions of leadership (Mayo, 1933; Barnard, 1938). The distinction between a chief executive who is a commander of substantive action and a chief executive who is a cultural symbol represents a false dichotomy. The leader interprets the organization's context for its members to create a shared meaning of action. For example, a study of the substantive actions of a new chief executive of a telephone operating company after deregulation had different meanings to the existing middle management who had been imbued with the values of the previous culture (Feldman 1986). Substantive actions had to be blended with symbolic actions to form a common understanding of what had to take priority in a changed business environment. Cultural shaping was required to prevent the officer corps from disintegrating into factions leading divergent corporate subcultures.

Management researcher John Kotter (1982) has specifically highlighted techniques for conquering the job uncertainty and dependence upon others which is particular to top executives. Kotter's research indicated that rather than relying upon the chain of command, executives create informal networks to gather information across levels and the continual reordering of the priorities on a changing common agenda. Overt decisions and formal orders are rare, while disjointed and short conversations are the vehicles for persuasion and change. It is first line supervisors and middle managers who are more concerned with the traditional management activities of coordination, planning, and decision making.

More important than the techniques of coalition building and networking, the chief executive is the reigning hero of the corporate culture. In this role, he or she embodies the spirit and values which provide others with a sense of collective purpose and group membership. This cultural function is far more sweeping than that which is appreciated by many economists and organizational theorists who see the firm as a passive institution which reacts to a dynamic environment.

While researchers such as Kotter and others have described the specific activities which top executives follow to circumvent their own bureaucracies, organizational theorist Edgar H. Schein (1985) described how the consequences of such managerial behaviors shape the underlying culture of a firm. The roles managers select shape culture through the following: (1) what leaders pay attention to through measurement and control; (2) how leaders react to specific incidents and crises; (3) the determination of membership status through the design of recruitment, selection, promotion, and dismissal policies; (4) the overt authority structures and flow of information; (5) the design of physical space like building architecture and office layout; (6) creating stories, legends, and myths which convey core values; and (7) formal statements of company philosophy.

BUSINESS HEROISM AND THE HORATIO ALGER MYTH

We have now come to appreciate chief executives as heroes within their own corporation. Their leadership may create or transform the firm's strategic purpose while shaping the culture of the membership. Furthermore, there is a corporate heroism which can transcend even the executive suite. American society at large has long balanced admiration and fear when considering business leaders. Folk heroes serve as a barometer of the social aspirations and expectations of individuals in a society. A decade ago, in the midst of both the highly publicized Watergate political scandals and the erosion of our international character through the tragic war in Vietnam, political leadership lost its heroic mantle. The major periodicals carried cover stories on "The Vanishing American Hero" (1975). Statesmen were no longer cast in the traditional heroic mold. Their fame was brief and their influence was limited. Comedians joked that, "one week a politician appears on the cover of *Time* while the next week he's doing time." Through such a decade the business leader had emerged as a folk hero as evidenced in surveys, periodicals, and best selling books.

Regardless of the actual power of chief executives, the heroic image within the firm is accompanied by heroic accountability and heroic rewards. According to research by Eugene Jennings of Michigan State University, chief executive turnover has more than doubled in the past 10 to 15 years (Prokesch, 1986: pp. 3-1 and 3-25; "Turnover. . .," 1983: pp. 104-110). Responsibilities over the secure employment of thousands of workers, long work days, the danger of wrong judgments, and the risk of an internal mishap over which the chief executive has little control can all be quite wearing. Increased pressure from the investment community as well as generally heightened public scrutiny over corporate behavior has greatly intensified these demands on chief executives (Sonnenfeld, 1980).

As compensation for these responsibilities, we see chief executives frequently earning the wages of celebrities. According to a *Business Week* ("Executive Pay. . .," 1988) survey, chief executives of large firms were paid an average of $1.8 million in 1987, including long-term compensation or $965,000 in just salary and bonus. Nine CEOs make more than $10 million. In fact, these wages are often justified in terms beyond the responsibilities of office or the actual performance of the firm. Rather, many leaders reference their wages by the wages of athletes and entertainers. Even outside board members acquiesce to chief executive requests for pay increases, since they frequently have similar salary expectations for themselves as top executives at other large firms. Board members also decide to lavish heroic rewards upon chief executives because they find it safer to placate a leader with whom they are familiar than face the risks of a new one. Furthermore, because chief executives are institutional figureheads, the costs of the presumably necessary royal life style are supported (Patton, 1983; O'Toole, 1985; O'Toole, 1984).

Despite the cries of some union leaders and dissident stockholders, these wages are met with little public reaction. This widespread acceptance was anticipated by political economist Thorstein Veblen (1899) decades ago when he pointed out that the average member of American society does not want to overthrow the wealthy but instead wants to become one of them. In the observations of Tocqueville and the stories of Horatio Alger, the American hero was revealed to be "a common man" who transcended humble origins.

The Horatio Alger material, in particular, made career success seem like it could be accessible to the average person. What is most interesting about this material is not who he was or what he wrote, but how our society uses it. The notion of the Horatio Alger myth is a demonstration of a social construction. His supposed "rags to riches" format was a conscious heavy borrowing from the works of Charles Dickens, Herman Melville, Mark Twain, and Benjamin Franklin. His formulaic stories were not justifications of wealth nor even of the meritocracy. These stories are not, as presumed to be, accounts of poor boys who, by honesty and industry, became millionaires. The stories described a moral hero who was only moderately successful in business, rather than a successful business hero who was

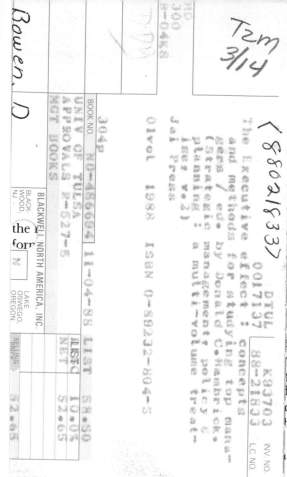

class respectability through

s stories does not compare
ly biographers in the 1920s
e because he and his family
e writers fabricated facts to
urces. Only a half century
ants as Malcolm Cowly and
Ierbert Mayes acknowledge
d that Alger, in fact, was a
who was a fugitive from
t and Bales, 1985). In mid-
isgrace. He tried in vain to
er briefly soared with the
later slid backwards as he
with the same formula. He
et. By the end, he had hired
yer would use Alger's name
grief upon Alger's death in
despite the popular myth to
ch. This victim of mistaken
he Second World War as a

long with other American
construct and maintain a
national identity. The selection of a particular occupation may have a great deal to do with the sources of societal uncertainty. Perhaps the emergence of business heroes in the early 1900s and then again 80 years later has to do with the perceived threat to individual mastery of a complex and changing economic system. Each time, new technologies and major structural shifts changed occupations and institutions. Business heroes help us to personalize the system and make it seem more familiar to the worried population. This heroic role can be found across American history. Heroes reduce social uncertainty through their visions and the example of their own careers. Heroes across ancient cultures regularly provided answers to the most fundamental questions of human existence such as: mortality; the general metaphysics governing the universe; territorial stability; and concepts of honor and loyalty.

This review shows a shifting focus of heroism in America while the mission has been consistent. When our nation experienced threats from warriors, our heroes were fighters—whether frontiersmen, cowboys, or soldiers. When these threats derived from the force of controlling bureaucracies of industry, our heroes were the figures who challenged bureaucracy and reversed its role so that it became an instrument of the individual rather than an oppressor of the individual. The role of business heroes in society then is, in part, to personalize and make understandable a complex and threatening economic system. There seem to be five conventional dimensions of heroism used to accomplish this social agenda. These will be discussed in the next section.

CORE DIMENSIONS OF BUSINESS HEROISM

The current adulation of top executives in society in general presents chief executives as swashbuckling iconoclasts in books and surveys. These figures have triumphed humble beginnings and career setbacks to ultimately achieve national prominence as industrial titans. They have skilfully navigated bureaucratic mazes, broken through traditional definitions of markets, and introduced new products and services. They promote sweeping visions of change in their firms and for society at large. Contrary to the sedate conservative image of corporate leaders of recent decades the reports on these leaders describe proud, even boastful, grand thinkers capable of executing courageous new plans which directly affect the livelihood of thousands.

While some of these leaders are widely admired, others receive sharp criticism. The notoriety of one auto executive for his alleged drug dealing and tax fraud indictments, the office romance of Bendix's William Agee and Mary Cunningham, the succession battles of Armand Hammer at Occidental Petroleum, William Paley of CBS, and Harold Geneen of ITT, as well as the "greenmailers" or "corporate raiders" such as T. Boone Pickens, Jr., Carl Ichan, and Ivan Boesky represent the negative portrayals of top executives. The activities of these figures have generated banner headlines in the daily press and have sparked national debate. Certainly, the controversial practices of these individuals do not rival the evil of the corrupt, turn-of-the-century robber barons, such as Jay Gould and Jim Fisk.

Many of the feared corporate leaders of today have been criticized for challenging the status quo of business conduct. They have created their own rules of fair play. The success of such chief executives has, for many, transformed their public images from near-villainous to near-heroic portraits on short notice.

Examples of such swings in chief executive image are far ranging. Frank Lorenzo of Texas Air was long criticized for his tough labor practices and ruthless takeover bids for other carriers. Now, as the winner and operator of such major carriers as Continental Airlines, Eastern Airlines, and People Express, Lorenzo is hailed as an industrial maverick and savior. Similarly, Ken Olsen of Digital Equipment, who served as chief executive since its founding 30 years ago, has faced harsh criticism for his stubborn resolve.

With several top level defections in recent years, analysts called for his retirement. Now, his rigidity is called tenacity and conviction as his visions of the firm prove to be a success.

This public fascination with the successes of private business leaders has been directed towards a changing elite. One particular breeding ground for new executive celebrities is high technology. Here, there have been many whiz kids who have achieved near mythic fame and great wealth by only their 20s and 30s. The names include Steven Jobs, who at age 29 founded Apple Computer, and Mitch Kapor, at age 34 founded the Lotus Development Corporation. Their colorful management styles and unconventional pasts (college dropout, transcendental meditation teacher, etc.) set them apart from many conventional industrialists. Their styles are, however, consistent with the avant-garde styles of their more senior high technology heroes, such as Robert M. Noyce, 58, the founder of Intel Semiconductors; H. Ross Perot, 55, the founder of Electronic Data Systems, and An Wang, the founder of Wang Laboratories.

To the current generations of readers, these names have great recognition. To future generations, some of these names may be recalled and others forgotten. These ambitious men all hope to have had a large impact on all parts of modern society. They also hope that their accomplishments will survive them. Certainly, their leadership styles will differ as well as will the robustness of their contributions. At the same time, there are some striking similarities in the paths followed by past business heroes and current ones. Their rise to celebrity stature was marked by a struggle to separate themselves from the crowd. Their descent, especially at late career, represents a dreaded possible return to anonymity.

One of the most apparent of these common traits of heroic stature was to have risen from humble origins. These industrialists have been portrayed as self-made successes having triumphed modest family situations. Computer pioneer An Wang was an immigrant from Shanghai. Chrysler's turnaround savior Lee Iacocca was the son of an Italian immigrant. Texas Air chairman and founder, Frank Lorenzo, was the son of a Spanish immigrant beautician in New York City. H. Ross Perot, the billionaire founder of Electronic Data Systems was the son of a horse trader (Kleinfield, 1986). He sold IBM computers before launching his own firm with $1,000 in personal savings. By 1984 it had grown to 15,000 famously dedicated workers when it was sold to General Motors for $2.5 billion. The profiles of business heroes throughout American history show a similar common touch.

A second common quality of these industrial heroes is that they have often triumphed over major career setbacks. Their resilience provided them with a further opportunity to demonstrate their leadership valor. Later in their careers, they point back proudly to the trials which they won along the way. Chrysler savior Lee Iacocca was fired in 1976 as President of Ford Motor

Company for what he claims was his insistence on the need for the firm to produce smaller cars. In 1974, H. Ross Perot, now America's wealthiest person, lost $60 million when two Wall Street investment houses he purchased both collapsed. Computer maker An Wang in 1986 still recalled his angry resentment of IBM's clever strong-armed practices which forced him to sell them his patented magnetic core memory thirty years earlier. Henry Ford's first two automobile firms, the Detroit Automobile Company of 1899 and the Henry Ford Motor Company of 1901 were both financial and market failures.

A third quality of such business heroes is that they have offered their firms sweeping strategic visions that were subsequently copied in other firms and adopted across industries. They introduced new technologies of production, they revived old business, discovered new markets and changed the standards of business conduct. After failing to convince his employer, Montgomery Ward, of the strategic value of expanding beyond the catalogue business into suburban department stores, Robert Wood led competitor Sears Roebuck into this important new market. H. Ross Perot left his employer IBM in 1962 when he became convinced of the importance of selling integrated information system design and software rather than merely hardware.

The required ego strength and inner confidence needed to stand up to critics of their destabilizing visions leads to a fourth heroic quality: a remarkable knack for self-promotion. They have accomplished a great deal and are rarely modest about their contribution. In public addresses by Apple founder Steven Jobs or Chrysler chairman Lee Iacocca, we can readily hear their bold statements of indispensibility in the creative shaping or overhaul of their firms. Dozens of chief executives have heralded their own accomplishments in recently published autobiographies. The list includes, Remington's Victor Kiam, cosmetics entrepreneur Estee Lauder, ITT conglomateur Harold Geneen, computer pioneer An Wang, financier Guy de Rothschild, Pepsi's restructurer in the 1940s Walter Mack, and Sony founder Akio Morita.

The auto industry has certainly provided its share of such reflective narratives on the success of its top executives. John DeLorean's *On a Clear Day You Can See General Motors* offered a maverick's vision of corporate life in the 1970s. It enjoyed enormous popularity even before his later criminal trials and business collapse. In running his own automaking firm, DeLorean converted his image from one of a hero to one of a villain. Lee Iacocca's blockbuster autobiography has sold over three million copies. It reports on his rise from modest origins to the presidency of the Ford Motor Company as well as on his resiliency upon his dismissal and finally his inspiring "can do" attitude in turning around Chrysler. The book, despite criticism over some of the author's bravado, has been a best seller since its 1984 publication.

A fifth common quality of these American business heroes is their sense of civic responsibility. The vision they held for transforming their firm and even their industry may tie into a larger societal mission. Thomas Edison, Henry Ford, and Andrew Carnegie were heavily involved in the public affairs of the nation as it entered the First World War.

Through personal philanthropy and political involvement, business heroes often display an evangelic zeal to transcend the boundaries of the corporation and reach a wider audience. Their books and personal statements ring out loud proclamations of their own approaches to manufacturing, finance, marketing, and human resource management as a suitable model for many other U.S. enterprises. For example, Lee Iacocca's autobiography extols virtues of self-reliance and personal resilience. He is active in many civic associations, and serves as a frequent spokesman for national industrial policy regarding basic "smokestack industries." He chaired the committee which planned the successful Statue of Liberty-Ellis Island Centennial Commission. As an ultimate statement of the crossover of heroic roles, Iacocca has been frequently mentioned by analysts as a Democratic presidential candidate.

We could cite the prominent examples of many other recent corporate chief executives who court active public leadership roles. J. Willard Marriott, Jr. divides his time between running his $3 billion lodging company, his deep involvement with the Mormon Church, and his chairmanship of several conservative business lobbying groups. H. Ross Perot of EDS is well known for his patriotic public activities, his conservative political involvements, his leadership of educational reform efforts and toughened drug laws, and his daring rescue mission to free U.S. citizens held hostage abroad.

Perhaps the greatest philanthropist among American business heroes was Andrew Carnegie. Carnegie virtually gave away the entire fortune he amassed from building U.S. Steel. The Carnegie Corporation of New York was founded in 1911 with $125 million of his U.S. Steel bonds. It was the first great open-ended foundation and served as the model for the later foundations of Rockefeller and Ford. Carnegie was worried that he might die before he completed his late-life philanthropic mission. The Carnegie Institute of Washington received $23 million and the Carnegie Institute of Technology in Pittsburgh received $22.3 million. The Carnegie Foundation for the Advancement of Teaching received $29 million. He created a novel pension system for retiring steel workers and college professors. He donated $10 million to the Hero Funds and $10 million to the Carnegie Endowment for International Peace. Carnegie built 2,811 free public libraries and donated 7,689 church organs. Carnegie also allocated tens of millions of dollars to various institutions around the world such as the Scottish Universities, the Sorbonne, and the Koch Institute of Berlin. Furthermore, he maintained a substantial private pension list which supported retiring

Presidents Grover Cleveland and William Howard Taft as well as the widows of Teddy Roosevelt and Cleveland. He also provided retirement pensions for many childhood friends and benefactors as well as for the telegraphers of the Civil War, a group neglected by veterans pensions.

If these leaders did not appear on their own, we would need to invent them. The great sociologist Max Weber (1947) described "charismatic leadership" as an interaction of personal attributes and social needs. Charisma was observed to be, "a certain quality of an individual personality by virtue of which he is set apart from ordinary men" (Weber, 1947: 245). Weber elaborated:

> an extraordinary quality of a person regardless of whether the quality is actual, alleged, or presumed. The legitimacy of charismatic rule rests upon the belief (of the governed) in magical powers, revelations, and hero worship. The source of those beliefs is the 'proving' of the charismatic quality through miracles, through victories, and through other successes, that is, through the welfare of the governed (Weber, 1947: 295).

Thus the hero's charismatic force is a product of the interaction between the governed's needs for miracles and the individual leader's success in meeting that need. The leader offers "miracles" to a corporation or to an entire society, and the followers offer the leader legitimacy in exchange.

HEROIC BARRIERS TO EXIT

We have learned in the previous section of the ingredients which serve as a recipe for heroism. Heroes believe that they have earned their stature through their deeds and sacrifice. Thus, they do not realize until their retirement that their position is, in part, a social creation. The hero's personal identity is so intertwined with his or her role that retirement represents a personal void.

When the great leader of the Second World War, Winston Churchill, retired as British Prime Minister in October 1951, he was 77, quite deaf, and had suffered two strokes. He had promised his cabinet that he would stay only a year after the last Parliamentary election and pass control to the capable Foreign Secretary Anthony Eden. When enticing international issues arose, Churchill reneged upon this commitment to his Tory party members (James, 1986). He suffered another stroke, but despite ill health, the pleas of his own cabinet, and his wife, Churchill struggled on in the job for another four and a half years.

Even given the vast differences in their external heroic roles, parallels can be safely drawn between a great political leader such as Winston Churchill and a corporate chief executive officer, if we limit the comparison to the internal psychodynamics of heroism. What does it mean to be someone who thinks of themself as a hero facing an untimely career end? Anthropologists and folklorists have drawn parallels between even more disparate folk heroes across cultures and across ages. For example, anthropologist Joseph Campbell's (1949) classic study, *The Hero with a Thousand Faces* uncovered universal patterns in the life stages of heroes. These life stages composed much of the heroic myth from rise, through adventures, to eventual decline. Campbell labelled the commonality across cultures of the life pattern the monomyth of the hero. This monomyth was composed of: a period of separation from society through calls to adventure and to the realization of superhuman talent; a period of continual trials through temptation, setbacks, and ultimate triumph; and finally, a period of reintegration into the mainstream of society.

It is in this final stage of reintegration back into society where the hero resists the process. The heroes are pressured to surrender the unique role which they feel they have created to become superhuman. Some heroes fear that in their retirement, the past may catch up with them through the delayed revenge of the vanquished. Others fear that their constituents will see their retirement as a career collapse. Campbell warned that often, "the hero of today becomes the tyrant of tomorrow" (Campbell, 1949: 353). The tyrant's inflated ego is a curse to himself. Regardless of the outward signs of strength and prosperity, the late career hero, as a tyrant, lives in fear of the threatening aggressions of his environment. The despotic defensiveness which marked the final days of Philippine President Ferdinand Marcos demonstrates this point well. In this case, a self-styled redeemer and professed humanitarian of the mid-1960s became overtly repressive and was overthrown as a bloody, avaricious martinet in the mid-1980s.

Some danger exists when even far more benevolent leaders become panicked at the realization of a quickly approaching termination of office. The desperate clinging to office of a seriously ill Woodrow Wilson, and the clever political scheming of the nation's only four-term president, Franklin Delano Roosevelt, are familiar reminders of the self-styled heroes' temptation to extend their reign. Political scientist Richard Neustadt (1964) warned that even leaders such as democratically elected U.S. presidents can come to believe in the lasting supremacy of power and thus destroy their power base in the process. He stated, "No one saves him from himself" (Neustadt, 1964: 83).

To master this fear of reintegration into society at late career, a top leader must come to terms with two addictive properties of the heroic role which I will refer to as heroic barriers to exit. One property is, most simply, the supreme member status which defines *heroic stature*. This refers to the leader's identification with his or her groups. Their sense of belonging to a group through the special distinction of a commanding office allows them to stand above the group, and thus be secured of a unique membership role.

With the late career loss of supremacy, declining heroes are uncertain as to how they still fit with their old groups—whether it be a team, a company, or a society at large. The second addictive property of leadership roles is the *heroic mission*. Late career, in general, is a time for reflection upon one's accomplishments and requires a coming to terms with a degree of success that has been reached. The chief executive, having established a superhuman yardstick by which to calibrate success, is often unable to appreciate the objective magnitude of his or her triumphs.

Heroic Stature

The first of these barriers to exit, the *heroic stature*, provides the chief executive a place in the firm as a core member who holds a distinct identity but who is nonetheless outside of the crowd. The leader, paradoxically, is never lost in the anonymity of the mass membership. The perspective a chief executive has on the firm, as well as the way his or her subordinates relate back, have been defined along the lines of "he's one of us, but different." Cultural artifacts and norms support the status distinctions between the leader and the subordinates. Some subordinates have projected personal feelings about past relationships with authority figures (e.g., parents, teachers, coaches, prior bosses, etc.) into this relationship. There are varied emphases upon the importance of perquisites of office such as chauffer-driven limousines and personal jet planes. Their mildest requests and suggestions are often translated into the echo of imperial commands by attendant clerks. They are respected and consulted by outside leaders and often quoted by the media. Chief executives can become so immersed in the trappings of office that it may be hard for some to imagine just how to interact with former subordinates and clients after they leave office.

Relinquishing the leadership title, then, leaves the chief executive without a ready identity in the firm. Research on group affiliation has suggested that we join groups for the purpose of being submerged within a larger group entity which provides such benefits as the power of collaborative efforts and a broad basis of reference and support (Schacter, 1959). Thus we have such common benefits from group membership as strength in numbers, the pooled variety of individual talents and knowledge, and the creation of norms or codes of conduct. Paradoxically, however, group membership provides more than the various benefits of group uniformity in that it also provides opportunities for approval and status which afford the individual high social visibility and identity. Thus groups can not only embrace individuals within a larger whole, but they can also help confirm a feeling of unique individuality for members. As a group leader, a corporate chief executive satisfies a need for personal recognition. This status is lost when the job is left behind.

Some theorists have suggested that this need for the leader to be singled out by the group represents a narcissistic drive which is stronger in leaders than for most others. The studies of political scientists Harold Lasswell (1930) and James David Barber (1965), as well as of psychologist Erik Erikson (1958), suggest that public leaders displace many personality affects of childhood into their later life career drives. For example, Barber has written,

> Intense political activity may represent either compensation for low self-esteem, usually resulting from severe deprivation in early life, or a specialized extension of high self-esteem, but seldom does it represent an ordinary or normal adaption to one's culture (Barber, 1965: 17).

Leaders diverse in disposition and activities were described in this research as having uncommonly emotional drives to stand apart from the crowd.

This desire for recognition has been traced through history as extensions beyond what were normal culturally fostered desires for fame. In his book *The Frenzy of Reknown*, literary scholar Leo Braudy (1986) argued that society always generates a subset of people anxious to live their lives in the public eye. These people court recognition on a grand scale in a belief that fame will ultimately liberate them from the suffocating expectations of immediate peers and offer them wider societal acceptance. By reaching a larger audience, the celebrity has merely exchanged one set of obligations for the lure of another set. To gain this greater fame, they rebuild their former private identities into their own creation of a more publicly salient image. Braudy began pointing out that the Greek word "hero" in Homer's works translated to "noble." Braudy used Alexander the Great's self-metamorphosis from Alexander III of Macedonia as a demonstration of how heroes recreate themselves during their pursuit of adventure.

> In recounting his extraordinary career, it hardly seems useful to separate the Alexander he created from the Alexander he became to others, or even from the Alexander he was to himself. Such distinctions assume that the inner nature is more real than the social self (Braudy, 1986: 38).

Alexander's military campaigns and other public achievements were carefully crafted to inflate his heroic identity. As with the facility of self-promotion of corporate heroes, Braudy wrote, "Kings have always been performers, but Alexander introduced the possibility that the king might be his own playwright and stage manager as well" (Braudy, 1986: 38).

Such a pursuit of fame is a manifestation of the urge to be unique. A famous person, however, is not only a successful private person, but also a public story of a private person. The hero manufactures a larger identity to help reach their ambitions. Sadly, heroes often lose contact with the original inner-self which preceded the current external identity as the group leader. They direct so much energy towards meeting the expectations of others to maintain this identity as well as to meet their own expectations, that they lose contact with an internal self-concept.

This movement between an inner, more autonomous self-concept and an external one more defined by group responsibilities and identification is not limited to leaders. Similar stages of cognitive development have been identified by psychologists Jean Piaget, Lawrence Kohlberg, Abraham Maslow, and Robert Keegan that suggest that most of us vacillate between periods in life where our orientation is embedded within a group or an institution (e.g., parents, school, employers, etc.) and periods when we break free from these shackles and gain release from institutional roles. At one point, there is a self which is within the organization while at another time, there is a self which pushes the organization. Robert Keegan (1985) theorized that by late life, a person's career has become less central in that a person *has* a career but no longer *is* a career.

The gradual shift to a more individual self-concept from a self-concept rooted in an institutional identification is far more difficult for a leader than for others. The movement between institutional and personal identities is frozen. The responsibilities of leader's roles keeps him trapped meeting the expectations of others. The leader does not have the time or freedom to look after his inner-self to the same extent. The heroic self-concept can so overwhelm his non-heroic, autonomous self-concept, he may lose touch with it forever.

An interesting illustration of this battle over the loss of status was provided by a 1983 meeting of several former world leaders. In August of that year, former President Gerald Ford hosted a gathering which included former President of France Valery Giscard D'Estaing; James Callaghan, former Prime Minister of Britain; and Malcolm Fraser, former Prime Minister of Australia. This group had governed a large slice of the industrialized world through the 1970s, but all were involuntarily retired by the 1980s. They reminisced over the past, complained about the present, and speculated over future world events. They each spoke wistfully over their lost identity. Prime Minister Callaghan commented, "I had to pinch myself last night and almost pinch the rest of them to remind ourselves that we were no longer in power" (Smith, 1983: 1). When President Giscard D'Estaing was asked how it felt to be out of power, he responded to an inquiring reporter, "How does it feel? About the same way you feel when you write a story that doesn't get in the paper!" (Smith, 1983: 1). These emeritus world leaders knew, as many corporate leaders know, that even as "has-beens," they needed their institutional identities.

Heroic Mission

Distinct from this feared loss of heroic status is the second barrier to exit: the feared loss of the *heroic mission*. The parting words of top executives frequently reveal the agonized confession of unrealized career goals. For example, consider the phrasing of the following final message to his shareholders by Donald C. Burnham, (1975) the retiring chief executive of Westinghouse. Well regarded by many for his accomplishments in office, he nonetheless confessed:

> Inasmuch as I step down from the position of chief executive officer as of the date of this letter, perhaps I may be excused for taking one brief look back at the corporation of July 1963, at which time I assumed leadership. The $2.3 billion corporation of that date has increased more than two and a half times in size. The $48.5 million in earnings of 1963 reached nearly $199 million in 1972 but have been sub-par during the two years just past.

> Naturally, I had hoped to yield the helm to my successor with profits at a record high. But I must be content with the knowledge that the company has taken bold steps to solve the energy, transportation, education, security, productivity, and other people problems of today. It has grown and developed into a far stronger organization than ever in its history, and the remedial groundwork laid during 1974 now provides a favorable platform for profit improvement (Burnham, 1975: 2).

In this candid letter, we see Burnham's disappointment at the close of his career at Westinghouse. His references to the organization's history suggested a searching for a niche in the records of Westinghouse that might last beyond his possibly unfulfilled reign. While he had not achieved as much as he had wanted, Burnham's statements reflected a desire to prove that he had left Westinghouse in better condition than he had inherited it, and better fortified for its future.

In part, this sentiment reflects what psychologist Erik Erikson (1963) has described as the late life tension between "integrity and despair." That is, in coming to terms with the gap between our life aspirations and our record of accomplishment, we either enjoy a feeling of "integrity" and completeness, or we are plagued by feelings of disappointment and despair. Beyond this common late life appraisal, chief executives as heroes have tougher going because they hold themselves to especially high standards of accomplishment. Several psychoanalysts such as Otto Rank, Ernest Becker, and Robert Jay Lifton have described the unusual need a leader has to justify him or herself as an object of primary value in the universe. In *The Denial of Death*, Becker wrote, "he must stand apart to be a hero—make the biggest possible contribution to world life—show that he counts more than anyone or anything else" (Becker, 1973: 4). This speaks to the very core motives of the hero. The hero seeks to make a contribution which will not be easily eroded by the sands of time.

Heroism, according to Becker, is thus a reflex to the terror of death. Frequently, the heroic myth across cultures actually describes a hero's return from the dead. The hero has a heightened awareness of his mortality. He or she struggles to master the destruction of death by seemingly immortal creations. The hero's legacy is an ultimate shield from the fear of death. In reviewing the classic folk heroes Gilgamesh and Odysseus, Rank (1932) explained:

> the problem is fundamentally similar: namely to attain personal immortality. Neither in primitive man nor in classical times does he actually achieve it. But he finds it ideologically in that his deeds, which he subserved in his attempt to gain immortality, have made him a hero whose fame lives on in the song of other generations (Rank, 1932: 215-216).

A society encourages an individual's pursuit of an heroic legacy because the hero's vision is a collective conception of immortality. For example, the chief executive's strategy for a firm is a plan to ensure the company's immortality as well as a permanent record of the chief executive's individual effort.

As chief executives sense the close of their career, many fear for the vulnerability of their heroic legacy. Will it survive the test of history? Will their dream outlive their reign, let alone their lifetime? These leaders have not hit plateaus by midcareer like most other workers. It is not until late career that their career mobility has slowed. Chief executives then begin to worry that they may not reach their ultimate career peaks but instead have hit a premature ceiling. Due to their prior clear pathway of success, many virtually face midlife and midcareer dilemmas at the same time which they confront late career trails of age.

This delayed realization of career limits, coupled with a heightened sense of mortality can arouse in chief executives the impulses which lead to stubborn assertions of command. They feel a life's work endangered and seek to prove their visions to be robust to the erosion of age. Scholars have suggested, for example, that Chinese Communist Party Chairman Mao Tse Tung's "Cultural Revolution" was, in part, a late career assertion of his heroic mission (Lifton, 1968). Mao's career had been that of a revolutionary. Throughout his recollections of his earlier activism, he showed a keen awareness of having been an "external survivor" with narrow personal escapes to safety. Meanwhile, his brothers, his first wife, and many colleagues were killed during the founding revolution of the late 1940s. He led the famous Long March 1934-1935 where 80 percent of the original group perished along a six thousand mile trek. By the mid-1960s, however, the aging of long triumphant colleagues and the complacency of the institutions which he created, indicated to him that his revolutionary works might not endure.

Thus a leader's frustration in late career is especially difficult to master. This is because he or she has selected far more difficult standards of accomplishment than most of us, but has not experienced final limits to personal abilities until late life. The degree of despair that an older person feels as he or she reflects upon a past career often has more to do with subjective goals established earlier in life than with actual, objective successes. No aspirations could be more ambitious than the leader's heroic dream of an immortal contribution. It is no wonder that many depart office with such difficulty, given the low likelihood of realizing such dreams. We will now turn directly to the attitudes chief executives report about their exits from office.

EXITING THE EXECUTIVE SUITE

In my survey of one hundred retiring chief executives of *Fortune* 500 firms, the *heroic status* variable was composed of 20 individual variables where affirmative responses for 12 variables corresponded with low identification with the heroic role and affirmative responses for the other nine variables corresponded with high identification with an heroic identity within the firm. The responses which contributed to this scale included chief executive self-reports on the following: whether they continued to hold an official position in the firm after retirement; whether they maintained an office in the firm's headquarters; whether they continued to serve on the firm's board of directors; and whether they continued to respond to public inquiries regarding the firm. The variables which composed an opposite scale which measured low identification with the *heroic status* of the leadership role included self-reported explanations of retirement as an opportunity to enjoy more time for themselves; an opportunity for long desired privacy; and finally, as an opportunity to spend time engaged in various new activities.

The second heroic barrier to exit, the sense of frustration with the *heroic mission*, was measured by five survey variables including their own statements of: regrets from a sense of facing an uncompleted mission; regrets over subsequent performance triumphs after they left; regrets over the performance of an individual successor; and regrets over the timing of the retirement decision.

The opposite scale was also created for this barrier to exit in that fulfillment with one's *heroic mission* was measured. This was assessed through seven affirmatively phrased items which reflected a high degree of personal satisfaction. These included responses indicating that the chief executive retired because he had contributed all that he could; that he retired because he had found other compelling community or business interests, or that he had no expressed difficulty at any time after retirement.

The final measure of a chief executive's identification with heroic stature was simply a subtraction of the negative scale from the positive scale. The same was true for the final measurement of a sense of fulfillment with their heroic mission. These 100 chief executives were compared to roughly 100 other non-CEO corporate officers from the same firms. I found that the chief executives did not significantly differ from those other top officers in terms of their sense of a completed mission, but chief executives were far more significantly attached to heroic stature in the firm.

This highly significant finding deserves some further reflection. It seems that those who were second-in-command of their firms, or at that general level, shared the same drive to create a lasting legacy with the chief executive. As one-time aspirants to the chief executive's throne, they too were ambitious people eager to create a lasting legacy. Those who ultimately became the supreme power in the firm, however, were showered with regal trappings of office that may have become addictive. Furthermore, guilt-ridden boards of directors or boards seeking continuity of command, often feel that they are making the transfer of power less painful to all, by allowing the departing chief executive to retain more of his executive privileges than are allowed to the second-in-command. Thus the chief executive often has the choice over whether to remain actively engaged in an effort to fortify the nearly severed links with a lost heroic role. The second-in-command is merely cut free. When asked how long it took to adjust to a life outside the executive suite, many non-CEO's stated, "About the time it took for the elevator to get from the penthouse to the lobby!" Not a single chief executive responded in that fashion.

A Typology of Departure Styles

In addition to examining these attitudes about their barriers to exit from executive stardom, the chief executives' specific exit activities were studied. Each of these chief executives was classified into one of four departure styles. These departure styles were based upon the pattern of activities they followed leading up to and through their retirement. The prior day-long interviews with roughly fifty chief executives were the source of four categories. While some executives consistently spoke in imperial, aristocratic ways with regard to succession, others used combative competitive terms, yet others spoke in paternalistic family tones, and a last group spoke in crisp, calculated political metaphors. Characteristic patterns of behavior were associated with the imagery which they selected to tell their personal career stories. The four categories which I derived from these interviews were labelled as follows: *Monarchs, Generals, Ambassadors,* and *Governors.*

The data which I used to sort my wider sample of 100 surveyed *Fortune* 500 chief executives into these four departure styles included:

1. The purpose and timing of the chief executive's exit
2. The expressed emotions over leaving office (e.g., resentment, loss, loneliness, eagerness, exhaustion, etc.)
3. The time and energy spent on ongoing contact maintained with the firm
4. The return to office after retirement
5. The length of time served on the board of directors
6. The attention to successors (e.g., period of grooming, timing of identification, timing of announcement, etc.)
7. The magnitude of involvement on outside corporate board directorships
8. The magnitude of involvement in new business ventures and officer positions
9. The length of one's reign as chief executive and their years in firm

Two independent sources of information were used to make these judgments: (1) a succession history constructed from a 25-year review of annual published shareholder proxy statements for each of the firms; and (2) the individual questionnaires from each surveyed chief executive. These chief executives were sorted into one of the four categories after having been individually evaluated by each of three independent raters. There was an 85 percent agreement among the raters.

Several brief definitions will help to reveal some striking links between the *heroic barriers to exit* discussed earlier in this article and the four distinctive departure styles. First, *Monarchs* are those chief executives who do not leave office until death or through an internal palace revolt. This palace revolt may be in the form of ultimata, the resignations of top officers, or the action of the board of directors. A second departure style which is marked by forcible exit is the style of the *General*. Here, the chief executive leaves office reluctantly, but quickly returns to office out of retirement to attempt to rescue the company from the real or imagined inadequacy of his or her successor. The generals enjoy serving as the returning savior and often hope to remain around long enough to take the firm and themselves toward even greater glory. The *Ambassadors,* by contrast, leave office quite gracefully and frequently serve as post-retirement mentors. They may remain on the board of directors for some time, but they do not try to sabotage the successor. The ambassadors provide continuity and counsel. The final group, the *Governors,* rule for a limited term of office and shift to other vocational outlets. Despite their fairly graceful exits, the governors maintain very little ongoing contact with their firm.

Table 1. Chief Executive Exit Barriers by Departure Styles

Departure Style	Exit Barrier	
	*Heroic Stature	**Heroic Mission
Monarchs	.75	-.125
Generals	.77	0.22
Ambassadors	.31	1.37
Governors	.46	0.48
F statistic =	10.18	3.46
	P < .00001	< .01

* greater number on scale indicates greater attachment to heroic stature
** greater number on scale indicates greater fulfillment or *less* frustration with heroic mission.

In comparing the heroic barriers to exit across these four departure styles, as reported in Table 1, both monarchs and generals are far more captured by the status of their positions. They find it hard to relinquish the respect and influence of office. Ambassadors were especially untroubled by a loss of status and hence were able to remain on the premises, while stripped of their power. In their continued willingness to serve the greater good of the group over their self-interest in status, ambassadors paradoxically have managed to preserve heroic respect from their former constituents. The elder statesman role has great potential power, if exercised with great caution.

Looking at the other barrier to exit, the fulfillment of one's *heroic mission*, again, monarchs and generals were far less ready to depart from their calling. Monarchs seemed to feel especially frustrated and generals somewhat less so. By contrast, ambassadors were particularly content with their record of accomplishment and no longer felt the need to prove themselves in battle. Thus it does indeed seem possible for those in heroic positions, such as a chief executive of a major U.S. corporation, to feel an ultimate sense of accomplishment.

CONCLUSIONS

Early in this article, we saw the changing nature of fame and heroism in society so that various occupations including corporate chieftains can enjoy widespread heroic appreciation by the greater community. In particular, we saw that corporate chief executives, at least within their own firms, are both treated as local heroes and come to believe in their own heroic myths. We also identified five common characteristics of the chief executive's heroic calling. In this chapter, we were reminded that heroes, even in late career, ride off into the sunset, not to obscurity, but rather in search of new adventures. Retirement suggests an abdication of heroic status and an abortive heroic mission. A chief executive may not be the omnipotent savior he or she purports to be. Thus an early exit may appear as a public confession of personal limitations.

Frequently, they feel pressed into leaving office with underutilized talents and a reservoir of continued energy. Consider the frustrations of Citicorp's chief executive Walter Wriston. After a 17-year term at the helm of the nation's leading commercial bank, Wriston was forced to retire when he reached a mandatory retirement age of 65—which he labelled "statutory senility" (Bender, 1985). He likened this exit to "stepping off the pier." His financial genius, imagination, and management savvy led to a complete redefinition of the nature of commercial banding in the converging sectors of the financial services industry. He championed deregulation of commercial banking to encourage the entry of these institutions into new service areas and geographic locations. Perhaps no single financier has had the same impact or public stature on the industry, short of J.P. Morgan.

Nonetheless, he has reported frustration in his present inability to secure another influential policy making position. As he put it, "The issue is: if you have your health, something I've been blessed with, what do you do the rest of your life? Some people get their golf clubs and sit on a beach" (Bender, 1985: 3-1). For him that is not the way to fill his days. Active as a director of eight corporations and involved with many philanthropic causes, he still yearns for more. Wriston stated:

> Undoubtedly, there will be something tomorrow or the day after, something in government, or outside of government and it's possible someone will say, "Why don't you give us a hand?" (Bender, 1985: 3-1).

Wriston's late career role models appear to be his father, who moved in and out of government, as well as John J. McCoy and W. Averell Harriman; people who moved into public service after successful private sector careers with assignments as: cabinet secretaries, ambassadors, agency chiefs, and Presidential trouble shooters.

Two exit barriers which chief executives must conquer to master their retirement are in evidence in such stories: the loss of heroic stature and the loss of a heroic mission. Heroic stature refers to the chief executive's identification with the power and the status of office. The key to mastery of this barrier depends on how immersed one has become in one's heroic institutional role. Sometimes the energies required to nurture a person's public persona divert energies needed to maintain a healthy independent self-concept.

The heroic mission refers to their lifelong career purpose. The key to mastery of this second barrier is to understand how they have come to terms with their own mortality and their definition of a lasting contribution. Perhaps Wriston's ready recall of late-career models, such as his father and others, only adds to the extraordinary high standards of accomplishment he has set for himself. Similarly, the despair in the annual report of Donald Burnham of Westinghouse represents unmet internal plans. None of these people seem to have left office and transferred to new lives with a complete feeling of accomplishment. They left haunted by a desire for different results or hungering for further opportunity. Similarly, history-shaping world leaders as Winston Churchill and recent, more modest world leaders such as President Gerald Ford, President Valery Giscard d'Estaing, Prime Minister James Callaghan, and Prime Minister Malcolm Fraser have shown profound nostalgia in having lost the spotlight of attention.

At the same time, however, we have seen that some chief executives do manage to begin anew and transcend the memory of what they have lost. In 1982, several prominent chief executives felt by their mid-50s that they outwardly agreed with their board that the time was right for a new corporate hero. William S. Sneath of Union Carbide retired at age 55, Harold J. Haynes of Chevron at 55, and Jack J. Crocker of Super Value Stores at 57. This public position can be read as an admission of poor performance by some, and an acquiescence to a strong board by others. It also can be read as an open acceptance of their limits and a welcomed change in command. For example, Crocker commented:

> I was right for the company during my time, but now I feel it needs someone more structured than I am. (President) Mike Wright will be a better man for the decade ahead than I would (Perham, 1982: 69).

This serves as a reminder that there are variations in how executives conquer these heroic barriers to exiting the executive suite. Some find new activities, others fight on, while still others accept their past record as a complete job well done. We found that a comparison of chief executives to their own second-in-command top officers showed that the non-CEO's had a similar dedication to the heroic mission but far less attachment to the heroic status of the executive role. Perhaps the job seizes a greater portion of the personal identity of the chief executive than the job filled by any other executive in the firm.

Irving Shapiro, the retired chief executive of DuPont, offered a valuable insight that may help to further understand the difference in these patterns. "Every CEO should remember that the position exists not for his benefit, but for the corporation's. It is his job to know when it is time to step down" (Perham, 1982: 69). Perhaps this is why some chief executives have managed to retire and yet preserve their heroic image, while others have unwittingly transformed themselves into late career villains.

ACKNOWLEDGMENTS

The material in this article is drawn from a fuller study of 300 retired top executives which appears in a book by the same author entitled, *The Heroes Farewell: What Happens When CEOs Retire*. New York: Oxford University Press, 1988.

REFERENCES

Aldrich, H.E. *Organizations and Environments.* Englewood Cliffs, NJ: Prentice-Hall, 1979.

Auletta, K. *The Art of Corporate Success.* New York: G.C. Putnam, 1984.

Barber, J.D. *The Lawmakers: Recruitment and Adaptation to Legislative Life.* New Haven, CT: Yale University Press, 1965.

Barnard, C.I. *Functions of the Executive.* Cambridge, MA: Harvard University Press, 1938.

Becker, E. *The Denial of Death.* New York: Free Press, 1973.

Bender, M. "Building a Life After Citicorp." *New York Times* 21 April 1985, pp. 3-11.

Bower, J.L. *The Two Faces of Managment.* Boston, MA: Houghton Mifflin, 1983.

Bower, J.L., and Weinberg, M. "Statecraft, Strategy and Corporate Leadership." Working paper, Harvard Business School, 1985.

Braudy, L. *The Frenzy of Reknown: Fame and Its History.* New York: Oxford University Press, 1986.

Burnham, D. C. "Letter from the Chairman." *1974 Annual Report, The Westinghouse Corporation.* Pittsburgh, PA: Westinghouse, 1975.

Campbell, J. *The Hero with a Thousand Faces.* Princeton, NJ: Princeton University Press, 1949.

Chandler, A.D. *The Visible Hand.* Cambridge, MA: Harvard University Press, 1977.

Cyert, R.M., and March, J. *A Behavioral Theory of the Firm.* Englewood Cliffs, NJ: Prentice-Hall, 1963.

DeLorean, J.Z. *On a Clear Day You Can See General Motors,* Grosse Point, MI: Wright Enterprises, 1979.

Drucker, P.F. *Innovation and Entrepreneurship.* New York: Harper & Row, 1985.

Emerson, R.W. *Self-Reliance.* Boston, MA: James Munroe, 1841.

Erikson, E. *Young Man Luther: A Study in Psychoanalysis and History.* New York: Norton, 1958.

Erikson, E. *Childhood and Society.* 2nd ed. New York: W.W. Norton, 1963.

"Executive Pay: Who Made the Most—And Why," *Business Week,* May 2, 1988, pp. 50-58.

Feldman, S.P. "Culture, Charisma, and the CEO: An Essay on the Meaning of High Office." *Human Relations* 19(3) (1986): 211-228.

Festinger, L. "A Theory of the Social Comparison Process." *Human Relations* 7 (2) (1954): 117-140.

Friedman, S.D., and Singh, H. "Why He Left: An Explanation of the Succession Effect." Paper presented at the 50th meeting of the Academy of Management, Chicago, IL, August 1986a.

Friedman, S.D., and Singh, H. "It Makes a Difference: Letter to the Editor." *The New York Review of Books* 23 October 1986b, p. 69.

Galbraith, J.K. "The Last Tycoon." *The New York Review of Books* 14 August 1986a, p. 3.

Galbraith, J.K. "Response." *The New York Review of Books* 23 October 1986b, p. 69.

Geneen, H. *Managing.* New York: Doubleday, 1984.

Hollie, P.G. "Well Past Age 65, They're Still Boss." *The New York Times* 29 July 1979, p. H-1.

Iacocca, L. *Iacocca: An Autobiography.* New York: Bantam, 1984.

James, R.R. *Anthony Eden—The Authorized Biography.* London: Weidenfeld and Nicolson, 1986.

Johnson, R. "Heineman Has a New Challenge at Northwest." *Wall Street Journal* 7 December 1983, p. 31.

Kanter, R.M. *The Change Masters.* New York: Simon & Schuster, 1983.

Keegan, R. *The Evolving Self.* Cambridge, MA: Harvard University Press, 1985.

Kleinfield, N.R. "The 'Irritant' They Call Perot." *The New York Times* 27 April 1986, pp. 3-1 and 3-81.

Kotter, J.P. *The General Managers.* New York: Free Press, 1982.

Lacey, R. *Ford: The Man and the Machine.* Boston, MA: Little Brown, 1986.

Lasswell, H.D. *Psychopathology and Politics.* New Haven, CT: Yale University Press, 1930.

Levinson, H., and Rosenthal, S. *CEO: Corporate Leadership in Action.* New York: Basic Books, 1985.

Lifton, R.J. *Revolutionary Immortality: Mao Tse Tung and the Chinese Cultural Revolution.* New York: Random House, 1968.

Mayo, E. *The Human Problems of an Industrial Civilization.* New York: MacMillan, 1933.

McMurty, L. *Lonesome Dove.* New York: Simon & Schuster, 1984.

Neustadt, R.E. *Presidential Power.* New York: John Wiley & Sons, 1960.

Nevins, A., and Hill, F.E. *Ford.* Vol. 1: *The Times, the Man, and the Company.* New York: Scribner's, 1954.

Nevins, A., and Hill, F.E. *Ford.* Vol. 2: *Expansion and Challenge: 1915-1933.* New York: Scribner's, 1957.

Nevins, A., and Hill, F.E. *Ford.* Vol. 3: *Decline and Rebirth: 1933-1962.* New York: Scribner's, 1963.

O'Toole, P. *Corporate Messiah: The Hiring and Firing of Million-Dollar Managers.* New York: Signet, 1985.

O'Toole, P. "Who Gets the Most Pay." *Forbes,* 4 June 1984, pp. 98-146.

Patton, A. "Why So Many Executives Make Too Much." *Business Week* 17 October 1983, pp. 24 and 26.

Perham, J. "Limiting a CEO's Tenure." *Dun's Business Month,* January 1982, p. 69.

Peters, T.J., and Waterman, R.H. *In Search of Excellence.* New York: Harper & Row, 1983.

Petric, P. "America's Most Successful Entrepreneur." *Fortune,* 27 October 1986, pp. 24-32.

Pfeffer, J., and Salancik, G. *The External Control of Organizations.* New York: Harper & Row, 1977.

Plumb, J.H. "Disappearing Heroes." *Business Horizons* 4 (Autumn) (1974): 104-110.

Prokesch, S. "America's Imperial Chief Executive." *The New York Times* 12 October 1986, pp. 3-1 and 3-25.

Rank, O. *Art and Artist: Creative Urge and Personality Development.* New York: Alfred A. Knopf, 1932.

Reich, R.B. "The Executive's New Clothes." *The New Republic* 13 May 1985, pp. 22-28.

Rustow, D.A. *Philosphers and Kings: Studies in Leadership.* New York: George Grazellas, 1970.

Schacter, S. *The Psychology of Affiliation, Experimental Studies of the Sources of Gregariousness.* Stanford, CA: Stanford University, 1959.

Scharhost, G., and Bales, J. *The Lost Life of Horatio Alger, Jr.* Bloomington, IN: Indiana University Press, 1985.

Schein, E.H. *Organizational Culture and Leadership.* San Francisco, CA: Jossey-Bass, 1985.

Schumpeter, J.E. *Capitalism, Socialism, and Democracy.* New York: Harper and Brothers, 1942.

Selznik, P. *Leadership in Administration.* Englewood Cliffs, NJ: Prentice Hall, 1957.

Sloan, A.E., Jr. *My Years with General Motors.* Cambridge, MA: Massachusets Institute of Technology Press, 1969.

Smith, T. "Leaders Emeritus Take a Look at the World." *The New York Times* 29 August 1983, p. 1.

Sonnenfeld, J. *Corporate Views of the Public Interest.* Boston: Auburn House, 1980.

Sonnenfeld, J. "Untangling the Muddled Management of Public Affairs." *Business Horizons,* December 1984.

"Turnover at the Top." *Business Week,* December 19, 1983, pp. 104-110.

"The Vanishing American Hero." *U.S. News and World Report* July 21, 1975, p. 22-26.

Veblen, T. *A Theory of the Leisure Class.* New York: The MacMillan Co., 1899.

Weber, M. *From Max Weber: Essays in Sociology.* Translated by H.H. Gerth, and C.W. Mills. New York: Oxford, 1946.

Weber, M. *Theory of Social and Economic Organization.* Translated by T. Parsons and A.M. Henderson. New York: Free Press, 1947.

"Where Have All the Heroes Gone?" *Newsweek* August 6, 1979, pp. 45-52.

Wyeliffe, D. "Where Have All the Leaders Gone?" *The New York Times* 31 July 1985, pp. C-1 and C-10.

BIOGRAPHICAL SKETCHES
OF THE CONTRIBUTORS

Gerard L. Brandon is completing his doctorate in industrial/organizational sychology at the Pennsylvania State University. He is currently employed with the consulting firm of Landy, Jacobs and Associates. His research interests lie in the areas of utility theory and testing and validation.

Robert B. Duncan is Provost of Northwestern University and James Allen Professor of Strategy and Organizations at the Kellogg Graduate School of Management. He earned his Ph.D. from Yale University. His areas of research are strategic management and the role of the CEO and top management team in strategy formulation.

John J. Gabarro is Professor and Chairman of Organizational Behavior and Human Resource Management at the Harvard Business School. He earned his DBA in organizational behavior at Harvard University. His areas of research are the development of working relationships, transition management and, more recently, executive leadership and succession.

Donald C. Hambrick is Samuel Bronfman Professor of Democratic Business Enterprise at the Graduate School of Business, Columbia University. He is also director of the School's Executive Leadership Research Center. He earned his Ph.D. from the Pennsylvania State University.

His areas of research are strategic management and the composition and processes of top management teams.

Anil K. Gupta is Associate Professor of Organizational Strategy and Policy at the College of Business and Management at the The University of Maryland at College Park. He earned his D.B.A. from Harvard University. His areas of research are strategy implementation within diversified firms, strategic leadership, and entrepreneurship.

Ellen F. Jackofsky is Assistant Professor of Organizational Behavior in the Edwin L. Cox School of Business Southern Methodist University. She earned her Ph.D. from the University of Texas-Dallas. Her areas of research are turnover, human resource management systems, and the dynamics of organizational climate.

John Kimberly is Professor of Management and Health Care Systems, Chairman of the Department of Management and a Senior Fellow in the Leonard Davis Institute of Health Economics in the Wharton School of the University of Pennsylvania. He received his Ph.D. degrees in Organizational Behavior from Cornell University. He is a specialist on problems of organizational change, innovation, and design. His most recent work has focused on problems of technology diffusion, organizational innovation and policy formulation in health care organizations.

Frances J. Milliken is an Assistant Professor of Management and Organizational Behavior at New York University. She received her Ph.D. in 1986 from the City University of New York. Her current research focuses on perception of organizational environments, environmental uncertainty, and strategic issue diagnosis.

Shelley R. Robbins is an Assistant Professor at the School of Business Administration at the University of Wisconsin at Milwaukee. She is a doctoral candidate at the Kellogg Graduate of Management at Northwestern University. Her areas of research are strategy formulation processes, strategic vision, and executive leadership.

Elaine Romanelli is Assistant Professor of Organization Behavior at the Fuqua School of Business, Duke University. She earned her Ph.D. from Columbia University in 1985. Her areas of research include new venture strategies, effects of founder backgrounds on strategy and venture team composition.

John J. Slocum, Jr. is the O. Paul Corley Professor of Organizational Behavior in the Edwin L. Cox School of Business, Southern Methodist University. He is the past President of the Academy of Management and editor of the *Academy of Management Journal.* He is the author of two books and more than 80 articles. His areas of research are career management and decision making by top managers.

Jeffrey Sonnenfeld is an associate professor at the Harvard Business School where he has taught since 1980. He has served on the editorial boards of the *Academy of Management Journal, The Journal of Occupational Behaviour,* and the *Academy of Management Executive.* He has won the Academy of Management Award for Research in Social Issues, the Richard D. Irwin Award for Business Research, the Hawthorne Award for Research in Social Relations, and the John Whitehead Fellowship for Research in Industry. His chapter is derived from research to appear in full in his forthcoming book, *The Hero's Farewell: The Retirement and Renewal of Chief Executives,* Oxford University Press.

William H. Starbuck is the ITT Professor of Creative Management and directs the doctoral program in business administration at New York University. He received his Ph.D. at Carnegie Institute of Technology. He has written about human decision making, bargaining, organizational growth and development, social revolutions, computer simulation, computer programming, accounting, business strategy, and organizational design.

Robert M. Steers is Professor of Management at the Graduate School of Management, University of Oregon. He earned his Ph.D. at the University of California, Irvine, and is a former President of the Academy of Management. His research interests include employee motivation and performance and comparative management.

Michael L. Tushman is Professor of Management and Director of the Innovation and Entrepreneurship Research Center at the Graduate School of Business, Columbia University. He earned his Ph.D. from the Sloan School of Management at M.I.T. His areas of research are strategic innovation, organization evolution and managing technology and R&D.

Gerardo R. Ungson is an Associate Professor of Management at the Graduate School of Management, University of Oregon. He earned his Ph.D. from The Pennsylvania State University. His areas of interest are strategic decision making and international competition in high technology.

Edward J. Zajac is an assistant professsor in the J.L. Kellogg School of Management, Northwestern University. He received his Ph.D. in organization and strategy at the Wharton School, University of Pennsylvania. His current research interests include the study of interorganizational strategies, corporate governance, and strategic control systems.